RACHAEL RAY'S BIG ORANGE BOOK

RACHAEL RAY'S BIG ORANGE BOOK

PHOTOGRAPHS BY TINA RUPP

Clarkson Potter/Publishers
New York

Published in the United States by Clarkson Potter/Publishers,
an imprint of the Crown Publishing Group, a division of
Random House, Inc., New York.

www.crownpublishing.com

www.clarksonpotter.com

Clarkson Potter is a trademark and POTTER with colophon
is a registered trademark of Random House, Inc.

Library of Congress Cataloging-in-Publication Data
is available upon request

ISBN 978-0-307-38319-8

Printed in the United States of America

Design by Amy Sly and Jennifer K. Beal Davis

10 9 8 7 6 5 4 3 2 1

First Edition

DEDICATED TO THE LOVED ONES I'VE LOST, THOSE GOOD EATERS, GOOD SOULS, AND ONE GOOD DOG WHO I CAN NO LONGER SIT AT THE TABLE WITH. IN MY DREAMS, WE ARE STILL TOGETHER AND THE TABLE IS AS FULL AS OUR HEARTS.

THANKS!

HUGE HUGS for the BIG help on the BIG ORANGE BOOK (I call him Bob, for short) and many thanks to the team of editors and artists who shape and style my recipes into lovely books, especially Pam Krauss and Amy Boorstein at Clarkson Potter, and Tina Rupp, Andrea Steinberg, and Deborah Williams (plus their assistants Elizabeth Drago, Teresa Horgan, Ivone Moutela, Jessica Gorman, and Alicia Steiling). Thanks also to my support system at all my homes away from home who test-kitchen my recipes and challenge me to make each dish tastier than the next. Thank you to the Food Network, EDWRR Magazine, and *Rachael Ray Show* staffs, especially Emily Rieger and our culinary team of Abigail Bodiker, Kara Vogt, and Patrick Decker. Thanks to my delicious family, including Isaboo, who is such a love and good eater, too. Special thanks to my mom and mother-in-law for the family memories and recipes they contributed to this book. Thanks to Michelle Boxer for her organizational acumen and the laughs! And thanks to my readers and viewers, who keep me employed and ever-hungry to do better.

CONTENTS

INTRODUCTION

The *Big Orange Book* is my biggest collection of recipes to date, but it's actually several small collections in one book. I always come up with recipes for television or print based on the feedback from readers and viewers who tell me what they are feeding themselves and their friends and families at home. They let me know what's working for them—and what they would like to see more of. Well, maybe you can't please all of the people all of the time, but I've given it my best shot here, with entire chapters devoted to Kosher meals, vegetarian meals, meals for one, entrée burgers, slow-it-down recipes that take a bit more than 30 minutes but are *definitely* worth it, family hand-me-down recipes, holiday menus, starters and apps, PLUS nearly 200 brand-new 30-minute meals—all in one BIG book. It's orange simply because orange is my favorite color. Orange is friendly and sparks my appetite for all things. The color orange makes me feel inspired, curious, and happy—the same words I would use to describe my love of food.

CAN DO!

All of these recipes are above all accessible to cooks of all skill levels. I have never set my bar anywhere above waist high in the kitchen because I don't think cooking a meal should be like running a marathon. I have friends who love the challenge of complicated cooking techniques and exotic ingredients, and I marvel at many of the meals I've enjoyed that were prepared by skilled chefs, professional and amateur alike. Still, while there are no fancy techniques to master here, turning out really good food that can be prepared by anyone at any time no matter where they live or shop feels and tastes like a new trick in and of itself. It's always been my belief that, with the right ingredients and easy methods, everyone can produce quality meals in a short (or relatively short) amount of time that will inspire the soul while they fill the stomach.

THERE'S EATING AND THEN THERE'S EATING.

I try to write recipes that take a bite outta life—food with a sense of humor and adventure. Today, I am striving to make the food I prepare in my home have social purpose as well. Thanks to independently owned small purveyors and farmers' markets cropping back into all of our communities, we have the opportunity to improve the quality of the food we eat as well as our quality of life while supporting and sustaining local, small growers. In my state alone, from the Bronx to the Adirondacks, every community has a grassroots effort of some sort to promote local growers and good-food awareness. The growing global food crisis and the rising costs associated with running a household and caring for a family have made cooking at home more often and supporting your local growers a strategic decision that makes good budgetary sense, too.

MY STUDY OF SLOW AND STEADY FOOD

While most of my recipes can be made in 30 minutes or less I still consider my cooking a relative of the slow-food tradition, because I make an effort to buy locally as much as I can and I try to savor every bite, sharing the food with family and friends. Sure, balance is hard to come by in my life, and I work many more hours than I rest, but even at 10 o'clock at night the act of preparing food is so satisfying and fulfilling to me that I finish each meal feeling more complete, uncompromised. Whether prepared fast or slow, food should be enjoyed, savored, and should inspire conversation, even if you are talking to yourself! I've worked out many tough decisions digesting my thoughts along with a dinner for one.

COOK, FEED, FUND

I also believe that everyone should have access to good food, and to that end I have established the Yum-o! organization to empower kids and their families to develop healthy relationships with food and cooking. Our goal is to teach families to cook, aid in the fight against hunger, and provide scholarships to fund cooking education across the country so that kids, their schools, and their families can make better choices in their eating habits. We want to see a country where everyone can experience the joys of food and cooking and live healthier lives as they do so. (For more information about Yum-o! and to check out the Yum-o! community, please visit www.yum-o.org.)

A NOTE ABOUT THE RECIPES IN THE BOOK

Some meals with more than one course or multiple components are broken into individual recipes so that the ingredient lists are easier to follow. These "square meals" are marked with a square orange symbol. Read through all the component recipes quickly before you start to cook. These menus are designed so that you can start the first recipe, then in the first pocket of time that recipe allows, begin the preparation of the next one. This is the method I use in cooking my 30-Minute Meals on Food Network, and once you've done it a few times it will become second nature. If you're new to 30-minute cooking, choose a meal that incorporates all the components in one recipe; these recipes let you know what to cook when so you use your time most efficiently and everything gets on the table at the same time.

30-MINUTE MEALS

SOUPS AND SAMMIES

QUICK PORK POZOLE

There are as many recipes for pozole stew as there are Mexican cooks, and they almost all contain slow-cooked pork or poached chicken in addition to dried corn kernels known as hominy. This fast ground-pork version is like a quick green weeknight chili. Don't forget to chill some Coronas.

Heat the EVOO in a high-sided skillet or medium soup pot over medium-high heat. Add the pork, season with the salt, pepper, allspice, and cumin, and brown for 3 to 4 minutes, crumbling and breaking up the meat with a wooden spoon. Add the onions, garlic, and jalapeños and stir to combine.

Halve the tomatillos, then place in the food processor and pulse until they are chopped into a chunky salsa. Stir the tomatillos into the skillet with the pork and cook for 10 minutes, stirring occasionally. Stir in the honey and adjust the salt and pepper, then stir in the hominy and stock. Heat through for another minute or two. Stir in the cilantro and turn off the heat. Douse the diced avocado with the juice of 1 lime. Squeeze the juice of the second lime over the pozole and stir.

Serve the soup in shallow bowls with some diced avocado, a handful of crushed chips, and some shredded lettuce on top.

SERVES 4

2 tablespoons **EVOO** (extra-virgin olive oil)

1½ pounds **ground pork**
Salt and **pepper**

½ teaspoon **ground allspice** (eyeball it in your palm)

1 teaspoon **ground cumin**, ⅓ palmful

1 large **onion**, finely chopped

3 to 4 **garlic cloves**, grated or finely chopped

2 **jalapeño peppers**, seeded and finely chopped

10 to 12 **tomatillos**, husked and rinsed

1 tablespoon **honey**

1 (15-ounce) can **hominy**, drained

3 cups **chicken stock**

A handful of fresh **cilantro**, chopped

1 **avocado**, diced

2 **limes**

2 cups **corn tortilla chips**, lightly crushed

½ heart of **romaine lettuce**, shredded

SOPA DA PEDRA ROCK SOUP

2 tablespoons **EVOO** (extra-virgin olive oil), plus some for drizzling

½ pound cooked **chorizo**, ham, or leftover cooked meat, diced

2 large **potatoes**, peeled and cubed

4 **celery stalks** from the tender heart, chopped

3 to 4 **carrots**, peeled and chopped

1 large **onion**, chopped

2 to 3 **garlic cloves**, chopped

1 **bay leaf**, fresh or dried

Salt and **pepper**

1 (15-ounce) can **chickpeas**, drained

1 rounded teaspoon **sweet paprika**

1 (15-ounce) can diced or crushed **tomatoes** or tomato sauce

2 tablespoons piquante or **hot sauce**

6 cups **chicken stock**, or 4 cups stock plus 2 cups water

2 cups **stale bread cubes**

A handful of fresh flat-leaf **parsley** or cilantro, chopped, for garnish

Rock soup is a recipe and a fable that exists in many different cultures, and it is especially dear to the Portuguese. Our thirty-something guide, Patricia, said it's one of her favorite "recipes" because there *is* no recipe: just add whatever's in your fridge or cupboard and stir. As the story goes (in case it's been a while), a clever beggar went door-to-door through a village bragging about his delicious specialty, something called Rock Soup. Each villager, excited about the mysterious recipe and vain enough to think he or she could improve it, offered the beggar chef an ingredient for the pot. In the end, the beggar had a soup fit for a king. When the townsfolk asked, "But where is the rock in this soup?" he replied, "I think I'll save it for the next pot." If I were living in Lisbon, here's what I might put in my Rock Soup.

Heat the EVOO in a soup pot over medium to medium-high heat. Add the chorizo or other meat and cook for 1 to 2 minutes, then add the vegetables, bay leaf, salt, and pepper and cook for 7 to 8 minutes to soften, stirring frequently. Add the chickpeas and season with the paprika. Stir in the tomatoes, hot sauce, and stock. Raise the heat, bring to a boil, then reduce the heat to a simmer and cook for 10 minutes, or until the potatoes are tender.

Place ½ cup of the bread cubes in each bowl and drizzle with EVOO. Ladle the rock soup over the bread and garnish with the chopped fresh herbs.

SERVES 4

KNOCKS 'N' BRATS STOUP

Cold beer, knocks 'n' brats. Nuff said. How 'bout dem Bears?

Heat 1 tablespoon of the EVOO and 2 tablespoons of the butter in the bottom of a soup pot over medium to medium-high heat. Add the onions and potatoes, season with salt and pepper, and cook for 6 to 7 minutes. Add the bay leaf, carrots, and cabbage. Cook for another 5 minutes, then season with the caraway, dill, and parsley. Stir in the beer and bring to a boil, then cook for 1 minute; stir in the mustard and stock. Bring to a bubble and reduce the heat to a simmer while you cook the sausage.

Place the knockwurst and bratwurst in a skillet with ¼ inch water and the remaining tablespoon of EVOO. Cook the sausage over medium-high heat until the liquid evaporates and the casings are brown and crisp, 12 to 15 minutes. Cut the sausages into 2-inch chunks.

Toast the bread and lightly butter it, then cut into croutons.

Ladle the stoup into 4 bowls and divide the sausage among them. Top with the croutons and serve.

SERVES 4

2 tablespoons **EVOO** (extra-virgin olive oil)

3 tablespoons **butter**

1 **onion**, thinly sliced

4 cups frozen shredded **hash brown potatoes**

Salt and **pepper**

1 **bay leaf**

1 cup shredded **carrots**

1-pound sack of shredded **cabbage** (coleslaw salad mix)

1 teaspoon **caraway seeds** (optional)

A handful of fresh **dill**, chopped

A handful of fresh flat-leaf **parsley**, chopped

1 bottle of **German lager** or whatever kind is in your fridge

¼ cup **spicy brown mustard**

4 cups **chicken stock**

3 **knockwurst**

3 **bratwurst**

4 slices of **pumpernickel** or rye

ONE-POT WONDER
CREAMY CHICKEN AND DUMPLING STOUP

The dumplings in this soup are not biscuit-based; it's store-bought gnocchi to the rescue! This super-fast, simple supper makes use of a classic combo of leek and potato in a fast version of an American classic.

Trim off the top 3 to 4 inches of the leeks, as well as the roots. Halve them lengthwise and cut them into ½-inch half-moons. Fill a large bowl with cold water and add the leeks, separating the layers to release the grit. Wipe off your cutting board and drain the leeks in a colander, giving them one extra rinse. Dry on a clean kitchen towel. Thinly slice the celery.

3 **leeks**

4 to 5 small **celery stalks**

2 tablespoons **EVOO** (extra-virgin olive oil)

Salt and **pepper**

1 **bay leaf**, fresh or dried

4 cups **chicken stock**

2 cups **heavy cream**

1 pound **chicken tenders**, diced

2 (12-ounce) packages fresh **gnocchi**

A handful of fresh flat-leaf **parsley**, finely chopped

1 teaspoon **sweet paprika**

3 tablespoons **dry sherry**

Heat the EVOO over medium heat in a soup pot or a Dutch oven. Add the leeks and celery to the pot and season with salt and pepper, add the bay leaf, and cook for 5 to 6 minutes to soften. Add the stock and raise the heat to bring to a boil. Stir in the cream and reduce the heat to a simmer. When the soup bubbles, add the chicken and gnocchi and cook for 5 to 6 minutes. The soup will become thick like a creamy stew. Adjust the salt and pepper and stir in the parsley, paprika, and sherry. Discard the bay leaf. Serve the stoup immediately.

SERVES 4

POTATO SOUP WITH THE WORKS

8 slices of **bacon**, chopped

4 **leeks**, white parts only, chopped

4 to 5 **garlic cloves**, chopped

8 sprigs of fresh **thyme**, leaves stripped from the stems

1 tablespoon **paprika**, plus additional for garnish

Salt and **pepper**

4 pounds **russet potatoes**, peeled and chopped

6 cups **chicken stock**

A dash of **hot sauce** (optional)

1 cup shredded extra-sharp **cheddar cheese**

1 cup shredded **Parmigiano-Reggiano**

Chopped **scallions**, for garnish

Sour cream, for garnish

This super soup tastes like a double-stuffed baked potato with the works. We served it to our TV audience the day we took the show to Bryant Park in Manhattan and did the first talk-show broadcast on ice.

In a large, heavy-bottomed pot, cook the bacon over medium-high heat until golden brown, 3 to 4 minutes. Remove the cooked bacon to a paper-towel-lined plate and reserve.

While the bacon cooks, fill a bowl with cold water and add the leeks. Swish vigorously to release the grit, then lift out the leeks and dry on a kitchen towel.

Add the leeks and garlic to the bacon fat and cook until tender, 4 to 5 minutes. Add the thyme, paprika, and salt and pepper, then add the potatoes and stock to the pot and bring up to a bubble over high heat. Reduce the heat to medium and simmer the potatoes until cooked through, 8 to 10 minutes. When the potatoes are tender, use a blender, a food processor, or an immersion blender to puree the soup until smooth.

Adjust the seasonings as needed with salt, pepper, and hot sauce, if desired. Serve the soup in a bowl or a mug topped with the two cheeses, the reserved bacon, a sprinkling of scallions, a dollop of sour cream, and a dash of paprika.

SERVES 4

SMOKY TOMATO SOUP WITH MINI GRILLED CHEESE AND BACON SAMMIES

1 tablespoon **EVOO** (extra-virgin olive oil)

4 slices **smoked bacon**, chopped

3 **garlic cloves**, chopped

1 **onion**, chopped

3 **celery stalks**, chopped

2 **carrots**, chopped

Salt and **pepper**

4 cups **chicken stock**

½ teaspoon **dried marjoram** or **oregano**

1 (28-ounce) can crushed **fire-roasted tomatoes**, partially drained (if you only have diced or whole fire-roasted tomatoes, don't sweat it; it all gets ground up later)

1 teaspoon **sugar**

2 teaspoons **hot smoked paprika**, ⅔ palmful

¼ cup **heavy cream**

Butter, for the skillet

16 slices of party-size rye, pumpernickel, or whole wheat **bread**, such as Pepperidge Farm

8 square slices of extra-sharp **cheddar cheese**, ¼ inch thick

3 tablespoons finely chopped fresh **chives**

1½ cups (a single-serving bag) **white cheddar popcorn**

Sammie nights are always fun; this one brings out the little kid in me.

Heat the EVOO in a medium soup pot over medium-high heat. Add the chopped bacon and cook until crisp, 2 to 3 minutes. Using a slotted spoon, transfer the crispy bacon to paper towels to drain and reserve for the mini grilled cheese and bacon sammies.

To the same pot, add the garlic, onions, celery, and carrots and season with salt and pepper. Cook for 5 to 6 minutes, until the vegetables are tender. Scoop the veggies into a food processor, add about ½ cup of the chicken stock and the marjoram, and puree until smooth. If the tomatoes you are using are whole or diced, add them to the processor with the veggies and puree.

Return the pureed veggies to the pot, place back over medium-high heat, and add the remaining chicken stock, the crushed or pureed fire-roasted tomatoes, the sugar, and the smoked paprika. Bring the soup up to a bubble, stir in the cream, and keep warm over low heat while you make the sammies.

Heat some butter in a large skillet over medium heat. While the butter is melting, lay 8 of the bread slices on a cutting board. Top each one with a slice of cheese, a sprinkle of the reserved bacon, some chives, and another slice of bread. Transfer 4 of the mini sammies to the hot skillet and cook until the sandwich is toasted on both sides and the cheese is melted. Repeat with the remaining 4 sammies.

Serve the smoky tomato soup with some popcorn floating on top and the grilled mini grilled cheese and bacon sammies alongside.

SERVES 4

ONE-POT WONDER
CACCIATORE STOUP
WITH TURKEY SAUSAGE MEATBALLS

Here's yet another twist on a winter favorite of mine: cacciatore. This fun, lighter version makes the traditional dish—which is usually prepared with rabbit or chicken—more accessible; it's easy on the palate *and* easy on time.

Heat the EVOO in a Dutch oven or soup pot over medium-high heat. Add the portabella mushrooms, peppers, and onions and cook until tender, 7 to 8 minutes. Season the vegetables with the red pepper flakes, salt, and black pepper.

While the vegetables cook, rip up the white bread and combine it with the milk in a mixing bowl; let it soak for 5 minutes. Add the turkey to the bowl along with the egg, cheese, parsley, garlic, and salt and pepper. Mix with your hands or a wooden spoon or rubber spatula.

Add the tomatoes to the pot with the mushrooms and break them up with a wooden spoon. Stir in the stock and raise the heat to bring the stoup to a boil. When the stoup boils, form the turkey mixture into 2-inch meatballs and drop them into the stoup as you make them. Cover the pot, reduce the heat, and simmer the meatballs in the stoup for 10 to 12 minutes. Serve in shallow bowls with crusty whole grain bread for mopping and extra cheese for topping.

SERVES 4

3 tablespoons **EVOO** (extra-virgin olive oil)

2 **portabella mushroom caps**, wiped clean and chopped into bite-size cubes

2 **cubanelle peppers** (light green, mild Italian peppers), seeded and chopped into bite-size pieces

1 large **red bell pepper**, seeded and chopped into bite-size pieces

1 large **onion**, chopped into bite-size pieces

½ to 1 teaspoon **crushed red pepper flakes**

Coarse salt and **black pepper**

3 slices of **white bread**

½ cup **milk**

1 pound **ground turkey breast**

1 **egg**

½ cup grated **Parmigiano-Reggiano** or **Pecorino** Romano cheese, a couple of handfuls, plus some to pass at the table

A handful of fresh flat-leaf **parsley**, finely chopped

2 **garlic cloves**, finely chopped

1 (28-ounce) can **San Marzano tomatoes** or whole canned plum tomatoes

4 cups **chicken stock**

Crusty whole grain bread, to pass at the table

PINCHIN' PENNIES

- GRILLED CHEESE ON PUMP
- SWEET 'N' "SAUER" CABBAGE SOUP

Nothin' stretches a buck like cabbage. This is not only a low-cost meal, it's like throwing your own personal Oktoberfest, any time you like.

Grilled Cheese on Pump

8 slices of **pumpernickel bread**

4 tablespoons (½ stick) **butter**, softened

8 teaspoons **Dijon mustard**

8 slices of **Emmentaler Swiss cheese**

2 large **dill pickles**, thinly sliced lengthwise

Heat a skillet over medium heat. Spread one side of all 8 slices of bread with butter. Spread the other side of 4 of the slices with mustard. Top each mustard-coated bread slice with a folded slice of Emmentaler, and place some pickle slices on top. Cover with a second slice of bread, buttered side up. Place the sandwiches in a hot skillet and cook for 3 to 4 minutes on each side, toasting and crisping the bread. Cut the sandwiches in half from corner to corner and serve.

SERVES 4

Sweet 'n' "Sauer" Cabbage Soup

2 tablespoons **EVOO** (extra-virgin olive oil)

½ pound **ham steak**, cut into ½-inch dice

1 **Savoy cabbage**, quartered, cored, and shredded

1 **onion**, quartered and thinly sliced

1 cup shredded **carrots**

2 cups frozen shredded **hash brown potatoes**

Salt and **pepper**

1 **bay leaf**, fresh or dried

2 cups **apple cider**

¼ cup **honey**

1 (14-ounce) can **white beans**, rinsed and drained

4 cups **chicken stock**

1-pound sack of **sauerkraut**, rinsed and drained

¼ cup chopped fresh **dill**

1 cup **sour cream**, to pass at the table

Heat the EVOO in a soup pot over medium-high heat. Add the ham and brown lightly for 2 to 3 minutes. Add the shredded cabbage to the pot and stir in the onions and carrots as you finish slicing and shredding them. Stir in the frozen hash browns and season the vegetables liberally with salt and pepper. Add the bay leaf, cider, honey, beans, and chicken stock. Cover the pot and bring the soup to a boil, then simmer uncovered for 10 minutes or until the vegetables are tender. Stir in the kraut and dill and adjust the seasoning. Serve the soup in shallow bowls topped with a spoonful of sour cream.

SERVES 4 TO 6

BALLPARK BURRITOS

When you can't make it to the ballpark for a real American baseball dog, these burritos stuffed with braised franks and all the fixin's are the next best thing. Try one of these three burrito wraps for your next seventh-inning stretch!

L.A. BALLPARK BURRITOS

To make the braised hot dogs: Place the franks in a skillet with ¼ inch water and a drizzle of oil. Bring the water to a boil, reduce the heat to a simmer, and allow the water to cook off while the dogs warm through. When the water has cooked off cover the pan loosely with foil to reduce spatter and allow the casings to crisp for 1 minute, shaking the pan a few times.

Combine the tomatillos, pickles, jalapeños, red onion, lime zest and juice, and cilantro in a bowl. Toss and season with salt.

Heat the beans in a small skillet over medium heat and season with the cumin, hot sauce, and salt.

Heat a skillet over medium to medium-high heat. Add one tortilla, heat until it blisters on one side, then turn it over in the pan. Top with one quarter of the cheese. When the cheese melts a little, transfer it to a plate. In the center of the tortilla, pile up one quarter of the beans, some shredded lettuce, one quarter of the salsa, and a hot dog. Tuck the ends in and wrap and roll the burrito. Make 3 more burritos in the same way. Have at it and play ball, dude!

SERVES 4

4 beef or pork **hot dogs**
  Drizzle of **EVOO** (extra-virgin olive oil)
4 **tomatillos**, husked, rinsed and chopped
2 **dill pickles**, chopped
1 **jalapeño**, seeded and finely chopped
¼ **red onion**, finely chopped
2 teaspoons **lime zest** plus the juice of 1 lime
¼ cup chopped fresh **cilantro**
  Salt
1 (15-ounce) can **black beans**, partially drained
1 teaspoon **ground cumin**
1 tablespoon **hot sauce**
4 large **flour tortillas**
1 cup shredded **Monterey Jack cheese**
1 cup shredded **lettuce**

N.Y. DELI BALLPARK BURRITOS

Heat the beans in a small pan over medium heat and bump up the flavor with the hot sauce, Worcestershire, and black pepper. Mix gently.

Combine the sauerkraut in a small pan with the mustard and beer. Bring to a boil, then simmer for 5 minutes.

Heat a tortilla in a skillet over medium-high heat until it blisters, flip it over, place a slice of Swiss on the tortilla, and let it melt for 1 minute. Transfer the tortilla to a plate and top the cheese with one quarter of the beans, some kraut, some raw chopped onion, and a dog. Tuck the edges of the burrito in, wrap, and roll. Make 3 more burritos in the same fashion.

SERVES 4

1 (16-ounce) can barbecued **baked beans**
2 teaspoons **hot sauce**
1 teaspoon **Worcestershire sauce**
  Black pepper
1 pound **sauerkraut**, rinsed and drained
¼ to ⅓ cup **dark spicy mustard**
1 cup **beer**
4 large **flour tortillas**
4 deli slices of **Swiss cheese**
1 small **white onion**, finely chopped
4 braised **hot dogs** (see above)

CHICAGO BALLPARK BURRITOS

If you are from Chi-town, feel free to substitute neon green relish for the sweet pickle relish.

Whisk the mustard, vinegar, and EVOO in a medium salad bowl. Add the lettuce, jalapeños, tomatoes, and onions to the bowl, toss to coat, and season with celery salt and pepper. One at a time, blister the tortillas on both sides in a dry pan. Build the burritos by piling some salad onto each burrito, topping with relish, and adding a pickle spear and a dog. Tuck in the sides, then wrap and roll the burrito. Repeat with the remaining ingredients.

SERVES 4

¼ cup **yellow mustard**

2 tablespoons **white wine vinegar**

¼ cup **EVOO** (extra-virgin olive oil)

1 heart of **romaine lettuce**, chopped

2 **jalapeños**, seeded and very thinly sliced

2 **tomatoes**, cut into wedges

½ **red onion**, thinly sliced

Celery salt

Black pepper

4 large **flour tortillas**

½ cup **sweet pickle relish**

4 large spears of half-sour, garlic, or **dill pickle**

4 braised **hot dogs** (see page 20)

PAT'S RABE STROMBOLI BREAD

Pat, the mother-in-law of a friend of mine at work, came to visit him one afternoon, and she stopped me in the hall to share this recipe. I added sausage to it (for my husband), but without sausage it makes an awesome vegetarian entrée as well.

Preheat the oven to 375°F. Halve the bread lengthwise and scoop out the insides.

Heat about 2 inches of water in a deep skillet over high heat and bring to a boil. Salt the water. Trim the ends off the broccoli rabe and cut into 3- to 4-inch pieces. Cook in the salted water, adding the rabes in stages as they wilt down—it's a mountain of greens! Reduce the heat and simmer for 5 minutes. Drain the broccoli rabe, rinse under cold water, and reserve.

Heat the EVOO in a large skillet over medium to medium-high heat. Add the sausage and cook, breaking it up into crumbles as it browns. Add the garlic and cook for 2 minutes, then add the rabe and heat through. Season with salt, pepper, and nutmeg to taste.

Fill the bread with the broccoli rabe and sausage and top with the Parmigiano, provolone, and mozzarella. Close up the sandwich, wrap in foil, and bake to melt the cheese, 12 to 15 minutes. Cut into thick portions and serve.

SERVES 4 TO 6

1 large loaf of **semolina bread**

Salt

2 bunches of **broccoli rabe**

3 tablespoons **EVOO** (extra-virgin olive oil)

1 pound bulk hot or sweet **chicken** or **pork sausage**

3 to 4 **garlic cloves**, chopped

Black pepper

Freshly grated **nutmeg**

1 cup grated **Parmigiano-Reggiano**

2 cups shredded **provolone**

8 thin slices of **mozzarella**

TILAPIA SAMMIES WITH
CITRUS HONEY SLAW

4 **tilapia fillets**, 6 to 8 ounces each

3 **limes**, 1 of them zested

Salt and **pepper**

All-purpose flour, for dredging

2 **eggs**, lightly beaten

½ sleeve of **saltine crackers**, ground up in the food processor (about 2 cups of crumbs)

2 teaspoons **smoked paprika**, ⅔ palmful

1 tablespoon **seafood seasoning**, such as Old Bay, a palmful

2 tablespoons plus ¼ cup **EVOO** (extra-virgin olive oil)

4 whole wheat **hoagie rolls**, split in half lengthwise

1 cup **sour cream**

1 **chipotle in adobo**, seeded and finely chopped, plus 1 teaspoon or so of the adobo sauce

2 teaspoons **hot sauce**

3 tablespoons **honey**

1 (16-ounce) bag of **slaw salad mix**

1 head **Bibb or romaine lettuce**, core removed, leaves separated and cleaned

1 large **beefsteak tomato**, thinly sliced

1 ripe **Hass avocado**, sliced

1 small **red onion**, sliced

1 **deli pickle**, thinly sliced lengthwise

This fish sammie is a real looker, supersized and spicy. If you usually get your fish sandwiches at the drive-thru, drive to the market and get these ingredients instead; you'll never eat fish in your car again.

Preheat the oven to 400°F or the broiler to high.

Season the fillets with lime zest, salt, and pepper. Set up three dishes on the counter: one with the flour, one with the eggs, and the third with the ground saltines, smoked paprika, and seafood seasoning. Bread the seasoned fish fillets by coating them first in the flour, then in the egg, and finally in the seasoned cracker crumbs.

Once all of the fillets have been breaded, place a large skillet over medium-high heat with about 2 tablespoons of EVOO. Once the oil is hot add the breaded fillets to the pan and cook until golden brown on each side and cooked through, 3 to 4 minutes per side. Remove the cooked fillets to a paper-towel-lined plate and squeeze the juice of half a lime over them so they soak up the lime juice while they're still hot.

While the fish fillets are cooking, place the split rolls onto a baking sheet and toast them in the hot oven until golden brown.

Combine the sour cream, chipotle, and adobo sauce in a small bowl and reserve.

In a medium mixing bowl, whisk together the juice of 2 limes, the hot sauce, and the honey. Whisk in the remaining ¼ cup of EVOO and some salt and pepper. Empty the bag of slaw mix into the dressing and give it a toss to coat.

Once the fish is cooked, assemble the sammies. Place the fish on the bottom of the rolls and top with lettuce and tomato. Douse the avocado with the juice of the remaining half lime. Top the tomato with avocado, onions, and pickle slices. Slather the roll tops with the flavored sour cream and set in place. Serve the sammies with the slaw alongside.

SERVES 4

BLTT: BACON, LETTUCE, TOMATO JAM, AND TUNA STEAK SANDWICHES

8 slices **peppered bacon**

2 tablespoons **EVOO** (extra-virgin olive oil), plus some for drizzling

1 small or medium **red onion**, chopped

2 **garlic cloves**, chopped

Salt and **pepper**

1 cup loosely packed tender sun-**dried tomatoes** (from a pouch, not oil-packed)

1 teaspoon **Worcestershire sauce**

2 tablespoons **aged balsamic vinegar**

2 tablespoons **brown sugar**, packed

4 (1-inch-thick) **tuna steaks**, 4 to 6 ounces each

1 tablespoon **grill seasoning**, such as McCormick's Montreal Steak Seasoning

2 teaspoons grated **lemon** or **orange zest**

1 tablespoon finely chopped fresh **rosemary**

4 **ciabatta rolls**, split in half, or 8 whole grain bread slices

8 leaves of **red leaf lettuce**

There's a great restaurant called 202 in Chelsea Market, home of Food Network and of the studio where we tape *30 Minute Meals*. Not only is the food and drink at 202 fresh, creative, and exceptional, half of the restaurant is filled with eccentric housewares and Nicole Farhi's clothing for men and women. At lunchtime, one of my favorites is a sammie with a tasty tomato jam like this one. At home I use it to make this awesome tuna BLT. It makes a delicious lunch or a simple dinner.

Preheat the oven to 375°F. Arrange the bacon on a slotted broiler pan and bake until crisp, 15 to 20 minutes. Remove the bacon from the oven and turn the oven to broil.

Heat 1 tablespoon of the EVOO in a small pot over medium-high heat. Add the onions and garlic and season with salt and pepper. Cook for 7 to 8 minutes, then add the sun-dried tomatoes, Worcestershire, vinegar, brown sugar, and ½ cup of water. Bring to a boil, then reduce the heat to a simmer and cook until a thick jam forms, 7 to 8 minutes, stirring occasionally.

Season the tuna with the grill seasoning, zest, and rosemary. Heat a skillet over medium-high heat with the remaining 1 tablespoon of EVOO. Cook the fish for 4 minutes, turning once, for rare to medium, or 8 minutes total for cooked-through fish.

While the fish cooks, toast the bread under the broiler.

To serve, drizzle the hot bread with EVOO. Place 2 lettuce leaves on 4 rolls and top each with a tuna steak, 2 bacon strips, halved and crisscrossed, and a pile of jam. Set the roll top in place and serve.

SERVES 4

THE ULTIMATE HAM AND CHEESE SANDWICH AND MIXED GREENS WITH RASPBERRY VINAIGRETTE

This sammie is like a *croque-monsieur* that hooked up for a one-night stand with a Monte Cristo. The result is the ultimate in ham-and-cheese sandwiches.

Place a medium pot over medium heat and melt 2 tablespoons of the butter. Sprinkle the flour over the melted butter and cook for about 1 minute. Slowly whisk the milk and mustard into the butter-flour mixture. Season the sauce with some fresh nutmeg, salt, and pepper, and cook for a minute or two until it thickens up.

Place 4 slices of the bread on the counter. Spread some of the sauce onto each slice of bread, then lay down 3 slices of ham per sammie, a couple slices of cheese, and another smear of sauce. Top each sandwich with the remaining bread slices.

Place a large skillet over medium-low heat and melt the remaining tablespoon of butter. Whisk the eggs in a high-sided dish. Dip the sandwiches in the egg and transfer them to the hot pan. Cook until golden brown, 3 to 4 minutes per side.

While the sandwiches are cooking, in the bottom of a salad bowl, whisk the raspberry jam, shallot, and vinegar. Whisking constantly, stream in the EVOO, then season the dressing with some salt and pepper. Toss the salad greens in the dressing and serve them up alongside the best ham and cheese you've ever had!

SERVES 4

3 tablespoons **butter**

2 tablespoons **all-purpose flour**

1 cup **milk**

2 tablespoons **Dijon mustard**

Freshly grated **nutmeg**

Salt and **pepper**

8 slices of **white bread**

12 slices of **deli ham**

8 slices of **Swiss** or **Gruyère cheese**

2 **eggs**

1 tablespoon **raspberry jam**

1 small **shallot**, minced

2 tablespoons **white vinegar**

⅓ cup **EVOO** (extra-virgin olive oil)

5 to 6 cups, a 10-ounce sack, of **mixed salad greens**

GYRO STEAK SANDWICH

2 pounds **London broil** or sirloin, at room temperature

EVOO (extra-virgin olive oil), for drizzling

Salt and **pepper**

1 cup plain **Greek yogurt**

1 small **garlic clove**, grated or minced

½ teaspoon **ground cumin** (eyeball it)

1 teaspoon **ground coriander**

Juice of 1 **lemon**

1 teaspoon **hot sauce**

¼ seedless **cucumber**, thinly sliced

2 vine-ripe **tomatoes**, seeded and chopped

1 heart of **romaine lettuce**, shredded

½ small **red onion**, thinly sliced

A couple handfuls of fresh flat-leaf **parsley leaves**

½ cup yellow **hot pepper rings**

4 large **Mediterranean flatbreads**

1 cup crumbled **feta**

Gyro, spiced ground lamb that is molded onto a giant rotisserie kebab, is hard to find if you do not live in a big city or near a good Greek diner. This simple sliced steak supper is a lean, mean knock-off of the big-city gyro pita. If you like these flavors as much as I do, check out the ground-meat gyro on page 74.

Heat the broiler to high and set the rack 6 inches from the heating element. Drizzle the meat with EVOO and season with salt and pepper. Broil the meat for 7 minutes on each side, then let it rest for 10 minutes.

In a small bowl, stir together the yogurt with the garlic, cumin, coriander, lemon juice, and hot sauce. Toss together the cukes, tomatoes, lettuce, and onions with the parsley and pepper rings. Char the flatbreads over an open flame on your stove or in a dry hot skillet. Slice the steak and serve the meat on a flatbread topped with some of the salad, sauce, and feta. Roll the flatbread around the gyro and wrap with foil or a piece of parchment to hold the sammie together while you're eating.

SERVES 4

HANDY-PASTO ANTIPASTO PIZZA

1 tube prepared **pizza dough**

2 cups shredded **provolone**

A couple of handfuls of grated **Parmigiano-Reggiano**

2 **garlic cloves**, grated or finely chopped

A few grinds of **black pepper**

A pinch of **red pepper flakes**

1 small heart of **romaine lettuce**, chopped

8 slices of **Genoa salami**, chopped

2 roasted **red peppers**, chopped

2 to 3 tablespoons chopped **banana pepper rings** or chopped hot peppers of any kind

A couple of **artichoke hearts** or marinated mushrooms, chopped

A handful of good-quality pitted green or black **olives**, coarsely chopped

Topped with all the makings of an antipasto platter, this white pizza with garlic makes a great starter or party snack cut into squares. Many of the antipasto toppers can be purchased by weight at the salad bar counter, so you only have to buy what you need.

Preheat the oven to 425°F. Press the dough onto a baking sheet and top with the cheeses, garlic, and black and red pepper. Bake for 15 to 18 minutes. Top the cooked pizza with the lettuce, salami, roasted peppers, hot peppers, artichokes or mushrooms, and olives. Cut into squares and serve.

SERVES 6 AS AN APPETIZER

PASTA

CHICKPEAS! THANK YOU!
BABA GANOUSH–HUMMUS PASTA

A few months ago I started cooking with whole wheat pasta because I was working on family-friendly recipes for my *Yum-o!* family cookbook. Whole wheat pastas are loaded with protein and fiber so it's a really easy way to help kids get more of both. I tried some whole wheat spaghetti for John and myself one night. The preparation was simple, just ten shallots and cheese dressed it, but from the first nutty-delicious bite I was hooked! (See That's Shallota Flavor Spaghetti, opposite.) The earthy flavor of chickpeas is a natural complement to whole wheat pasta, too. Here I let a couple of dip-n-spread favorites inspire a hearty vegetarian sauce.

Salt

1 pound **whole wheat penne**

¼ cup **EVOO** (extra-virgin olive oil)

4 **garlic cloves**, finely chopped or grated

1 teaspoon **crushed red pepper flakes**

1 (15-ounce) can **chickpeas**

1 medium **eggplant**, peeled and chopped

2 teaspoons **ground cumin**

2 teaspoons **ground coriander**

Black pepper

1 cup **vegetable stock**

¼ cup **tahini paste**

Juice of 1 **lemon**

½ cup fresh flat-leaf **parsley leaves**, coarsely chopped

4 **scallions**, thinly sliced on an angle

¼ cup **pine nuts**

Bring a large pot of water to a boil for the pasta. When it boils, salt the water, add the pasta, and cook to al dente. Heads up: you will need to save 1 ladleful of the starchy pasta cooking water before you drain the pasta.

While the water comes to a boil, heat the EVOO in a deep skillet over medium heat. Add the garlic and red pepper flakes, cook for 1 to 2 minutes, then add the chickpeas and eggplant and stir to coat with the garlicky oil. Season the chickpeas and eggplant with the cumin, coriander, and salt and pepper, then stir in the stock. Cover and cook for 10 minutes until the eggplant is tender. Stir in the tahini paste and lemon juice and transfer to a food processor. Process the chickpea and eggplant mixture until almost smooth, then transfer to a large pasta bowl.

Drain the pasta, reserving a ladle of starchy cooking liquid. Add the pasta water to the sauce, then add the pasta and toss with the sauce. Top with the parsley, scallions, and pine nuts.

SERVES 4

THAT'S SHALLOTA FLAVOR SPAGHETTI

2 tablespoons **EVOO** (extra-virgin olive oil)

2 tablespoons **butter**

2 **garlic cloves**, finely chopped

10 big **shallots**, halved then thinly sliced

Salt and **pepper**

1 pound **whole wheat spaghetti**

A generous handful of fresh flat-leaf **parsley**, chopped

1 cup grated **Parmigiano-Reggiano**

Made with ten shallots per pound of whole wheat spaghetti, this pasta dish delivers unbelievable flavor—it's a knockout! It's like a bowl of French onion soup, hold the broth. Serve it up with sautéed broccoli rabe or a simple green salad.

Heat the EVOO with the butter over medium-low heat in a skillet with high sides. Add the garlic and shallots and season with salt and pepper, then cook gently until caramelized, about 20 minutes, stirring occasionally.

Meanwhile, bring a large pot of water to a boil for the pasta. Salt the water very liberally, then add the spaghetti and cook to al dente. When the pasta is nearly done, add 2 ladles of the starchy cooking water, about 1 cup, to the shallots and stir. Drain the pasta and add it to the shallots. Add the parsley and cheese and more pepper to taste. Toss for a minute or two to allow the pasta to absorb the sauce, then serve. Wow! Talk about yum-o!

SERVES 4

CREAMY PARSLEY AND PISTACHIO FETTUCCINE

Salt

1 pound **fettuccine pasta**

1 **lemon**

¾ cup **heavy cream**

1 packed cup fresh flat-leaf **parsley leaves**

¼ cup shelled natural **pistachio nuts**, lightly toasted (see Note, page 102)

⅓ cup grated **Parmigiano-Reggiano**

1 large **garlic clove**, grated or minced

3 tablespoons **EVOO** (extra-virgin olive oil)

Black pepper

This one will make you want to make out, so be careful who you serve it to.

Bring a large pot of water to a boil. Salt it, add the pasta, and cook to al dente.

Zest the lemon and combine it with the cream in a small sauce pot. Heat over medium-low heat until hot but not boiling.

Place the parsley leaves, nuts, cheese, and garlic in a food processor. Squeeze the zested lemon into the bowl. Turn the processor on and stream in the EVOO with the motor running to make a pesto.

Drain the pasta.

Place the pesto in the bottom of a large pasta serving bowl and season with salt and pepper. Stir the hot cream into the pesto, then add the hot pasta and toss to combine. Adjust the salt and pepper. Serve with a green salad.

SERVES 4

BELIEVE IN BACON
- AMERICAN-ITALIAN ALL'AMATRICIANA
- FENNEL AND CELERY SLAW

Spaghetti all'Amatriciana—with pancetta, onion, garlic, and tomato—is an old favorite. This is an American-Italian cousin of the Italian classic, a smoky, salty, satisfying supper. I use cassarecci pasta, a shape similar to cavatelli, but any tubular pasta is fine.

American-Italian all'Amatriciana

Bring a large pot of water to a boil for the pasta. Salt the water, add the pasta, and cook to al dente.

While the pasta water is heating up, heat the EVOO in a deep skillet over medium-high. Add the bacon and crisp for 4 to 5 minutes, then add the onions and garlic and cook to soften, 5 to 6 minutes. Stir in the stock, then the tomatoes, and season with pepper to taste. Simmer the sauce for 15 minutes. Toss the drained pasta with the sauce and parsley. Serve topped with shredded sharp white cheddar.

SERVES 4 TO 6

Salt

1 pound **whole wheat cassarecci**, rigatoni, or penne pasta

1 tablespoon **EVOO** (extra-virgin olive oil)

6 slices of lean **peppered bacon**, chopped

1 large **red onion**, chopped

4 **garlic cloves**, finely chopped or grated

1 cup **chicken stock**

1 (28-ounce) can crushed **fire-roasted tomatoes**

Black pepper

A handful of fresh flat-leaf **parsley**, chopped

Shredded **sharp white cheddar**, to pass at the table

Fennel and Celery Slaw

Mix the vinegar and sugar in the bottom of a salad bowl and whisk in the EVOO. Add the slaw mix. Chop the fennel fronds and add to the cabbage, then quarter the fennel bulb, cut away the core, and thinly slice the bulb. Add to the cabbage. Add the celery and basil to the salad, toss to combine, and season liberally with salt and pepper.

SERVES 4

3 tablespoons **white wine vinegar**

2 teaspoons **sugar**

⅓ cup **EVOO** (extra-virgin olive oil)

½ pound shredded **slaw salad mix**

1 **fennel bulb**, trimmed (reserve a handful of the feathery fronds)

4 **celery stalks** from the heart, thinly sliced on an angle

10 fresh **basil leaves**, thinly sliced

Salt and **pepper**

ROASTED PASTA ALLA NORMA WITH ORANGE AND ARUGULA SALAD

I love the classic pasta alla Norma, but making the roasted version cuts way back on the amount of oil you have to use. This way I can have seconds!

Preheat the oven to 400°F.

Cut 4 to 5 slits on one side of the eggplant and place it slit side up on a rimmed baking sheet.

Trim off the top third of the head of garlic, exposing the cloves. Place the garlic on a piece of aluminum foil, drizzle with a tablespoon of the EVOO, wrap it up, and place it and the eggplant in the oven. Roast them both for about 45 minutes, until the eggplant looks like a flat tire and the garlic is tender.

When the eggplant and garlic have been in the oven for 15 minutes, put the grape tomatoes on a rimmed baking sheet, drizzle them with a tablespoon of the EVOO, and season with salt and pepper. Roast in the oven for about 30 minutes.

Place a large pot of water over high heat with a lid on it and bring up to a boil. Once it is boiling, salt the water and add the pasta; cook to al dente. Heads up: right before draining the pasta, ladle about 1 cup of the pasta cooking water into the bottom of a large pasta bowl.

While the pasta is cooking, use a sharp knife to cut the ends and the skin off the orange. Slice it into disks. Arrange the arugula on a serving platter and scatter the orange and onion slices on top. Squeeze the lemon half directly over the orange slices, drizzle with the remaining 2 tablespoons of EVOO, and season with salt and pepper.

When the vegetables are all roasted, split the eggplant open and scoop the roasted flesh into the serving bowl with the pasta water. Add the roasted tomatoes. Squeeze the roasted garlic flesh from the papery skins into the bowl with the eggplant and tomatoes. With a large wooden spoon or a potato masher, smash up the eggplant, tomatoes, and garlic until thoroughly combined. Season with some salt and pepper, add the pasta and basil, and toss for a minute. Serve in shallow bowls topped with lots of grated or crumbled ricotta salata.

SERVES 4

1 large, firm **eggplant**

1 large head of **garlic**

4 tablespoons **EVOO** (extra-virgin olive oil)

2 pints **grape tomatoes**

Salt and **pepper**

1 pound **cavatappi** (hollow corkscrew-shaped pasta) or other short-cut pasta

1 softball-size seedless **orange**

1 (6- to 8-ounce) bag of **arugula**

¼ **red onion**, thinly sliced

Juice of ½ **lemon**

1 cup fresh **basil**, 20 leaves, torn into pieces

⅓ pound **ricotta salata cheese**

BEEF AND GORGONZOLA GNOCCHI WITH ESCAROLE SALAD

4 tablespoons **EVOO** (extra-virgin olive oil)

1 pound **ground sirloin**

Salt and **pepper**

1 large **onion**, chopped

2 **garlic cloves**, finely chopped

¾ cup **dry white wine**

1 cup **chicken stock**

10 fresh **sage leaves**, chopped

1 cup crumbled **Gorgonzola**

1 (12- to 16-ounce) package **gnocchi**, fresh or frozen

A handful of fresh flat-leaf **parsley**, finely chopped

1 tablespoon **grainy mustard**

Juice of ½ **lemon**

1 head of **escarole**, cleaned and coarsely chopped

Meat and potatoes, Italian style, in minutes! The quality of the prepared gnocchi available in markets has really improved over the last few years. I love to use them because the dumplings cook up quickly and are so comforting.

Bring a large pot of water to a boil over high heat for the pasta.

While the water is coming to a boil, heat 1 tablespoon of the EVOO in a medium skillet over medium-high heat. Add the sirloin, season with salt and pepper, and cook until it is very well browned, about 5 minutes, breaking it up into bite-sized crumbles with a wooden spoon.

Add the onion and garlic to the pan and soften for 5 minutes; adjust the salt and pepper, add the wine to the pan, and stir for 1 minute. Stir in the stock and sage, then add the Gorgonzola. Reduce the heat to low.

Salt the boiling water well and add the gnocchi. Cook for 2 to 3 minutes until they float, then drain well and add to the skillet with the beef and cheese. Toss to combine. Top with the chopped parsley.

For the salad, combine the mustard with the lemon juice and the remaining 3 tablespoons of EVOO in a salad bowl. Season with salt and pepper. Add the escarole and toss to coat with the dressing. Serve alongside the gnocchi.

SERVES 4

PASTA E FAGIOLI AL FORNO
WITH LEMON-PEPPER SALAD

Pasta e Fagioli is a dish I revisit over and over, trying to play around with methods for it so I can keep making it new to me. Here, the classic soup turns into a baked pasta dish. Loosen your belts and open wide. Have your blankies ready for a family nap.

Pasta e Fagioli al Forno

Bring a large pot of water to a boil, salt it, cook the pasta to just shy of al dente.

Chop the pancetta into ¼ inch dice.

While pasta cooks, heat a skillet with EVOO over medium to medium-high heat. Add pancetta, cook 2 to 3 minutes then add celery, carrot, onions, garlic, rosemary, thyme and bay leaf to the skillet, season with salt and pepper. Saute the vegetables until tender, 6 to 7 minutes. Add beans and heat them through. Stir in ½ cup wine, simmer 30 seconds more and turn off heat. Remove bay leaf.

While vegetables cook, place a small sauce pot over medium heat, add butter, melt butter then whisk in flour and cook 1 minute then whisk in milk. Season sauce with salt, pepper, and nutmeg and reduce 4 to 5 minutes, stir in half the grated cheese, turn off heat and adjust seasoning.

While sauce cooks, place a rack in the middle of the oven and Preheat the broiler to high.

Drain pasta and return to the pot, toss with white bean mixture and sauce, stir to coat, transfer to a casserole dish, top with remaining cheese and place in oven to brown, 5 minutes.

SERVES 6

Salt

1 pound **penne rigate** or whole wheat penne

¼ pound **pancetta**, 3 to 4 slices thick cut like bacon

1 tablespoon **EVOO** (extra-virgin olive oil)

2 **celery stalks** from the heart with leafy tops, chopped

1 **carrot**, peeled and chopped

1 **onion**, peeled and chopped

2 to 3 large **garlic cloves**, finely chopped

2 sprigs fresh **rosemary**, finely chopped

3 to 4 sprigs fresh **thyme**, finely chopped

1 fresh **bay leaf**

Pepper

1 (15-ounce) can small **white beans**, "Roman" beans, such as Goya brand, or cannellini beans, rinsed and drained

½ cup **dry white wine**

2 tablespoons **butter**

2 tablespoons **all-purpose flour**

2 cups **milk**

Finely grated **nutmeg**, to taste

1½ cups grated **Pecorino Romano**

Lemon-Pepper Salad

Zest the lemon into a bowl. Add the juice of the lemon to the bowl with pepper, whisk in EVOO then season the dressing with salt to taste, toss the tomatoes and greens with dressing and adjust seasoning.

SERVES 6

1 **lemon**

1 teaspoon coarse **black pepper**

⅓ cup **EVOO** (extra-virgin olive oil)

Salt

½ pint **yellow tomatoes**, halved or 2 vine ripe yellow tomatoes, seeded and chopped

2 hearts **romaine lettuce**, shredded or chopped

SPRING-SUMMER ZITI

2 tablespoons **EVOO** (extra-virgin olive oil)

3 large **shallots**, thinly sliced

3 large **garlic cloves**, grated or finely chopped

1 (28-ounce) can **San Marzano plum tomatoes**

Salt and **pepper**

4 sprigs of fresh **tarragon**, leaves removed, chopped

½ cup fresh **basil**, 10 leaves, thinly sliced

1 pound **ziti rigate** (with lines)

1 pound thin **asparagus**, trimmed of woody ends, chopped into 1½-inch pieces on an angle

1 cup **frozen peas**

1 cup **ricotta cheese**

1 cup grated **Parmigiano-Reggiano**

1 teaspoon **lemon zest**

½ pound fresh **mozzarella**, thinly sliced

Baked ziti is a seasonal meal for most of us, hearty fall and winter fare. I, for one, am sick and tired of living half my months without my ziti. Here is a fake-baked ziti so light and lovely in flavor you can serve it all spring and summer long. A light tomato sauce with tarragon and basil surrounds the ziti at the bottom and on the top of the serving dish. The pasta is tossed with asparagus tips, sweet ricotta, tender peas, and Parmigiano. Have tissues handy. This one might bring you to tears.

Preheat the oven to 400°F.

Place a large pot of water over high heat and bring to a boil to cook the pasta.

While the water is coming to a boil, heat the EVOO in a medium-high-sided skillet over medium heat. Sauté the shallots and garlic for 3 to 4 minutes, then stir in the tomatoes and crush them with a wooden spoon or potato masher. Season the sauce with salt and pepper to taste, cook for 5 minutes more, then stir in the tarragon and basil and remove from the heat.

While the sauce is simmering, salt the boiling water and cook the pasta to just under al dente—a nice bite left to it. After the pasta has been cooking for 5 minutes, add the asparagus and frozen peas to the pot for a minute or 2 before draining. Drain the pasta and veggies.

Add the ricotta, half the Parmigiano cheese, and the lemon zest to the hot pasta pot. Return the hot pasta to the pot and stir to coat evenly.

Pour half the tomato sauce into a large baking dish. Add all of the ziti and top with the remaining tomato sauce. Dot the top of the dish with mozzarella and sprinkle with the remaining Parmigiano. Bake until the top is brown and bubbly, about 12 minutes.

SERVES 6

SAUSAGE MUSHROOM RAGÙ AND RIGATONI

Pasta is always a favorite when you are trying to please a crowd. This spicy, earthy comfort dish could easily feed a hungry mob. Round out this meal with either wilted spinach or a spinach salad.

Bring a large pot of water to a boil for the pasta. When the water comes to a rolling boil, salt it and cook the pasta to al dente.

While the water is heating, heat 1 tablespoon of the EVOO over medium-high heat in a large, deep skillet with high sides. When the oil ripples, add the sausage and crumble and brown it for 5 minutes. Remove the sausage to a bowl. Drain off the fat, then add the remaining tablespoon of EVOO to the skillet and the mushrooms. Cook the mushrooms until they begin to brown, about 5 minutes, then add the onions and garlic. Season with salt, pepper, and sage, and cook to soften, about 5 minutes. Stir in the beef stock and tomatoes and return the sausage to the sauce. Bring the sauce to a bubble, reduce the heat to medium-low, and simmer for 10 minutes.

Drain the pasta and return it to the pot; toss with 2 cups of the sauce and the cheese. Mound portions of pasta in shallow bowls and top with more sausage and mushroom sauce. Pass additional cheese at the table.

SERVES 6

Salt

1 pound **rigatoni** or whole wheat rigatoni

2 tablespoons **EVOO** (extra-virgin olive oil)

1½ pounds bulk hot or sweet **Italian sausage**

4 large **portabella mushroom caps**, wiped clean and chopped in 1-inch dice

1 **onion**, chopped

4 **garlic cloves**, chopped

Black pepper

5 to 6 **sage leaves**, thinly sliced

2 cups **beef stock**

1 (28-ounce) can San Marzano **tomatoes**

1 cup grated **Pecorino Romano** cheese, plus some to pass at the table

TIP: Always salt the water for pasta after it has come to a full rolling boil. Salting it before you heat it will make it take longer to reach a boil, and it can also pit the interior surfaces of your pots.

PASTA WITH TUNA-TOMATO HERB SAUCE

Salt

1 pound medium **pasta shells**

¼ cup **EVOO** (extra-virgin olive oil)

2 to 3 large **garlic cloves**, finely chopped or grated

5 to 6 whole **anchovy fillets** or 1 rounded tablespoon of anchovy paste

1 pound fresh **tuna steaks**, diced into ½-inch pieces

1 pint ripe **cherry tomatoes**

Black pepper

1 sprig fresh **rosemary**, finely chopped

¼ cup fresh flat-leaf **parsley**, a handful, chopped

½ cup **white wine**

¼ cup fresh **basil**, 5 to 6 leaves, torn or shredded

This is a combination of many of my favorite Sicilian flavors. The sauce begins with *aglio e olio,* garlic and oil and anchovies. The tuna, cherry tomatoes, and herbs take this dish to another level. I can eat the whole panful by myself—that's my Sicilian appetite!

Place a large pot of water over high heat and bring it to a boil. Salt the water and cook the pasta to al dente.

While the pasta is boiling, place a large skillet over medium-low heat with about ¼ cup EVOO, 4 turns of the pan. Gently cook the garlic and anchovies 3 to 4 minutes until the anchovies melt away into the oil and garlic is tender and very fragrant. Raise the heat to medium-high and add the tuna and tomatoes and season with black pepper, rosemary and parsley. Toss 5 to 6 minutes to burst the tomatoes and cook the tuna. Stir in the wine and cook a minute or two.

Drain the pasta and combine with the sauce and basil. Serve immediately.

SERVES 4

NEW YORK DELI MAC 'N' CHEESE

Salt

1 pound **cavatappi**, hollow corkscrew-shaped pasta, or other short-cut

3 tablespoons **butter**, plus extra to butter bread

3 tablespoons **all-purpose flour**

1 cup **chicken stock**

2 cups **milk**

¼ cup **spicy deli mustard**

1½ cups shredded **sharp white cheddar cheese**

1½ cups shredded **Swiss cheese**

½ pound **pastrami**, chopped

4 slices **rye bread**, toasted and buttered, finely chopped

Black pepper

Mac 'n' cheese meets pastrami on rye—hold the pickle.

Preheat the broiler to high or oven to 400°F.

Place a large pot of water over high heat and bring it to a boil to cook the pasta. Once at a boil, add some salt and the pasta and cook it until al dente.

While the pasta is cooking, heat a medium skillet over medium heat and add the butter. When the butter melts, add the flour and cook for a minute, stirring. Whisk in the stock, milk, and spicy mustard and bring to a bubble. Stir in two-thirds of cheese in a figure-eight motion. Fold in the pastrami. Adjust the seasonings.

Drain the cooked pasta well and combine with the sauce. Pour into a 9 x 13-inch baking dish and top with the crumbled rye toast and remaining cheeses. Sprinkle with black pepper. Brown under the broiler for 3 to 5 minutes.

SERVES 6

VENETIAN MAC 'N' CHEESE WITH RADICCHIO AND SHRIMP

This dish is based on baked pasta au gratin I had in Venice with my hubby, John. There it was served as a starter course, but at home it takes center plate!

Bring a big pot of water to a boil for the pasta. Salt the water, add the pasta, and cook to al dente.

While the pasta is working, melt the butter in a medium sauce pot over medium heat. Whisk in the flour, cook for a minute or so, then whisk in the chicken stock and then the half-and-half. Season the sauce with salt, pepper, and a little nutmeg and simmer for 6 to 7 minutes to thicken. Adjust the seasonings.

Heat the EVOO in a skillet over medium heat. Add the anchovy paste, if using, and the garlic, cook for a minute, then add the shrimp and radicchio. Raise the heat a touch and cook for 3 to 4 minutes, until the shrimp is pink and firm and the radicchio is tender.

Preheat the broiler.

Stir the Parmigiano into the white sauce. Drain the pasta and toss with the white sauce, shrimp, and radicchio. Pour into a casserole or serving dish. Sprinkle the pasta with the asiago and brown under the broiler for 2 to 3 minutes. Serve immediately.

SERVES 4

Salt

1 pound medium **pasta shells**

2 tablespoons **butter**

2 tablespoons **all-purpose flour**

1 cup **chicken stock**

1½ cups half-and-half or whole **milk**

Black pepper

A little freshly grated **nutmeg**

2 tablespoons **EVOO** (extra-virgin olive oil)

1 teaspoon **anchovy paste** (optional)

2 to 3 **garlic cloves**, finely chopped or grated

1 pound medium **shrimp**, peeled, deveined, and tails removed

2 small or medium heads of **radicchio**, shredded

1 cup grated **Parmigiano-Reggiano**

1 cup shredded **asiago cheese**

BUFFALO CHICKEN CHILI MAC

2 tablespoons **EVOO** (extra-virgin olive oil)

2 pounds boneless skinless **chicken breasts**, cut into small bits

1 large **carrot**, peeled and finely chopped

1 large **onion**, chopped

3 **celery stalks**, finely chopped

5 large **garlic cloves**, finely chopped or grated

1 tablespoon sweet **smoked paprika**

1 **bay leaf**

Salt and **pepper**

2 cups **chicken stock**

¼ to ½ cup **hot sauce**, depending on how hot you like it

1 (15-ounce) can crushed **tomatoes**

1 pound **whole wheat elbow macaroni**

½ cup shredded **pepper Jack cheese**

½ cup crumbled **blue cheese**

2 **scallions**, ends trimmed, thinly sliced

This healthy combo of two of my favorite comfort foods is packed with the robust flavor of chili, heart-healthy whole wheat pasta, and the creamy tang of two cheeses. Using stronger-flavored cheeses like pepper Jack and blue lets you cut back on the amount you need while stretching the flavor into every bite, giving you a much healthier bang for your buck. To make cutting the chicken easier, place it in the freezer for about 15 minutes until it firms up slightly but isn't frozen through.

Preheat the broiler and bring a large pot of water to a boil over high heat for the pasta.

Place a large pot over medium-high heat and add the EVOO. Add the chicken bits and brown them, stirring often, for 5 to 6 minutes. Add the carrot, onion, celery, garlic, paprika, and bay leaf and season with salt and pepper. Cook the veggies, stirring frequently, until tender, 3 to 4 minutes. Add the chicken stock and scrape up any brown bits from the bottom of the pot. Add the hot sauce and crushed tomatoes, and bring up to a bubble. Reduce the heat and simmer the chili for 8 to 10 minutes to let the flavors come together and thicken slightly.

While the chili is simmering, salt the boiling water, add the pasta, and cook until al dente. Drain the pasta and toss it into the chili, then transfer everything to a 9 x 13-inch casserole dish. Discard the bay leaf. Sprinkle the cheeses evenly over the top and place the dish under the broiler until the cheeses have melted and the top is golden brown, 2 to 3 minutes.

Sprinkle the sliced scallions over the top and watch this one disappear in no time.

SERVES 6

SOUTH PHILLY CHEESESTEAK MAC 'N' CHEESE WITH ITALIAN SALAD

Yet another take on mac 'n' cheese, made even more rib-sticking with roast beef from the deli.

For the mac 'n' cheese

Salt

1 pound **cavatappi pasta**, hollow ridged corkscrews

2 tablespoons **EVOO** (extra-virgin olive oil)

2 large **onions**, thinly sliced

Black pepper

3 tablespoons **butter**

3 tablespoons **all-purpose flour**

3 cups **milk**

2 cups shredded **provolone**

½ cup **beef stock**

¾ pound thinly sliced deli **roast beef**, coarsely chopped

¼ cup fresh flat-leaf **parsley**, chopped

For the salad

4 **roasted red peppers**, chopped into bite-size pieces

A generous handful of **hot peppers** or hot pepper rings, chopped

1 (15-ounce) can quartered **artichoke hearts**, drained

1 head of **romaine lettuce**, core removed, leaves chopped

1 teaspoon dried **oregano**

1 **garlic clove**, grated or minced and pasted

3 tablespoons **red wine vinegar**

⅓ cup **EVOO** (extra-virgin olive oil)

Salt and **pepper**

For the mac 'n' cheese: Place a large pot of water over high heat and bring it to a boil. Salt the water, add the pasta, and cook to al dente. Drain the pasta and return it to the pot.

While the pasta water is coming to a boil, heat the EVOO in a large skillet over medium to medium-high heat. Add the onions, season with salt and pepper and cover with a lid or piece of aluminum foil for 2 to 3 minutes to get them going. Remove the lid or foil and continue cooking the onions until tender and lightly caramelized, 12 to 15 minutes, stirring occasionally.

While the onions are caramelizing, melt the butter in a medium pot over medium-high heat. Sprinkle the flour over the melted butter and cook the mixture for about 1 minute, stirring constantly. Whisk the milk into the butter-flour mixture slowly and bring up to a bubble to thicken, about 5 minutes. Remove the pot from the heat and stir in 1½ cups of shredded cheese, then season with salt and pepper and reserve.

Preheat the broiler.

To the skillet with the onions, add the beef stock and the roast beef. Stir over medium heat just to warm through.

Add the cheese sauce and the onion–roast beef mixture to the pot with the drained pasta and toss everything to combine. Return the pasta mixture to the skillet or to a 9 x 13-inch casserole dish and top with the remaining 1½ cups cheese. Place under the broiler until bubbly, 2 to 3 minutes. Garnish with the parsley.

For the salad: toss all the veggies together in a salad bowl. Mix the oregano and grated garlic with the vinegar in a small bowl, then whisk in the oil in a slow stream. Toss the dressing with the salad and season with salt and pepper.

SERVES 6, EASILY

LASAGNA—NOW!

TWO-SAUCE WEEKNIGHT LASAGNA BOWLS AND BEANS-AND-GREENS SALAD

Classic lasagna in my family is made by layering thin lasagna noodles, preferably egg pasta, with layers of *besciamella* (white sauce) and a light meat sauce. Here, curly short-cut pasta is tossed with the white sauce and then topped with a rich meat sauce for mixing in, making it an anytime meal.

Bring a large pot of water to a boil for the pasta. Salt the water, add the pasta, and cook to al dente.

While the pasta water comes to a boil, heat 2 tablespoons of the EVOO in a medium sauce pot over medium-high heat. Add the pancetta and cook for 2 to 3 minutes to render the fat, then add the meat and break it up as it browns. When the meat has begun to caramelize and develops a nice brown color, 4 to 5 minutes, add the carrot, onions, 2 cloves of chopped garlic, allspice, salt and pepper, and bay leaf. Cook for 3 to 4 minutes more to soften the onions and carrots, then stir in the tomato paste and cook for 2 minutes. Add the wine and cook for 1 minute, then stir in the stock and reduce the heat to a simmer.

While the red sauce cooks, cut the peeled whole garlic clove in half and rub the inside of a medium sauce pot with it. Add the butter and melt over medium heat. Add the flour and whisk together for a minute or so, then whisk in the milk and bring to a bubble. Reduce the heat and season the sauce with salt, pepper, and nutmeg; cook for 8 to 10 minutes to thicken.

In a large bowl combine the lemon zest and juice, peeled garlic, mustard, ¼ cup of EVOO, salt, pepper, and a pinch of nutmeg. Toss with the greens and beans.

Toss the pasta with the white sauce and the ½ cup of grated cheese. Serve the pasta in individual bowls and top each serving with a ladle of meat sauce for mixing in.

SERVES 4

Salt

1 pound curly short-cut **pasta** such as campanelle or fiore

2 tablespoons **EVOO** plus ¼ cup (extra-virgin olive oil)

⅛ pound **pancetta**, chopped

¾ pound **ground beef, pork, and veal mix** or ¾ pound ground beef

½ **carrot**, peeled and grated

1 small to medium **onion**, chopped

4 **garlic cloves**, 3 chopped or grated, 1 peeled

½ teaspoon ground **allspice**

Black pepper

1 **bay leaf**

3 tablespoons **tomato paste**

½ cup **dry red wine**

2 cups **beef stock**

3 tablespoons **butter**

3 tablespoons **all-purpose flour**

2 cups **milk**

Freshly grated **nutmeg**

1 teaspoon grated **zest** and juice of 1 **lemon**

2 teaspoons **Dijon mustard**

1 large or 2 small heads of **escarole**, cleaned and dried, coarsely chopped

1 (15-ounce) can **butter beans**, rinsed and drained

½ cup grated **Parmgiano-Reggiano**, plus some to pass at the table

CHICKEN

ITALIAN CHICKEN AND DUMPLINGS

If you love chicken fricassee, chicken and biscuits, or chicken and dumplings, this is a flavorful Italian take on the theme. Here, basil pesto, a kid favorite, is stirred into the light gravy, and fresh potato gnocchi tossed in lemon butter stands in for the dumplings. Wow!

5 tablespoons **EVOO** (extra-virgin olive oil)

2 pounds **chicken tenders**, diced into bite-size pieces

5 tablespoons **butter**

12 large **white mushrooms**, sliced

1 cup shredded **carrots**

4 **celery stalk**s from the heart, very thinly sliced

1 large **onion**, chopped

1 fresh **bay leaf**

Salt and **pepper**

3 tablespoons **all-purpose flour**

3 cups **chicken stock**

1 cup fresh **basil leaves**

A generous handful of fresh flat-leaf **parsley leaves**

A handful of **pine nuts**, lightly toasted (see Note, page 102)

A couple handfuls of grated **Parmigiano-Reggiano**

Zest of 1 **lemon**

2 (10- to 12-ounce) packages fresh **gnocchi**

Place a large pot of water on to boil for the gnocchi.

Heat a pot or deep skillet with 1 tablespoon of the EVOO over medium-high heat. Add the chicken and cook until lightly browned on both sides, 3 to 4 minutes total. Transfer the chicken to a plate and add another tablespoon of EVOO and 2 tablespoons of the butter to the pan. When the butter melts, add the mushrooms, carrots, celery, onions, and bay leaf, and season with salt and pepper. Cook for 5 minutes to soften the veggies, then sprinkle in the flour and cook for 2 minutes. Whisk in 2½ cups of the stock, slide the chicken and any juices on the plate back into the pot, and simmer until the sauce has thickened and the chicken is cooked through, 5 to 7 minutes.

Place the remaining ½ cup stock in a food processor with the basil, parsley, pine nuts, cheese, and salt and pepper. Turn the processor on and pour in the remaining 3 tablespoons of EVOO with the motor running.

Melt the remaining 3 tablespoons of butter in a skillet over medium heat and add the lemon zest.

Salt the boiling water and add the gnocchi. Cook the gnocchi until they float to the surface, then drain and add to the lemon butter. Toss the gnocchi in the lemon butter for 2 to 3 minutes, until light golden at the edges.

Remove the chicken from the heat, discard the bay leaf, and stir in the pesto sauce. Serve the chicken topped with lemon-butter dumplings in shallow bowls.

SERVES 4 TO 6

CHICKEN PARMIGIANA

1 cup **all-purpose flour**

2 **eggs**, lightly beaten

½ cup **bread crumbs**

1 cup grated **Parmigiano-Reggiano**

¼ cup chopped fresh flat-leaf **parsley** (about a handful)

5 tablespoons **EVOO** (extra-virgin olive oil), plus more as needed

4 **chicken breast halves**, 1½ to 2 pounds

Salt and **pepper**

3 to 4 **garlic cloves**, finely chopped

1 teaspoon **crushed red pepper flakes**

1 small yellow **onion**, finely chopped

1 teaspoon dried **oregano**

1 (28-ounce) can diced or crushed **fire-roasted tomatoes**

½ cup chopped fresh **basil** (a couple of handfuls), plus additional for garnish

1 cup shredded **smoked fresh mozzarella**

Need I say more? Serve with a green salad or chopped vegetable salad with oil and vinegar.

Preheat the broiler.

Set up three dishes on your countertop: one with the flour, one with the eggs, and a third with the bread crumbs, half the grated Parm, and the parsley combined.

Heat 3 tablespoons of the EVOO in a large skillet over medium-high heat. While the pan is heating up, season the chicken cutlets with salt and pepper, and coat each one in the flour, then in the egg, and lastly in the cheesy bread crumbs.

Once the oil is hot, cook 2 of the chicken cutlets until they are golden brown and cooked through, 3 to 5 minutes per side depending on how thick they are. Transfer the cooked cutlets to a paper-towel-lined plate and repeat with the remaining 2 cutlets, adding more oil to the pan if needed.

While the chicken is cooking, place a medium pot on the stove over medium heat. Add the remaining 2 tablespoons of EVOO. Add the garlic, red pepper flakes, chopped onion, oregano, salt, and pepper. Cook for 7 to 8 minutes, stirring often, until the veggies have softened. Add the tomatoes and heat them through, about 2 minutes. Remove the pot from the heat and stir in the basil, then season the sauce with salt and pepper.

Spread a layer of the sauce in a casserole dish. Layer the chicken on top and cover with the remaining sauce. Sprinkle with the remaining grated Parmigiano and the mozzarella. Brown the casserole under the broiler until the cheese has melted and is light golden brown, about 3 minutes.

Garnish with additional basil and serve.

SERVES 4

30-MINUTE MEAL FOR THE GRILL
LEMON-GARLIC-HERB CHICKEN WITH GRILLED PROSCIUTTO-WRAPPED ASPARAGUS AND PESTO THREE-BEAN SALAD

My husband loves the grill so much that he and his friends go outside in the dead of winter to make themselves Fred Flintstone steaks in the snow. This is a simple, flavorful meal that you can make in a grill pan or skillet if you want to keep yourself and your food indoors.

Heat a grill or grill pan to medium or medium-high. Fill a small skillet with about 1 inch of water and bring to a boil.

Grate the garlic onto a cutting board and add a couple teaspoons of salt. Mash into a paste with the flat of a knife.

Add salt to the boiling water and cook the green beans for 1 minute, then drain and cool under cold running water. Set aside.

Reserve one fifth of the pasted garlic, about 1 clove, and transfer the rest to a shallow dish. To the dish, add the zest of 2 lemons, the fennel seed, the chopped thyme, rosemary, and parsley, ¼ to ⅓ cup of the EVOO, and some black pepper. Stir with a fork to combine, then add the chicken pieces and turn to coat evenly. Grill the chicken for 12 to 15 minutes, until the juices run clear.

While the chicken grills, drizzle the asparagus with a touch of EVOO and season with salt and pepper. Divide the asparagus into 4 piles and roll 2 layered slices of prosciutto around each pile to form bundles. Add to the grill with the chicken and cook for 7 to 8 minutes, until the prosciutto is crisp and the spears are tender.

Place the basil and mint leaves in a food processor with the nuts. Add some salt and pepper and turn the processor on. Stream in ¼ to ⅓ cup of the EVOO to form a thick sauce. Transfer the sauce to a large bowl and stir in the reserved garlic paste and the grated Parmigiano. Add the cooled green beans and the canned beans to the bowl and stir to combine. Adjust the seasoning.

Remove the chicken from the grill and squeeze the juice of 1 of the zested lemons over the meat.

Serve each diner a chicken breast and thigh with an asparagus bundle and some bean salad alongside.

SERVES 4

5 **garlic cloves**, peeled

Salt

¼ to ⅓ pound fresh **green beans**, trimmed and cut into 2-inch pieces

2 **lemons**

1 teaspoon **fennel seed**

5 to 6 sprigs of fresh **thyme**, leaves stripped and finely chopped

3 to 4 sprigs of fresh **rosemary**, leaves stripped and finely chopped

A handful of fresh flat-leaf **parsley**, finely chopped

½ to ⅔ cup **EVOO** (extra-virgin olive oil), plus some for drizzling

Black pepper

4 boneless skinless **chicken breast halves**

4 boneless skinless **chicken thighs**

1 pound **asparagus**, tough ends trimmed

8 slices of **prosciutto**

1 cup fresh **basil leaves**, about 20

½ cup fresh **mint leaves**, 5 to 6 stems

A handful of **pine nuts**, 3 to 4 tablespoons, lightly toasted (see Note, page 102) and cooled

½ cup grated **Parmigiano-Reggiano**

1 (15-ounce) can **cannellini beans**, rinsed and drained

1 (15-ounce) can **chickpeas**, rinsed and drained

BBQ SPICED CHICKEN, SALSA SALAD, AND PUMPKIN-CHIPOTLE POLENTA

1 tablespoon **grill seasoning**, such as McCormick's Montreal Steak Seasoning

2 tablespoons **chili powder**

½ tablespoon **ground cumin**, ½ palmful

1 tablespoon **ground coriander**, a palmful

3 tablespoons **dark brown sugar**, packed

4 boneless skinless **chicken breast halves**

4 tablespoons **EVOO** (extra-virgin olive oil)

4 plum **tomatoes**, chopped

1 yellow **bell pepper**, seeded and chopped

1 **red onion**, chopped

Juice of 2 **limes**

A handful of fresh **cilantro leaves**, chopped

Salt and **pepper**

2 cups **chicken stock**

1 cup **milk** or half-and-half

1 **chipotle in adobo**, finely chopped, and 2 teaspoons adobo sauce

¾ cup **quick-cooking polenta**

1 (15-ounce) can **pumpkin puree**

2 tablespoons **honey**

2 tablespoons **butter**

This BBQ dry-rub works equally well on pork chops or pork tenderloin. Polenta is a creamy, easy alternative to potatoes and rice.

Heat a grill pan over medium-high heat or heat an outdoor grill.

Mix the grill seasoning, chili powder, cumin, coriander, and brown sugar in a large resealable plastic bag. Coat the chicken with 1 tablespoon of the EVOO and add it to the bag, turning to coat the chicken evenly in the spices. Let the chicken hang out for a few minutes.

Chop and combine the tomatoes, bell pepper, and onions in a salad bowl.

Place the chicken on the grill pan or grill and cook for 6 to 7 minutes on each side.

Dress the salad with the lime juice and the remaining 3 tablespoons of EVOO. Add the cilantro and season with salt and pepper.

Heat the stock and milk or half-and-half in a large sauce pot with the chipotle and adobo sauce. Whisk in the polenta and cook for 2 to 3 minutes to thicken, then stir in the pumpkin puree and heat to warm through. Stir in the honey and butter and season with salt and pepper.

Serve the polenta topped with the chicken and with the salsa salad alongside.

SERVES 4

BUCKET O' CHICKEN WITH BUTTERMILK DIP

4 cups **buttermilk**

2 **garlic cloves**, grated

1 tablespoon **hot sauce**, plus more to taste

¼ cup fresh flat-leaf **parsley**, a generous handful, chopped

¼ cup fresh **dill**, a handful, finely chopped

2 to 3 tablespoons finely chopped fresh **chives**

Juice of 1 **lemon**

Salt and **pepper**

2 pounds **chicken tenders**

Canola oil, for shallow frying

2 cups **all-purpose flour**, plus more as needed

8 **scallions**, roots trimmed

¾ cup **sour cream**

Assorted **raw vegetable sticks**: seedless cucumber, celery, carrots, red bell pepper

Everyone craves fried chicken sometimes; there's just no way around it. If you're gonna succumb, don't hit the drive-thru; make it at home. Here's a once-in-a-while treat for game night or movie night.

In a large bowl, mix together the buttermilk, garlic, hot sauce, parsley, dill, chives, and lemon juice, and season with salt and pepper. Set aside about one-third of the mixture; reserve for the dipping sauce.

Season the chicken with salt and pepper and place it in a shallow dish or large resealable plastic bag. Pour about half of the remaining seasoned buttermilk over the chicken pieces, then cover the dish with plastic wrap or seal the bag and marinate for 10 minutes.

Place a medium, high-sided skillet over medium to medium-high heat. Add an inch of canola oil to your pan and get it hot. Place two high-sided dishes on the counter and fill one with flour and the other with the remaining buttermilk mixture. Dip the trimmed scallions into the buttermilk, then into the flour, then back into the buttermilk and back into the flour. Once they're double-coated, fry them in batches in the oil until they are golden brown all over; don't crowd the pan. Transfer them to a paper-towel-lined plate to drain.

When the scallions are fried, remove the chicken from the marinade and discard the marinade. Dip and coat the chicken strips and fry until golden and cooked through, 5 to 6 minutes. Change the oil if it gets too gritty with flour dust.

Put your chicken strips and scallions on a platter or pile them into a paper bucket (they're available at party stores). Mix the sour cream into the reserved buttermilk mixture to thicken it up and add salt and pepper and hot sauce to taste. Serve the chicken with the dip and veggie sticks alongside.

SERVES 4

M.Y.O.T.O.
TANDOORI CHICKEN WITH MASHED CHICKPEAS AND PEPPER AND ONION SALAD

One of the joys of living in New York City is the wide variety of ethnic restaurants we can choose from. One I love is called Tamarind; their huge clay tandoor ovens give everything cooked in them an unmistakable flavor. Out of necessity, though, John and I had to learn how to make our own takeout for nights away from the big city. For a regular oven, this is a pretty good substitute for the real thing. Make sure your oven is really clean, otherwise it will smoke at this temperature.

Preheat the oven to 500 to 550°F, or as high as your oven goes. Cover a rimmed baking sheet with foil and set a baking rack on top if you have one; it's not necessary but use it if ya got it.

Place the yogurt in a shallow dish and stir in the ginger, 3 of the grated garlic cloves, the chili powder, coriander, paprika, turmeric, cardamom, cumin, and 2 tablespoons of the EVOO. Season the chicken with salt and pepper and coat in the sauce. Arrange on the baking sheet and roast for 20 to 25 minutes, until the juices run clear.

Heat 1 tablespoon of the EVOO in a medium skillet over medium heat. Add the remaining grated garlic. Pulse or chop the chickpeas in a food processor, then add to the garlic oil and season with salt and pepper. Mash with the chicken stock and tahini and reduce the heat to low.

In a bowl combine the red onions, bell peppers, chopped hot peppers and 2 tablespoons of the juice from the jar, cilantro leaves, the juice of 1 lime, the remaining tablespoon of EVOO, and salt and pepper to taste.

Cut the remaining lime into wedges.

Warm and crisp the pitas in the hot oven during the last few minutes the chicken is roasting.

Serve the chicken with lime wedges to squeeze over the top and the mashed chickpeas alongside. Top the chicken with the pepper and onion salad. Cut the pitas in half and pass at the table.

SERVES 4 TO 6

1 cup plain **Greek yogurt**

2-inch piece of fresh **gingerroot**, peeled and grated

4 **garlic cloves**, grated

1 tablespoon **chili powder**

2 teaspoons **ground coriander**, ⅔ palmful

1 teaspoon **smoked paprika**

½ teaspoon **ground turmeric**

1 teaspoon **ground cardamom**

1 teaspoon **ground cumin**

4 tablespoons **EVOO** (extra-virgin olive oil)

4 boneless skinless **chicken thighs**

3 boneless skinless **chicken breast halves**, cut in half across

Salt and **pepper**

2 (15-ounce) cans **chickpeas**, drained

½ cup **chicken stock**

¼ cup **tahini paste**

1 small **red onion**, very thinly sliced

1 **yellow bell pepper**, seeded and thinly sliced

Hot banana pepper rings, chopped, juice reserved

A handful of fresh **cilantro leaves**, chopped

2 **limes**

4 **pita breads**

FRENCH WHITE BURGUNDY CHICKEN AND EGG NOODLES

1 tablespoon **EVOO** (extra-virgin olive oil)

4 slices of good-quality **bacon**, chopped

½ cup plus 2 tablespoons **all-purpose flour**

2 pounds **chicken tenders**, cut into 1½- to 2-inch pieces

Salt and **pepper**

½ pound **button mushrooms**, quartered

3 **celery stalks** from the heart with leafy tops, chopped

1 **carrot**, peeled and chopped

2 **parsnips**, peeled and chopped

2 tablespoons fresh **thyme**, chopped (4 to 5 sprigs)

4 tablespoons (½ stick) **butter**

2 cups **French white burgundy wine** (⅔ bottle)

1 cup **chicken stock**

2 cups frozen **pearl onions**

1 pound **extra-wide egg noodles**

Freshly **grated nutmeg**

A handful of fresh flat-leaf **parsley**, finely chopped

I love beef in burgundy sauce—a dish for which my mom holds the title of master craftswoman. But, I ask you, why should beef have all the fun? This chicken and white burgundy makes a hearty favorite appropriate for all seasons.

Bring a pot of water to boil for the egg noodles.

Heat the EVOO in a Dutch oven over medium-high heat. Add the bacon and crisp for 5 minutes; transfer to a bowl with a slotted spoon, leaving the fat in the pan.

While the bacon crisps, scatter ½ cup of the flour on a shallow dish. Season the chicken pieces with salt and pepper and toss in the flour to coat. Add the chicken to the hot bacon drippings, shaking off the excess flour as you go. Lightly brown the chicken, about 3 minutes on each side, then remove. Add the mushrooms to the same pan and as they cook, add the celery, carrots, and parsnips. Season with salt, pepper, and thyme. Cook the vegetables for 5 to 6 minutes, until tender, then scoot the vegetables off to the sides of the pan. Add 2 tablespoons of the butter to the well in the center of the pan, and when it melts whisk in the remaining 2 tablespoons of flour. Whisk the wine into the roux, shake the pan to combine, then stir in the stock. Return the chicken to the pan and stir in the pearl onions. Simmer for 10 minutes, then adjust the seasoning. Stir in the reserved bacon.

Salt the boiling water and add the egg noodles. Cook to al dente, with a bite left to them. Drain the noodles and return them to the hot pot. Add the remaining 2 tablespoons of butter and toss to melt the butter and coat the noodles. Season the noodles with nutmeg, salt, and pepper to taste and garnish with the parsley.

Serve the chicken over the noodles.

SERVES 6

CHUTNEY AND CHEDDAR–STUFFED CHICKEN BREASTS WITH BLTP (BACON, LEEK, AND TOMATO POTATOES)

People often ask me where I get the inspiration for my recipes, and the truth is that it comes to me in all kinds of crazy places and crazy ways. Take this menu. I was reading a magazine at the hair salon—shocker, right? Anyhoo, I saw a bit of business about one of my favorite actors, Pierce Brosnan, who rattled off a few of his potato recipes. They inspired me to create these BLTPs. The chicken just came to me after that. And there you have it!

2 pounds **small potatoes**. such as Red Bliss, fingerling, or baby Yukon Gold

4½ tablespoons **EVOO** (extra-virgin olive oil)

Salt and **pepper**

1 pint **grape tomatoes**

4 boneless skinless **chicken breast halves**

4 tablespoons prepared **chutney**

8 slices of **sharp white cheddar**

4 slices of thick-cut **bacon**, chopped

2 **leeks**, white and light green parts only, cleaned and thinly sliced

1 cup **chicken stock**

Preheat the oven to 425°F.

Halve the potatoes and scatter them on a rimmed baking sheet. Drizzle them with 2 tablespoons of the EVOO and season with salt and pepper. Toss them to coat evenly and move them to one end of the baking sheet. Roast the potatoes for 10 minutes, then remove the baking sheet from the oven and scatter the tomatoes over the empty half of the pan. Drizzle them with 1 tablespoon of EVOO and season with salt and pepper. Turn the potatoes with a spatula and return the pan to the oven to continue roasting for another 15 minutes.

Once the tomatoes go into the oven, place the chicken breasts on a cutting board and use a paring knife to cut a pocket into one side of each of them. Spread about 1 tablespoon of chutney inside each pocket and 2 slices of cheddar. Season each breast with salt and pepper.

Heat 1 tablespoon of EVOO in a large ovenproof skillet over medium-high heat and sear the chicken breasts until golden brown, 3 to 4 minutes per side.

Transfer the skillet to the oven to finish cooking the chicken, about 8 minutes.

Once the chicken goes into the oven, heat the remaining 1½ teaspoons EVOO in another large skillet over medium-high heat. Add the bacon and cook until the bacon starts to brown, 3 to 4 minutes. Add the leeks and cook until tender, another 3 to 4 minutes.

When the vegetables have finished roasting, transfer the potatoes to the skillet with the bacon and leeks, add the chicken stock, and stir everything up together. Fold in the roasted tomatoes and season with salt and pepper.

Serve up the cooked chicken breasts with a scoop of BLTP alongside.

SERVES 4

TIP: If your pan is not oven-safe, cover the handle of the pan with 2 layers of foil to protect it.

SPANISH CHORIZO & CHICKEN CHILI

1 tablespoon **EVOO** (extra-virgin olive oil)

2 pounds **ground chicken**

½ pound **Spanish chorizo**, cut into medium dice

2 medium **onions**, chopped

4 **garlic cloves**, finely chopped or grated

Black pepper

1 rounded tablespoon **hot smoked paprika**

1 rounded teaspoon **ground cumin**

¼ cup **dry sherry** or ½ cup Spanish wine such as Rioja

2 cups **vegetable juice**, such as V8 brand

2 to 3 cups **chicken stock**, depending on how thick you like your chili

¼ cup fresh flat-leaf **parsley**, coarsely chopped

5 to 6 jarred **piquillo peppers** (mild Spanish roasted peppers) or 4 roasted **red bell peppers**

Salt

Hot sauce

1 cup grated **Manchego cheese**

½ cup slivered **almonds**, toasted (optional); see Note, page 102

John and I love this dish, sort of a cross between Spain and the Southwest. Why not serve it up at a tapas party? Fill espresso cups with the chili and garnish, and serve with a demitasse spoon.

Heat the EVOO in a large skillet or chili pot over medium-high heat. Once the oil is hot, add the chicken and brown it for 5 to 6 minutes then add the chorizo and cook 2 to 3 minutes more to render the fat.

Stir in the onions and garlic, season with the pepper, paprika, and cumin, then cook until the onions are tender, 5 to 6 minutes more. Stir in the sherry or wine, stir for 1 minute, then add the vegetable juice, 2 cups of the stock, the parsley, and the peppers. Simmer for a couple of minutes more to combine the flavors, then taste for salt or hot sauce. Add more stock if you like your chili thinner. Serve the chili garnished with the cheese and almonds.

SERVES 4 AS AN ENTRÉE, UP TO 12 AS A TAPA

CHICKEN AND CHORIZO ROMESCO WITH SPANISH POTATOES AND KALE

My take on romesco sauce—a classic from Catalonia—has a smoky twist. It is also delicious with strong-flavored fish or pork.

Heat 2 tablespoons of the EVOO in a medium skillet over medium to medium-high heat. Add the garlic and lightly brown for 2 to 3 minutes, then add the bread cubes and toss occasionally until toasted, 10 minutes.

While the bread toasts, place the potatoes in a large pot and cover with water. Bring to a boil, season with salt, and cook for 15 minutes, or until tender. In a medium pot simmer the kale in salted water for 10 minutes; drain the kale and potatoes and return the potatoes to the pot.

Once the bread is toasted, scoot it off to the side and warm the nuts (Marconas come toasted) for a couple of minutes. Place the garlic, croutons, and nuts in a food processor and add the peppers, tomatoes, sherry vinegar, and salt and pepper. Turn the processor on and stream in ⅓ cup of the EVOO. Return the sauce to the skillet and keep it warm over low heat.

Cut the chicken breasts or thighs into 3 chunks apiece, then season with the citrus zest, smoked paprika, salt and pepper, and parsley. Heat a tablespoon of the EVOO in a nonstick skillet over medium-high heat. Add the chorizo and cook it for 1 minute to render the fat, then add the chicken and cook for 8 to 10 minutes, turning occasionally, until browned and cooked through.

When you are ready to serve, mash the potatoes with the stock and cheese. Fold in the kale, and adjust the salt and pepper.

Pour a pool of romesco sauce onto a dinner plate and top with a mound of potatoes and kale and chunks of chicken and chorizo. Olé!

SERVES 4

3 tablespoons plus ⅓ cup **EVOO** (extra-virgin olive oil)

4 **garlic cloves**, thinly sliced

2 cups **crusty bread cubes**

4 large **russet potatoes**, peeled and coarsely chopped
Salt

1 bunch of **kale**, stemmed and coarsely chopped

½ cup **Spanish Marcona almonds** or toasted blanched almonds (see Note, page 102), sliced

1 cup jarred **piquillo peppers** or roasted red peppers

1 (15-ounce) can **fire-roasted tomatoes**, drained

2 tablespoons **sherry vinegar**
Black pepper

4 boneless skinless **chicken breast halves** or thighs

2 teaspoons grated **orange zest** or **lemon zest**

1 teaspoon **sweet smoked paprika**

A handful of fresh flat-leaf **parsley**, finely chopped

¾ pound **Spanish chorizo**, cut into 8 pieces on the diagonal

1 cup **chicken stock**

1 cup shredded **manchego cheese**

CHORIZO BASICS Many people are confused about chorizo, a term for the spiced pork sausage used in various Spanish and Mexican dishes. Some markets carry both Mexican and Spanish varieties, and they cannot be used interchangeably, so check the recipe before purchasing to make sure you are choosing the correct type. Most Mexican chorizo is raw and can be removed from its casings and crumbled like Italian sausage. It must be cooked before eating. Spanish chorizo is dry-cured and can be sliced and eaten as is or cut into smaller pieces and sautéed briefly to render some of its fat. If you cannot find Spanish chorizo, Portuguese linguica is a good substitute.

HALFTIME HERO: CHILI SUIZAS BAKE

3 large **poblano peppers**

2 tablespoons **EVOO** (extra-virgin olive oil)

2 pounds **ground chicken**

1 **onion**, chopped

1 **jalapeño**, seeded and finely chopped

4 **garlic cloves**, finely chopped

12 large or 16 small to medium **tomatillos**, peeled, rinsed, and halved

¼ cup fresh **cilantro**, a handful

2 cups **chicken stock**

2 teaspoons **honey**

Salt and **pepper**

Juice of 1 **lime**

½ cup **crème fraîche**

3 cups lightly crushed **tortilla chips** (whole grain tortilla chips, such as flax seed tortillas, add a wonderful texture and flavor)

1 cup shredded **Swiss cheese** (buy a piece that weighs about ⅓ pound)

1 cup shredded **Monterey Jack cheese** (buy a piece that weighs about ⅓ pound)

When your gang gathers at your place to watch the next big game, hit them with this one. It's definitely not your average chili. It tastes like chicken enchiladas Suizas, a mild recipe developed by Swiss immigrants living in Mexico. Traditionally that dish consists of pulled, stewed chicken rolled in tortillas and topped with tomatillo sauce, Mexican cream, and Swiss cheese. This version is simple to make and faster than the original but is every bit as flavorful.

Heat the broiler to high. Place the poblanos under the hot broiler and char until blackened on all sides, 10 to 12 minutes. Leave the door of the oven cracked to allow the steam to escape. Place the peppers in a bowl and cover it tightly with plastic wrap. Allow the peppers to steam until they are cool enough to handle. Leave the oven on broil.

While the peppers char, heat the EVOO in a high-sided ovenproof skillet over medium-high heat. Add the chicken and brown lightly, 3 to 4 minutes, then stir in the onions, jalapeño, and garlic. Cook for 5 minutes to soften the onions. While the mixture cooks, place the tomatillos and cilantro in a food processor and process until smooth. Pour the tomatillos into the chicken mixture and stir to combine. Stir in the chicken stock and honey, season with salt and pepper, and simmer the chili for 10 minutes.

When the poblano peppers have cooled, remove the seeds, chop the peppers, and stir into the chili. Remove the chili from the heat and stir in the lime juice. Spoon dollops of crème fraîche onto the chili, spacing them evenly across the pan. Cover the surface with a layer of crushed chips and top with the Swiss and Monterey Jack cheeses. Place under the broiler just until brown and bubbly, 30 seconds to 1 minute. Serve directly from the hot skillet, spooning the chili and topping into shallow dinner bowls. Touchdown!

SERVES 6

BRAZILIAN CHICKEN CUTLETS WITH RAW TROPICAL SAUCE

I came up with this Brazilian-style chicken cutlet with raw sauce, a twist on the classic Milanese, for Helio Castroneves, the Indy 500 and *Dancing with the Stars* champ. I am such a sucker for *DWTS*. This chicken is so delish, it makes your stomach dance with excitement.

Preheat the oven to 250°F.

Prepare the raw sauce by combining the mango, plum tomatoes, red onion, cilantro, lime juice, hot sauce, salt, and pepper in a medium mixing bowl. Stir gently to combine.

Flatten the chicken breasts into cutlets by butterflying each piece open then pounding it out ¼ inch thick.

Set up three shallow dishes on the counter. To one dish add the flour, to the second add the eggs and beat with a splash of water, and to the third add the bread crumbs, grated Parmigiano-Reggiano, granulated garlic, and lemon zest.

Bread the cutlets by first tossing them in the flour, then dipping them in the beaten egg, then coating them in the bread crumb mixture.

Heat 2 tablespoons of EVOO in a large skillet over medium-high heat. Once the oil is hot, cook the cutlets in batches until golden brown on each side and cooked through, 4 to 5 minutes per side, adding more oil to the pan as needed between batches. As each cutlet finishes cooking, transfer it to a baking sheet and keep warm in the oven while the others cook.

Serve the cutlets with the raw sauce on top and lemon wedges to squeeze over the cutlets if desired.

SERVES 4

1 large, ripe **mango**, pitted and chopped

4 **plum tomatoes**, seeded and chopped

½ medium **red onion**, chopped

¼ cup (about a palmful) **cilantro**, chopped

Juice of 1 **lime**

A few dashes **hot sauce**

Salt and **pepper**

4 boneless, skinless **chicken breast halves**

1 cup **all-purpose flour**

2 **eggs**

½ cup **bread crumbs**

½ cup grated **Parmigiano-Reggiano**

1 teaspoon **granulated garlic**

1 **lemon**, zested and cut in wedges

4 tablespoons **EVOO** (extra-virgin olive oil), plus more as needed

HONEY MUSTARD CHICKEN TENDERS AND BUTTERMILK SMASHED POTATOES

Here's another take on tenders paired with the flavor of ranch dressing. But you have to eat your broccoli, too.

Preheat the oven to 250°F.

Place the potatoes in a medium pot and cover them with cold water. Bring the water to a boil, salt it, then reduce the heat to medium-high and cook until the potatoes are tender, 15 to 20 minutes.

In a shallow dish, combine the honey and Dijon mustard. Add the chicken to the dish and season with salt and pepper. Turn the tenders to coat the chicken in the honey mustard.

Place the bread crumbs in a second shallow dish, then add the coated chicken tenders to the dish a few at a time, covering them completely with bread crumbs (press down on the chicken to make sure the crumbs stick).

In a large skillet heat about an inch of canola oil over medium-high heat. When the oil is hot, fry the chicken tenders a few at a time until golden brown on each side and cooked through, about 3 minutes on each side. Repeat until all the chicken is cooked, placing the finished pieces on a rimmed baking sheet in the oven to keep warm and crispy. (If you have a wire cooling rack, place it on top of the baking sheet for extra-crispy chicken.)

Heat an inch of water in a pan with a lid. When it boils, salt the water and add the broccoli. Reduce the heat to a simmer and cover the pan to trap the steam. Cook for 5 minutes or until the broccoli is just about tender but still bright green. Drain the broccoli and keep warm in the pan.

When the potatoes are cooked through, drain them and return them to the pot. Mash the potatoes to the desired consistency with the buttermilk, sour cream, hot sauce to taste, parsley, dill, chives, salt, and pepper.

Serve the chicken fingers alongside some taters and broccoli spears.

SERVES 4

5 large **russet potatoes**, peeled and chopped into large chunks
Salt
½ cup **honey**
½ cup **Dijon mustard**
2 pounds **chicken tenders**
Black pepper
2 cups **bread crumbs**
Canola oil, for frying
1 head of **broccoli**, trimmed and cut into spears
½ cup **buttermilk**
3 tablespoons **sour cream**
Hot sauce
2 tablespoons fresh flat-leaf **parsley**, about a palmful, chopped
2 tablespoons fresh **dill**, about a palmful, chopped
1 tablespoon fresh **chives**, ½ palmful, chopped

CHICKEN AND GARLIC-HERB POTATO SHEPHERD'S PIE

2½ to 3 pounds **Idaho potatoes**, peeled and cut into chunks

Salt

1 tablespoon **EVOO** (extra-virgin olive oil), plus more for drizzling

2 pounds **chicken breast**, cut in ½ inch dice

Black pepper

1 cup store-bought shredded **carrots**, chopped

1 cup frozen **peas**

1 small bunch **scallions**, thinly sliced

2 tablespoons **butter**

2 tablespoons **all-purpose flour**

½ cup **white wine**

1½ cups **chicken stock**

1 tablespoon **Dijon mustard**

6 sprigs of **tarragon**, leaves removed and chopped, about 2 tablespoons

1 5-ounce package soft **garlic and herb cheese**, such as Boursin

2 **egg yolks**

¼ cup flat-leaf **parsley**, a handful, chopped

¼ cup **milk** or **chicken stock**, enough to loosen up the potatoes

Paprika, for garnish

This is a decidedly light cousin to heavy beef or lamb and potato pies. This meal is perfect for spring and fall suppers. I taught it first as an easy Mother's Day supper.

Preheat the broiler, place an oven rack at the center of the oven.

Place the potatoes in a medium pot and cover with cold water. Bring to a boil, salt the water and cook until tender, 12 to 15 minutes.

While the potatoes are cooking, place a large skillet over medium-high heat with about 1 tablespoon of EVOO. Add the chicken, season it with salt and pepper and cook until golden brown and cooked through, 6 to 7 minutes. Remove the chicken from the pan to a casserole dish, add a drizzle of EVOO to the pan, then add the carrots, peas, and scallions. Season the veggies with salt and pepper and cook until tender, about 2 minutes. Scoot the vegetables over to one side and melt in the butter. Sprinkle the flour over the butter and cook for about 1 minute, stirring. Whisk in the white wine, cook 1 minute, then whisk in the chicken stock and cook for 1 minute to thicken. Season the sauce with mustard and tarragon then salt and pepper to taste. Pour the sauce and vegetables over the chicken in the casserole and combine.

Drain the potatoes and return them to the hot pot, then mash with the herb cheese, egg yolks, parsley, milk or chicken stock, salt and pepper. Spread the potatoes over the chicken in the casserole dish.

Put the dish under your broiler until the top is golden brown, 3 to 5 minutes. Garnish with paprika.

SERVES 4 TO 6

FOUR-SIDED SQUARE MEAL

- MASHED SWEET 'N' BITTER POTATOES
- TRADITIONAL SUPPER STUFFING WITH CIDER GRAVY
- SMOKY GREENS WITH CRANBERRIES

I'm an unconventional girl, but I do enjoy an occasional square meal. This one literally has four side dishes that come together to form a well-balanced dinner: potatoes, stuffing, gravy, and greens.

Mashed Sweet 'n' Bitter Potatoes

Cover the potatoes with water in a medium pot and bring to a boil. Salt the water and cook the potatoes for 12 to 15 minutes until tender. Drain the potatoes. Return the same pot to the stove and warm the stock over medium heat. Whisk in the butter and marmalade. Add the potatoes and mash; they should be a bit chunky. Season with salt and pepper and a few dashes of hot sauce. Serve immediately.

SERVES 4 TO 6

2 pounds **sweet potatoes** (2 to 3 large), peeled and sliced or cubed

Salt

½ cup **chicken stock**

2 tablespoons **butter**

¼ cup **orange marmalade**

Black pepper

A couple dashes of **hot sauce**

Traditional Supper Stuffing with Cider Gravy

Preheat the oven to 325°F and scatter the bread on a rimmed baking sheet. Season with the poultry seasoning and bake to toast the bread cubes, 10 to 12 minutes.

Quarter the unpeeled apples and cut away the cores. Chop the apples into bite-size pieces.

Heat 3 tablespoons of the butter in a large skillet over medium heat. When the butter melts, add the apples, onions, celery, and bay leaf, season with salt and pepper, and cook until tender, 7 to 8 minutes. Add the chicken to the skillet, combine with the vegetables, and heat through for 2 to 3 minutes. Fold in the bread cubes and moisten with about 2 cups of the chicken stock.

4 to 5 cups farmhouse-style **crusty bread** cut into 1-inch cubes

1 teaspoon **poultry seasoning**, ⅓ palmful

4 McIntosh, Golden Delicious, Gala, or Honey Crisp **apples**

6 tablespoons (¾ stick) **butter**

2 **onions**, chopped into bite-size pieces

6 **celery stalks** from the heart, chopped into bite-size pieces

1 fresh **bay leaf**

Salt and **pepper**

Meat from 1 large rotisserie **chicken**, cubed

4 cups **chicken stock**

3 tablespoons **all-purpose flour**

1 cup **apple cider**

A handful of fresh **flat-leaf parsley**, chopped

While the stuffing cooks, melt the remaining 3 tablespoons of butter in a saucepan over medium heat. Whisk in the flour, cook for a minute or so, then whisk in the cider and the remaining 2 cups of chicken stock. Season the sauce with salt and pepper to taste, and simmer for 4 to 5 minutes to thicken. Stir in the parsley.

Serve the stuffing doused with ½ cup of the gravy and with Smoky Greens with Cranberries and Mashed Sweet 'n' Bitter Potatoes alongside.

SERVES 4

Smoky Greens with Cranberries

½ tablespoon **EVOO** (extra-virgin olive oil)

4 slices of hickory or applewood **smoked bacon**, chopped

1½ pounds **kale**, washed and dried

Salt and **pepper**

A little freshly grated **nutmeg**

A handful of dried sweetened **cranberries**

2 cups **chicken stock**

Heat a high-sided skillet over medium-high heat. Add the EVOO and bacon and cook until the bacon is crisp, 5 to 6 minutes. Strip the kale from the stems while the bacon crisps up. Coarsely chop the kale and add it to the pan, adding as much as will fit, then adding more as it wilts into the pan. Season the greens with salt, pepper, and a little nutmeg. Scatter in the cranberries and stir in the stock. Simmer the greens for 10 minutes over medium-low heat to plump the cranberries and sweeten the greens. Stay warm!

SERVES 4

ESCAPE THE MUNDANE

- BACON-WRAPPED CHICKEN WITH BLUE CHEESE AND PECANS
- RED WINE RICE WITH GRAPES
- SAVORY SWISS CHARD

Really, this meal sells itself. I make a variety of drunken pasta dishes—pasta cooked in red wine rather than water, a Tuscan tradition. My smart husband asked me one night why I had never made a drunken rice. Look for drunken risotto soon, too!

Bacon-Wrapped Chicken with Blue Cheese and Pecans

Preheat the oven to 375°F.

Butterfly the chicken breast halves by cutting horizontally across the breast but not all the way through. Open the breasts up like a book and pound them lightly between sheets of parchment paper or plastic wrap. Peel away the paper and season the meat with salt and pepper.

Cover the seasoned chicken cutlets with blue cheese crumbles, pecans, and scallions in equal amounts. Roll the chicken around the filling, then wrap each roll with a strip of bacon, securing it with a wooden toothpick. Season the outside of the rolls with pepper.

Heat the EVOO in an ovenproof skillet over medium-high heat. Add the chicken rolls and brown evenly all over, 5 to 6 minutes. Transfer the skillet to the oven and cook the chicken for 10 minutes, or until cooked through.

When the chicken is almost done, melt the butter in small saucepan over medium heat. Whisk in the flour and cook for a minute, then whisk in the stock. Cook for a minute to thicken, then whisk in the half-and-half and mustard, and season with salt and pepper. Reduce the heat to low.

Serve the halved chicken rolls with the red wine rice and savory Swiss chard. Pour the gravy over the top.

SERVES 4

4 boneless skinless **chicken breast halves**
Salt and **pepper**
1 cup **blue cheese** crumbles
½ cup toasted chopped **pecans**
2 **scallions**, sliced on an angle
4 slices of good-quality center-cut **bacon**
1 tablespoon **EVOO** (extra-virgin olive oil)
2 tablespoons **butter**
2 tablespoons **all-purpose flour**
1 cup **chicken stock**
½ cup **half-and-half** or cream
2 tablespoons **grainy mustard**

Red Wine Rice with Grapes

Bring the wine to a boil in a saucepan with the bay leaf and EVOO. Stir in the rice, cover, and reduce the heat to a simmer. Cook the rice for 15 minutes, then stir in the grapes and parsley. Turn off the heat, cover, and let stand for 5 minutes. Discard the bay leaf before serving.

SERVES 4

1¾ cups **dry red wine**
1 fresh or dried **bay leaf**
1 tablespoon **EVOO** (extra-virgin olive oil)
1 cup **white rice**
1 cup halved red **seedless grapes**
A handful of fresh flat-leaf **parsley**, chopped

Savory Swiss Chard

2 tablespoons **EVOO** (extra-virgin olive oil)

1 teaspoon **Worcestershire sauce**

1 large bunch of **Swiss chard**, stemmed and coarsely chopped

¼ teaspoon freshly grated **nutmeg**

½ teaspoon **sweet smoked paprika** or ground cumin

Salt and **pepper**

½ cup **chicken stock**

Heat the EVOO in a large skillet over medium-high heat. When the oil is hot, add the Worcestershire and wilt the greens into the pan. Season the greens with nutmeg, paprika or cumin, salt, and pepper. Add the chicken stock, simmer for a few minutes until tender, then serve.

SERVES 4

BEEF, LAMB, AND PORK

GRAPE-STUFFED BALSAMIC SAUSAGE MEATBALLS WITH FLATBREAD AND RICOTTA CHEESE

This may sound like an odd combo, but it's one of my favorite recipes and dates back to Columbus: roasted pork or sausage with grapes and vinegar. The meatballs are sophisticated in flavor and easy to execute. Before you dismiss the pairing of grapes and sausage as too weird, consider this: Have you ever dipped salty sausage or bacon into maple syrup? Sweet and savory flavors work together and will leave you happy, really happy.

Heat an outdoor grill to medium or preheat the oven to 400°F.

Using your hands, combine the meat with the fennel seeds, grill seasoning, red pepper flakes, garlic, and balsamic vinegar. Divide the mixture into 4 parts; you will be making 3 meatballs from each. To stuff a meatball, take a handful of meat and press a grape into the center, then roll the meat around the grape. Form 12 balls and coat with about 2 tablespoons of the EVOO. Thread them onto metal skewers if using the outdoor grill; place on a rimmed baking sheet if you're using the oven. Grill for 17 to 18 minutes with the lid closed, turning occasionally, or roast in the oven for 16 to 18 minutes, until the balls are firm.

Combine the greens and herbs with the lemon juice, about 1 tablespoon of the EVOO, and salt and pepper. Combine the ricotta with the honey and black pepper to taste. Char the bread when the meatballs come off the grill, or soften and char it under the hot broiler or over the flame of your gas burners.

To serve, pile 3 meatballs onto each flatbread along with some greens and ricotta.

SERVES 4

2 pounds **ground pork** or turkey

2 teaspoons **fennel seeds**, ⅔ palmful

1 tablespoon **grill seasoning**, such as McCormick's Montreal Steak Seasoning

1 teaspoon **crushed red pepper flakes**

1 large **garlic clove**, minced or grated

3 tablespoons **aged balsamic vinegar** (eyeball it)

12 red or black **seedless grapes**

3 tablespoons **EVOO** (extra-virgin olive oil)

2 cups **arugula**, chopped

1 cup fresh **basil**, 20 leaves, torn

1 cup fresh flat-leaf **parsley** leaves, coarsely chopped

Juice of ½ **lemon**

Salt and **pepper**

1 cup **ricotta cheese**

2 tablespoons **honey**

4 Mediterranean **flatbreads**

SWEDISH MEATBALLS AND EGG NOODLES

4 tablespoons (½ stick) **butter**

1 medium **onion**, finely chopped

2 tablespoons **all-purpose flour**

1 cup **beef stock**

1 cup **chicken stock**

Salt and **pepper**

2 slices of **white bread**, torn

¼ cup **milk**

½ pound **ground beef**

½ pound **ground pork**

½ pound **ground veal**

1 **egg**

1 teaspoon **ground allspice**

1 pound **egg noodles**

5 **gingersnap cookies**, ground up in the food processor

2 tablespoons **currant, lingonberry, or grape jelly**

2 tablespoons **sour cream**

½ cup (about 2 handfuls) fresh flat-leaf **parsley**, chopped

2 **dill pickles**, chopped

Little kids love this one—and this big kid still makes it from time to time, as well.

Place a large pot of water over high heat and bring it up to a boil.

Place a large pan over medium-high heat and melt 2 tablespoons of the butter. Add the onions to the pan and cook until tender, 5 to 6 minutes. Sprinkle the flour over the pan, stirring to incorporate, and cook for about 1 minute. Whisk the beef and chicken stocks into the pan and bring the liquid up to a bubble to thicken it slightly. It won't get too thick; you want a thinner gravy for this dish.

Once the gravy comes up to a bubble, season with salt and pepper, turn the heat down to low, and simmer while you prepare the meatballs.

In a small bowl, combine the bread and milk. Soak the bread briefly, then squeeze out the excess liquid. In a medium mixing bowl, combine the ground meats, egg, milk-soaked bread, and ground allspice. Season with salt and pepper, and mix everything up with your hands to combine evenly.

Using a spoon, a small ice cream scoop, or your hands, portion the meat mixture into walnut-size balls. As you shape them, drop the meatballs into the pan of simmering gravy. Once all of them are in the pan, increase the heat to medium and simmer the meatballs in the gravy, stirring occasionally, until cooked through, about 10 minutes.

Salt the boiling water, add the egg noodles, and cook to al dente.

Stir the ground gingersnaps into the gravy with the meatballs, and cook for about 1 minute to thicken. Stir jelly and sour cream into the gravy and keep warm over low heat until the noodles are done.

Drain the noodles and return them to the pot they were cooked in. Add the remaining 2 tablespoons of butter and the parsley to the pot and stir to melt the butter and evenly coat the noodles.

To serve, spoon some noodles onto a dinner plate and top them off with a scoop of meatballs and gravy. Sprinkle a handful of chopped pickles over the top and serve with your favorite salad.

SERVES 4

ROASTED LAMB MEATBALLS WITH HONEY-ROSEMARY POLENTA AND TANGY RED ONION AND FIRE-ROASTED TOMATO SAUCE

4 slices of **whole wheat bread**, crusts removed, crumbled

3 cups **chicken stock**

1½ pounds **ground lamb**

Salt and **pepper**

1 **egg**, lightly beaten

2 large **garlic cloves**, peeled and grated or finely chopped

EVOO (extra-virgin olive oil) for drizzling, plus 1 tablespoon

1 medium **red onion**, finely chopped

2 tablespoons **aged balsamic vinegar**

1 (28-ounce) can crushed **fire-roasted tomatoes**

1 cup **milk** or half-and-half

1 cup **quick-cooking polenta**

1 tablespoon **butter**, cut into small bits

1 tablespoon finely chopped fresh **rosemary**, a couple of sprigs

2 tablespoons **honey**

In my family, lamb was a special-occasion meat. Today, lamb makes its way into many of my weeknight meals—especially in the form of lamb burgers and meatballs. Ground meat is an affordable way to bring the flavor of special meals into everyday menus.

Heat the oven to 400°F.

In a mixing bowl, combine the bread with about ⅓ cup of the stock to moisten it. Add the lamb to the bowl and season with salt and pepper; add the egg and garlic and mix gently with your hands. Form the mixture into 8 large meatballs about 2½ inches in diameter and place on a nonstick baking sheet. Lightly drizzle the meatballs with EVOO, rolling to coat on all sides, and arrange them 2 inches apart. Roast the meatballs for 15 minutes, until cooked through.

While the meatballs cook, heat the 1 tablespoon of EVOO in a medium sauce pot over medium heat. Add the red onions, season with salt and pepper, and cook for 8 to 10 minutes to soften. Add the vinegar to the onions and cook for 1 minute, or until somewhat reduced. Stir in about ⅔ cup of the stock, then add the tomatoes. Bring the sauce to a bubble and adjust the seasoning. Reduce the heat a little, then simmer for 10 minutes.

In a sauce pot with a lid, combine the remaining 2 cups of stock and the milk or half-and-half and bring to a boil. Whisk in the polenta and reduce the heat to low. Cook the polenta for 2 to 3 minutes, whisking frequently, until it develops a dense but spoonable consistency. As the polenta begins to thicken, stir in the butter, rosemary, and honey, and season with salt and pepper. If it gets too "tight," add a little water or more milk to the polenta.

Spoon the polenta into shallow bowls and make a well in the center. Place two meatballs in each well and spoon the sauce over the top.

SERVES 4

SPRING RISOTTO AND LAMB CHOPS WITH ROASTED VEGETABLES

Easy, elegant, flavorful—this one is a great last-minute meal for entertaining.

Preheat the oven to 400°F.

Toss the tomatoes, scallions, and green beans with the balsamic, about 2 tablespoons of the EVOO, and salt and pepper. Spread on a rimmed baking sheet and roast for 20 minutes.

Warm the stock in a small pot over low heat. Heat about 2 tablespoons of the EVOO in a skillet with deep sides and add the onions, and garlic. Add the rice and stir over medium to medium-high heat for 2 to 3 minutes to toast it while you are sweating the garlic and onions. Add the wine and cook until it has evaporated, 1 minute. Season the rice with salt and pepper. Add the stock a ladle at a time, stirring and allowing the rice to absorb the liquid before adding more. Continue to cook for 18 minutes, adding stock as needed; the total cook time will be 22 minutes. While the risotto cooks, puree half of the peas with the herbs, salt, and pepper in a food processor. When the risotto has about 5 more minutes to cook, stir in the pureed peas and the remaining whole peas. When the risotto is done, stir in the butter and then the grated cheese.

Once you've got the risotto going, heat a skillet over high heat and flatten each chop a bit using a meat mallet or the heel of your hand. Season the chops with salt and pepper and drizzle with the remaining tablespoon of EVOO. Cook the chops for 2½ minutes on each side for rare, 4 minutes on each side for well done. Allow the meat to rest for a couple of minutes.

Serve the risotto with the chops alongside and scatter the roasted vegetables over both.

SERVES 4

1 pint **grape tomatoes**

4 **scallions**, coarsely chopped

½ pound **green beans**, stem ends trimmed, cut into 1-inch pieces

1 tablespoon aged **balsamic vinegar**

5 tablespoons **EVOO** (extra-virgin olive oil)

Salt and **pepper**

4 cups **chicken stock**

1 small **onion**, chopped

3 to 4 **garlic cloves**, finely chopped

1½ cups **arborio rice**

½ cup **dry white wine**

1 pound **frozen green peas**, defrosted

A handful of fresh **mint**

A handful of fresh flat-leaf **parsley**

2 tablespoons **butter**, cut into small pieces

½ cup grated **Parmigiano-Reggiano**, a couple of handfuls

8 **lamb rib chops**

BROILED LAMB RIB CHOPS WITH SALSA VERDE, MIXED BEANS WITH LEMON-CAPER BUTTER, AND MASHED POTATOES WITH PEAS

2 pounds **new potatoes**, halved

Salt

1 (10-ounce) package **frozen peas**, defrosted

8 **lamb rib chops**

Black pepper

½ cup fresh **mint** leaves

1 cup fresh flat-leaf **parsley**

1 cup fresh **basil**, 20 leaves

1 **garlic clove**

1 **shallot**, coarsely chopped

3 tablespoons **red wine vinegar**

¼ to ⅓ cup **EVOO** (extra-virgin olive oil)

½ pound **yellow string beans**, stem ends trimmed

½ pound **green string beans**, stem ends trimmed

Zest and juice of 1 **lemon**

2 tablespoons **capers**, drained and chopped

1 tablespoon **butter**

1 cup **ricotta cheese**

Preheat the broiler.

Place the new potatoes in a pot and cover them with cold water. Place the pot over high heat with some salt and bring it up to a boil. Reduce the heat to medium and simmer the potatoes until tender, 12 to 15 minutes. Drop in the peas during the last minute of cooking time to heat through.

While the potatoes are cooking, season both sides of the lamb chops with salt and pepper and place them on a broiler pan.

Make the salsa verde by combining the herbs, garlic, shallot, and vinegar in a food processor. Pulse the machine to chop everything up and then turn it on and stream in the EVOO until the mixture is the consistency of pesto. Season it with salt and pepper and set aside.

Broil the chops to your desired doneness, about 4 minutes per side for medium rare.

When your potatoes are just about ready, fill a lidded pan with about 1 inch of water and place it over high heat. When the water is at a rolling boil, drop the beans in and cover them. Cook the beans until they're crisp-tender, 3 to 4 minutes. Drain off the water, then add the lemon zest and juice, capers, and butter to the pan. Toss the beans to coat well and season with salt and pepper.

Once the potatoes are tender, drain the potatoes and peas and return them to the pot they were cooked in to dry out. Add the ricotta to the spuds and mash them up, and season with salt and pepper.

Serve everything up family style, passing the green sauce at the table to pour over the chops.

SERVES 4

GROUND GYRO PLATTER DELUXE

John loves a good gyro platter deluxe. When we are in the country, we have no diners and no delivery, so we have no gyros. Or should I say, we *had* no gyros…

Preheat the oven to 425°F.

Defrost the spinach in the microwave for about 5 minutes on high.

Place the lamb in a bowl. Add the grill seasoning, 2 teaspoons of the cumin, the chili powder, coriander, oregano, cinnamon, and feta crumbles. Wring the spinach dry in a clean kitchen towel and add it to the lamb. Combine well and form the mixture into two 2½- to 3-inch-wide rolls on a baking sheet. Coat the lamb with the EVOO.

Place the fries on a second baking sheet and bake with the lamb for 20 minutes.

Mix the yogurt, garlic, tahini, lemon juice, and the remaining ½ teaspoon of ground cumin in a small bowl.

In a small sauce pot melt the butter over medium heat. Whisk in the flour and cook for 1 minute. Add the Worcestershire sauce and whisk in the stock. Season the gravy with salt and pepper and cook for 5 minutes until somewhat reduced and thickened.

Soften the pita over an open gas flame or under the broiler.

Slice the lamb loaves into ¼-inch slices. Spread some of the yogurt mixture on the pitas and top with 2 slices of lamb loaf, tomatoes, cucumbers, and hot peppers. Serve 2 pitas per person. Serve the fries with gravy for dipping alongside.

SERVES 4

1 (10-ounce) package frozen chopped **spinach**

2 pounds **ground lamb**

2 tablespoons **grill seasoning**, such as McCormick's Montreal Steak Seasoning, a couple of palmfuls

2½ teaspoons **ground cumin**

1 tablespoon **chili powder**, a palmful

1 tablespoon **ground coriander**, a palmful

1 teaspoon dried **oregano**, ⅓ palmful

2 to 3 pinches of **ground cinnamon**

1 cup **feta crumbles**

2 tablespoons **EVOO** (extra-virgin olive oil)

1 sack of frozen **waffle-cut fries**

1 cup plain **Greek yogurt**

1 small **garlic clove**, grated

2 to 3 tablespoons **tahini paste**

Juice of 1 **lemon**

2 tablespoons **butter**

2 tablespoons **all-purpose flour**

2 teaspoons **Worcestershire sauce**

2 cups **chicken stock**

Salt and **pepper**

8 **pita breads**

2 vine-ripe **tomatoes**, thinly sliced

½ **cucumber**, thinly sliced

Hot pepper rings or sliced banana peppers, drained

COCIDO (SPANISH STEW WITH CABBAGE AND MEATBALLS)

1 tablespoon **EVOO** (extra-virgin olive oil)

½ pound **Spanish chorizo**, halved lengthwise then sliced ½ inch thick

1 small head or ½ large head (no more than 1 pound total) of **Savoy cabbage**, shredded

2 **leeks**

1 large **carrot**, peeled and grated

Salt and **pepper**

1 (15-ounce) can **chickpeas**, drained

6 cups **chicken stock**

¾ to 1 pound boneless skinless **chicken thighs** or **chicken tenders**, cut into bite-size pieces

¾ pound **ground beef, pork, and veal mix**

½ cup plain **bread crumbs** or 1 slice of stale bread, crumbled

1 teaspoon **sweet smoked paprika**

¼ teaspoon **ground cinnamon**

A few grates of fresh **nutmeg**

½ cup fresh flat-leaf **parsley**, 2 handfuls, chopped and divided

1 **egg**, beaten

2 cups **fideos** (see Note) or medium egg noodles

Zest of 1 **lemon**

2 **garlic cloves**, finely chopped

2 firm plum **tomatoes**, halved, seeded, and finely chopped

From tiny villages to big cities and everywhere in between in Spain—especially in and around Madrid—every family has a beloved recipe for this traditional stew. I live in New York, but here's my stab at it.

Heat the EVOO in a Dutch oven or soup pot over medium to medium-high heat. Add the chorizo and cook for 2 to 3 minutes to render some of the fat, then remove to a bowl with a slotted spoon. To the drippings, add the cabbage and cook and turn to wilt it down. While the cabbage wilts, trim the top 3 to 4 inches and root ends of the leeks, then halve them lengthwise and slice them thin. Swish in a large bowl of water to release the grit. Repeat if the leeks are especially sandy. Wipe down your work area. Pat the clean leeks dry on a kitchen towel and add to the cabbage with the grated carrot. Season with salt and pepper and sweat the vegetables for 3 to 4 minutes. Add the chickpeas and chicken stock to the pot, cover, and bring to a boil.

When the stew boils, uncover the pot and reduce the heat a bit, but keep it at a low boil. Stir in the chicken.

Place the ground meat in a bowl and top with the bread crumbs or crumbled bread. Season the mixture with paprika, cinnamon, nutmeg, salt, and pepper. Add a handful of the parsley to the bowl and add the egg. Using your hands, combine the ingredients, then form the mixture into 1-inch meatballs, adding them to the soup as you go. Wash your hands well. Simmer the meatballs for 5 minutes, then stir in the pasta and simmer for 5 minutes more. Turn off the soup.

While the soup cooks, combine the remaining parsley with the lemon zest, garlic, and chopped tomatoes in a small bowl.

Serve the cocido in shallow bowls topped with spoonfuls of the tomato mixture to stir in.

SERVES 4 TO 6

NOTE *Fideo* is the Spanish word for "noodle." In Mexico it refers to a type of fine pasta similar to angel hair; in Spain it refers to very short noodles used in place of rice in some dishes.

STEAK HOUSE SHEPHERD'S PIE WITH TOMATO AND SHRIMP SALAD WITH HORSERADISH DRESSING

I must admit I have a weakness for old-school steak houses, and New York has several good ones. I always order an aged cut of meat with onions and mushrooms alongside, a tomato salad with bacon, and a shrimp cocktail with extra horseradish. Here I've repackaged the whole experience in a new, and much more affordable, way.

Steak House Shepherd's Pie

Place the potatoes in a pot, cover them with cold water, and bring to a boil. Season the water with salt and cook the potatoes until tender, 12 to 15 minutes. Heads up: save a ladle of the starchy cooking water just before draining. Return the drained potatoes to the pot you cooked them in to dry them out a little.

While the potatoes cook, heat an ovenproof skillet with high sides over medium-high heat. Add the EVOO and the bacon. Crisp the bacon and remove to a paper-towel-lined plate. Add the ground sirloin to the pan and brown for 4 to 5 minutes, breaking the meat up as you go. Add the onions and mushrooms and cook until tender, 6 to 7 minutes more, then season with salt and pepper.

While the meat cooks, melt the butter in a small sauce pot over medium heat. Whisk in the flour, cook for 2 minutes, then whisk in the beef stock and add the Worcestershire. Season the sauce with salt and pepper, simmer for 6 to 7 minutes to thicken, then add to the skillet with the beef mixture.

Preheat the broiler.

Temper the egg yolk by beating it with the reserved starchy potato cooking water. Add the egg yolk and sour cream to the warm potatoes, then fold in the blue cheese crumbles and the chives. Season the potatoes with salt and pepper, then spread them over the meat in an even layer. Sprinkle the potatoes with paprika and slide the pan under the broiler to crisp and brown the potatoes, 2 to 3 minutes. Serve immediately right from the hot skillet.

SERVES 4 TO 6

2 pounds **Idaho potatoes**, peeled and cut into chunks

Salt

Drizzle of **EVOO** (extra-virgin olive oil)

4 slices of good-quality **bacon** or peppered bacon, chopped

2 pounds **ground sirloin**

1 **onion**, chopped

½ pound **button mushrooms**, quartered

Black pepper

2 tablespoons **butter**

2 tablespoons **all-purpose flour**

1½ cups **beef stock**

2 tablespoons **Worcestershire sauce**

1 **egg yolk**

3 tablespoons **sour cream**

½ pound **Maytag blue cheese**, crumbled

3 to 4 tablespoons chopped fresh **chives**

1 teaspoon **paprika**

Tomato and Shrimp Salad with Horseradish Dressing

2 **beefsteak tomatoes**, sliced

12 jumbo **shrimp** (12 to 16 count), cooked and chilled

¾ cup **sour cream**

Juice of ½ **lemon**

1 teaspoon **hot sauce**

A few dashes of **Worcestershire sauce**

2 tablespoons prepared **horseradish**

1 **celery stalk**, finely chopped

Arrange the tomatoes on a platter and arrange the shrimp down the middle. Combine the remaining ingredients in a small bowl. Pour a strip of the creamy dressing across the serving platter.

SERVES 4

FRENCH ONION SLICED STEAK WITH GRUYÈRE SAUCE AND GREEN BEANS

I had a chance to visit the set of that great TV comedy *The New Adventures of Old Christine.* The cast and crew raved about the food their chef dished up. That day it was French onion soup with sirloin steak—delish! I got the idea to make the same, minus the broth, with a simple broiled, sliced steak topped with mounds of soft, sweet onions. In a wink 'n' nudge to soup with a cheesy crouton top, the steak and onions get a dousing of Gruyère gravy. Ooh-la-la!

4 tablespoons **EVOO** (extra-virgin olive oil), plus some for drizzling

4 tablespoons (½ stick) **butter**

2 softball-size **yellow onions**, thinly sliced

1 **bay leaf**

1 teaspoon ground dried **thyme**

Salt and **pepper**

1 **London broil** (about 2 to 3 pounds, enough for 4 people)

1 pound **green beans**, ends trimmed

Juice of ½ **lemon**

2 tablespoons **all-purpose flour**

½ cup **chicken stock**

½ cup **milk**

1 cup shredded **Gruyère cheese**

Preheat the broiler.

In a large sauté pan over medium-high heat, heat 2 tablespoons of the EVOO and 2 tablespoons of the butter. When the butter is melted, add the sliced onions, bay leaf, thyme, salt, and pepper and cook for about 20 minutes, or until the onions are melted down, caramelized, brown, and sweet.

While the onions are cooking, place the steak on a broiler pan and coat it generously with 2 tablespoons of the EVOO, salt, and pepper. Broil for 15 minutes, turning once, for medium. Let the steak rest for 5 minutes to settle the juices.

In a medium skillet, bring 2 inches of water to a boil. Salt the water, add the green beans, and cook for 3 to 4 minutes, until crisp tender. Drain and return the beans to the pan. Dress the beans with the lemon juice, a drizzle of EVOO, salt, and pepper.

In a medium skillet over medium-high heat, melt the remaining 2 tablespoons of butter. Add the flour to the melted butter and cook for about 1 minute. Whisk in the chicken stock and milk and season with salt and pepper. Let it come up to a bubble and thicken, 3 to 4 minutes, then turn off the heat. Add the cheese and stir in a figure-eight motion until combined.

Slice the steak and divide it among 4 dinner plates. Top with the onions and pour some cheese sauce over the top. Serve the lemon green beans alongside.

SERVES 4

GINGER FLANK STEAK WITH WASABI SMASHED POTATOES AND SESAME-SOY GREEN BEANS AND PEPPERS

Meat and potatoes is a place where we can all get stuck in a rut, making the same recipes over and over again. What's up? Wasabi is what's up! These spicy potatoes will de-fog your brain, and the ginger flank steak will snap you out of that same-old strip-steak-and-sauce you've been eating once a week.

Preheat a grill pan or indoor/outdoor grill to high.

Combine the ginger, ¼ cup of the tamari, lime juice, 3 tablespoons of the oil, and grill seasoning in a large shallow dish. Add the meat to the marinade, turn to coat evenly, and let stand for 10 minutes.

While the flank steak marinates, place the potatoes in a pot and cover with water. Bring to a boil, salt the potatoes, and cook until tender, 10 to 12 minutes. Drain the potatoes and return them to the hot pot. Use a potato masher to smash the potatoes with the cream and wasabi to your preferred consistency and heat level. Adjust the salt to taste.

Remove the steak from the marinade and pat dry. Grill the meat for 6 to 7 minutes on each side, for medium-rare to medium. Let the meat rest for 5 minutes, then thinly slice on an angle against the grain.

While the potatoes and meat cook, cut the green beans into 2-inch pieces on an angle, and place in a skillet. Add an inch or two of water, salt it, and bring to a boil. Cook the beans for 5 minutes, then drain. Return the skillet to the burner and add the remaining vegetable oil. Heat the pan over high heat until the oil smokes. Add the beans and bell peppers and stir-fry for 2 minutes. Add the remaining tamari and the sesame oil, toss, and transfer to a serving dish. Sprinkle with the sesame seeds.

Finely chop the scallions together with the cilantro and lime zest.

Serve the meat over a mound of smashed potatoes and garnish with a generous sprinkling of the chopped scallion-cilantro-lime zest. Serve the sesame-soy green beans and peppers alongside.

SERVES 4

3 inches of fresh **gingerroot**, peeled and grated

¼ cup plus 3 tablespoons **tamari** (aged soy sauce)

Zest and juice of 2 **limes**

5 tablespoons **vegetable oil** (eyeball it)

2 tablespoons **grill seasoning**, such as McCormick's Montreal Steak Seasoning

2 pounds **flank steak**

2½ to 3 pounds **Idaho potatoes**, 4 large **potatoes**, peeled and cut into chunks

Salt

¼ to ⅓ cup **heavy cream**

1 to 2 tablespoons **wasabi paste** (how hot do ya like it?)

¾ pound **green beans**, ends trimmed

Salt

1 **red bell pepper**, seeded and thinly sliced

2 teaspoons **sesame oil**

1 tablespoon **sesame seeds**

4 **scallions**, trimmed of root ends

A handful of fresh **cilantro leaves**

SWEET 'N' SOUR SIRLOIN STIR-FRY WITH RANCH MASHED POTATOES AND WARM SESAME SLAW

1¼ to 1½-pound piece of **sirloin**, 1 inch thick

2½ pounds **Idaho potatoes**, peeled and cubed

Salt and **pepper**

5 tablespoons **vegetable**, **peanut**, or canola oil

1 large **red bell pepper**, seeded and sliced

1 large **green bell pepper**, seeded and sliced

1 bunch of **scallions**, green and white parts, cut into 2- to 3-inch pieces on an angle

2 cups **frozen shelled edamame**

3 tablespoons **brown sugar**

3 tablespoons **soy sauce**

¼ cup **yellow mustard**

¼ cup **ketchup**

1 small head of **red cabbage**, shredded

3 tablespoons **rice wine vinegar**

3 tablespoons **honey**

3 tablespoons toasted **sesame seeds**

1 tablespoon **sesame oil**

⅔ cup **buttermilk**

A few dashes of **hot sauce**

A handful of fresh flat-leaf **parsley**, chopped

A handful of fresh **dill**, chopped

A handful of fresh **chives**, chopped

Create a stir! This is an all-American twist on traditional Asian-style stir-fry. The "special sauce" can be thrown together with items we all have on our kitchen shelves.

Pop the meat in the freezer for a few minutes to firm it up for slicing.

Place the potatoes in a pot and cover with cold water. Bring to a boil, salt the water, and cook the potatoes until tender, 12 to 15 minutes. Drain the potatoes and return them to the hot pot.

Halve the steak lengthwise, then slice the meat very thin across the grain. Season with salt and pepper. Heat 3 tablespoons of the oil in a very large skillet over high heat. When the oil ripples and begins to smoke, add the meat and stir-fry until browned, about 3 minutes. Add the bell peppers and stir-fry for 2 minutes, then add the scallions and edamame and cook for 2 minutes more. Stir together the brown sugar, soy, mustard, and ketchup and pour over the stir-fry for the last minute of cooking.

Heat the remaining 2 tablespoons of vegetable oil in a large skillet over high heat. Stir-fry the cabbage for 5 minutes, then dress with salt and pepper, vinegar, honey, sesame seeds, and sesame oil. Toss to combine and serve warm.

Mash the potatoes with the buttermilk, salt and pepper, hot sauce, parsley, dill, and chives. Adjust the seasoning and serve with the stir-fry on top. Serve the sesame slaw alongside.

SERVES 4

30-MINUTE GERMAN GOURMET
SLICED STEAKS WITH SAUERBRATEN GRAVY, ONION HASH BROWNS, AND SPICED RED CABBAGE

6 tablespoons **EVOO** (extra-virgin olive oil)

2 tablespoons **butter**

4 cups frozen shredded **hash brown potatoes**

2 **onions**, 1 quartered and thinly sliced, 1 chopped

Salt and **pepper**

1 small or ½ large head of **red cabbage**, shredded

2 teaspoons **caraway seeds**

2 teaspoons **paprika**

1 fresh **bay leaf**

2- to 2½-pound piece of **London broil** (bottom round) steak

2 tablespoons **brown sugar**, packed

2 tablespoons **red wine vinegar**

1 cup **beef stock**

¼ cup **heavy cream**

1 cup **apple cider** or juice

¼ cup **grainy mustard**

Traditional sauerbraten is marinated for days and braised for hours. This broiled, sliced steak supper is ready in minutes, and the stovetop gravy captures much of the slow-cooked flavors of the original.

In a medium skillet over medium heat combine 2 tablespoons of the EVOO with the butter. When the butter melts into the oil, add the hash browns and thinly sliced onions. Season with salt and pepper and cook for 7 to 8 minutes. Turn with a spatula and press to crisp the potatoes. Cook for 7 to 8 minutes longer.

Heat 2 more tablespoons of the EVOO in a large skillet over medium to medium-high heat. Add the cabbage, caraway, paprika, salt, and pepper and cook, stirring occasionally, for 12 to 15 minutes, until the cabbage is tender.

While the cabbage and potatoes are working, preheat the broiler. Heat a small skillet over medium heat with the remaining 2 tablespoons of EVOO. Add the chopped onions and the bay leaf, salt, and pepper, and cook for 8 minutes, or until the onions are soft and sweet, stirring occasionally.

Pat the meat dry and season with salt and pepper. Broil the meat for 10 to 15 minutes total, turning once, for medium-rare to medium-well doneness. Let the meat rest for 5 minutes, then thinly slice against the grain.

While the meat rests, add the brown sugar and vinegar to the softened onions and stir for 1 minute. Add the beef stock and bring to a bubble. Reduce the heat under the gravy to low and stir in the cream.

Stir the apple cider or juice together with the mustard and pour over the red cabbage. Stir over medium heat for 1 minute to combine, then turn off the heat.

Remove the bay leaf from the gravy and discard. Serve the cabbage and hash browns next to the sliced steak topped with gravy.

SERVES 4

INDIAN SPICED BEEF AND WARM CURRY POTATO SALAD, TANGY "CREAMED" SPINACH

This meal is fun because it can adapt to your choice of protein—beef, chicken, or lamb. The spice rub will coat four 6- to 8-ounce portions of chicken breasts and thighs or rib lamb chops. You can make double or triple the spice rub and keep it in a plastic storage bag for up to three months.

For the creamed spinach: Defrost the spinach in the microwave one box at a time, 6 to 7 minutes on defrost each. Wring well in a clean kitchen towel, squeezing out all of the water. Move forward preparing the meat and potatoes while the defrost cycles are going on. When the spinach is ready, add the EVOO to a skillet, then sweat the onion for 5 minutes over medium heat. Add the spinach and stir in the yogurt. Season the spinach with salt and pepper and simmer for 5 minutes over low heat.

For the spice rub: Combine the ingredients and season the meat liberally. Let stand for 15 minutes. Heat a skillet with the 2 tablespoons of EVOO over medium-high heat. Add the meat and cook chicken for 12 minutes, turning once; cook steak or lamb for 7 minutes turning once for rare and up to 12 minutes for well done. Allow the meat to rest before slicing.

For the potato salad: Once the meat has been seasoned with the rub, place the potatoes in a pot and cover with water, bring to a boil, and season with salt. Cook the potatoes until tender, about 12 minutes.

While the potatoes cook, heat the 2 tablespoons of EVOO in a large skillet over medium to medium-high heat. Add the bell pepper, onions, and garlic and cook for 7 to 8 minutes; stir in the chickpeas, curry paste, and stock and season with salt. Dissolve the chutney into the sauce, then fold in the peas. Drain the potatoes and add to the pan, then adjust the seasoning. Stir in the chopped scallions.

Serve the meat with additional chutney. Spoon the potato-vegetable salad and creamed spinach alongside.

SERVES 4

Tangy "Creamed" Spinach

- 2 (10-ounce) boxes chopped **frozen spinach**
- 1 tablespoon **EVOO** (extra-virgin olive oil)
- 1 small **onion**, finely chopped
- 1 cup plain **Greek yogurt**
- **Salt** and **pepper**

Spice Rub

- 1 tablespoon **ground cumin**
- 1 tablespoon **ground coriander**
- 1 teaspoon **ground turmeric**
- 1 teaspoon **ground allspice**
- 1 teaspoon **smoked paprika**
- 1 tablespoon **grill seasoning**, such as McCormick's Montreal Steak Seasoning

- 4 6-ounce portions 1-inch-thick **beef sirloin**
- 2 tablespoons **EVOO** (extra-virgin olive oil)

Curry Potato Salad

- 4 large **Idaho potatoes**, peeled and cut into ½-inch cubes
- **Salt**
- 2 tablespoons **EVOO** (extra-virgin olive oil)
- 1 **red bell pepper**, seeded and chopped
- 1 **onion**, chopped
- 2 **garlic cloves**, chopped
- 1 (15-ounce) can **chickpeas**, drained
- 2 rounded tablespoons **curry paste**, mild or hot
- 2 cups **chicken stock**
- ¼ cup **mango chutney**, plus more to pass at the table
- 1 cup frozen **peas**
- 4 **scallions**, chopped

WEEKNIGHT POT ROAST

2-pound **London broil** (about 1½ inches thick)

4 tablespoons **EVOO** (extra-virgin olive oil)

4 tablespoons (½ stick) **butter**

1 pound **cremini** or **button mushrooms**, quartered

1 medium **onion**, chopped

1 **garlic clove**, chopped

3 **carrots**, peeled and cut into 1-inch slices

3 **parsnips**, peeled and cut into 1-inch slices

1 **bay leaf**

6 sprigs of fresh **thyme**

½ cup (about a handful) chopped fresh flat-leaf **parsley**

1 pound baby **Yukon Gold potatoes**, cut in half depending on size

4 cups **beef stock**

Salt and **pepper**

2 tablespoons **all-purpose flour**

1 tablespoon **Worcestershire sauce**

1 tablespoon **Dijon mustard**

Prepared **horseradish**

Loaf of **crusty bread**

Who would have thought that you could have slow-cooked weekend flavor Monday through Friday? It's easy. Make it. Gather the family around the table.

Preheat the broiler. Take the steak out of the refrigerator and let it come up to room temperature.

In the meantime, heat 2 tablespoons of the EVOO and 2 tablespoons of the butter in a medium sauce pot over medium-high heat. Once the butter is melted, add the mushrooms and cook for about 5 minutes, until brown. Add the onions, garlic, carrots, parsnips, and herbs. Cook until the veggies are tender, 7 to 8 minutes. Add the potatoes and 3 cups of the stock plus 1 cup of water. Bring up to a bubble, then reduce the heat and simmer for 20 minutes.

As the liquid simmers, place the London broil on a broiler pan. Rub it with the remaining 2 tablespoons of EVOO and season it generously with salt and pepper. Broil the meat about 6 inches from the flame for 15 minutes, turning it once. Remove the meat from the broiler and let it rest for about 5 minutes.

While the meat is resting, melt the remaining 2 tablespoons of butter in a small skillet over medium-high heat. Add the flour and cook for about 1 minute. Whisk in the remaining cup of stock, the Worcestershire sauce, and mustard. Once the mixture is thickened, add it to the sauce pot with the veggies.

Thinly slice the meat and top with the gravy-soaked vegetables. Serve with a dollop of prepared horseradish on top and a nice hunk of crusty bread with butter on the side.

SERVES 4

GRILLED VEAL OR PORK CHOPS WITH MARSALA FIG SAUCE, LEMON-RICOTTA ORZO, AND CELERY AND MUSHROOM SALAD

4 (1½-inch-thick) bone-in **veal** or **pork chops**

4 teaspoons **grill seasoning**, such as McCormick's Montreal Steak Seasoning

2 teaspoons **fennel seeds**

2 teaspoons **ground coriander**

16 **dried figs**, coarsely chopped

⅔ cup **Marsala wine**

4 to 5 sprigs of fresh **thyme**

Black pepper

6 tablespoons **EVOO** (extra-virgin olive oil)

Salt

½ pound **orzo**

1 (10-ounce) box **frozen peas**

1 heart of **celery**, thinly sliced on an angle, 3 to 4 cups

4 large **portabella mushroom caps**, thinly sliced

1 cup fresh flat-leaf **parsley leaves**

Zest and juice of 2 **lemons**

2 cups **ricotta cheese**

Parmigiano-Reggiano, for shaving

The marriage of flavors in this meal reminds me of the scents and smells of my own wedding celebrations in Tuscany.

Bring a large pot of water to a boil for the pasta, and preheat the oven to 375°F.

Pat the chops dry. Mix the grill seasoning, fennel seeds, and coriander and rub the mixture into the chops.

In a small pot over medium-low heat combine the figs, Marsala, and thyme. Season with some pepper and simmer gently for 15 minutes to reduce the liquid.

Heat about 2 tablespoons of the EVOO in a skillet over medium-high heat. When the oil smokes, sear the chops for 2 minutes on each side, then transfer the skillet to the oven to finish cooking the chops for about 10 minutes.

Salt the boiling water, add the orzo, and cook to al dente. During the last minute of cooking time, add the frozen peas to the water.

While the pasta cooks, combine the celery and mushroom caps in a bowl with the parsley leaves.

In a pasta bowl, combine the lemon zest with the ricotta cheese and season with salt and pepper.

Dress the celery and mushrooms with the lemon juice and the remaining 4 tablespoons (¼ cup) of EVOO. Season with salt and pepper and top with lots of shaved Parm.

Drain the orzo and peas and add to the lemon-ricotta mixture. Toss to combine and adjust the salt and pepper to taste.

Serve the chops with the figs and sauce on top and the lemon-ricotta orzo and celery and mushroom salad alongside.

SERVES 4

UPTOWN PORK CHOPS AND APPLE SAUCE

- ROASTED PORK TENDERLOINS WITH ESCALLOPED APPLES
- SAUTÉED MINI VEGETABLE MEDLEY
- CHEESY POTATO AND SHARP CHEDDAR HASH

Many of us have friends or family who come to town unexpectedly or are lucky enough to have unexpected reasons to celebrate from time to time. For those occasions, here's a tasty supper that can make even an average day more festive. If you go to a good butcher, get him to trim up the tenderloins for you.

Roasted Pork Tenderloins with Escalloped Apples

Preheat the oven to 425°F.

Combine the grill seasoning, lemon zest, and thyme in a small bowl, then coat the tenderloins with the mixture. Drizzle with the EVOO and rub into both sides of the chops. Place the pork on a rimmed baking sheet and roast for 25 minutes. Let the pork rest for 10 minutes to allow the juices to settle, then slice on an angle.

Melt the butter in a skillet over medium heat. Add the apples and sauté for 12 to 15 minutes, until very tender. Season with a pinch of salt, then sprinkle the flour over the apples and toss to combine. Squeeze the lemon juice over the apples and sweeten with the sugar.

Arrange the apples over the pork to serve.

SERVES 4 TO 6

1 tablespoon **grill seasoning**, such as McCormick's Montreal Steak Seasoning

2 teaspoons grated **lemon zest**

2 tablespoons fresh chopped **thyme**

2 tablespoons **EVOO** (extra-virgin olive oil)

2 **pork tenderloins** (1 package), 1½ to 2 pounds total, trimmed of all silver skin and sinew

3 tablespoons **butter**

5 Gala, Honey Crisp, or Golden Delicious **apples**, quartered, cored, and sliced

Salt

2 tablespoons **all-purpose flour**

2 tablespoons **lemon juice**

2 tablespoons **sugar**

Sautéed Mini Vegetable Medley

Halve the squash. Heat the EVOO in a large skillet over medium-high heat. Sauté the squash for 5 minutes, then add the onions and tomatoes, season the vegetables with salt and pepper, and cook for 5 to 7 minutes until the tomatoes begin to burst and the onions are heated through. Toss the herbs with the vegetables and transfer to a serving dish.

SERVES 4 TO 6

1 pound assorted mini pattypan and/or baby zucchini **squash**

3 tablespoons **EVOO** (extra-virgin olive oil)

1 cup frozen **pearl onions**

1 pint **cherry tomatoes**

Salt and **pepper**

3 to 4 tablespoons chopped fresh **dill**

A handful of fresh flat-leaf **parsley**, chopped

Cheesy Potato and Sharp Cheddar Hash

2 tablespoons **EVOO** (extra-virgin olive oil)

2 tablespoons **butter**

1 large **onion**, chopped

5 cups frozen **hash brown potatoes**

Salt and **pepper**

Freshly grated **nutmeg**

1 cup crumbled or grated **extra-sharp white cheddar cheese**

Heat the EVOO and butter in a large skillet over medium-high heat. Add the onions and cook for 2 to 3 minutes, until they begin to soften. Add the potatoes, season with salt and pepper, and cook for 20 minutes, turning occasionally, until the potatoes are brown and crispy. Season with nutmeg to taste and add the cheese. Turn the mixture with a spatula to melt the crumbles and crisp the cheese a bit, 1 minute. Transfer to a serving dish.

SERVES 4 TO 6

TRAVEL FOOD DIARY: LISBON, PORTUGAL
PORK IN THE ALENTEJO STYLE WITH CHORIZO AND MUSSELS

2 **pork tenderloins**, 1½ to 2 pounds total

Salt and **pepper**

2 tablespoons **EVOO** (extra-virgin olive oil)

1 rounded teaspoon **sweet paprika**

⅓ pound **chorizo**, casings removed, chopped

2 **carrots**, peeled and chopped

1 **onion**, chopped

4 **garlic cloves**, chopped

½ cup **dry white wine**

1 cup **chicken stock**

24 **mussels**, scrubbed well

2 to 3 tablespoons chopped fresh **cilantro**

Crusty bread, for mopping

This dish was actually served to a friend of mine at a tiny restaurant on a small graffiti-covered side street of Lisbon. (I ordered the cod cakes.) The restaurant had no sign; it didn't need one. The cluster of hungry locals waiting for tables outside was sign enough that the food would be traditional and "made right." Thanks to Chris for letting me taste his dinner four or five times so I could get it right, too.

Trim the pork of all connective tissue and cut it into ½-inch-thick slices. Season the pork with salt and pepper.

Heat the EVOO in a large skillet over medium-high heat. When the oil smokes, add the pork and brown on one side for 3 to 4 minutes. Turn the meat, season with the paprika, and cook for 2 minutes more to brown the second side. Remove the pork slices to a plate. Add the chorizo to the skillet and cook for 1 to 2 minutes to render some of the fat, then add the vegetables and cook for 7 to 8 minutes to soften, stirring frequently. Return the pork to the pan and deglaze with the wine, scraping up any brown bits with a wooden spoon. Stir in the stock, scatter the mussels around the pan, add the cilantro, and gently stir. Put a lid on the skillet and cook until the mussels open, 3 to 4 minutes. Discard any mussels that do not open. Serve immediately in shallow bowls, with bread for mopping.

SERVES 4

PORK CHOPS IN TANGY FIRE-ROASTED TOMATO SAUCE WITH BACON PEA POLENTA

Every time I cook a simple pork chop supper I ask myself why I don't cook these more often. They're tasty, and, as they say—they're the other white meat. The spicy sauce on these chops is balanced nicely with the sweet and smoky polenta.

Place a large skillet over medium-high heat with 2 tablespoons of EVOO. Season the pork chops with salt and pepper and sear them in the hot pan until they're golden brown on both sides, about 3 minutes per side. Once they are golden, remove the chops to a plate and cover them with foil. To the same pan the chops were cooked in, add the garlic and scallions. Cook until the scallions begin to get tender, 3 to 4 minutes.

While the scallions are cooking, heat the remaining tablespoon of EVOO in a medium pot over medium heat. Once it is hot, add the chopped bacon and cook until the bacon is crispy, 5 to 6 minutes.

Once the scallions are tender, add the vinegar, brown sugar, and tomatoes to the pan. Bring the sauce up to a bubble and return the pork chops to the pan. Finish cooking the pork chops in the sauce, 3 to 4 minutes.

When the bacon is crispy, remove it from the pot with a slotted spoon and reserve. Pour off all but about 1 tablespoon of the rendered fat, add the chicken stock, milk, and peas to the pot, and bring everything up to a bubble. Whisking constantly, gradually add the polenta to the pan and cook, still whisking, until the polenta has thickened up, 2 to 3 minutes. Season the polenta with salt and pepper and stir in the Parmigiano-Reggiano and reserved bacon.

Serve the polenta alongside the chops and top with the tomato sauce.

SERVES 4

3 tablespoons **EVOO** (extra-virgin olive oil)

4 (1-inch-thick) bone-in **pork chops**

Salt and **pepper**

2 **garlic cloves**, finely chopped or grated

1 bunch of **scallions**, cut into 1-inch pieces

4 strips of **smoky bacon**, chopped

2 tablespoons **white wine vinegar**

2 tablespoons **brown sugar**

1 (28-ounce) can diced **fire-roasted tomatoes**

1½ cups **chicken stock**

1½ cups **milk**

1 (10-ounce) package frozen **peas**

1 cup **quick-cooking polenta**

1 cup grated **Parmigiano-Reggiano**

SPICY-SWEET WATERMELON AND WATERCRESS SALAD WITH GRILLED HOT AND SOUR SHRIMP

Although I've written many recipes encouraging you to make your own take-out food so that you can control the salt, fat, and quality of ingredients in what you're eating, *everyone* orders takeout occasionally. So you *must* have leftover packets of Chinese condiments in your junk drawer. This recipe is a great way to use them up.

Combine the vinegar, honey, and hot mustard in a salad bowl. Toss the watermelon, watercress, scallions, and bell pepper with the dressing and season with salt and pepper to taste.

Combine the hot sauce, duck sauce, and soy sauce in a small bowl. Heat the oil in a skillet over high heat. Add the shrimp to the hot oil and stir-fry for 3 minutes, or until pink and firm. Add the soy sauce mixture to the shrimp and toss to coat. Season with salt and pepper and squeeze the lime over all. Serve the shrimp on a bed of the watermelon salad.

SERVES 4

¼ cup **rice wine vinegar**

3 tablespoons **honey**

2 tablespoons **Chinese hot yellow mustard** (2 packets)

3 cups seedless yellow or red **watermelon** cut in bite-size dice

2 bunches of **watercress**, tough stems trimmed, coarsely chopped

4 **scallions**, thinly sliced on an angle

1 small **red bell pepper**, seeded and chopped

Salt and **pepper**

2 teaspoons **hot sauce**

3 tablespoons **duck sauce** (3 packets)

2 tablespoons **soy sauce** (2 packets)

2 tablespoons **canola** or **peanut oil**

1 pound large **shrimp**, peeled and deveined, tail on

1 **lime**, halved

PRAWNS WITH AÇORDA (SAVORY BREAD PORRIDGE WITH GARLIC AND CILANTRO)

This is serious comfort food, Portuguese style. If you're a fan of *ribollita,* the thick Tuscan bread and vegetable soup, you will LOVE this dish, which is pronounced "ah-sord-ah." You'll know the bread porridge is done when the stirring spoon can stand upright in the pot by itself—just like it would in a good ribollita. (Skip lunch if this is supper; you'll need to save room!)

1 **bay leaf**, fresh or dried

1 **lemon**

Salt

5 to 6 cups torn stale **chewy bread**

2 tablespoons **EVOO** (extra-virgin olive oil)

2 to 3 **garlic cloves**, finely chopped

2 to 3 tablespoons fresh **cilantro leaves**, coarsely chopped

1 **egg**, beaten (optional)

20 **prawns** or jumbo shrimp (12 to 16 count), peeled and deveined

Fill a medium pot with water. Add the bay leaf, then cut the lemon in half and squeeze the juice into the pot and throw in the squeezed halves. Bring to a boil.

In a second pot bring about 4 cups of water to a rolling boil over high heat. Salt the water. Add the bread chunks and cook, stirring and mashing them, for 5 to 6 minutes, until a thick porridge forms. Remove from the heat and stir in the EVOO, garlic, and cilantro. If using the egg, add it now and stir vigorously into the bread porridge. Adjust the seasoning.

Once the bread porridge is simmering, add the shrimp to the lemon–bay leaf water and season with salt. Cook the shrimp until pink and firm, 3 to 4 minutes, then drain.

Serve the *açorda* in shallow bowls and arrange 5 prawns around each portion.

SERVES 4

GRILLED SHRIMP AND "GRITS" WITH SPICY 'SCAROLE SALAD

20 jumbo **shrimp** (12 to 16 count), peeled and deveined, tail on

About ½ cup **EVOO** (extra-virgin olive oil)

2 tablespoons **grill seasoning**, such as McCormick's Montreal Steak Seasoning

1 tablespoon **lemon zest** plus juice of 2 **lemons**

2 teaspoons **sweet smoked paprika**

1 teaspoon **cayenne pepper**

1 (24-ounce) tube prepared **polenta**, plain or sun-dried tomato flavor

Salt and pepper

1 small **garlic clove**, grated or finely chopped

1 tablespoon **grainy mustard**

1 medium-large head of **escarole**, cleaned and dried, coarsely chopped

1 (15-ounce) can **butter beans**, rinsed and drained

The term "grits" is not used literally here: instead of ground hominy, this recipe utilizes polenta logs, a store-bought, fully cooked cousin that is ready for the grill.

Heat your grill to medium-high or preheat a ridged grill pan on the stovetop.

Place the shrimp in a shallow dish and pour about 2 tablespoons of the EVOO over them. Sprinkle in the grill seasoning, lemon zest, paprika, and cayenne and toss the shrimp to coat them evenly in the oil and spices.

Slice the polenta into 12 pieces about ½ inch thick on a little bit of an angle. Brush the polenta with a little of the EVOO and season with salt and pepper.

Combine the grated garlic with the juice of 1½ lemons, the mustard, and about 3 tablespoons of the EVOO. Toss the escarole and drained beans with the dressing and season with salt and pepper.

Grill the shrimp and polenta discs about 3 minutes on each side (if using an outdoor grill, keep the lid closed while cooking). The shrimp should be pink and firm and the polenta evenly marked. Squeeze the juice of the remaining ½ lemon over the shrimp. Serve 5 shrimp and 3 polenta discs per person with the escarole salad alongside.

SERVES 4

SPANISH SHRIMP AND CHORIZO SKEWERS WITH ESPECIAL COUSCOUS

2 teaspoons **sweet smoked paprika**, ⅔ palmful

2 **garlic cloves**, finely chopped or grated

A generous handful of fresh flat-leaf **parsley**, chopped

Zest and juice of 1 **lemon**

2 to 3 tablespoons **hot sauce** (eyeball it)

¼ cup **EVOO** (extra-virgin olive oil)

16 jumbo **shrimp** (12 to 16 count), deveined, peeled, tail on

2 cups **chicken stock**

1½ teaspoons **ground turmeric**, ½ palmful

A couple of pinches of **saffron threads** or 1 packet of powdered saffron

1 cup **frozen peas**

4 **scallions**, white and green parts, finely chopped

2 cups **couscous**

A handful of fresh **cilantro**, finely chopped

¼ cup sliced **almonds**, toasted, see Note, page 102

¼ cup **green olives with pimiento**, chopped

¾ pound smoked **Spanish chorizo**, casings removed, cut on an angle into 12 pieces about 1½ inches thick

If you enjoy paella, this dish delivers many of the same complex flavors but is much faster to make—so you'll eat sooner. Look for Spanish chorizo in the packaged meats aisle.

Heat an outdoor grill to medium-high or preheat the broiler with the rack 8 inches from the heat.

Combine the paprika, garlic, parsley, and lemon juice in a shallow bowl. Add the hot sauce and 3 tablespoons of the EVOO, then add the shrimp and toss to coat. Let the shrimp marinate for 10 minutes.

While the shrimp marinate, bring the stock, the remaining tablespoon of EVOO, the lemon zest, turmeric, saffron, peas, and scallions to a boil. Stir in the couscous, turn off the heat, and let stand for 5 minutes. Add the cilantro, almonds, and olives, and fluff with a fork.

Thread 4 shrimp with 3 pieces of chorizo per metal skewer, nestling the sausage in the natural curve of each shrimp. Grill or broil for 7 to 8 minutes, turning once.

To serve, make a bed of couscous on each dinner plate. Top with a skewer and pull the skewer away from the shrimp and chorizo, leaving them resting on top of the couscous.

SERVES 4

HALITUT WITH CORN CHOWDER GRAVY AND SOUR CREAM AND CHIVE MASHED POTATOES

I love corn chowder; I could eat a whole pot of it by myself. To keep myself from doing so, I invented this gravy to pour over lean fish. (All things in moderation, right?)

Place the potatoes in a large pot with water to cover and bring to a boil over high heat. Salt the water and cook the potatoes for 12 to 15 minutes, or until tender.

While the potatoes are cooking, get the corn chowder gravy started. Heat ½ tablespoon of the EVOO in a medium pot over medium-high heat. Add the bacon and cook until golden, 3 to 4 minutes. Add the onions, celery, and sprigs of thyme and sauté the veggies with the bacon until they become almost tender, 5 to 6 minutes. Add the bell pepper and corn and season with salt, pepper, and hot sauce. Cook for 3 to 4 minutes more. Sprinkle the flour over the veggies and cook for 2 to 3 minutes, then add the chicken stock and milk. Cook until thickened to a gravy-like consistency, a couple of minutes.

Meanwhile, heat a large nonstick skillet over medium-high heat with 1 tablespoon of the EVOO for the fish.

While the gravy is thickening, check the potatoes. If they have finished cooking, drain them, and then pop them back into the hot pot. Add the sour cream, chives, salt, and pepper and mash them well with a potato masher. Cover to keep warm.

Season the halibut fillets with salt and pepper and add them to the preheated skillet. Let them get crispy and golden brown on one side, about 5 minutes. Flip them over and cook them for 2 minutes more, or until just cooked through.

Serve the halibut alongside the potatoes and top all with the corn chowder gravy. Garnish with the parsley.

SERVES 4

4 large **Idaho potatoes**, about 3 pounds, peeled and cut into large chunks (1 big potato per person)

Salt

1½ tablespoons **EVOO** (extra-virgin olive oil)

4 slices of **bacon**, diced

1 medium **onion**, finely chopped

2 **celery stalks** from the heart with leaves attached, finely chopped

3 sprigs of fresh **thyme**

¼ **red bell pepper**, seeded and chopped into small dice

1 (10-ounce) box **frozen corn** or 3 to 4 ears fresh corn (kernels cut from the cob)

Black pepper

Hot sauce

2 tablespoons **all-purpose flour**

1 cup **chicken stock**

1 cup **milk** or half-and-half

½ to ⅔ cup **sour cream** or reduced-fat sour cream

3 tablespoons **chives**, finely chopped

4 **halibut fillets**, 6 ounces each, skin removed

2 tablespoons finely chopped fresh flat-leaf **parsley**

TILAPIA WITH BALSAMIC BROWN BUTTER AND CREAMY FARFALLE WITH BACON, TOMATO, AND PEAS

3 tablespoons **EVOO** (extra-virgin olive oil)

5 slices of center-cut **bacon**, chopped

1 medium **onion**, chopped

12 white **mushrooms**, thinly sliced

Salt and **pepper**

1 (28-ounce) can **San Marzano tomatoes**

4 **tilapia fillets**, 6 to 8 ounces each

½ cup **all-purpose flour**

1 pound **farfalle** (bow-tie pasta)

1 (10-ounce) box **frozen peas**

¼ cup **mascarpone cheese**

3 tablespoons **butter**

¼ cup **balsamic vinegar**

½ cup fresh **basil leaves**, shredded or torn

This meal is based on family favorites of my friend Vicki. Balsamic butter is a balance of nutty and sweet flavors, while the pasta balances smoky and sweet flavors. This one is dedicated to her mom, Gilda. She was a wonderful cook and obviously a terrific mom as well; she did a great job with Vick.

Bring a large pot of water to a boil for the pasta.

Heat 1 tablespoon of the EVOO in a deep large skillet over medium-high heat. Add the bacon and cook for 3 to 4 minutes to crisp. Add the onions and mushrooms to the skillet, season with salt and pepper, and cook until tender but not browned, 5 minutes. Add the tomatoes, crushing them up with a wooden spoon, and simmer on low heat for 15 minutes.

Season the fish with salt and pepper. Dust the fish with flour and shake off the excess. Heat the remaining 2 tablespoons of EVOO in a large skillet over medium-high heat. Cook the fish for 4 minutes on each side, until cooked through. Remove the fish from the skillet to a platter and cover loosely with foil to keep warm.

While the fish cooks, salt the boiling water and add the pasta. Cook to al dente.

Stir the peas into the sauce. Bring it back to a bubble and stir in the mascarpone cheese. Adjust the seasoning.

Add the butter to the pan the fish cooked in. Brown the butter over medium heat for 2 to 3 minutes, then stir in the balsamic vinegar and simmer for a minute or two to reduce by half. Pour the brown butter sauce over the fish.

Drain the pasta, toss with the sauce, and wilt the basil into the pasta. Serve the fish with the pasta alongside.

SERVES 4

PORTUGUESE-STYLE ROASTED COD WITH TOMATOES, STOVETOP POTATOES, AND CUT GREEN BEANS

There are hundreds of Portuguese recipes for codfish, as *baccalau* is the national dish. This is a translation of my favorite cod dinner on my first visit to Lisbon, which I made earlier this year.

1 medium to large **onion**, quartered and thinly sliced

4 **garlic cloves**, chopped

EVOO (extra-virgin olive oil) for drizzling, plus 5 tablespoons

Salt and **coarse pepper**

1 (28-ounce) can diced **tomatoes**

4 large **cod fillets**, center-cut from the widest part of the fish (the fillets should be 2 to 3 inches thick if possible and weigh 7 to 8 ounces each)

4 slices **Serrano ham** or prosciutto di Parma (ask for thicker slices rather than shaved pieces at the deli, but no more than ⅛ inch thick), halved

2 large **russet potatoes**, peeled and thinly sliced into ¼-inch-thick rounds

1 pound **green beans**, stem ends trimmed

Crusty bread, to pass at the table

Preheat the oven to 425°F and place a cast-iron pan or other heavy, oven-safe dish in the oven to preheat.

While the oven and pan preheat, place a sauce pot over medium heat and soften the onions and garlic in about 2 tablespoons of the EVOO for 8 minutes. Season with salt and pepper, add the tomatoes, and stir.

When the pan has heated for 10 minutes, rinse the fish and pat dry. Drizzle the fillets with EVOO and set into the hot dish. Roast the fish for 7 to 8 minutes, then remove the dish from the oven. Top each fillet with some of the tomatoes. Place a half ham slice on top of the tomato sauce on each fillet. Return to the oven for another 8 to 10 minutes to finish cooking the fish. The ham will crisp and darken as the fish cooks.

Once the fish goes into the oven, heat the remaining 3 tablespoons of EVOO over medium to medium-high heat in a large skillet. Add the potatoes and cook, turning occasionally, for 15 to 20 minutes, until tender and browned. Season with salt.

Bring 1 inch of water to a boil in a pan with a lid. While it heats, cut the green beans on an angle. Salt the water, add the beans, and cook for 5 minutes or until crisp-tender; drain.

Make a bed of beans on 4 dinner plates and top each with a cod fillet, sauce, and ham. Serve the potatoes alongside and pass the bread for mopping up the sauce.

SERVES 4

MY-OH-MAHI!
THAT'S a GOOD FISH TACO

¼ cup **canola oil**

1 **jalapeño pepper**, seeded and finely chopped

1 small or medium **red onion**, ¼ finely chopped, the remainder thinly sliced

1 **garlic clove**, minced or grated

1 (15-ounce) can **black beans**, drained

1 teaspoon **ground cumin**, ⅓ palmful

Salt and **pepper**

½ cup **mango chutney**

2 **limes**

2 tablespoons **hot sauce**

3 tablespoons **honey**

A handful of fresh **cilantro**, finely chopped

½ medium head of **red cabbage**, shredded

4 **mahimahi fillets**, 6 ounces each

1 tablespoon **grill seasoning**, such as McCormick's Montreal Steak Seasoning

8 **corn tortilla taco shells**

8 **flour tortillas**

1 cup **crème frâiche**

My friend Charlie told me about his special fish tacos, and now they are mine, too. They are like a double-decker taco, with a soft flour tortilla wrapped around a crispy corn taco shell, giving them a crazy texture.

Heat a tablespoon of the oil in a skillet over medium heat and add the jalapeño, finely chopped red onion, and garlic. Cook for 3 to 4 minutes, then add the beans and cumin and mash together. Season the beans with salt and pepper and fold in the chutney. Reduce the heat to low to keep warm, stirring now and then to keep them from burning. If the beans dry out before you are ready to use them, add a splash of water.

Zest one of the limes and set aside. Combine the juice of both limes, the hot sauce, honey, 2 tablespoons of the canola oil, salt, and pepper with the sliced onions, cilantro, and shredded cabbage. Toss to combine.

Heat an outdoor grill to medium or preheat the broiler. Season the fish with the remaining tablespoon of oil, 2 teaspoons of lime zest, and the grill seasoning. Cook the fish on the grill with the lid closed or under the broiler for 8 minutes total, until cooked through, turning once.

Crisp the taco shells and blister the tortillas on the grill or in the oven. Glue the softened flour tortillas onto the crisp taco shells with a few spoonfuls of mashed black beans. Fill each tortilla-wrapped taco shell with half a piece of fish, flaked, and top with some cabbage slaw and crème frâiche. Serve 2 tortilla-wrapped tacos per person.

SERVES 4

GREEN ONION HALIBUT WITH BBQ BACON TOMATO SAUCE AND HONEY-MUSTARD POLENTA

Halibut is quite a firm fish, and this recipe can stand up to the outside grill. The green onions are so flavorful your friends will be green with envy for the recipe.

Preheat the oven to 400°F. On a rimmed baking sheet, coat the tomatoes with 1 tablespoon of the EVOO and season with salt and pepper. Roast the tomatoes for 15 minutes, or until they burst.

Season the fish with the lime zest, salt, and pepper, then coat in 1 to 2 tablespoons of the EVOO. Roll the fish evenly in the chopped green scallions.

Heat a sauce pot with a drizzle of EVOO over medium-high heat. Add the bacon and crisp it up, about 3 minutes, then add the garlic and onions to the skillet and cook for 5 minutes to soften. Add the vinegar and brown sugar, stir, then add the hot sauce. Add the roasted tomatoes and mash them with a wooden spoon or potato masher. Add a splash of water and keep warm over low heat.

Heat a drizzle of EVOO in a nonstick skillet over medium-high heat. Add the fish and cook for about 5 minutes until well browned; turn and cook until the other side is brown and the fish is firm.

While the fish cooks, heat 2 cups water and the milk in a medium pot and bring to a bubble. Whisk in the polenta and cook until it thickens, about 3 minutes. Turn off the heat and whisk in the butter, honey, and mustard; season with salt and pepper.

Serve the fish topped with the BBQ bacon tomato sauce, with the polenta alongside.

SERVES 4

1 pint **grape tomatoes**

2 to 3 tablespoons **EVOO** (extra-virgin olive oil), plus some for drizzling

Salt and **pepper**

4 skinless **halibut steaks** or fillets, skin removed, 6 to 8 ounces each

Zest of 1 **lime**

6 **scallions**, roots and 2 inches of tough ends trimmed, finely chopped

2 slices of **smoky bacon**, chopped

2 **garlic cloves**, grated or chopped

1 small **onion**, red or yellow, chopped

2 tablespoons **balsamic vinegar** (eyeball it)

2 tablespoons **brown sugar**, packed

2 teaspoons **hot sauce** (eyeball it)

1 cup **milk**

1 cup **quick-cooking polenta**

2 tablespoons **butter**

3 to 4 tablespoons **honey**

3 tablespoons **Dijon mustard**

TOASTING NUTS

Toast nuts in a dry skillet over medium-high heat for 6 to 7 minutes, stirring or tossing often, just until lightly golden. Remove the toasted nuts from the skillet immediately, as the heat of the skillet will continue to toast the nuts. Cool completely. Alternatively, you can spread the nuts on a baking sheet and toast them in a 350°F oven or toaster oven, stirring once or twice.

GRILLED FISH AND VEGETABLE KEBABS AND COUSCOUS WITH MINT PESTO

2 pounds **halibut**, cut into 1-inch chunks

2½ **lemons**

2 teaspoons **hot sauce**

2 tablespoons plus ¼ cup **EVOO** (extra-virgin olive oil)

Salt and **pepper**

1 package fresh **bay leaves**

2 **red bell peppers**, seeded and chopped into 2-inch pieces

2 **yellow bell peppers**, seeded and chopped into 2-inch pieces

2 **red onions**, cut into wedges

2 pints multi-colored **cherry tomatoes**

1¾ cups **chicken stock**

½ cup pitted **green olives**, chopped

1½ cups **couscous**

¼ cup **pine nuts**, toasted (see Note, opposite)

1 cup fresh flat-leaf **parsley leaves**

½ cup fresh **mint leaves**, a couple of handfuls

1 **garlic clove**

½ cup grated **Parmigiano-Reggiano**

8 **Mediterranean flatbreads** or large pitas

For the yogurt sauce

1 cup plain **Greek yogurt**

2 to 3 inches of **seedless cucumber**, peeled and grated

1 small **garlic clove**, grated or minced

Grated zest and juice of ½ **lemon**

1 teaspoon **ground cumin**

Salt and **pepper**

I made this dish for the lovely Kate Hudson when she stopped by our show and stayed to hang out in the kitchen. She is as beautiful on the inside as she is on the outside, truly a fun girl. Plus, I discovered we have more than a few things in common: we love to cook, we love indie music (we both married indie rockers), and we both blow off going to the dentist far too often. In a kinda odd coincidence, we both admit to having temporary crowns that are crumbling because rather than two weeks, we've had ours for two years . . . and counting. Kate the Great, this one is for you.

Preheat the outdoor grill or a stovetop grill pan to medium-hot .

Toss the fish in a large bowl with the juice from 2 lemons, the hot sauce, 1 tablespoon of the EVOO, and salt and pepper. Skewer 2 pieces of fish onto a metal skewer followed by a bay leaf. Continue adding fish and bay leaves to make 3 skewers of fish.

Thread the red and yellow bell pepper chunks and the onion wedges onto 2 skewers and dress with another tablespoon of the EVOO, salt, and pepper. Thread the cherry tomatoes on one or two skewers.

Place the pepper-onion skewers on the grill, turning after a couple of minutes. After 4 minutes, place the fish skewers on the grill with the veggies. Rotate the fish skewers a quarter turn every 2 minutes. After the first turn, add the tomatoes on their skewers. Continue to cook all the skewers, turning occasionally; the peppers and onions will cook in about 12 minutes, the fish in 8, and the tomatoes in 5 to 6 minutes total.

While the skewers are cooking, bring 1½ cups of the chicken stock to a boil in a medium saucepan. Slice half a lemon into disks and add to the stock, then add the olives. Bring the stock to a boil, stir in the couscous, turn off the heat, and let stand for 5 minutes.

To a food processor, add the pine nuts, parsley, mint, garlic, Parmigiano, the remaining ¼ cup of stock, salt, and pepper. Turn the processor on and stream in about ¼ cup EVOO. Stir the pesto into the cooked couscous.

For the yogurt sauce: In a small bowl, mix together the yogurt, cucumber, garlic, lemon zest and juice, cumin, salt, and pepper.

Fluff the couscous with a fork and place the couscous on a platter. Top with the fish and vegetable kebabs and remove the skewers. Fill the flatbreads or pitas with fish, vegetables, and yogurt sauce as you eat.

SERVES 4

CARBONARA PASTA-FRITTATA PIE AND TOMATO-CUCUMBER SALAD

My mom still remembers my grandpa Emmanuel's favorite breakfast. He would take leftover cold pasta, fry it in olive oil, then pour eggs over top with a sprinkle of cheese. My husband never met Emmanuel but this kind of meal is why they would have loved each other so—neither would have been able to get enough of it!

Bring a large pot of water to a boil for the pasta. When it boils, salt the water liberally and add the pasta. Cook the pasta for 3 to 4 minutes or according to package directions; drain.

Preheat the oven to 400°F.

Heat 3 tablespoons of the EVOO in an ovenproof medium skillet over medium heat. Add the pancetta and crisp for 3 to 4 minutes, then add the garlic and cook for a minute or two. Beat the eggs with the milk and season with a little salt and lots of black pepper. Add the drained pasta to the skillet and combine with the pancetta mixture. Scatter half the parsley into the pasta and pour the eggs over the mixture. Let the eggs settle and begin to firm up, then transfer the pan to the oven. Bake the frittata for 10 minutes, then remove from the oven and sprinkle the cheese on top. Return to the oven and bake for another 3 to 4 minutes, until golden.

Combine the tomatoes, cucumber, and red onion with the remaining parsley. Dress the salad with the remaining 3 tablespoons of EVOO and season liberally with salt and pepper.

Cut the frittata into 4 wedges and serve with salad alongside.

SERVES 4

Salt

1 (¾-pound) package fresh **linguine**

6 tablespoons **EVOO** (extra-virgin olive oil)

¼-pound chunk of **pancetta**, chopped

3 to 4 **garlic cloves**, chopped

8 **eggs**

½ cup **milk** or half-and-half

Black pepper

A couple of handfuls of fresh flat-leaf **parsley**, finely chopped

1 cup grated **Romano cheese**

4 **plum tomatoes**, halved lengthwise and sliced into half-moons

½ **seedless cucumber**, halved then sliced into half-moons

½ small to medium **red onion**, thinly sliced

MONTE CRISTO FRITTATA, WARM PINEAPPLE WITH CRYSTALLIZED GINGER, AND PUMPERNICKEL BREAD WITH HONEY-ROSEMARY RICOTTA

3 tablespoons **EVOO** (extra-virgin olive oil), plus some for drizzling

½ pound (½-inch-thick) **ham steak**, chopped

½-pound slice of deli-cut or rotisserie **turkey breast**, chopped

4 **scallions**, white and green parts, chopped

12 large **eggs**

¼ cup **milk** or half-and-half

A few dashes of **hot sauce**

Salt and **pepper**

2 tablespoons **butter**

4 cups frozen shredded **hash brown potatoes**

1 medium **yellow onion**, peeled and grated

8-ounce piece of **Emmentaler cheese**, grated

8 slices **pumpernickel bread**, with raisins if available

2 cups **ricotta cheese**

3 tablespoons **honey**

4 to 5 sprigs of fresh **rosemary**, finely chopped

Coarsely ground **black pepper**

1 fresh **pineapple**, peeled and cored

4 to 5 pieces **crystallized ginger**, grated or very thinly sliced

Eggs are a great go-to for breakfast, lunch, or dinner and an affordable way to stretch a buck or entertain a friend or two. Monte Cristo sandwiches combine turkey, ham, and cheese on egg-coated bread; here the original inspires an easy, hearty egg pie.

Preheat the oven to 375°F.

Heat 2 tablespoons of the EVOO in an ovenproof 10-inch nonstick skillet over medium to medium-high heat. Add the ham and turkey and cook for 3 to 4 minutes, then add the scallions and cook for 1 to 2 minutes more. Beat the eggs with the milk or half-and-half, hot sauce, salt, and pepper. Pour the eggs over the meats and scallions and cook for a few minutes, lifting the edges as they set to allow the uncooked egg to run underneath. Transfer to the oven.

While the turkey and ham are heating through, heat a second nonstick skillet with the remaining tablespoon of EVOO and the butter over medium heat. Add the potatoes and grated onion and cook for 7 to 8 minutes. Season the hash browns with salt and pepper. Turn and press the potatoes down to brown and crisp.

Remove the frittata from the oven after 5 to 6 minutes, once the eggs have set on top but are still a bit soft at the center. Cover the frittata with the cheese and bake for 5 to 6 minutes more until golden on top. Let stand for a few minutes.

Switch the oven to broil and lightly toast the bread on each side. Stir the ricotta together with the honey and rosemary and lots of coarse black pepper. Top the toast with heavy dollops of ricotta. Leave the broiler on.

Cut the pineapple into spears. Arrange the pineapple on a baking sheet and broil for 2 to 3 minutes, or until just beginning to char. Sprinkle with the ginger.

Cut the frittata in wedges and serve with the potatoes and pineapple, passing the cheesy toasts at the table.

SERVES 4

MIGHTY MIGAS

Austin, Texas, is home to the best *migas* I've ever tasted. I make this egg and tortilla dish when I get homesick for the coolest city in that great state of Texas.

Place a large skillet over medium-high heat with 2 tablespoons of EVOO. Add the chorizo to the pan and cook, breaking the meat up with a wooden spoon, until the chorizo begins to get crispy, 4 to 5 minutes. Add the torn tortillas to the pan and cook until crispy and golden brown, 4 to 5 minutes. Add the onions, jalapeño, and garlic to the pan and cook until the veggies begin to get tender, 5 to 6 minutes.

Once the veggies are tender, add the eggs and hot sauce to taste to the pan and cook, stirring occasionally, until the eggs are close to your desired doneness. Season the eggs with salt and pepper and stir in the tomatoes, avocado, lime juice, and cheese. Continue cooking until the eggs are finished scrambling. Serve the *migas* topped with a dollop of sour cream.

SERVES 4

2 tablespoons **EVOO** (extra-virgin olive oil)

⅓ pound raw **Mexican chorizo**, casings removed

4 (6-inch) **corn tortillas**, torn into bite-size pieces

1 medium **onion**, chopped

1 **jalapeño**, seeded and chopped

2 to 3 **garlic cloves**, finely chopped or grated

8 **eggs**, lightly beaten

Hot sauce

Salt and **pepper**

2 **plum tomatoes**, seeded and diced

1 ripe **Hass avocado**, diced

Juice of 1 **lime**

1 cup shredded **smoked cheddar** or Monterey Jack cheese

½ cup **sour cream**

TORTILLA AND TOMATO TOAST

In Spain, tortillas are egg pies, like a big flat omelet that is cooked in olive oil. They are DELISH! My fave is potato tortilla served with *chapata,* toasted bread that you smush tomato all over. Olé!

Heat the EVOO in a medium skillet over medium heat. Add the potatoes and onion, salt them, and cook for about 15 minutes, turning them every 2 to 3 minutes, until tender but not brown.

Preheat the broiler.

Whisk up the eggs and cream or milk and season with salt. Pour the eggs over the potatoes. Let the omelet settle and get firm at the edges, then place the skillet under the broiler until the tortilla is firm and golden. Remove the tortilla from the oven to cool but leave the broiler on.

Place the bread on a baking sheet and toast under the broiler. Cut the tomatoes in half and squish and rub their guts all over the toasted bread. Drizzle the bread with EVOO and season it with salt.

Slice the tortilla into 4 wedges and serve with the tomato toast.

SERVES 4

¼ cup **EVOO** (extra-virgin olive oil), plus some for drizzling

2 **potatoes**, peeled and thinly sliced

1 **onion**, peeled and thinly sliced

Salt

8 **eggs**

¼ cup **heavy cream** or whole milk

8 slices **crusty bread**

2 really ripe **tomatoes**

GREEN EGGS AND HAM BLD

- ROOT VEGETABLE PATTIES
- GREEN EGGS AND HAM
- SPICED SUGAR GRAPEFRUIT HALVES

This is one of the things I (and lots of my chef friends) often whip up when dining solo but it's too good to keep to yourself; it's great for a brunch crowd.

Root Vegetable Patties

Combine all of the ingredients except the oil in a bowl. Heat 2 tablespoons of the oil in a large nonstick skillet, then drop 4 mounds of the vegetable mixture into the pan using about half of the veggie mix. Flatten each mound a bit. Cook the patties for 3 to 4 minutes on each side. Drain the patties on paper towels and make 4 more patties, adding more oil to the pan as needed. Serve at room temperature.

SERVES 4

2 **parsnips**, peeled and grated

1 large **carrot**, peeled and grated

2 cups frozen shredded **hash brown potatoes**

3 **scallions**, chopped

A handful of fresh flat-leaf **parsley**, finely chopped

2 tablespoons **all-purpose flour**

1 **egg**, beaten

Salt and **pepper**

¼ cup **canola oil**

Green Eggs and Ham

Preheat the oven to 375°F.

Melt the butter in a medium skillet over medium heat. Add the shallots and cook for 2 to 3 minutes, until tender. Roll the defrosted spinach in a clean kitchen towel and wring to squeeze out the liquid. Add the spinach to the skillet, then stir in the cream and season with salt, pepper, and a little nutmeg. Cook the mixture, stirring occasionally, until the cream has thickened, about 5 minutes. Adjust the seasoning to your taste.

Fold each slice of ham or prosciutto in half and use them to line 8 cups of a 12-cup nonstick muffin tin. Spoon a heaping tablespoon of the creamed spinach into each of the cups, then crack an egg into each one, making sure it stays whole. (Hint: if you're worried about breaking the egg yolk, crack the egg into a small bowl first, then slide it into the muffin cup.) Season the tops of the eggs with salt and pepper and bake until set, about 15 minutes. Allow the baked eggs to cool in the muffin cups for a couple of minutes before removing them from the pan. Serve immediately, 2 per person.

SERVES 4

1 tablespoon **butter**

1 large **shallot**, finely chopped

1 (10-ounce) box **frozen chopped spinach**, defrosted

⅓ to ½ cup **heavy cream** (eyeball it)

Salt and **pepper**

Freshly grated **nutmeg**

8 slices of **deli ham** or prosciutto di Parma

8 **eggs**

Spiced Sugar Grapefruit Halves

2 ruby red **grapefruits**, halved

2 tablespoons **brown sugar**

2 teaspoons **grill seasoning**, such as McCormick's Montreal Steak Seasoning

Preheat the broiler.

Arrange the grapefruit halves on a broiler pan. Combine the brown sugar and grill seasoning and sprinkle onto the grapefruits. Broil the grapefruit halves until the sugar melts and becomes bubbly, about 4 minutes.

SERVES 4

FARMERS' MUFFIN STUFFIN' HASH AND EGGS

2 large bakery-bought **corn muffins**, split

3 tablespoons **butter**, softened

1 tablespoon **EVOO** (extra-virgin olive oil)

1 (12-ounce) package **andouille sausage**, casings removed, diced

1 medium **onion**, chopped

1 **green bell pepper**, seeded and chopped

2 to 3 **celery stalks** from the heart with leafy greens, chopped

2 to 3 **garlic cloves**, chopped

Salt and **pepper**

1 cup **chicken stock**

2 cups crumbled or shredded **cheddar cheese**

8 **eggs**

1 tablespoon **hot sauce**

2 **scallions**, chopped

I love a farmers' omelet with peppers, onions, ham, potatoes, and cheese. Here's a twist that's supper-worthy.

Spread the split muffins with half the softened butter and brown the muffin halves, cut side down, in a hot skillet over medium heat, 3 to 4 minutes. Remove the muffins and reserve; wipe the crumbs from the pan.

Add the EVOO to the skillet and raise the heat a little. Add the sausage bits and cook just until crisp at the edges, 2 to 3 minutes. Add the onions, peppers, celery, and garlic to the pan and season with salt and bell pepper. Cook for 5 to 6 minutes to tenderize the vegetables, then crumble in the muffins. Moisten the stuffing with the stock and heat through, 1 to 2 minutes. Cover the stuffing with the cheese and tent the pan with aluminum foil. Turn off the heat.

Heat the remaining butter in a medium nonstick skillet over medium heat. Beat the eggs with the hot sauce and season with salt and pepper. Scramble the eggs to your preferred degree of doneness.

Serve piles of the stuffing topped with some scrambled spicy eggs and garnish with the scallions.

SERVES 4

WINNING WAFFLES
- SAVORY WAFFLES WITH PAPRIKA SAUSAGES
- EGGS WITH PEAS AND SHALLOTS

Because I do not bake, I always have to borrow baking powder and baking soda from my neighbors. I measure everything with my morning coffee cup and the teaspoon that I stir my first cup with. Even if you bake and have legit measuring devices on hand, you might want to refrain from using them because these waffles rule, but only if you make them my way. Serve with lingonberry syrup.

Savory Sour Cream–Chive Waffles and Paprika Sausages

Preheat a waffle iron, and preheat the oven to 200°F.

Warm the preserves in a saucepan with the cloves, cinnamon, lemon juice, and ⅓ cup water over low heat. Remove the cloves and cinnamon stick and discard. Set the syrup aside.

Mix the dry ingredients and chives in a mixing bowl and make a well in the middle. Mix the milk, sour cream, eggs, and half the melted butter together in a bowl, then pour into the well. Beat the wet ingredients into the dry with a few swift turns, but do not overmix the batter.

In a medium bowl mix the ground meat with the fennel, paprika, parsley, and grill seasoning.

Brush the waffle iron with a little of the remaining butter and cook the waffles, keeping the finished waffles warm and crisp in the oven. The batter should fill a 4-section iron 3 times, making 12 waffles.

While the waffles cook, form eight 2- to 3-inch sausage patties. Heat the EVOO in a large skillet. Add the patties to the hot skillet and cook for 3 to 4 minutes on each side.

Serve 3 waffles and 2 sausage patties per person, with lingonberry syrup drizzled over the top.

SERVES 4

- 1 cup **lingonberry preserves**
- A couple of **whole cloves**
- 1 **cinnamon stick**
- 1 tablespoon fresh **lemon juice**
- 1½ cups **all-purpose flour**
- 1½ teaspoons **baking powder**
- 1½ teaspoons **baking soda**
- ¼ teaspoon **salt**
- 2 teaspoons **sugar**
- A little freshly grated **nutmeg**
- ¼ cup chopped fresh **chives**
- 1 cup **milk**
- 1 cup **sour cream**
- 2 large **eggs**
- 4 tablespoons melted **butter**
- 1 pound **ground pork**, chicken, or turkey breast
- 2 teaspoons **fennel seeds**
- 2 teaspoons **paprika**
- A handful of fresh flat-leaf **parsley**, finely chopped
- 1 tablespoon **grill seasoning**
- 1 tablespoon **EVOO** (extra-virgin olive oil)

Eggs with Peas and Shallots

Melt the butter in a medium skillet over medium heat. Add the shallots and cook for 3 to 4 minutes, until softened. Whisk the eggs with the salt and pepper and add to the skillet with the shallots. Stir in the crumbled Boursin and peas, and cook for 3 to 4 minutes until the eggs are firming up but not yet dry. Serve immediately.

SERVES 4

- 2 tablespoons **butter**
- 1 large **shallot**, very thinly sliced
- 8 **eggs**
- **Salt** and pepper
- 1 package **Boursin cheese**
- 1 cup frozen green **peas**, thawed

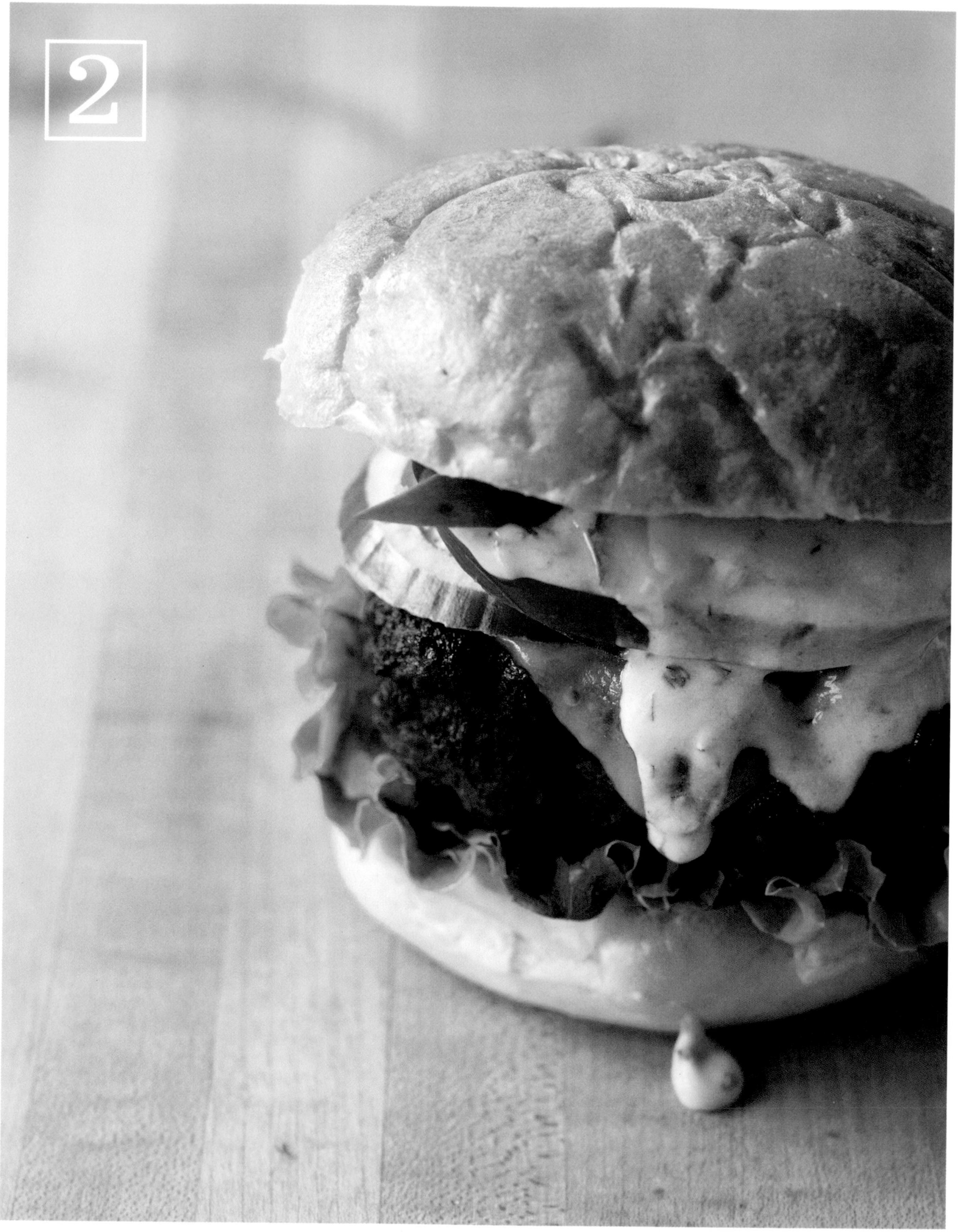
2

ENTREE BURGERS

Burgers have become a true passion of mine. Over the years I have become fascinated with what a burger is and what it can be. Here are my latest recipes for what I call entrée burgers. These are simple meals that often boast surprisingly sophisticated flavors. I love to entertain with my entrée burgers, and I make many of them in miniature versions as cocktail party offerings—who doesn't love a slider? Come on, think outside the bun and try a patty of something completely different!

SOUTH BY SOUTHWEST
7-LAYER SLIDERS

Based on the classic 7-layer Tex-Mex party dip, these spicy beef sliders are only 2½ inches wide but when stacked up with 6 other layers they stand tall! Inside the bun are refried beans, a spicy burger, cheese, lime guacamole, yellow mustard and yellow tomato salsa, olives, and tangy sour cream. Look for mini brioche or potato rolls if your market's bakery section does not make mini burger buns. Split packaged dinner rolls work in a pinch as well.

Each recipe yields 12 mini sliders, or 6 supper-size burgers.

Heat the beans in a small skillet over medium-low heat. Thin them out with a splash of water so they can heat through without becoming pastelike.

Preheat a large skillet over medium-high heat.

Use your hands to combine the meat and chili powder, smoked paprika, grated onion, 2 cloves of garlic, grill seasoning, and beer. Score the meat into 4 portions with the side of your hand and form three 3-inch patties from each section, yielding 12 mini sliders. Drizzle EVOO over the burgers and place them in the hot skillet over medium-high heat. Cook the burgers for 6 minutes, turning once, for medium doneness. (To make a double batch, roast the burgers on a rimmed baking sheet at 375°F for 7 to 8 minutes.)

In the last minute of cooking time place 2 mini slices of cheese on each burger and tent the pan with foil to melt the cheese.

While the burgers cook, mash the avocado with the lime zest and juice, half the cilantro, half the red onion, the remaining clove of garlic, half of the chopped jalapeño, and salt to taste.

Toss the tomatoes in a bowl with the remaining cilantro, red onion, and jalapeño, salt to taste, and the mustard to make a salsa.

In a separate bowl combine the sour cream with the hot sauce and cumin.

To assemble the sliders, layer as follows: bun bottom, a spoonful of beans spread around, a beef patty with cheese, lettuce, guacamole, salsa, sour cream, olives, and bun top.

MAKES 12

1 (15-ounce) can vegetarian (lard-free) spicy **refried beans**

2 pounds **ground sirloin**

1 tablespoon **chipotle chili powder** or chili powder, a palmful

1 tablespoon **sweet smoked paprika**, a palmful

3 to 4 tablespoons grated **onion**

3 **garlic cloves**, minced or grated

1½ tablespoons **grill seasoning**, such as McCormick's Montreal Steak Seasoning, 1½ palmfuls

1 cup **beer**—whatever the cook is drinkin'

EVOO (extra-virgin olive oil), for drizzling

6 slices of **pepper Jack cheese** from the deli counter, quartered to make 24 little squares

1 large ripe **Hass avocado**

1 teaspoon grated **lime** zest

Juice of 2 **limes**

3 tablespoons finely chopped fresh **cilantro**

½ small or medium **red onion**, finely chopped

2 **jalapeños**, seeded and finely chopped

Salt

2 medium **yellow tomatoes**, seeded and chopped

¼ cup **yellow mustard** (eyeball it)

1 cup **sour cream**

1 tablespoon **hot sauce** (eyeball it)

1 teaspoon **ground cumin**

12 **mini buns**, split

Shredded lettuce

½ cup **green olives** with pimientos, chopped

BLUE-RUGULA BURGERS WITH RADICCHIO-PASTA SALAD

This burger is topped with buttery blue cheese, spicy arugula, and sweet 'n' spicy onions. It's a combo that can't be beat, but it can be matched: the pasta salad's dressing features a favorite flavor combo of mine, orange and oregano. The pasta is tossed with the sweet-tangy dressing, bitter red greens, and onions. It may not be for everyone but it's definitely for me.

Blue-Rugula Burgers

Heat 1 tablespoon of the EVOO and the butter in a large skillet over medium heat. Add the onions, season with salt and pepper and cook until caramelized and sweet, about 20 minutes, stirring now and then. Stir the brown sugar and a splash of water into the onions, then add the mustard, combine, and turn off the heat.

Using your hands, combine the meat with the garlic, Worcestershire, parsley, and salt and pepper and mix well. Form the mixture into 4 patties, making them thinner at the center and thicker at the edges for even cooking. Cook the patties for 8 minutes, turning once, for medium doneness, 1 to 2 minutes less for rare, or 1 to 2 minutes more for medium-well done. In the last minute of cooking time, top the burgers with a few slices of the cheese.

Serve the burgers on the buns topped with some arugula and mustard-glazed onions.

SERVES 4

- 2 tablespoons **EVOO** (extra-virgin olive oil)
- 1 tablespoon **butter**
- 1 large **onion**, chopped
  Salt and **pepper**
- 1 tablespoon **brown sugar**, packed
- ¼ cup spicy **brown mustard**
- 1½ pounds **ground sirloin**
- 2 **garlic cloves**, grated or finely chopped
- 1 tablespoon **Worcestershire sauce** (eyeball it)
  A handful of fresh flat-leaf **parsley**, finely chopped
- ½ pound **Cambazola blue cheese**, thinly sliced
- 4 **crusty rolls**, split and lightly toasted
- 2 handfuls of fresh **arugula leaves**, coarsely chopped

Radicchio-Pasta Salad

Bring water to a boil, salt it and cook pasta to al dente.

In a mixing bowl, whisk together the orange marmalade, oregano, mustard and vinegar. Stream the EVOO into dressing while whisking and season dressing with salt and pepper. Pull off 8 of the outer leaves of radicchio. Form serving cups for the pasta salad out of the leaves using 2 leaves to form each bowl. Chop the remaining radicchio. Toss the radicchio and pasta and onions with the dressing to combine. Serve in the lettuce bowls.

SERVES 4

- **Salt**
- ½ pound **orrechiette**, cooked to al dente
- 2 tablespoons **orange marmalade**
- 1 teaspoon **oregano**, ⅓ palmful or 2 sprigs fresh, finely chopped
- 1 rounded teaspoon **Dijon mustard**
- 2 tablespoons **red wine vinegar**
- ⅓ cup **EVOO** (extra-virgin olive oil)
- **Salt** and **pepper**
- 1 head **radicchio**
- ½ small **red onion**, chopped

PHILLY CHEESE STEAK SLOPPY JOES
AND SOUTH PHILLY SALAD

4 tablespoons **EVOO** (extra-virgin olive oil)

1 pound **ground sirloin**

1 softball-sized **onion**, chopped

Salt and **pepper**

¼ cup **steak sauce**

1 cup **beef stock**

2 tablespoons **butter**

2 tablespoons **all-purpose flour**

1 cup **milk**

1 cup shredded **provolone**

2 **romaine lettuce hearts**, chopped

¼ pound chunk **Genoa salami**, diced

A handful of **cherry tomatoes**, halved

3 tablespoons chopped **hot cherry peppers** or sliced yellow pepper rings

2 tablespoons **red wine vinegar**

4 **Portuguese rolls** or club rolls, split

If you love cheesesteaks but don't live near a good Philly steak stand, here's the Joe for you! This one is a real winner wherever you live, but I think even Philly natives will approve.

Heat 1 tablespoon of the EVOO in a large skillet over medium-high heat. Add the meat to the hot pan and brown it for 5 to 6 minutes, breaking up the meat with a spoon. Add the chopped onion and season the onions and meat with salt and pepper. Cook until the onions are tender, 5 to 6 minutes more. Stir in the steak sauce and beef stock, bring the mixture up to a bubble, and cook for 2 minutes more.

While the meat is cooking, melt the butter in a small skillet or pot over medium heat. Stir in the flour and cook for about 1 minute, then whisk in the milk and let it come up to a bubble. Add the cheese, stirring in a figure-eight pattern, then turn off the heat.

Toss the lettuce with the diced salami, tomatoes, hot peppers and dress with a couple tablespoons vinegar and the remaining 3 tablespoons EVOO, season with salt and pepper.

Serve sloppy meat on the roll bottoms and top with ¼ of the super thick provolone cheese sauce, set roll top in place. Serve the salad alongside.

SERVES 4

COBB SALAD TURKEY BURGERS AND OVEN FRIES

My friend Janet Annino asked if I could turn a Cobb salad into a burger. Here's my best shot at putting a few of her favorite things on a bun.

Preheat the oven to 400°F.

Place the potato wedges on a rimmed baking sheet and dress them with 2 tablespoons of the EVOO—eyeball it. Season the potatoes liberally with grill seasoning. Roast the fries until very crispy, 45 to 50 minutes, turning once.

Place the bacon on a slotted pan or rimmed baking sheet and bake until crisp, about 15 minutes. Transfer to a paper-towel-lined plate and cool.

While the potatoes are roasting, combine the blue cheese, sour cream, chives, hot sauce, lemon juice, and salt and pepper in a food processor or blender and process until almost smooth, about 30 seconds. Transfer to a small bowl.

Place the sun-dried tomatoes in a small bowl and cover with very hot water. Let stand for 5 minutes, then drain and chop the tomatoes.

Place the turkey in a mixing bowl and season with grill seasoning. Add the sun-dried tomatoes, garlic, and parsley to the bowl and combine well, using your hands.

Heat the remaining tablespoon of EVOO in a nonstick skillet over medium-high heat. Add a small bit of the meat mixture—a patty the size of a quarter—and cook for a minute on each side; taste the mini burger and adjust the seasonings as needed. Form the rest of the mixture into 4 large patties, making them thinner at the center and thicker at the edges to prevent burger bulge. Cook the burgers for 6 to 7 minutes on each side.

Slice the avocado thin and dress with the juice of the lime and some salt.

Place the burgers on the English muffin bottoms and top with the sliced avocado, sliced eggs, pickles, and red onions. Slather blue cheese dressing on the muffin tops and set atop the burgers. Spoon any extra blue cheese dressing over the potatoes on the side.

SERVES 4

4 large **Idaho potatoes**, scrubbed and cut into 10 wedges each

3 tablespoons **EVOO** (extra-virgin olive oil)

Grill seasoning, such as McCormick's Montreal Steak Seasoning

8 slices of **smoky bacon**

1 cup crumbled **blue cheese**

1 cup **sour cream**

2 tablespoons finely chopped fresh **chives**

2 teaspoons **hot sauce**

2 tablespoons fresh **lemon juice**

Salt and **pepper**

8 to 10 **sun-dried tomatoes**

2 pounds **ground turkey breast**

2 **garlic cloves**, finely chopped or grated

¼ cup fresh flat-leaf **parsley leaves**, chopped

1 **Hass avocado**, pitted and flesh scooped from the skin

1 **lime**

4 sandwich-size **English muffins**, toasted

2 hard-boiled **eggs**, peeled and sliced

1 large **deli pickle**, thinly sliced lengthwise

4 thin slices of **red onion**

WELSH RAREBIT BURGERS

8 slices of good-quality **bacon**

1½ pounds lean **ground sirloin**

1 **shallot**, minced

A handful of fresh flat-leaf **parsley**, finely chopped

Coarse black pepper

Salt

A drizzle of **EVOO** (extra-virgin olive oil)

2 tablespoons **butter**

2 tablespoons **all-purpose flour**

1 tablespoon **dry mustard** or 1 rounded tablespoon prepared English mustard

1 teaspoon **hot sauce**

2 tablespoons **Worcestershire sauce**

¾ to 1 cup **Guinness stout**, just over half a bottle (what *will* you do with the remainder?)

1 pound shredded sharp yellow **cheddar cheese**

8 slices of **pumpernickel bread**

1 cup chopped fresh **watercress leaves**, 1 small bunch

4 thick slices of **beefsteak tomato**

Salt-and-vinegar potato chips

When I was a kid my mom made a great rarebit, a tangy cheese sauce made from porter or stout, egg, mustard, and hot sauce. Mom always poured her sauce over toasted pumpernickel, sprinkled it with bacon bits, and served it with sliced tomatoes.

Preheat the oven to 350°F and place the oven rack 6 inches from the heat source. Arrange the bacon on a slotted broiler pan and bake for 15 to 18 minutes, until very crisp. When you remove the bacon from the oven, switch on the broiler.

Use your hands to combine the meat with the shallots, parsley, lots of black pepper, and a little salt. Divide the mixture into 4 equal portions and form each portion into a patty. Drizzle some of the oil into a cast-iron skillet or nonstick pan and place over high heat. When the oil smokes, add the burgers and cook for 3 minutes on each side for medium-rare. Add a minute more per side for each degree of doneness past that.

In a small pot, melt the butter over medium heat. Whisk in the flour and cook, stirring occasionally, for 3 minutes, or until light brown. Season the roux with the mustard, hot sauce, and Worcestershire, then whisk in the Guinness and stir together for 1 to 2 minutes, until thickened. Turn the heat to low and stir in the cheese in a figure-eight motion until smooth.

Arrange the pumpernickel slices on a foil-lined baking sheet and toast lightly on each side under the hot broiler—less than 1 minute. Pour the Welsh rarebit sauce evenly over the toasts. Return the toasts to the broiler until the cheese is brown and bubbly, 2 minutes. Place a burger on each of 4 slices and top with a handful of watercress, a crisscross of 2 bacon slices, and a slice of tomato seasoned with salt and pepper. Top with a second slice of cheesy toast, cheese side down. The result will be a patty melt fit for a king (or for the Queen of England). Pile a few salt-and-vinegar chips alongside.

SERVES 4

EVERYTHING SALMON BURGERS WITH HONEY-DIJON POTATO SALAD

If you love Sunday because it means everything bagels with cream cheese and smoked salmon, this is your cheat—good for every other day of the week.

Everything Salmon Burgers

1½ pounds skinless **salmon fillet**, cut into large chunks

1 tablespoon **grill seasoning**, such as McCormick's Montreal Steak Seasoning

1 tablespoon **poppy seeds**

1 tablespoon **sesame seeds**

2 tablespoons **dehydrated onion flakes**

¼ cup fresh **dill**, finely chopped

EVOO (extra-virgin olive oil), for drizzling

½ cup **cream cheese**, softened

3 **scallions**, chopped

½ cup **sour cream**

1 tablespoon **lemon juice**

4 crusty **Kaiser rolls**

Green leaf lettuce

Sliced beefsteak **tomato**

Sliced **red onion**

Place the salmon in a food processor and pulse to coarse-grind the fish. Transfer the fish to a mixing bowl and season with the grill seasoning, poppy and sesame seeds, onion flakes, and dill. Use your hands to mix, then divide into 4 equal portions and form each portion into a patty.

Heat a drizzle of EVOO in a large skillet over medium-high heat.

Cook the burgers for 3 minutes on each side for a pink center, 4 to 5 minutes on each side for fully cooked.

While the burgers cook, combine the cream cheese with the scallions. Fold in the sour cream and lemon juice. Split and lightly toast the rolls

Serve the burgers on the toasted buns topped with lettuce, tomato, red onion, and some of the cream cheese sauce.

SERVES 4

Honey-Dijon Potato Salad

2 pounds small **red-skin potatoes**

Salt

¼ cup **honey**

¼ cup **Dijon mustard**

2 tablespoons **cider vinegar**

⅓ cup **EVOO** (extra-virgin olive oil)

Black pepper

6 **radishes**, quartered

½ medium **red onion**, chopped

3 to 4 **celery stalks**, chopped

1 cup chopped **watercress**

Quarter the potatoes and place in a medium pot with water to cover. Bring to a boil, and salt the water. Boil potatoes until just tender, 12 to 15 minutes. Drain the potatoes and place on a baking sheet for 5 minutes to cool and dry.

Combine the honey, mustard, and vinegar in a bowl, then whisk in the EVOO. Season with salt and pepper. To the bowl add the radishes, onions, celery, cress or parsley, and the potatoes. Toss the potato salad, adjust the salt and pepper, then serve.

SERVES 4

AUDACIOUS, HERBACEOUS BEEF BURGERS WITH HONEY-MUSTARD CREAM SAUCE

These burgers are packed with garden herbs and stuffed with a tangy surprise. Serve with a garden salad or oil-and-vinegar-dressed slaw on the side.

Heat an outdoor grill to medium-high or preheat a grill pan or nonstick skillet with a liberal drizzle of EVOO over medium-high heat.

Use your hands to combine the beef in a bowl with the parsley, dill, chives, Worcestershire, and salt and pepper. Score the meat into 4 equal portions with the side of your hand. Grab one portion and press about 2 rounded tablespoons of cheese into the center, forming a burger around the cheesy center filling. Drizzle the patties with oil for outdoor grilling or add to the hot oil in the skillet if you're cooking on the stovetop. Cook the burgers for 4 to 5 minutes on each side for medium doneness and to allow the heat to transfer through to the cheesy centers.

In a small bowl combine the honey with the mustard and sour cream, and season with salt and pepper.

Pile the burgers on the bun bottoms and top with lettuce, cucumber, radish, and onion. Spread the honey-mustard sauce on the bun tops and set into place.

SERVES 4

EVOO (extra-virgin olive oil), for drizzling

1½ pounds **ground sirloin**

A generous handful of fresh flat-leaf **parsley**, finely chopped

A generous handful of fresh **dill**, finely chopped

3 to 4 tablespoons chopped fresh **chives**

1 tablespoon **Worcestershire sauce** (eyeball it)

Salt and **pepper**

5 to 6 ounces **goat cheese** or 1 package Boursin cheese

3 tablespoons **honey**

¼ cup **Dijon mustard**

⅓ cup **sour cream**

4 whole wheat crusty **Kaiser rolls**, split and lightly toasted

4 **red or green leaf lettuce leaves**

¼ **seedless cucumber**, thinly sliced

4 **radishes**, thinly sliced

4 very thin slices of **red onion**

BETTER BURGERS The best way to combine burger ingredients is with your hands, mixing the meat and flavorings quickly but thoroughly. Use the side of your hand to score the meat into 4 equal portions, and form each portion into one or more patties, as directed. When forming burger patties, make them thinner in the center than at the side, as the centers tend to plump and bulge as the patties cook.

GAUCHO BURGER

Charred Pico de Gallo

6 **plum tomatoes** or small vine-ripe tomatoes in assorted colors

2 **jalapeño peppers**

1 small or medium **red onion**, cut into 6 slices

1 teaspoon grated **lime zest**

Juice of 1 **lime**

A generous handful of fresh **cilantro**, chopped

Coarse salt

Burgers

1½ to 2 pounds **lean ground sirloin**

1 tablespoon **ground cumin**, a palmful

1 tablespoon **ground coriander**, a palmful

2 tablespoons **chili powder**, a couple of palmfuls

1 tablespoon **grill seasoning**, such as McCormick's Montreal Steak Seasoning, a palmful

2 teaspoons **Worcestershire sauce** (eyeball it)

2 **garlic cloves**, grated or finely chopped

½ cup **beer** (eyeball it)

2 tablespoons **EVOO** (extra-virgin olive oil; eyeball it)

8 slices deli-sliced **pepper Jack cheese**

1 **romaine lettuce heart**, shredded

4 **cornmeal-crusted Kaiser rolls**, split and toasted

Fancy flavored **tortilla chips**, to pass at the table

When it begins to heat up outside, I find people split into two groups. There's the group that wants to ready themselves for swimwear season and "cut back," subsisting on flavored waters until they reach their target weight. Then there are the gauchos. Gauchos are cowboys and cowgirls who get more active as the days get longer. At the end of those first warm days of almost-summer, this burger is a sure-fiery hit for people who keep their appetite up as the temperature rises.

For the pico de gallo: Preheat the broiler or outdoor grill. Char the tomatoes, peppers, and onions all over. If using the broiler, halve and seed the tomatoes and peppers, place on a broiler pan, and char the skin side only. If using the outdoor grill, char the vegetables first and then seed them. Chop the tomatoes, finely chop the peppers, coarsely chop the onions, and combine them in a bowl. Stir in the lime zest, lime juice, cilantro, and salt to taste.

For the burgers: If you are not using an outdoor grill, heat a grill pan or a large skillet over medium-high heat. Use your hands to combine the beef, spices, Worcestershire, garlic, and beer in a bowl. Score the mixture into 4 equal portions with the side of your hand and form each portion into a large patty. Make the burgers more shallow at the centers than at the edges to battle burger bulge as the patties cook up. Drizzle the burgers with the EVOO and cook for 5 minutes on each side for medium-rare (the centers will be pink). Place 2 slices of cheese over each burger during the last few minutes of cooking, and tent the burgers with foil or close the grill lid to help melt the cheese.

Pile some shredded lettuce on the bun bottoms, top with the burgers, then pile on the pico de gallo and set the bun tops in place. Pass the chips at the table.

SERVES 4 GAUCHOS

STEAK PIZZAIOLA BURGERS

3 tablespoons **EVOO** (extra-virgin olive oil)

2 large **onions**, thinly sliced

Salt and **pepper**

3 tablespoons **tomato paste**

¾ cup **dry red wine**

2 pounds **ground sirloin**

½ cup **pepperoni**, finely chopped

¼ cup fresh flat-leaf **parsley**, a generous handful, chopped

1 teaspoon dried **oregano**, ⅓ palmful

1 teaspoon **crushed red pepper flakes**

4 tablespoons (½ stick) **butter**

3 to 4 **garlic cloves**, finely chopped or grated

4 slices of **sesame semolina bread**, about 1 inch thick

½ to ¾ cup grated **Parmigiano-Reggiano**

8 deli slices **provolone**

I came up with this recipe for The Donald. Mr. Trump enjoys a nice steak and appreciates a good pizza. Here, my recipe for steak pizzaiola gets ground up into a BIG, BOLD, and BADASS burger. Serve with a side salad of your choice.

Heat 2 tablespoons of the EVOO in a large pan over medium-high heat. Add the onions and season with salt and pepper. Cover the onions with a piece of aluminum foil and cook, stirring occasionally, until they start to soften, 2 to 3 minutes. Remove the foil and continue cooking until fully softened, another 5 to 6 minutes.

Add the tomato paste to the pan and cook, stirring occasionally, until it smells sweet and has caramelized, 2 to 3 minutes. Add the wine and scrape the pan with a wooden spoon to loosen any browned bits that may be stuck to the bottom. Cook until the wine has almost completely evaporated, 1 minute. Turn off the heat and reserve.

While the onions cook, place a large skillet over medium-high heat with the remaining tablespoon of EVOO. In a large mixing bowl, use your hands to combine the ground sirloin, pepperoni, parsley, oregano, and red pepper flakes. Season the meat with salt and pepper, then score the meat into 4 parts using the side of your hand. Form 4 large patties thinner in the center than at the edges for even cooking and to prevent the burgers from bulging. Cook for 4 to 5 minutes per side for medium doneness.

Preheat the broiler.

While the burgers are cooking, heat the butter and garlic together in a small pot over medium heat. When the butter melts, remove the pot from the heat to infuse the butter with the garlic flavor. While the butter is melting, place the bread slices on a baking sheet and toast them under the broiler until golden brown on each side. Brush the toasts with the garlic butter and sprinkle with the grated cheese. Place the toasts back on the baking sheet and top each with one of the burgers. Divide the onion mixture among the four burgers and top each one with 2 slices of cheese. Slide the burgers under the broiler to melt the cheese, 2 to 3 minutes.

Serve the burgers with a knife and fork, and with your favorite salad on the side.

SERVES 4

DENVER MILE-HIGH BURGERS

Denver is the mile-high city because of its altitude. These burgers are a mile high thanks to loads of toppings. Good luck getting your mouth around this one.

Preheat the oven to 375°F.

Arrange the bacon slices on a slotted broiler pan and bake for 15 minutes, or until crisp.

While the bacon is cooking, grind up the ham in a food processor; it shouldn't be too fine. In a bowl, use your hands to combine the ground ham and the ground turkey with the grill seasoning, hot sauce, scallions, and parsley. Form 4 large patties, making them a little thinner at the center as the burgers will plump as you cook them.

Heat 2 tablespoons of the EVOO in a large, nonstick skillet over medium to medium-high heat. Add the burgers and cook for about 15 minutes, 7 to 8 minutes on each side.

While the burgers are cooking, heat the remaining 2 tablespoons of EVOO in a second skillet over medium-high heat. Add the onions and bell peppers to the skillet and season them with salt and pepper. Place a piece of foil over the onions and peppers and press down to smother them. Cook until soft, about 10 minutes, stirring the veggies every few minutes. Stir in the chili sauce and reduce the heat to keep the mixture warm.

To serve, place the burgers on bun bottoms, and top each with 2 slices of bacon and a mound of onions and peppers. Set the bun tops in place and enjoy!

SERVES 4

8 slices of good-quality **bacon**

⅓ to ½ pound cooked **deli ham**, coarsely chopped

1½ pounds **lean ground turkey breast**

1 tablespoon **grill seasoning**, such as McCormick's Montreal Steak Seasoning

1 teaspoon **hot sauce**

4 **scallions**, finely chopped

A handful of fresh flat-leaf **parsley**, finely chopped

4 tablespoons **EVOO** (extra-virgin olive oil)

1 large **onion**, sliced

1 **green bell pepper**, seeded and sliced

1 **red bell pepper**, seeded and sliced

Salt and **pepper**

1 cup **chili sauce**

4 **Kaiser rolls**, split and toasted

CASABLANCA BURGERS

All the flavors of Moroccan lamb sausage in a patty topped with cool, creamy yogurt sauce. You'll make it again, Sam!

Heat an outdoor grill to medium-high or heat a large skillet or grill pan over medium-high heat.

Use your hands to combine the meat with the harissa, fennel seeds, garlic, lemon zest, coriander, cumin, cinnamon, and salt and pepper in a bowl. Score the meat into 4 equal portions with the side of your hand and form

1½ pounds **ground lamb**

2 tablespoons **harissa** or red chili paste

2 teaspoons **fennel seeds**

2 **garlic cloves**, grated or finely chopped

2 teaspoons grated **lemon zest**

½ tablespoon **ground coriander**, ½ palmful

½ tablespoon **ground cumin**, ½ palmful

2 pinches of **ground cinnamon**

Salt and **pepper**

EVOO (extra-virgin olive oil) for drizzling, plus 3 tablespoons

1 cup plain **Greek yogurt**

A generous handful of fresh **mint**, finely chopped

A generous handful of fresh **cilantro**, finely chopped

2 **scallions**, finely chopped

2 tablespoons **white wine vinegar** or cider vinegar

½ cup **mango chutney**, such as Major Grey's

½ pound **slaw salad blend**, ½ sack

½ medium **red onion**, thinly sliced

4 **crusty rolls**, split

each portion into a large patty, making them thinner at the centers and thicker at the edges to prevent burger bulge. Drizzle each patty with EVOO.

Grill or pan-fry the burgers for 7 to 8 minutes total, turning once for medium-rare to medium doneness, a couple minutes less for rare, and 2 minutes longer for medium-well.

While the burgers cook, in a bowl combine the yogurt, mint, cilantro, scallions, and a little salt.

Combine the vinegar, chutney, and about 3 tablespoons of EVOO in a blender or food processor. Blend to form a smooth dressing. In a salad bowl, toss the slaw mix and red onions with the dressing, and season with salt and pepper.

Top each bun bottom with a pile of chutney cabbage, a burger, and some yogurt sauce. Add the bun top and serve.

SERVES 4

FALAFEL BURGERS

2 (15-ounce) cans **chickpeas**, drained and rinsed

1 small red **onion**, chopped

2 **garlic cloves**, grated or finely chopped

1 large handful of fresh flat-leaf **parsley**, chopped

3 to 4 tablespoons **all-purpose flour**

1 tablespoon **ground cumin**

1 tablespoon **ground coriander**

1 tablespoon **chili powder**

1½ teaspoons **ground turmeric**

Salt and **pepper**

¼ cup **vegetable oil**

½ cup **tahini paste**

Zest and juice of 2 **lemons**

4 sandwich-size **pita pockets**

1 to 1½ cups shredded **romaine lettuce**

½ **seedless cucumber**, sliced

¼ to ½ cup **hot peperoncini peppers**, depending on how hot you like it, sliced

2 **vine-ripe tomatoes**, sliced

These patties are more tender in texture than a traditional falafel, with the same great flavors.

Preheat the oven to 300°F.

Pat the beans dry with paper towels and place them in the food processor. Add the onion, garlic, parsley, flour, cumin, coriander, chili powder, turmeric, and salt and pepper along with the beans and process until fairly smooth. It will be very thick so you can form it into patties.

Preheat a large nonstick skillet with the oil. Form the bean mixture into 4 large patties and cook for 3 minutes on each side.

While the patties are cooking, get the sauce started. Scoop the tahini paste into a medium mixing bowl and add 3 tablespoons water and the lemon zest and juice, and season with salt and pepper.

Cut open an edge of each pita to form big pockets, then wrap them in foil and place them in the oven to warm for 3 minutes or so.

Open up the pitas and spoon a couple of tablespoons of tahini sauce into each. Stuff some shredded lettuce, cucumbers, peppers, and tomatoes into each pita, then slide in a falafel burger and enjoy! Pass extra tahini sauce at the table.

SERVES 4

TURKEY BACON DOUBLE CHEESE BURGERS WITH FIRE-ROASTED TOMATO SAUCE AND CITRUS SLAW

3½ tablespoons **EVOO** (extra-virgin olive oil), plus ⅓ cup

8 slices of **turkey bacon**

2 teaspoons grated **lime zest**

3 **limes**

1 tablespoon **chipotle chili powder**

1½ teaspoons **sweet smoked paprika**

2 **scallions**, finely chopped

A handful of fresh **cilantro**, finely chopped

3 pounds **ground turkey breast**

Salt and **pepper**

½ **red onion**, chopped

2 tablespoons **brown sugar**

1 tablespoon **Worcestershire sauce**

1 tablespoon **grainy mustard**

1 (15-ounce) can diced **fire-roasted tomatoes**, lightly drained

¼ cup **orange marmalade**

Juice of 1 **lemon**

2 to 3 teaspoons **hot sauce**

1-pound sack of shredded **slaw salad mix**

8 slices of **pepper Jack cheese**

4 large sandwich-size **English muffins**, lightly toasted

2 **dill pickles**, thinly sliced lengthwise

I love taking naughty food—such as a bacon double cheese burger—and making it nice. This big beautiful burger will fill you up and then some, but it will keep you in the same size jeans. Nice!

Heat ½ tablespoon of EVOO in a large nonstick skillet over medium to medium-high heat and add the turkey bacon. Cook until crisp, about 3 minutes on each side. Remove the bacon to a paper-towel-lined plate.

While the bacon cooks, combine the zest and juice of 2 limes with the chipotle, chili powder, paprika, scallions, and cilantro in a large bowl. Add the turkey to the bowl and season with salt and pepper. Use your hands to mix the turkey with the seasonings, then use the side of your hand to score the mixture into 4 portions. From each, form 2 patties, for a total of 8. Heat a tablespoon of EVOO in the same skillet, place the first 4 patties in the pan and cook for 3 to 4 minutes on each side over medium-high heat. Transfer the patties to a plate and cover with foil to keep warm.

While the first batch of burgers cooks, heat 1 tablespoon of EVOO in a saucepot over medium-high heat. Add the onions and cook to soften, 3 to 4 minutes. Season the onions with salt and pepper, then add the brown sugar and stir until it dissolves. Add the Worcestershire, mustard, and tomatoes and let the sauce cook on low while you cook the second batch of burgers.

While the second batch of burgers cooks, remove the lid from the marmalade jar and heat the marmalade in the microwave for 15 seconds to liquefy it. Spoon the marmalade into a bowl, then whisk in the lemon juice and juice of the remaining lime, hot sauce, and ⅓ cup EVOO. Toss the slaw mix with the dressing and season with salt and pepper.

Add another tablespoon of EVOO and the remaining burgers to the skillet and cook for 3 to 4 minutes on each side. Top each with a slice of cheese and 2 pieces of bacon, then top with the reserved patties and the remaining 4 pieces of cheese. Tent the pan with foil and melt the cheese over medium heat for 1 minute.

Serve the bacon double cheese burgers on English muffins topped with sliced pickles and the fire-roasted tomato sauce. Serve with citrus slaw on the side.

SERVES 4

TURKEY BURGERS WITH ZUCCHINI RELISH ON SOURDOUGH ENGLISH MUFFINS

Use your hands to combine the turkey in a bowl with the poultry seasoning, parsley, grill seasoning, and mustard. Score the meat into 4 equal portions with the side of your hand and form each portion into a large patty, thinner at the center than the edges. As the burgers cook they will plump in the middle and even out on top to make a flat, thick burger.

Heat the EVOO in a nonstick skillet over medium-high heat and cook the patties for 6 to 7 minutes on each side until the juices run clear. Top the burgers with slices of cheese in the last few minutes of cooking. Tent the pan loosely with foil to help melt the cheese.

While the burgers cook, combine the zucchini with the bell pepper, onion, thyme, hot sauce, lime juice, and salt. Toast the split muffins and butter them.

Serve the burgers on the English muffins topped with lettuce and lots of zucchini relish.

SERVES 4

2 pounds **ground turkey breast**

2 teaspoons **poultry seasoning**

A handful of fresh flat-leaf **parsley**, finely chopped

1 tablespoon **grill seasoning**, such as McCormick's Montreal Steak Seasoning

1 tablespoon **Dijon mustard**

1 tablespoon **EVOO** (extra-virgin olive oil)

½ pound **sharp white cheddar cheese**, sliced

1 small **zucchini**, finely chopped

¼ **red bell pepper**, seeded and finely chopped

½ small **red onion**, finely chopped

2 tablespoons fresh **thyme** leaves, finely chopped

2 teaspoons **hot sauce**

Juice of 1 **lime**

Salt

4 jumbo sourdough **English muffins**, split

Softened **butter**, for English muffins

4 **red lettuce leaves**

BUFFALO TURKEY BURGERS WITH BLUE CHEESE GRAVY AND CHILI FRIES

4 big **Idaho potatoes**, cut lengthwise into 6 wedges

4 tablespoons **EVOO** (extra-virgin olive oil)

1 teaspoon **chili powder**

1 teaspoon **ground cumin**

½ teaspoon **cayenne pepper**

Salt and **pepper**

2 pounds ground **turkey breast**

A palmful of **grill seasoning**, such as McCormick's Montreal Steak Seasoning

¼ cup **hot sauce**

¼ cup (about a palmful) chopped fresh **chives**, plus extra chopped chives for garnish

¼ cup (about a handful) fresh flat-leaf **parsley**, chopped

2 **garlic cloves**, grated

3 tablespoons **butter**

3 tablespoons **all-purpose flour**

3 cups **milk**

1 cup **blue cheese**

4 **kimmelweck rolls** or 4 thick slices of rye bread, slightly toasted

3 **celery stalks**, cut into sticks

3 **carrots**, peeled and cut into sticks

These open-face burgers taste great on kummelweck rolls, but unfortunately they're made only in the Buffalo-Rochester area. The kummelweck—sometimes spelled "kimmelweck"—is basically a Kaiser roll topped with lots of pretzel salt and caraway seeds. (The name means "caraway roll" in German.) If you find them, reserve the tops for burgers and save the bottoms to make fresh croutons or bread crumbs later in the week.

Preheat the oven to 450°F.

Place the potato wedges on a rimmed baking sheet, drizzle with about 2 tablespoons of the EVOO, and sprinkle with the chili powder, cumin, cayenne pepper, and salt and pepper. Toss to coat. Roast the potatoes for 40 to 45 minutes, until crispy and cooked through, turning once or twice.

In a large bowl, use your hands to combine the turkey, grill seasoning, hot sauce, chives, parsley, garlic, and salt and pepper. Score the meat into 4 equal portions with the side of your hand, and form each portion into a large patty, thinner at the center than at the edges. As the burgers cook they will plump in the middle and even out on top to make a flat, thick burger.

Heat a large skillet over medium-high heat with the remaining 2 tablespoons of EVOO. Fry the burgers for about 5 minutes on each side, until cooked through.

Melt the butter in a medium skillet over medium-high heat. Sprinkle the flour over the butter and cook for about 1 minute. Whisk the milk into the roux and season with salt and pepper. When the milk comes up to a bubble and has thickened, take the pan off the heat and stir the cheese into the sauce in a figure-eight motion.

To serve, place the top of the roll or a slice of rye bread on a plate, and top with the burger and some chopped chives. Serve the potato wedges, celery and carrot sticks, and a cup of warm blue cheese dip garnished with chopped chives for each person alongside.

SERVES 4

If you're a creature of habit who always orders a club sandwich, stick your toe outside the comfort zone and try this entrée burger twist.

Tur-Chicken Club Burgers

Preheat the oven to 375°F. Arrange the bacon strips on a slotted broiler pan and bake until crisp, 15 to 20 minutes.

Use your hands to combine the meats in a bowl with the paprika, poultry seasoning, grill seasoning, parsley, and shallots. Score the meat into 4 equal portions with the side of your hand, and form each portion into a patty. Make them thinner at the center and thicker at the edges for even cooking. Heat the EVOO in a large skillet over medium to medium-high heat. Cook the burgers for 14 to 15 minutes, turning once.

Pour the buttermilk into a bowl and stir in the garlic, lemon juice, hot sauce, chives, and salt and pepper.

Split and toast the rolls.

Place a burger on each bun bottom and top with 2 slices of the bacon and 2 lettuce leaves. Season the tomatoes, arrange them on top of the lettuce, and top with 2 avocado slices. Slather the bun tops with the buttermilk dressing and set in place.

SERVES 4 REALLY HUNGRY PEOPLE

8 slices of good-quality **bacon**

1 pound **ground turkey breast**

1 pound **ground chicken**

1 teaspoon **paprika** or **sweet smoked paprika**

2 teaspoons **poultry seasoning**, ⅔ palmful

1 tablespoon **grill seasoning**, such as McCormick's Montreal Steak Seasoning, a palmful

A handful of chopped fresh flat-leaf **parsley**

1 large **shallot**, finely chopped

2 tablespoons **EVOO** (extra-virgin olive oil)

1 cup **buttermilk**

1 large **garlic clove**, grated or minced

1 tablespoon fresh **lemon juice**

1 teaspoon **hot sauce**

3 tablespoons chopped fresh **chives**

Salt and **pepper**

4 crusty **whole wheat Kaiser rolls**

8 **green leaf lettuce leaves**

8 slices of **ripe tomato**

8 slices of **Hass avocado**

Green Potato Salad

Place the potatoes in a pan with water to cover. Bring to a boil, salt the water, and cook until the potatoes are just tender, 12 to 15 minutes. Drain the potatoes and return them to the hot pot to dry out for a minute or two. Transfer the potatoes to a bowl and gently combine with the scallions and salsa. Serve warm or chilled.

SERVES 4 TO 6

2 pounds **Idaho potatoes**, peeled and cut into bite-size cubes

Salt

4 **scallions**, white and green parts, chopped

1½ cups prepared **salsa verde**

BISTRO NIGHT AT HOME

- PROVENÇAL CHICKEN BURGERS WITH PISSALADIÈRE TOPPING
- ROASTED BEANS AND TOMATOES

Here, the burgers carry the flavor of a traditional French sausage. They are topped with cheese and with caramelized onions flavored with olives and anchovies—the topping of *pissaladière,* my favorite savory French tart. Ooh-la-la!

Provençal Chicken Burgers with Pissaladière Topping

2 tablespoons **EVOO** (extra-virgin olive oil)

2 tablespoons **butter**

2 large **onions**, very thinly sliced

Salt and **pepper**

⅓ cup pitted **black olives**, such as niçoise or kalamata, chopped

1 tablespoon **anchovy paste**

2 pounds **ground chicken**

1 tablespoon dried **herbes de Provence**, a healthy palmful

2 teaspoons **fennel seeds**, ⅔ palmful

2 teaspoons grated **lemon zest**

2 **garlic cloves**, minced

4 slices of **Swiss cheese**

4 **crusty rolls**, split and lightly toasted

4 **red or green leaf lettuce leaves**

Combine 1 tablespoon of the EVOO and the butter in a skillet over medium heat. Add the onions to the pan, season with salt and pepper, and cook slowly for 20 minutes to caramelize the onions a golden brown. Stir in the olives and anchovy paste and cook for 2 minutes more. Remove from the heat.

While the onions cook, in a bowl use your hands to combine the chicken with the herbes de Provence, fennel seeds, lemon zest, garlic, and salt and pepper. Score the meat into 4 equal portions with the side of your hand, and form each portion into a large patty. Heat the remaining tablespoon of EVOO in a large nonstick skillet over medium-high heat, and cook the patties for 6 minutes on each side. During the last 2 minutes of cooking time, place a slice of cheese on each burger and loosely tent the pan with aluminum foil to melt the cheese. Serve the burgers on buns topped with lettuce and caramelized onion topping, with some olive-oil potato chips and roasted beans and tomatoes alongside.

SERVES 4

Roasted Beans and Tomatoes

1 pound **green beans**, stem ends trimmed

1 pint **cherry tomatoes**

EVOO (extra-virgin olive oil), for drizzling

Salt and **pepper**

Preheat the oven to 450°F with an empty rimmed baking sheet on an upper rack. Coat the beans and tomatoes with EVOO and season them with salt and pepper. Pour the beans and tomatoes onto the hot baking sheet and roast for 22 to 25 minutes, until tender and caramelized.

SERVES 4

GUILTLESS PLEASURES

- SLOPPY HOT WING JOES
- SMASHED POTATO SKINS

I cannot provide enough figure-friendly replacements for the artery-clogging guilty pleasure of Buffalo-style hot wings. Here's one more to add to your arsenal in the battle of the bulge. The potatoes taste like skins with sour cream and the works, but they are broiled, not fried. The bacon is baked on a slotted broiler pan so the fat drains away. The sour cream is replaced with buttermilk, which is tangy but made from skimmed milk. I use super-sharp cheddar cheese, so a little goes a long way!

Sloppy Hot Wing Joes

2 tablespoons **EVOO** (extra-virgin olive oil)

2 pounds **ground chicken**

2 **carrots**, peeled and grated

4 **celery stalks**, chopped

1 **onion**, finely chopped

2 **garlic cloves**, finely chopped

Salt and **pepper**

2 tablespoons **red wine vinegar**

2 tablespoons **brown sugar**

1 tablespoon **Worcestershire sauce**

¼ to ⅓ cup **hot sauce**

1 cup **tomato sauce**

1 cup **chicken stock**

6 quality **burger rolls**

1 cup **blue cheese** crumbles

2 large **dill pickles**, chopped

Heat the EVOO in a large skillet over medium-high heat. Add the meat and cook for 5 to 6 minutes, breaking it up with a wooden spoon as it cooks. Add the carrots, celery, onions, and garlic, season with salt and pepper, and cook for 7 to 8 minutes more. Combine the vinegar, brown sugar, Worcestershire, hot sauce, tomato sauce, and stock in a mixing cup and pour over the contents of the pan. Mix thoroughly, and simmer for a few minutes more.

Split the rolls and toast under the broiler or in a toaster oven. Pile the sloppy Buffalo-style filling onto buns and top with blue cheese crumbles and chopped pickles.

SERVES 6

Smashed Potato Skins

6 slices of **bacon**

2½ pounds small **potatoes**, unpeeled

Salt

1 cup **buttermilk**

¼ cup chopped fresh **chives**

½ cup grated **sharp cheddar cheese**, yellow or white

Black pepper

Preheat the oven to 350°F. Arrange the bacon on a slotted broiler pan and bake for 12 to 15 minutes, until crisp. Let the bacon cool for a few minutes, then chop into small bits.

Halve the potatoes and place them in a medium pot with water to cover. Bring the water to a boil, season the water with salt, and cook the potatoes until tender, about 15 minutes. Drain the potatoes and return them to the hot pot. Mash the potatoes with the buttermilk, chives, and cheddar, then season with salt and pepper. Fold in the bacon and serve.

SERVES 6

HAM BURGER

This burger tastes like a Sunday-supper of glazed baked ham with pineapple. The idea for it came from a big, sweet ham in my life—my talented and always hungry hubby, John. Honey, open wide and ham it up!

Serve this with an oil and vinegar slaw salad.

Grind the ham in a food processor, pulsing on and off until finely chopped, and place in a bowl. Add the pork, drizzle with the syrup, and season with the cloves, mustard, allspice, paprika, hot sauce, and grill seasoning. Use your hands to combine the mixture. Score the meat into 4 equal portions with the side of your hand and form each into a large patty.

Heat 1 tablespoon of the EVOO in a large nonstick skillet over medium-high heat. Add the pineapple to the hot oil and cook for 2 to 3 minutes to caramelize each side. Transfer the pineapple to a plate, wipe the pan clean, and add the remaining tablespoon of EVOO. Cook the burgers for 12 to 14 minutes until cooked through, turning occasionally. Toast the rolls while the burgers cook.

Serve the burgers on buns topped with lettuce, pineapple, red onion, and chutney.

SERVES 4

¾ pound **honey-roasted or other sweet ham** from the deli, coarsely chopped

1 pound lean **ground pork**

2 tablespoons pure **maple syrup**

A pinch of **ground cloves**

½ teaspoon **dry mustard** or 2 rounded teaspoons **prepared yellow mustard**

1 teaspoon **ground allspice**, ⅓ palmful

1½ teaspoons **sweet paprika**, ½ palmful

2 teaspoons **hot sauce**

1 tablespoon **grill seasoning**, such as McCormick's Montreal Steak Seasoning, a palmful

2 tablespoons **EVOO** (extra-virgin olive oil)

4 (1-inch-thick) slices of cored fresh **pineapple**

4 **Kaiser rolls**, split and lightly toasted

8 **red leaf lettuce leaves**

Thinly sliced **red onions**, for topping

1 cup **prepared mango** or pineapple chutney

VEGETARIAN MEALS

I am always a little surprised to be asked by viewers or readers to write more veggie meals, as several nights a week in my own home we are meat-free. A fair percentage of my meals have always been vegetarian because my diet includes many vegetables, beans, and grains. Additionally, I have been aware for the past several years of the growing pressure on those living in households where one member, be it a child, a partner, or otherwise, is a vegetarian and the others are not. Here are some delicious meals, all of which I make in my own home for my husband (a *huge* meat eater) to everyone's satisfaction. Once you've worked your way through these, thumb through the book to find other meals that can be adapted easily: swap vegetable or mushroom stock for chicken or beef broth, omit pancetta or bacon, swap tofu for animal protein. Have fun eating your veggies!

WINTER GREENS PASTA

In Italy my mom and I shared a panini stuffed with a salty combination of greens, anchovies, and capers. It was so delish we gobbled it up. Here it is in the form of a pasta dish. I chose to use whole wheat pasta because the nutty flavor balances the deepness of the greens, but it is tasty with semolina pasta as well.

Bring a large pot of water to a boil over high heat to cook the pasta. Once the water is boiling, season with salt, add the pasta, and cook to al dente. Heads up: you'll need to reserve about 1 cup of the pasta cooking water before draining the pasta.

Once the pasta water is almost to a boil, start the greens. Heat the EVOO in a large skillet over medium heat. Add the garlic, anchovies, and red pepper flakes and cook, stirring every now and then, until the anchovies have completely melted, 3 to 4 minutes. Turn the heat up to medium-high and add the escarole and spinach. Season the wilted greens with black pepper and nutmeg.

When the pasta is drained, add the reserved cup of pasta cooking water, the capers, lemon zest and juice, arugula, and the drained pasta to the pot you used to cook the pasta. Add the wilted greens. Toss over medium-high heat for 1 minute to combine.

SERVES 4

Salt

1 pound whole wheat **spaghetti**

¼ cup **EVOO** (extra-virgin olive oil)

5 to 6 large **garlic cloves**, grated or finely chopped

5 to 6 **anchovy fillets**

1 teaspoon **crushed red pepper flakes**

2 heads of **escarole**, leaves separated from the core, washed, and coarsely chopped

1 pound **spinach**, thick stems removed, leaves coarsely chopped

Black pepper

Freshly grated **nutmeg**

3 tablespoons drained **capers**

Zest and juice of 1 **lemon**

3 cups **arugula leaves**

RED AND GREEN LASAGNA

Here's a cheery holiday offering to take to a friend's house or to make for any new parents in your life; lasagna is a bottomless pan that keeps the eaters fed as long as need be. The red sauce looks like marinara but it is really a thick sauce of sun-dried tomatoes and pureed roasted red peppers.

Preheat the oven to 400°F.

Reconstitute the sun-dried tomatoes by placing them in a small heat-proof bowl and pouring hot water over them. Let them sit while you prepare the sauce.

Place a medium sauce pot over medium-high heat with 2 tablespoons of the EVOO. Add the onions, half of the garlic, and the marjoram to the pot and cook until the onions begin to soften, about 5 minutes; season with salt and pepper. While the onions simmer, place the roasted peppers in a food processor and process until pureed and smooth. Add the crushed tomatoes to the pot with the onions, reduce the heat to medium, and bring the sauce up to a bubble. Drain the reconstituted sun-dried tomatoes and coarsely chop them. Add them to the sauce along with the basil and pureed roasted peppers. Simmer the sauce until it thickens up, 7 to 8 minutes. Adjust the seasonings.

While the sauce is simmering, wash out the bowl of the food processor. Make a spinach pesto by combining the spinach, pine nuts, and the remaining garlic in the food processor. Pour in the vegetable stock and pulse the machine until a very thick paste forms. Season the pesto with salt, pepper, and nutmeg, and add ½ to ¾ cup of the grated Parm to the bowl. With the processor on, stream in the remaining ½ cup of EVOO. Transfer the pesto to a mixing bowl and stir in the ricotta cheese, egg, and extra yolk.

Assemble the lasagna by ladling a little of the red sauce into the bottom of a 13 x 9-inch baking dish. Top the red sauce with a layer of lasagna noodles and cover those with a thin layer of the spinach pesto mixture. Layer red and green with pasta until all of the sauce and pasta are used. Top the lasagna with the provolone and remaining Parm. Cover the pan with foil and bake for 45 minutes, then remove the foil and bake 15 minutes more, or until the cheese is bubbly and brown.

SERVES 8

10 to 12 **sun-dried tomatoes**, about ½ cup (not oil-packed)

½ cup plus 2 tablespoons **EVOO** (extra-virgin olive oil)

1 medium **onion**, finely chopped

4 **garlic cloves**, finely chopped or grated

1 teaspoon dried **marjoram** or oregano

Salt and **pepper**

8 **roasted red peppers** from a jar

1 (28-ounce) can **crushed tomatoes** or crushed fire-roasted tomatoes

A handful of fresh **basil leaves**, shredded or torn

2 pounds **spinach**, trimmed of thick stems

1 cup **pine nuts**, toasted (see Note, page 102)

½ cup **vegetable stock**

Pinch of **nutmeg**

1 cup grated **Parmigiano-Reggiano**

1 (32-ounce) container **whole-milk ricotta cheese**

1 **egg** plus 1 **egg yolk**

2 boxes **no-boil lasagna noodles**

2 cups shredded **provolone cheese**

ROASTED GARLIC AND TOMATO RATATOUILLE PASTA

1 head of **garlic**

3 tablespoons **EVOO** (extra-virgin olive oil)

1 medium **eggplant**, peeled and cut into ¾-inch dice

2 medium **zucchini**, trimmed, quartered lengthwise and chopped into ¾-inch dice

2 **red bell pepper**s, seeded and chopped into ¾-inch dice

1 medium **onion**, chopped into ¾-inch dice

2 to 3 sprigs of fresh **rosemary**, leaves stripped and finely chopped

5 to 6 sprigs of fresh **thyme**, leaves stripped and chopped

Salt and **pepper**

1 pint **grape tomatoes**

1 pound **whole wheat penne**

½ cup fresh flat-leaf **parsley**, a couple of handfuls, chopped

½ cup grated **Parmigiano-Reggiano**, a couple handfuls, plus more to pass at the table

Did you see the animated feature *Ratatouille*? I watched it on a long flight when I had forgotten my iPod at home and had exhausted my brain and my computer on work. I just wanted to drift off, and I thought a "kids' film" would provide the distraction I needed to fall sleep. Guess what? I LOVE THAT RAT! I laughed, I cried, I got looks from all my fellow passengers; but the humble, chubby rodent chef had me at his love of stinky cheese. I immediately wrote this dish in homage to my new short, hairy French friend, Remy. Uh huh huh huh, *c'est magnifique!*

P.S. You'll also find a version of this recipe in *Yum-O!,* my cookbook for kids and families to benefit our charity, Yum-o, but I simply could not put together a vegetarian collection and leave this one out.

Preheat the oven to 450°F.

Cut the top third off the head of garlic, exposing all of the cloves. Tear off a large square of aluminum foil and place the garlic in the center. Drizzle about ½ tablespoon EVOO over the head, wrap it in the foil, and place it in the oven. Roast until golden in color and tender, about 45 minutes.

Once the garlic has been in the oven for 10 minutes, place a large pot of water over high heat and bring to a boil.

While the water comes to a boil, place the eggplant, zucchini, bell peppers, and onions on a rimmed baking sheet. Coat the vegetables with 2 tablespoons of the EVOO and season with the rosemary, thyme, and salt and pepper. Place the tomatoes on a separate rimmed baking sheet and dress with ½ tablespoon EVOO and salt and pepper. Roast the vegetables and tomatoes for 25 to 30 minutes.

About 10 minutes before the vegetables come out of the oven, salt the boiling water, add the penne, and cook to al dente. Heads up: before draining the pasta reserve ¾ to 1 cup of starchy cooking liquid, a ladleful.

Unwrap the roasted garlic and let it cool enough to handle, 5 minutes. Squeeze out all of the roasted cloves into a large pasta bowl. Add the tomatoes and mash together. Add the starchy pasta cooking liquid to the bowl and stir to combine into a sauce. Add the roasted veggies, pasta, parsley, and grated Parmigiano to the bowl and toss to combine. Adjust the seasoning and serve with extra cheese at the table.

SERVES 4

BEET RISOTTO

4 medium **beets**, scrubbed, stems and root ends trimmed, tender greens washed and chopped (discard tough or bruised leaves)

4 tablespoons **EVOO** (extra-virgin olive oil)

Salt and **pepper**

4 cups **vegetable stock**

1 tablespoon **butter**

1 medium **onion**, finely chopped

2 **garlic cloves**, finely chopped or grated

2 cups **arborio rice**

½ cup **dry white wine**

½ cup grated **Parmigiano-Reggiano**, plus some to pass at the table

Juice of ½ **lemon**

Optional garnishes: **pomegranate seeds, crumbled ricotta salata, smoked ricotta salata, or goat cheese**

This rich, ruby-hued supper is a true jewel of a meal. It is simple and satisfying yet deceptively deep in taste and texture. If you've never thought of rice as sexy before, make this for someone you love—you'll get your groove on for dessert!

Preheat the oven to 400°F.

Place the beets on a large piece of aluminum foil and drizzle with EVOO, about 1 tablespoon. Season with salt and pepper and fold the foil into a pouch. Roast the beets inside the pouch until tender, about 45 minutes. Allow the beets to cool for 10 minutes, then gently rub the skins off with paper towels. Transfer the beets to a food processor and puree them until smooth. Reserve the puree until the risotto is finished cooking.

Combine 2 cups of water and the stock in a sauce pot and bring to a boil. Reduce the heat to low to keep the stock warm.

Heat 2 tablespoons of the EVOO and the butter in a medium high-sided skillet over medium-high heat. Add the onions and garlic and sauté until the onions begin to get tender, about 5 minutes. Add the arborio rice and toast it, stirring constantly for 2 to 3 minutes more. Add the wine and cook until the liquid has been absorbed, 1 minute.

Add a few ladles of the warm stock to the rice and stir. Cook until the liquids have been absorbed, then add another ladle of stock. Continue cooking and adding the stock, stirring vigorously each time you add the stock to form a creamy risotto. When the rice is almost done, season with salt and pepper and stir in the beet puree. Cook a couple minutes longer, until the rice is creamy and tender but still slightly al dente. It should take about 18 minutes in total. Stir in the Parmigiano and taste to adjust the seasonings.

Dress the beet greens with the lemon juice, salt and pepper, and the remaining tablespoon of EVOO.

To serve, top shallow bowls of risotto with a few of the dressed greens. Top with one of the garnishes, if you like.

SERVES 4

POPEYE RISOTTO WITH BEEFY BALSAMIC MUSHROOMS

Olive Oyl was too skinny. If you ask me, Popeye should have given her some of that spinach with cheese and extra EVOO on top. This would have been a great date meal for the two of them. It works for John and me—but anything involving good food always does. Eat your greens and stay off the corncob pipes. *Toot! Toot!*

Bring 2 cups of the stock and 2 cups water to a boil in a saucepan; reduce the heat to low to keep warm.

Add as much spinach as possible to a food processor with a ladle of the stock that's heating up. Pulse the spinach to a puree and add more until all the spinach fits into the processor bowl. Season the spinach with a little nutmeg, salt, and pepper and add the pine nuts and cheese to the bowl as well; pulse to combine, then stream in another ladle of liquid and the ¼ cup EVOO. Turn off the processor and adjust the seasonings. Reserve.

Place a large skillet with high sides over medium-high heat and add 1 tablespoon of the butter and 1 tablespoon of the EVOO. Add the onions and chopped or grated garlic, and sauté until the onions begin to get tender, 4 to 5 minutes. Add the arborio rice and toast it in the pan, 2 minutes. Add the wine and cook until all the liquid is absorbed, about 1 minute. Add a few ladles of stock to the pan and stir to combine; cook until all of the liquid is absorbed, then stir in more stock. The risotto will take about 18 minutes total to cook to al dente. Each time you add liquid, stir vigorously. This makes your risotto creamy and starchy.

While the risotto is cooking, heat the remaining tablespoon of EVOO and tablespoon of butter in another skillet over medium to medium-high heat. Add the mushrooms and cracked garlic clove to the hot pan and cook until tender and dark, 10 to 12 minutes. Season with salt and pepper and deglaze the pan with the balsamic vinegar, scraping up any brown bits with a wooden spoon. Cook for 30 seconds, then turn off the heat.

Stir the spinach mixture into the risotto in the last 2 minutes of cooking time and taste to adjust the seasoning. Top bowlfuls of risotto with beefy mushrooms and serve.

SERVES 4

4 cups **vegetable stock**

2 pounds **spinach**, stems removed

Freshly grated **nutmeg**

Salt and **pepper**

⅓ cup **pine nuts**, toasted (see Note; page 102)

½ cup grated **Parmigiano-Reggiano**, a couple of handfuls, plus some for passing at the table

¼ cup plus 2 tablespoons **EVOO** (extra-virgin olive oil)

2 tablespoons **butter**

1 small **onion**, finely chopped

2 **garlic cloves**, finely chopped or grated, plus 1 clove peeled and cracked

2 cups **arborio rice**

½ cup **dry white wine**

4 large **portabella mushroom caps**, brushed clean of dirt and sliced ½ inch thick

2 tablespoons **aged balsamic vinegar**

VEGITARI-ASIAN FEAST
HOISIN NOODLE BOWLS, ROASTED MUSHROOM TERIYAKI AND CUCUMBER-SESAME SALAD

Salt

1 pound **whole wheat spaghetti**

Juice of 4 **limes**

3 tablespoons **rice wine vinegar**

3 tablespoons **honey**

1 tablespoon **toasted sesame oil**

1 seedless **cucumber**, thinly sliced

1 **red onion**, thinly sliced

3 tablespoons toasted **sesame seeds**

2 pounds mixed **fresh mushrooms**, such as shiitake, oyster, and cremini

¼ cup **teriyaki sauce**

1 bunch of **scallions**, cut into 2-inch pieces

4 tablespoons **vegetable oil**

1 tablespoon **grill seasoning**, such as McCormick's Montreal Steak Seasoning

1 **red bell pepper**, seeded and thinly sliced

1 cup **snow pea pods**, thinly sliced

3 to 4 **garlic cloves**, grated or finely chopped

2 inches of fresh **gingerroot**, peeled and grated

1 (10-ounce) package **frozen shelled edamame**

¼ cup **hoisin sauce** (available on the Asian foods aisle of the market)

1 to 2 tablespoons **Asian chili sauce** or **hot sauce**

¼ cup fresh **cilantro leaves**, chopped

A handful of fresh **mint leaves**, finely chopped

This menu came out of word play. I was playing around with the term "vegetarian" and my head went down the random tangent of a menu that was meat-free and full of Asian flair and flavors: vegetari-Asian. So silly, I know, but nevertheless it is a tasty meal.

Bring a large pot of water to a boil for the pasta. Salt the water, add the spaghetti, and cook to al dente. Heads up: you will need to reserve ½ cup of the starchy pasta water before draining the pasta.

Preheat the oven to 450°F.

Combine the juice of 2 of the limes with the rice wine vinegar, honey, and sesame oil in a large bowl. Add the cucumber and one quarter of the red onion, season with salt, and toss to combine. Sprinkle with the sesame seeds.

Coarsely chop the mushrooms and place in another bowl. Drizzle the mushrooms with the teriyaki sauce and combine with the scallions, 2 tablespoons of the vegetable oil, and the grill seasoning. Toss to combine. Spread the mushrooms on a nonstick baking sheet and bake for 20 minutes, turning once. Scrape the mushrooms into a bowl.

Heat the remaining 2 tablespoons of vegetable oil in a large skillet over high heat. When it's very hot, add the bell peppers, the remaining red onion, the pea pods, garlic, and ginger and stir-fry for 2 minutes. Add the edamame and heat through, 2 to 3 minutes more. Add the hoisin, the remaining lime juice, the chili sauce, and the reserved starchy pasta cooking liquid to form a sauce. Add the drained spaghetti and toss over medium-high heat for a minute to coat with the sauce. Turn off the heat and toss in the cilantro and mint. Serve the noodles in bowls with the mushrooms and the cucumber salad as side dishes.

SERVES 4

JAW-DROPPINGLY DELICIOUS ASPARAGUS PENNE

Salt

1 pound **thin asparagus**, trimmed of ends

1 pound **whole wheat penne pasta**

1 tablespoon **EVOO** (extra-virgin olive oil)

2 tablespoons **butter**

2 large **garlic cloves**, minced

2 tablespoons **all-purpose flour**

¾ cup **vegetable stock**

¾ cup **half-and-half**

2 tablespoons **Dijon mustard**

2 teaspoons grated **lemon zest**

Black pepper

2 tablespoons fresh **tarragon**, finely chopped, a couple of sprigs

Juice of 1 **lemon**

Grated **Parmigiano-Reggiano**

I have smuggled contraband over the Canadian border, and I am *not* sorry. If you work the Canadian-U.S. border and you are reading this, turn the page and forget what you've read because the contraband I bring across is necessary for recipes like this to occur. I smuggled over the thinnest asparagus I have ever seen in my life from the Jean-Talon Market in Montreal. I shared my stash with my mom. This is what she made with hers. Not many moms are psyched about kids who grow up to be smugglers. Mine's the exception.

Bring a large pot of water to a boil. Salt the water. Drop the asparagus in for 2 minutes, then remove, drain, and chop into 2-inch pieces. Add the pasta to the water and cook to al dente.

To a skillet placed over medium heat, add the EVOO and butter. When the butter melts into the oil, add the garlic and gently cook for 2 to 3 minutes, then sprinkle the flour into the pan and cook for 1 minute, stirring. Whisk in the stock, half-and-half, mustard, and lemon zest. Season the sauce with salt, pepper, and tarragon, and cook for 2 to 3 minutes to thicken. Add the lemon juice, and gently toss the asparagus and pasta with the sauce to coat. Turn off the heat and adjust the salt and pepper to taste, then top with grated cheese and serve.

(Uh, yeah, I know. It's really good.)

SERVES 4

AUSTIN MAC 'N' CHEESE SUIZAS

This vegetarian mac 'n' cheese tastes just like enchiladas Suizas—a tangy green sauce and pulled chicken dish with Swiss cheese and Mexican crema on top, minus the chicken, of course. Here, the Swiss and Monterey Jack cheese sauce is layered with tangy tomatillo sauce. The mac 'n' cheese is topped with crushed tortillas and spicy pepper Jack cheese.

Bring a large pot of water to a boil. Season the water with salt, add the pasta, and cook to al dente.

Heat the EVOO over medium-high heat in a sauce pot. Place the tomatillos in a food processor and process into coarse salsa. Add the onions, garlic, and jalapeños to the pot and cook for 5 minutes; stir in the tomatillos, season with salt and the cumin, and stir in the honey. Simmer over low heat for 10 minutes. Stir in the cilantro and lime juice.

Preheat the broiler.

Melt the butter over medium heat in a saucepan. Whisk in the flour and cook for 1 minute. Whisk in the vegetable stock and milk, season with salt and pepper, and cook for about 5 minutes to thicken. Stir in the Swiss and Monterey Jack cheeses.

Drain the pasta and toss with the cheese sauce. Place half the mac 'n' cheese in a 9 x 13-inch baking dish and top with half the tomatillo salsa. Spoon in the remaining mac 'n' cheese and top with the remaining salsa, the crushed chips, and the pepper Jack cheese. Brown the top under the broiler. Pass the crème frâiche or sour cream at the table.

SERVES 6

Salt

1 pound **cavatappi** (hollow ridged corkscrew-shaped pasta), or other short-cut pasta

1 tablespoon **EVOO** (extra-virgin olive oil)

12 **tomatillos**, husked, rinsed, and dried, then coarsely chopped

1 medium **onion**, chopped

2 to 3 **garlic cloves**, finely chopped or grated

2 **jalapeños**, seeded and finely chopped

1 teaspoon **ground cumin**

2 teaspoons **honey**

A handful of fresh **cilantro**, finely chopped

Juice of 1 **lime**

3 tablespoons **butter**

3 tablespoons **all-purpose flour**

1 cup **vegetable stock**

2 cups **whole milk**

Black pepper

1 cup shredded **Swiss cheese**

1 cup shredded **Monterey Jack cheese**

2 cups crushed flax seed or other specialty **tortilla chips**

1 cup shredded **pepper Jack cheese**

1 cup **crème frâiche** or sour cream

SUPER SOUP 'N SALAD

- GO GREEN VEGETABLE SOUP
- VEGETABLE-PITA FATTOUSH

Here's a meal in minutes that is perfect for the last few rainy, cool nights of spring.

Go Green Vegetable Soup

Preheat the oven to 400°F. On a rimmed baking sheet, toss the tomatoes in 1 tablespoon of the EVOO and season with salt and pepper. Roast the tomatoes for 15 minutes, or until they burst. Remove the tomatoes from the oven and turn the oven to broil.

Heat the remaining tablespoon of EVOO in a high-sided skillet or medium soup pot. Add the scallions to the hot pan and wilt for 2 minutes. Add the stock and bring to a simmer. Add the green beans and asparagus, return to a simmer, and cook for 2 to 3 minutes. Add the spinach and stir until it is wilted. Season the soup with salt and pepper and remove it from the heat. Wilt in the arugula.

Toast the bread under the broiler until crisp on both sides. Rub each slice of toast with ½ clove of garlic. Place a garlic toast in each soup bowl and ladle vegetable soup over the toast. Pass lots of cheese for topping at the table.

SERVES 4

1 pint **grape tomatoes**

2 tablespoons **EVOO** (extra-virgin olive oil)

Salt and **pepper**

5 to 6 **scallions**, cut on an angle in 1½-inch lengths

5 cups **vegetable stock**

½ pound **green beans**, trimmed and cut on an angle into 1½-inch pieces

1 bundle of **thin asparagus**, trimmed and cut on an angle into 1½-inch pieces

½ pound **spinach**, stemmed and coarsely chopped

1 bundle of **arugula**, thick stems removed, chopped

4 (1-inch-thick) slices of **crusty bread**

2 **garlic cloves**, halved

Parmigiano-Reggiano, for passing at the table

Vegetable-Pita Fattoush

Combine the garlic, lemon juice, and EVOO in a salad bowl. Add the bell peppers, onions, parsley, mint, and pita chips to the bowl and toss. Season the salad with salt and pepper and serve.

SERVES 4

1 **garlic clove**, grated or finely chopped

Juice of 2 **lemons**

⅓ cup **EVOO** (extra-virgin olive oil)

1 **green bell pepper**, seeded and chopped

1 **red bell pepper**, seeded and chopped

1 medium **red onion**, chopped

1 cup fresh flat-leaf **parsley** leaves, chopped

½ cup fresh **mint** leaves, chopped

2 cups **pita chips**, such as Stacy's, in a Mediterranean flavor or plain, lightly crushed

Salt and **pepper**

CORN AND SALSA TORTILLA SOUP

3 **poblano peppers**

6 **corn tortillas**, halved, then cut into ½-inch strips

3 tablespoons **canola or vegetable oil**

1 teaspoon **ground cumin**

Salt

6 ears **corn on the cob**, kernels scraped from cob, or 2 (10-ounce) boxes of frozen kernels

1 medium **red onion**, chopped

3 to 4 **garlic cloves**, chopped

Black pepper

1 (15-ounce) can diced or crushed **fire-roasted tomatoes**

4 cups **vegetable stock**

1 **Hass avocado**

1 **lime**, cut into 4 wedges

4 tablespoons **sour cream**

2 tablespoons chopped fresh **cilantro**

Take advantage of fresh corn on the cob as many months of the year as you can get it. When fresh corn is nowhere to be found, though, frozen kernels are just fine, Sprout. This zesty soup is a great vegetarian version of a classic chicken tortilla soup.

Preheat the broiler and char the poblanos on a broiler pan on all sides until blackened, 10 to 12 minutes. Place in a bowl and cover the bowl with plastic wrap. When the poblanos are cool enough to handle, after about 10 minutes, peel, seed, and chop them.

While the peppers are under the broiler, toss the tortillas in a bowl to coat with 1 tablespoon of the oil, season with the cumin, and toss again. Spread the tortillas onto a baking sheet. When the poblanos come out of the oven, switch the oven to 400°F. Bake the tortillas for 10 minutes, or until golden, then salt them as soon as they come out of the oven.

While the poblanos are under the broiler and you're waiting for the tortillas to go in, heat the remaining 2 tablespoons of oil in a large high-sided skillet or medium soup pot over medium-high heat. Add the corn and cook until the corn begins to char at the edges and caramelize, 10 to 12 minutes. Add the onions and garlic, season with salt and pepper, and cook for 5 to 6 minutes, until the onions are softened. Stir in the tomatoes and stock and add the poblanos when they are chopped. Adjust the salt and pepper.

Divide the chips among 4 soup bowls.

Halve the avocado and remove the pit. Use a spoon to scoop the flesh out of the skin, and dice it. Divide the avocado among the 4 soup bowls and squeeze a lime wedge over each serving. Ladle the soup over the avocado and chips and garnish with the sour cream and cilantro.

SERVES 4

RED AND GREEN WINTER STOUP

¼ cup **EVOO** (extra-virgin olive oil)

2 large **russet potatoes**, peeled and thinly sliced

2 medium-large **onions**, quartered and thinly sliced

2 to 3 sprigs of fresh **rosemary**, finely chopped

Salt and **pepper**

1 **bay leaf**, fresh or dried

4 cups **vegetable stock**

1 bunch of **kale**, stripped from thick veins and stems and coarsely chopped

1 (28-ounce) can **crushed tomatoes** or crushed fire-roasted tomatoes

3 large **roasted red peppers**, drained well

4 (2-inch-thick) slices **crusty whole grain bread**, cut on a bias

2 large **garlic cloves**, peeled and halved

1 cup shredded **Asiago cheese**

A stoup is thicker than a soup and thinner than a stew, and always comforting because of the hearty texture. The color of this meal adds to the overall appeal. It can brighten up a dark and cloudy day.

Heat the EVOO in a medium soup pot over medium to medium-high heat. Add the potatoes and onions and season with the rosemary, salt and pepper, and bay leaf. Cook the potatoes and onions, gently stirring frequently, for 7 to 8 minutes to soften. Add the stock to the pot and bring to a boil, 2 to 3 minutes. Wilt in the kale in bunches, 1 to 2 minutes, then stir in the tomatoes.

Preheat the broiler.

Puree the peppers in a food processor and stir into the soup pot. Reduce the heat to medium-low and simmer for 10 minutes; adjust the seasoning and remove the bay leaf.

While the stoup simmers, toast the bread under the broiler on both sides, then rub the hot crispy bread with the cut garlic and top with the cheese. Melt the cheese under the broiler, about 1 minute.

Serve the stoup in shallow bowls. The toast can be placed at the bottom of the bowl, if you like soaked bread that you can cut with your spoon, or you can float it up on top if you like it crunchy.

SERVES 4

THE MUST-HAVE MINESTRONE

The greatest MUST in any vegetarian diet is a great minestrone—a mighty one. The name means, literally, a really BIG bean soup. Try this and become a legend tonight!

Adding a rind of Parmigiano-Reggiano to the soup as it simmers really deepens the flavor. When you've finished grating up your next wedge, hang on to that rind!

Heat a soup pot over medium heat with 2 tablespoons of the EVOO. Add the chopped onion to the hot oil but reserve the finely chopped ¼ onion. Add the garlic, to the onions along with the carrots, celery, and bay leaf; season with the red pepper flakes, marjoram, and salt and pepper and sauté to soften the vegetables, 8 to 10 minutes.

Add the beans, and season with salt and pepper and the rosemary. Stir in the tomato paste and cook for 2 minutes, or until the paste smells sweet. Stir in the wine, cook for 1 minute, then stir in the stock and 2 cups water. Wilt in the greens and bring the soup to a boil. Add the pasta and cook to al dente, about 8 minutes. Adjust the seasonings. Serve bowlfuls of the soup topped with a drizzle of EVOO, a sprinkle of finely chopped raw onion, and Parmigiano. Use bread for mopping up your bowl.

SERVES 6

2 tablespoons **EVOO** (extra-virgin olive oil), plus some for drizzling at the table

1 **onion**, ¾ chopped, ¼ finely chopped

4 **garlic cloves**, finely chopped or grated

2 **carrots**, shredded

4 **celery stalks** from the heart, chopped

1 fresh **bay leaf**

½ teaspoon **crushed red pepper flakes**, lightly crushed in your palm

1 teaspoon dried **marjoram** or oregano, ⅓ palmful

Salt and **pepper**

1 (15-ounce) can **red kidney beans**, drained

1 (15-ounce) can **cannellini beans**, drained

1 (15-ounce) can **chickpeas**, drained

2 to 3 sprigs of fresh **rosemary**, leaves stripped and finely chopped

¼ cup **tomato paste**

½ cup **dry white wine**

4 cups **vegetable stock**

1 bunch of **kale** or chard, thick vein removed and leaves coarsely chopped

½ pound **whole wheat elbow pasta**

Grated **Parmigiano-Reggiano**, for topping

1 loaf of **crusty bread**

CHIPOTLE–PUMPKIN–BLACK BEAN SOUP WITH CRANBERRY SOUR CREAM AND APPLE-JALAPEÑO SALSA

- 2 tablespoons **EVOO** (extra-virgin olive oil)
- 1 large **onion**, finely chopped
- 2 large **garlic cloves**, grated or finely chopped
- 1 **chipotle pepper in adobo**, finely chopped and mashed up, plus 1 tablespoon adobo sauce
- 1 bottle of **Negra Modelo** or other Mexican beer
- 1 (15-ounce) can **pumpkin puree**
- **Salt** and **pepper**
- 1½ teaspoons **ground cumin**, ½ palmful
- 2 pinches of **ground cinnamon**
- 3 cups **vegetable stock**
- 1 (21-ounce) can **black beans**, rinsed and drained
- 1 **green apple**, finely chopped
- 1 **jalapeño pepper**, seeded and finely chopped
- ½ small **red onion**, finely chopped
- A handful of fresh **cilantro**, finely chopped
- Juice of 1 **lime**
- ¼ cup **whole berry cranberry sauce**, such as Ocean Spray brand
- ½ cup **sour cream**
- A couple of generous handfuls of **tortilla chips**, lightly crushed

Soup is our go-to food when either John or I don't feel well. This one is spicy; it'll clean out your sinuses and then some! Eat two bowlsful and feel better, fast. Of course, it is equally tasty when you're healthy!

Heat the EVOO in a medium soup pot or high-sided skillet over medium-high heat. Add the onions, garlic, and chipotle in adobo and cook for 5 to 6 minutes, stirring frequently. Add the beer to the pot and boil until it is reduced by half, 2 to 3 minutes. Stir in the pumpkin and season with salt and pepper, the cumin, and the cinnamon. Add the stock and beans. Bring the soup to a bubble, reduce the heat to low, and simmer for 10 minutes.

In a bowl combine the chopped green apple with the jalapeño, red onion, cilantro, lime juice, and salt to make a salsa. Stir together the cranberry sauce and sour cream in a second bowl.

Top each bowlful of soup with some of the crushed chips, salsa, and sour cream.

SERVES 4

GRILLED VEGETABLE CHILI

Here is a hearty, healthy use of the grill in a meat-free meal.

Heat a grill to medium-high heat. Lightly brush all the vegetables with EVOO and season with salt and pepper. Cook for 4 minutes on each side, or until marked and tender, with the lid down; remove to a platter.

Heat the remaining EVOO, a couple of tablespoons, in a medium pot over medium to medium-high heat. Add the garlic and jalapeños and cook for 2 to 3 minutes, add the beans to heat through, and begin chopping the grilled vegetables into ½-inch dice, adding them to the pot as you work. Season the vegetables with the chili powder, paprika, and salt and pepper. Stir in the tomato paste and cook for 2 minutes. Stir in the beer and reduce for 30 seconds, then stir in the stock and simmer the chili for a few minutes. Stir in the lime juice and cilantro. Serve with the crushed chips and some cheese on top. Garnish with the scallions.

SERVES 4

2 **zucchini**, sliced ½ inch thick on the diagonal

1 large **red bell pepper**, halved and seeded

1 large **yellow bell pepper**, halved and seeded

2 large **portabella mushrooms**

1 **red onion**, peeled and sliced ¾ inch thick

½ cup **EVOO** (extra-virgin olive oil)

Salt and **pepper**

2 to 3 **garlic cloves**, grated or chopped

2 **jalapeño peppers**, seeded and finely chopped

1 (15-ounce) can **black beans**

2 tablespoons **chili powder**, a couple of palmfuls

2 teaspoons **sweet smoked paprika**, ⅔ palmful

3 tablespoons **tomato paste**

1 cup **beer**

2 cups **vegetable stock**

Juice of 1 **lime**

A handful of fresh **cilantro** leaves, finely chopped

Flax seed or other specialty **tortilla chips**, crushed

2 cups shredded **smoked cheddar** or pepper Jack cheese

2 to 3 **scallions**, finely chopped or thinly sliced

BLACK BEAN CHILI

4 large **poblano peppers**

2 tablespoons **EVOO** (extra-virgin olive oil)

1 **jalapeño pepper**, seeded and finely chopped

1 large **onion**, chopped

4 **garlic cloves**, finely chopped or grated

Salt and **pepper**

1 bottle of **Mexican beer**, such as Negra Modelo

2 (15-ounce) cans **black beans**

2 tablespoons **chili powder**, a couple palmfuls

1½ teaspoons smoked **paprika**, ½ palmful

1½ teaspoons **ground cumin**, ½ palmful

½ teaspoon **ground allspice** (eyeball it in your palm)

1 (15-ounce) can **crushed or diced fire-roasted tomatoes**

2 cups **vegetable stock**

1 **lime**, halved

Toppings

Hot sauce

Sour cream, to pass at the table

½ cup chopped fresh **cilantro**, to pass at the table

4 **scallions**, finely chopped

2 cups lightly crushed **tortilla chips** such as flax seed or sesame seed

1 cup shredded **smoked cheddar** or pepper Jack cheese

This chili is so smoky, hearty, and spicy that even the carnivores will forget there's no meat in it. This recipe has cojones—no bull.

Preheat the broiler to high.

Char the poblanos under the broiler to blacken their skins evenly all over, 12 to 15 minutes, turning as needed. Keep the oven door cracked so you do not give yourself a poblano facial each time you open the door and release the hot steam. Place the charred poblanos in a bowl, cover with plastic wrap, and let stand for 10 minutes. Once the peppers have cooled enough to handle, peel and seed them, then coarsely chop and reserve.

Heat the EVOO in a medium pot over medium-high heat. Add the jalapeños, onions, and garlic to the pan, season with salt and pepper, and cook until tender, 6 to 7 minutes. Stir the beer into the pot, scraping up any brown bits from the bottom of the pan. Boil the beer until reduced by half, 1 to 2 minutes, then add 1 can of black beans. Mash them into the onions with a potato masher or wooden spoon, then stir in the second can of beans, leaving them whole. Add the chopped poblanos to the chili and season with the chili powder, smoked paprika, cumin, and allspice. Stir in the tomatoes and stock. Bring the chili up to a bubble, add salt to taste, then reduce the heat to a simmer and cook the chili for 8 to 10 minutes to thicken. Squeeze in the lime juice and remove the chili from the heat.

Pass your choice of hot sauce, sour cream, cilantro, scallions, tortilla chips, and cheese at the table to top the chili.

SERVES 6 TO 8

SLOPPY VEG-HEAD JOE

1 tablespoon **canola** or **vegetable oil**

2 **jalapeño peppers**, seeded and finely chopped

1 red, green, or yellow **bell pepper**, seeded and chopped

1 **red onion**, chopped

2 large **garlic cloves**, chopped

1 (21-ounce) can **black beans**, drained and rinsed

1 teaspoon **ground cumin**

1 teaspoon **ground coriander**

Salt and pepper

1 (15-ounce) can diced **fire-roasted** or **chunky-style crushed tomatoes**

1 rounded tablespoon **brown sugar**

1 tablespoon **Worcestershire sauce** (see Note) or vinegar, any kind

1 **lime**

4 **crusty rolls**, split and lightly toasted

2 large **dill pickles**, chopped

A handful of fresh **cilantro** leaves, chopped

Over the last several years I've probably typed up and taught dozens of takes on the American classic, good ole sloppy Joes. I am stupefied that it took me this long to come up with a meat-free buddy. Here ya go, meet Sloppy Veg-head Joe.

Heat the oil in a skillet over medium-high heat. To the hot oil, add the jalapeños, bell peppers, onions, and garlic and cook until tender, 7 to 8 minutes. Fold in the black beans, cumin, and coriander and season to taste with salt and pepper. Stir in the tomatoes, brown sugar, and Worcestershire or vinegar and simmer the mixture for a few minutes to combine the flavors. Squeeze the lime juice into the pan and stir. Serve the joe mixture on buns with chopped pickles and cilantro to top and a couple of chips or a green salad alongside.

SERVES 4

NOTE Worcestershire sauce contains everything but the kitchen sink, including anchovies. I love it, but if you follow a strict vegetarian diet you might prefer to substitute vinegar.

GRILLED VEGETABLE MUFFALETTA

For veg-heads, attending a cookout usually spells a meal of potato and macaroni salads. This is a hearty GIANT sammie filled with grill flavor. It is a vegetarian version of an Italian meat sammie topped with olive salad. This loaf of bread stuffed with a garden of charred vegetables will really please a meat eater or a meat free-er alike.

Heat a grill or grill pan to medium-high heat. Lightly brush the vegetables with EVOO and season with salt and pepper, then grill until marked and tender, 3 to 4 minutes on each side (if using a grill, keep the lid down). Reserve 3 to 4 tablespoons EVOO for the pesto.

Place the spinach in a food processor with the nuts and season with salt, pepper, and nutmeg. Add the Parmigiano and stock and turn on the processor; drizzle in 3 to 4 tablespoons of the EVOO to form the pesto. Adjust the seasoning and transfer to a bowl.

Rinse the processor bowl and return it to its base. Pulse-chop the giardiniera and olives into a relish.

Cut the top off the bread and scoop out the insides. Spread half the pesto on the bottom of the loaf, pile in half of the grilled vegetables, pour on the remaining pesto, fill the loaf with the rest of the vegetables, and top with the provolone. Spread the underside of the top of the bread loaf with the relish and set into place; press down to set the ingredients. Cut into wedges and serve.

SERVES 4

- 1 medium **eggplant**, sliced ½ inch thick
- 1 **zucchini**, sliced ½ inch thick on the diagonal
- 1 large **red bell pepper**, seeded and quartered lengthwise
- 2 **cubanelle peppers** (Italian mild light green) peppers, seeded and halved lengthwise
- 2 large **portabella mushrooms**
- 1 **red onion**, peeled and sliced ¾ inch thick
- ½ to ⅔ cup **EVOO** (extra-virgin olive oil)
- **Salt** and **pepper**
- 1 pound **spinach**, stemmed
- A handful of **pine nuts**, toasted (see Note, page 102)
- A little freshly grated **nutmeg**
- ½ cup grated **Parmigiano-Reggiano**, a couple of handfuls
- ½ cup **vegetable stock**
- 1 cup **giardiniera** (hot pickled vegetable salad)
- ½ cup **pitted green olives**
- 1 round of **crusty bread**, 8 to 9 inches wide
- ¼ pound deli-sliced **provolone**

BROCCOLI AND CHEDDAR STUFFED TATERS

I have always been partial to stuffed potatoes and here they take center plate. Eat either these stuffed taters or Ranch-Style Stuffed Taters with a salad alongside.

Preheat the oven to 425°F.

Scrub the potatoes of any excess dirt and prick them each several times with a fork. Place them on a baking sheet, drizzle with EVOO, and season with salt and pepper, tossing lightly to coat. Bake until tender, 45 to 60

- 4 **BIG Idaho potatoes**
- **EVOO** (extra-virgin olive oil), for drizzling
- **Salt** and **pepper**
- 1 head of **broccoli**, trimmed of tough stems and cut into small chunks
- ½ cup **sour cream**
- 1 cup **vegetable stock**
- 1½ cups shredded **cheddar cheese**

minutes depending on the size of the potato. Remove the baked potatoes from the oven and let cool enough to handle.

While the potatoes are cooling, place a skillet with 1 inch of water over high heat and bring to a boil. Salt the water and reduce the heat to a simmer, then add the broccoli and cook for 3 to 4 minutes, until tender. Drain the broccoli.

Cut the potatoes in half lengthwise and scoop the insides out into a mixing bowl, leaving a thin layer of flesh still intact. Try not to pierce the skin of the potato. Add the sour cream, stock, and ½ cup of the cheddar to the bowl and mash the potatoes; season with salt and pepper. Fold the broccoli into the potatoes and refill the potato skins. Top with a little extra cheese, a couple of tablespoons per skin. Place them back into the oven to melt the cheese, about 5 minutes. Serve them up with your favorite salad alongside.

SERVES 4

RANCH-STYLE STUFFED TATERS

4 BIG **Idaho potatoes**

EVOO (extra-virgin olive oil), for drizzling

Salt and **pepper**

1 pint **grape tomatoes**

⅔ cup **buttermilk**

⅓ cup **sour cream**

1 **garlic clove**, grated or minced

A few dashes of **hot sauce**

2 tablespoons chopped fresh flat-leaf **parsley**

2 tablespoons chopped fresh **dill**

2 tablespoons chopped fresh **chives**

1 cup shredded **sharp cheddar cheese**

Preheat the oven to 425°F.

Scrub the potatoes of any excess dirt and prick them each several times with a fork. Place them on a baking sheet, drizzle with EVOO, and season with salt and pepper. Bake the potatoes until tender, 45 to 60 minutes depending on the size of the potato. Remove the baked potatoes from the oven and let cool enough to handle.

When the potatoes have about 10 minutes left in the oven, place the tomatoes on a rimmed baking sheet and drizzle EVOO over them. Season them with salt and pepper and roast them in the oven until they collapse, about 15 minutes.

While the potatoes are cooling, combine the buttermilk, sour cream, garlic, hot sauce, and herbs in a small mixing bowl and season with salt and pepper to taste.

Cut the potatoes in half lengthwise and scoop the insides out into a mixing bowl, leaving a thin layer of flesh still intact on each half. Try not to pierce the skin of the potato while doing so. Add the ranch mixture to the potato flesh and mash lightly to mix everything together. Adjust the seasonings to taste. Divide the filling among the skins.

Place the potato skins back onto a baking sheet and sprinkle the cheese over each of them. Place them back into the oven to melt the cheese, 4 to 5 minutes. Top each potato with some of the roasted tomatoes and serve them up with your favorite salad alongside.

SERVES 4

EGGPLANT STEAKS PARMIGIANA ALLA RINGO

Here's a BIG day at the office: a Beatle drops by with his mates, sings a song for you, then sits down at your kitchen table for a chat. During his visit to our show, my *good friend* Ringo Starr told me that he makes a wonderful pesto. He is a vegetarian, so I created this recipe in honor of his appearance. (Incidentally, the album, *Liverpool 8*, kicks ass, as did he, Dave Stewart, and the band.)

Preheat the oven to 375°F.

Heat ¼ cup of the EVOO in a large skillet over medium-high heat.

Line up three shallow dishes on your counter. Add the flour to the first, the eggs to the second, and the bread crumbs, grated cheese, parsley, lemon zest, and garlic to the last. Beat the eggs with a splash of water.

Cut the top and bottom off the eggplants, slice the skin off of each side, then cut each eggplant lengthwise into 4 steaks, each 1 to 1½ inches thick. Coat all 8 steaks first in the flour, then in the beaten egg, and finally in the cheesy bread crumbs.

Working in 2 batches, brown 4 of the breaded eggplant steaks in the hot oil until golden, about 2 minutes on each side, then lay them on a baking sheet and place in the oven to stay warm. (If you place the eggplant steaks on a wire rack set onto the baking sheet they will get extra crispy.) Wipe out the pan and heat the remaining ¼ cup of EVOO. Repeat the browning process, then transfer all the steaks to the oven and finish cooking through, 10 minutes.

While the eggplant steaks are in the oven, heat the tomatoes and their juices in a small sauce pot over medium-high heat. Mash up the tomatoes with a potato masher or wooden spoon, season with salt and pepper, and stir in the tomato paste. Once the tomatoes come up to a bubble, simmer for 5 minutes, then remove from the heat. Stir in the pesto.

Remove the steaks from the oven and switch on the broiler.

On the baking sheet, stack one eggplant steak topped with a little sauce, then another steak, another ladle of sauce, and one quarter of the provolone. Make 8 stacks total. Brown the eggplant stacks under the broiler to melt the cheese. Serve 2 stacks per person.

SERVES 4

½ cup **EVOO** (extra-virgin olive oil)

1 cup **all-purpose flour**

3 **eggs**

1 cup seasoned **bread crumbs**

1 cup grated **Parmigiano-Reggiano**

¼ cup fresh flat-leaf **parsley**, a generous handful, chopped

1 teaspoon **lemon zest**

4 **garlic cloves**, finely chopped or grated

2 medium, firm **eggplants**

1 (28-ounce) can **San Marzano tomatoes**

Salt and **pepper**

2 tablespoons **tomato paste**

⅓ cup store-bought or homemade **pesto**

1 cup shredded **provolone**

EGGPLANT STEW WITH HONEY AND GOLDEN RAISIN POLENTA

One of my family recipes for a classic Sicilian appetizer, caponata, has been reinvented in many of my books. We love the dish so much that we have always eaten it as an entrée with polenta or pasta, or on sandwiches with melted provolone. Here I go again with another tasty entrée version.

Place the dried mushrooms and 2 cups of the stock in a small pot over medium-low heat.

Heat the EVOO in a Dutch oven or high-sided skillet over medium to medium-high heat. Add the garlic, red pepper flakes, onions, carrots, cubanelle and bell peppers, and eggplant to the pot as you chop them. Season with salt and pepper and cover the pot; sweat the vegetables for 10 to 12 minutes, stirring occasionally, then uncover and stir in the balsamic vinegar. Use a slotted spoon to scoop the reconstituted dried mushrooms out of the soaking water, and add them to the pot. Pour in all but the last few tablespoons of mushroom stock, which may have a little loose grit from the dried mushrooms. Add the tomatoes to the pot and break up with a wooden spoon. Simmer over low heat for a few more minutes; adjust the salt and pepper.

While the veggies are sweating down, in a medium saucepan slowly heat the remaining 2 cups of stock with the milk, raisins, and rosemary over medium-high heat. When it just simmers, whisk in the polenta and stir for 3 minutes, or until thickened. Remove from the heat and stir in the honey, butter, and cheese.

Pile some polenta in shallow bowls and spoon the stew around the polenta.

SERVES 6

1 ounce dried **porcini mushrooms**, coarsely chopped

4 cups **vegetable stock**

¼ cup **EVOO** (extra-virgin olive oil)

4 **garlic cloves**, chopped

1 teaspoon **crushed red pepper flakes**

1 **red onion**, chopped into bite-size pieces

1 large **carrot**, peeled and thinly sliced

2 **cubanelle peppers** (light green mild Italian peppers), seeded and chopped into bite-size pieces

1 **red bell pepper**, seeded and chopped into bite-size pieces

2 **eggplants**, half the skin peeled in strips, cut into bite-size cubes

Salt and **pepper**

2 tablespoons **aged balsamic vinegar**

1 (28-ounce) can whole **San Marzano tomatoes**

1 cup **milk**

A handful of **golden raisins**

2 sprigs of fresh **rosemary**, leaves stripped and finely chopped

1 cup quick-cooking **polenta**

3 tablespoons **honey**

2 tablespoons **butter**

½ cup grated **Parmigiano-Reggiano** or Romano cheese

ROASTED CAULIFLOWER CURRY
WITH TOASTED ALMOND RICE

1 cup sliced **almonds**

5 tablespoons **EVOO** (extra-virgin olive oil)

1½ cups **basmati rice**

Salt and **pepper**

5 cups **vegetable stock**

1 head of **cauliflower**, cut into bite-size florets

1 large **onion**, sliced

3 large **garlic cloves**, chopped

2 inches of fresh **gingerroot**, peeled and finely grated or chopped

1 **Granny Smith apple**, peeled, cored, and chopped

2 tablespoons **curry powder**, 2 palmfuls

¼ cup **half-and-half** or **heavy cream**

5 **plum tomatoes**, seeded and cut into quarters lengthwise

1 (10-ounce) box **frozen peas**

A handful of fresh **cilantro leaves**, coarsely chopped

I see cauliflower and almonds over and over again on lists of what foods we should all be eating more of for various health benefits. This easy Indian-style supper is really a year-round super supper!

Preheat the oven 400°F.

Place a large high-sided skillet over medium-high heat. Add the sliced almonds to the skillet and toast, stirring frequently, until golden. Reserve.

Place a sauce pot over medium-high heat with about 1 tablespoon of the EVOO. Add the rice, season with salt and lots of pepper, and stir to coat and toast, 1 minute. Add 3 cups of the vegetable stock and bring the rice up to a boil, cover, reduce the heat to a simmer, and cook for 18 minutes.

Arrange the cauliflower on a rimmed baking sheet, drizzle with a couple tablespoons of the EVOO, and season with salt and pepper. Toss to coat and transfer to the oven to roast for 15 minutes, or until the cauliflower is lightly browned and tender.

While the cauliflower is roasting, return the pan you toasted the nuts in to the stove over medium-high heat and add 2 tablespoons of EVOO. Once it is hot, add the onions, garlic, ginger, apple, curry powder, and salt and pepper. Cook, stirring frequently, for 5 minutes. Add the remaining 2 cups of vegetable stock and bring up to a bubble. Transfer the mixture to a food processor and puree until smooth, then return it to the skillet over medium-low heat and add the half-and-half. Continue to simmer while you are waiting for the cauliflower to finish roasting. Once the cauliflower is done, transfer it to the curry sauce along with the tomatoes and peas, and continue to simmer for about 2 more minutes. Add the cilantro and stir to combine.

Add the toasted almonds to the rice and fluff the rice with a fork while distributing the almonds. Divide the rice among 4 bowls and top with the roasted cauliflower curry.

SERVES 4

SMOKY CHIPOTLE AND BLACK BEAN CHILAQUILES

Chilaquiles are a great use-up for stale tortillas. It's a vegetarian dish that I make all the time and I am a meat eater. Its big flavor will knock you out, plus the ingredients are inexpensive, so if you are on a budget (or just a cheapskate when it comes to grocery shopping) this one's for you!

Preheat the oven to 400°F.

Stack the corn tortillas on top of one another and slice them into strips about an inch thick. Place into a mixing bowl and dress the tortillas with about 2 tablespoons oil, cumin, coriander and zest of a lime. Evenly coat the tortilla strips then transfer them to a baking sheet. Bake the strips until they're crispy and golden brown, 12 to 15 minutes, remove them from the oven, then sprinkle with salt.

While the tortillas are crisping up in the oven place a medium skillet over medium-high heat with about 1 tablespoon of vegetable oil. Toss the red onion and garlic into the pan and cook for 3 to 4 minutes to soften them up. Add the chipotle peppers along with the adobo sauce and the tomatoes. Season with salt and pepper and stir to combine. Heat through then transfer the mixture to a food processor and pulse a couple of times, you want a salsa-like consistency. Set aside.

Place a second skillet over medium-high heat and add the butter. Add the corn to the melted butter and cook until golden brown and caramelized, 10 minutes.

While the corn is cooking, place the same skillet the onion and tomatoes were cooked in back over medium-high heat with about 1 tablespoon of vegetable oil. Add in one can of black beans and heat them through. Using a wooden spoon or potato masher, mash the beans to a paste, then stir in the second can of beans and season with the hot sauce and salt to taste.

Assemble the *chilaquiles* by ladling half of the salsa into a 9 x 13-inch casserole dish. Arrange the toasted corn tortilla strips in the dish and top them with the black beans, followed by the corn and the remaining salsa. Cover your *chilaquiles* with shredded cheeses, bake for 8 to 10 minutes until top is bubbly and lightly browned. Remove the casserole from the oven and squeeze the juice from the lime over the top and garnish with scallions and chopped cilantro or parsley. Dot with sour cream and serve.

SERVES 4

8 6-inch **corn tortillas**

4 tablespoons **vegetable or other light oil**

1 tablespoon ground **cumin**, a palmful

1 tablespoon ground **coriander**, a palmful

Zest and juice of 1 **lime**

Salt

1 medium **red onion**, chopped

3 **garlic cloves**, finely chopped or grated

2 **chipotle peppers** in adobo sauce, seeded and chopped, plus 1 tablespoon adobo sauce

2 (15-ounce) cans or 1 28-ounce can **diced fire-roasted tomatoes**, drained

Black pepper

2 tablespoons **butter**

3 cups **corn kernels**, freshly scraped off 4 cobs or, **frozen** kernels

2 (15-ounce) cans **black beans**, drained

Hot sauce, to taste

¾ cup shredded **Monterey Jack cheese**

¾ cup shredded smoked **cheddar cheese**

4 **scallions**, thinly sliced on a bias

¼ cup **cilantro** or flat-leaf parsley leaves, a handful, finely chopped

1 cup **sour cream**

MUSHROOM RAGOUT

¼ cup **EVOO** (extra-virgin olive oil)

1 pound **cremini mushrooms**, quartered

½ teaspoon **ground allspice**

1 fresh **bay leaf**

1 teaspoon dried **marjoram** or oregano

Black pepper

1 medium **carrot**, peeled and grated or finely chopped

2 **celery stalks** from the heart, finely chopped

1 medium **onion**, finely chopped

4 to 5 **garlic cloves**, chopped or grated

1 **cubanelle pepper** (Italian light green mild frying pepper), seeded and chopped

1 roasted **red bell pepper** from a jar, seeded and chopped

Salt

3 tablespoons **tomato paste**

1 cup **red wine**

2 cups **vegetable or mushroom stock**

2 (15-ounce) cans **stewed tomatoes**

Worcestershire sauce, optional (see Note, page 161)

1 pound **whole wheat penne**

½ cup fresh **basil leaves**, 10 leaves, shredded or torn

½ cup grated **Parmigiano-Reggiano**, plus some to pass at the table

Mushrooms can be as hearty and satisfying as meat because as they cook they develop bold, earthy, beefy flavors. This is a hearty but heart-healthy alternative to meat sauce. I season the ragout with a bit of Worcestershire, but strict vegetarians will want to omit it (see Note, page 161).

Bring a large pot of water to a boil for the pasta.

In a high-sided skillet, heat the EVOO over medium-high heat. When the oil ripples, add the mushrooms, allspice, bay leaf, marjoram, and black pepper and cook until the mushrooms darken and become tender, 6 to 7 minutes. Add the carrots, celery, onions, garlic, and cubanelle and bell peppers and season with salt. Cook for 6 to 7 minutes more, then stir in the tomato paste and cook for a minute. Add the wine and stir with a wooden spoon to scrape up any brown bits from the bottom of the pan. Cook for 1 minute to reduce the wine, then stir in the stock and tomatoes. Bring the sauce to a boil, then reduce the heat to a simmer. Season with Worcestershire and salt and pepper to taste. Simmer for 10 minutes more, then discard the bay leaf.

While the ragout is cooking, salt the boiling water and cook the penne to al dente. When the pasta is done, drain it and return it to the hot pot. Toss with half the sauce, the basil, and the ½ cup of grated cheese. Top bowlfuls of pasta with the remaining sauce and pass more grated cheese at the table.

SERVES 4

KOSHER MEALS

For some time readers, especially younger readers in families who keep kosher, have been asking me how they can adapt my recipes to fit their dietary needs. I usually suggest they just omit nonkosher ingredients such as pancetta or bacon from a sauce or stew, or that they swap out vegetable or mushroom stock for chicken or beef broth in a dish that also contains dairy. With some creativity, a trait that is second-nature to many kosher cooks, most any recipe in the book could be converted—pardon the pun. The recipes in this section, however, are good to go for kosher cooks just as they are, no adaptations required. (There are also some good choices for kosher meals in the vegetarian section of this book, too.)

If you didn't grow up around families who kept kosher you might be under the misconception that eating kosher food seems like a sacrifice in some way. Well, that idea isn't kosher! This small collection of recipes alone runs the gamut from Broken Florentine Lasagna Bake to Mediterranean Grilled Tuna Steaks with Sicilian-Style Potato and Sun-Dried Tomato Salad, Apricot and Cipollini Braised Chicken to Wild Mushroom Beef Meat Loaf with Horseradish Gravy, proof that *any* cuisine can be kosher and tasty, too.

RED WALDORF SALAD

I love beets, and if you like sweet beets too, this totally tasty all-red salad is for you! Your tongue will turn red, but your mouth will be happy.

Preheat the oven to 400°F.

Drizzle just a little EVOO over the beets, then wrap them in foil. Roast the beets for 35 to 40 minutes or until tender. Let them cool for a few minutes, then rub off the skins with a paper towel—they'll come off like magic! Drizzle oil on your hands first to make washing them a little easier. Chop the beets on a rubber or plastic cutting board; the beets will permanently stain a wooden board.

Next, combine the cranberry sauce and vinegar in the bottom of a shallow bowl. Whisk in the ¼ cup EVOO and season the dressing with salt and pepper. Add the beets and apples to the bowl, then the grapes, onions, celery, and walnuts. Toss the salad together for a minute or two until everything in the salad is tinted red!

Place 2 lettuce leaves in each of 4 bowls. Fill the lettuce leaves with red salad and top each with 1 cup shredded chicken. Delish!

SERVES 4 BEET-LOVIN' PEOPLE

EVOO (extra-virgin olive oil) for drizzling, plus ¼ cup

4 large **red beets**, tops and root ends trimmed, washed

½ cup **whole berry cranberry sauce**

2 tablespoons **red wine vinegar**

Salt and **pepper**

2 Honey Crisp or Gala **apples**, peeled and chopped

1 cup **red seedless grapes**, halved

¼ red **onion**, chopped

4 small **celery stalks** from the heart, chopped

½ cup **walnut pieces**, lightly toasted (see Note, page 102)

8 **red leaf lettuce** leaves

4 cups shredded or diced **chicken**, from 1 rotisserie chicken

---

SAMMIE NIGHT
JON'S GRILLED TUNA SALAD

This simple, heart-healthy sammie was invented by my friend Jon, a single man who has recently become Master and Commander of his kitchen.

Heat a drizzle of EVOO in a grill pan or skillet over medium-high to high heat until the oil smokes. Add the tuna and cook for 2 minutes on each side for rare and 4 minutes on each side for cooked-through fish. Remove from the heat and let the fish rest for a minute or two, until it is cool enough to handle.

Preheat the broiler.

2 tablespoons **EVOO** (extra-virgin olive oil), plus some for drizzling

2 **tuna steaks**, 6 ounces each

3 tablespoons drained **capers**

3 to 4 **hot pickled cherry peppers** or peperoncini, seeded and chopped

½ small or medium **red onion**, chopped

2 **celery stalks** from the heart, chopped or very thinly sliced

1 small bunch of **arugula**, coarsely chopped

Juice of 1 **lemon**

Black pepper

2 (8-inch) pieces of **baguette** or 4 large slices of Italian bread, toasted

Black or green olive tapenade, pesto, or sun-dried tomato spread (optional)

Chop the tuna into small dice. Combine the tuna with the capers, hot peppers, onion, celery, arugula, lemon juice, 2 tablespoons of EVOO, and black pepper to taste. Toast the split baguette or bread under the broiler until golden. Dot with tapenade, pesto, or sun-dried tomato spread, if using, and pile the tuna salad onto the bread.

SERVES 2

MEDITERRANEAN GRILLED TUNA STEAKS AND SICILIAN-STYLE POTATO AND SUN-DRIED-TOMATO SALAD

2 pounds **red-skin potatoes**, sliced ½ inch thick

Salt

⅓ cup **EVOO** (extra-virgin olive oil), plus some for drizzling

4 **tuna steaks**, 6 to 8 ounces each

2 tablespoons finely chopped fresh **rosemary**

Zest and juice of 1 **lemon**

Black pepper

¾ cup soft, loosely packed **sun-dried tomatoes**, available in pouches in the produce department

2 teaspoons **anchovy paste**

1 large **garlic clove**, grated or minced

½ **red onion**, chopped

3 to 4 **celery stalks** from the heart, finely chopped

½ cup pitted **Sicilian olives**, coarsely chopped

3 tablespoons drained **capers**

½ cup fresh flat-leaf **parsley leaves**, coarsely chopped

This meal is simple, hearty, flavorful, and packed with many of my favorite Sicilian ingredients.

Preheat a grill or grill pan over medium-high heat.

Place the potatoes in a pot and cover with cold water. Bring to a boil, salt the water, and cook for 12 to 15 minutes, until just tender.

Drizzle a little EVOO over the tuna, then season it with the rosemary, lemon zest, and salt and pepper.

Place the sun-dried tomatoes in a bowl. Ladle a cup of the boiling potato water over the tomatoes to soften them. Steep for 10 minutes, then drain and thinly slice the tomatoes.

In a bowl, combine the anchovy paste, garlic, lemon juice, and about ⅓ cup EVOO. Drain the potatoes and return to the hot pot to dry them out for a minute. Toss the potatoes with the dressing and the onion, celery, olives, capers, and parsley. Season the salad with pepper and taste to see if it needs salt; both the capers and the anchovy paste are salty on their own.

Grill the fish for 3 minutes on each side for medium-rare, up to 10 minutes total for fully cooked fish. Serve the fish with a mound of the salad alongside.

SERVES 4

COLD CHICKEN SATAY NOODLES

This meal comes together in a snap because it uses a store-bought chicken. The salty-nutty sauce goes especially well with the nutty flavor of whole-grain pastas.

Bring a large pot of water to a boil. Salt the water liberally, then add the pasta and cook to al dente. Run the cooked pasta under cold water to cool. Drain well.

While the water comes to a boil and the pasta cooks, heat the peanut butter in the microwave in 10-second intervals until softened. Place in a large bowl with the honey and warm water. Whisk in the tamari, garlic, lime juice, and hot sauce, then whisk in the oil in a slow stream. Add the noodles, veggies, and peanuts to the bowl and toss until the ingredients are well mixed. Serve the noodles in shallow bowls topped with the chicken and cilantro.

SERVES 4

Salt

1 pound **whole wheat spaghetti**

¼ to ⅓ cup smooth or chunky **peanut butter** (eyeball it)

2 tablespoons **honey**

¼ cup **warm water** (eyeball it)

¼ cup **tamari** (eyeball it)

1 **garlic clove**, finely chopped

Juice of 2 **limes**

1 teaspoon **hot sauce** (eyeball it)

3 tablespoons **peanut or sunflower oil** (eyeball it)

A handful of shredded **carrots**

4 **scallions**, thinly sliced on an angle

1 cup **spinach**, thinly sliced

¼ cup chopped **peanuts**

2 cups shredded store-bought **rotisserie chicken**

2 tablespoons chopped fresh **cilantro** or flat-leaf parsley

BROKEN FLORENTINE LASAGNA BAKE

Much easier to make than the traditional layering process, this dish is a dream—rich, simple, and delish. And with three pounds of greens, it's full of iron and vitamins.

Preheat the oven to 375°F.

Melt the butter in a medium pot over medium heat. Sprinkle the flour over the melted butter, whisk to combine, and cook for about 1 minute. Slowly whisk the milk into the butter-flour mixture, season with salt, pepper, and nutmeg, and cook for a couple of minutes to thicken. Stir in half the Parmigiano (about ¾ cup). Set the sauce aside.

Heat the EVOO in a large cast-iron skillet over medium-high heat. Toss in the cracked clove of garlic and cook for a minute or two to release its aroma and flavor. Add the chard and cook, turning occasionally to wilt down, 2 minutes. Add the spinach a few handfuls at a time, wilting each batch before adding more. Season the greens with salt and pepper.

Break the pasta sheets into large pieces. Toss them into the pan with the greens and give them a good stir to incorporate them. Pour the sauce into the skillet, stirring again to incorporate everything evenly. Smooth the top down and sprinkle the remaining ¾ cup Parmigiano into the skillet. Cover the skillet with foil, transfer to the oven, and bake the lasagna for 30 minutes. Remove the foil from the pan and let it finish cooking uncovered for about 15 more minutes to brown the cheese.

SERVES 4

4 tablespoons (½ stick) **butter**

4 tablespoons **all-purpose flour**

3 cups **milk**

Salt and **pepper**

Freshly grated **nutmeg**

1½ cups grated **Parmigiano-Reggiano**

2 tablespoons **EVOO** (extra-virgin olive oil)

1 **garlic clove**, cracked away from its skin

1 bunch of **green chard**, stems removed, leaves coarsely chopped

2 pounds **spinach**, stems removed, leaves coarsely chopped

1 box **no-boil lasagna noodles**

GNOCCHI WITH FRESH CHICKEN SAUSAGE AND BROCCOLI RABE

Salt

1 (12- to 16-ounce) package fresh or frozen **gnocchi**

2 bunches of **broccoli rabe**, stem ends trimmed and coarsely chopped

4 tablespoons **EVOO** (extra-virgin olive oil)

1½ pounds fresh **Kosher Italian chicken sausage links**, casings removed

1 small **onion**, finely chopped

3 large **garlic cloves**, finely chopped or grated

¼ teaspoon **crushed red pepper flakes**

Zest and juice of 1 **lemon**

Crusty bread

Who can knock gnocchi? It's fast, easy, and delish! Here, the classics, sausage and rabes, come together to round out our round dumpling dinner. Make sure that your chicken sausages are Kosher and not made with pork casings.

Bring a large pot of water to a boil over high heat to cook the gnocchi. Once the water is boiling, add some salt, add the gnocchi, and cook according to package directions. Right before draining, remove and reserve about 1½ cups of the cooking liquid.

While the water for the gnocchi is coming to a boil, bring 2 inches of water to a boil in a large high-sided skillet. Add some salt and the broccoli rabe and simmer for 5 minutes; drain and reserve. Return the skillet to the stove and heat 2 tablespoons of EVOO over medium-high heat. Add the chicken sausage and break it up with the back of a spoon or a potato masher while it cooks and browns, 6 to 7 minutes. Add the onions, garlic, and red pepper flakes to the sausage and continue to cook for another 3 to 4 minutes or until the onions start to get tender. Remove the sausage and onions from the skillet and reserve. Add the remaining 2 tablespoons of EVOO and heat it up. Add the drained gnocchi to the skillet and brown lightly for a couple of minutes. Return the sausage and onions and reserved broccoli rabe to the pan. Toss to combine and add the reserved pasta cooking liquid. Turn the heat up to high and simmer for 1 to 2 minutes. Stir in the lemon zest and juice and serve with the bread.

SERVES 4

SPANISH SPAGHETTI

Among the many nice things that happened to me in 2007, I got to visit Spain for the first time for my Food Network show *Tasty Travels*. After flight delays, lost equipment and luggage, and many hours in cars, planes, and assorted lines, the crew and I (and our luggage) all ended up in Barcelona. The first meal I had was small toasts topped with piquillo peppers, anchovies, and black olives, and I thought this topping would be great on spaghetti! (You can take the Sicilian-American to Spain but you can't . . .) Viva Spanish Spaghetti, one of my new faves.

Preheat the oven to 350°F.

Heat a large pot of water to a boil for the pasta. Salt the water, then add the spaghetti and cook to just shy of al dente. The pasta will continue to cook for a minute or two when you add it to the sauce. Reserve a cup of the starchy cooking water when you drain the pasta.

Scatter the nuts on a baking sheet and lightly crush them. Toast the nuts in the oven for 10 to 12 minutes until golden and fragrant; your nose will know when they are done. Transfer to a small bowl to cool, and reserve.

Heat the EVOO in a large, deep skillet over medium-low to medium heat. Add the garlic and anchovies or anchovy paste to the warm oil and cook for 5 to 6 minutes until the garlic is tender and the anchovies have melted into the oil completely, stirring with a wooden spoon to break up the fish. (Once they melt into the oil, the anchovies will taste more like salted nuts and less like salty fish. Both flavors are appealing to me, but if you think you don't care for anchovies, try this dish and change your mind.)

While the anchovies and garlic are working, place the piquillo or red peppers in a food processor and puree them into a paste. Stir the peppers into the garlic-anchovy oil and stir over medium heat until they are warmed through. Season with black pepper to taste.

Stir the reserved pasta cooking liquid into the sauce, then add the pasta. Toss the pasta and sauce together over medium heat for a minute or two to allow the pasta to suck up the sauce. Toss in the olives and nuts, toss again, and transfer the pasta to a serving platter or shallow dinner bowls.

SERVES 4

Salt

1 pound **spaghetti**

½ cup **slivered or sliced almonds**, to pass at the table

¼ cup **EVOO** (extra-virgin olive oil)

4 **garlic cloves**, finely chopped

6 to 8 **flat anchovy** fillets or 2 teaspoons anchovy paste

8 to 10 **piquillo peppers** (see Note), drained, or 4 roasted red peppers

Black pepper

1 cup loosely packed pitted good-quality **black olives**, finely chopped

PIQUILLO PEPPERS

are mild Spanish red peppers that are available roasted and peeled in jars. You can find them in more and more markets, including my Price Chopper in Glens Falls, New York; but if they're not available, regular roasted red peppers are a very close substitute.

SPAGHETTI WITH SARDINE-FENNEL SAUCE AND SPINACH SALAD

Salt

1 pound **spaghetti**, regular or whole wheat

6 tablespoons **EVOO** (extra-virgin olive oil)

1 medium **onion**, chopped

3 **garlic cloves**, finely chopped or grated

1 tin **sardines**, drained and chopped

1 **fennel bulb** with fronds

A generous handful of **golden raisins**

½ to ¾ cup **dry white wine**

1 cup **chicken stock**

1 (15-ounce) can **Italian crushed tomatoes**

Black pepper

¼ cup **pine nuts**

1 tablespoon **grainy mustard**

1 tablespoon **balsamic vinegar**

6 cups chopped **spinach** or baby spinach leaves

½ **red onion**, very thinly sliced

1 tablespoon **butter**

My husband loved the sound of a canned sardine sauce he saw in a local Italian market. We've been making the same sardine pasta at our house forever: sardines and spaghetti with garlic and bread crumbs, delish but a bit old hat. So this one's for you, honey; we're out of our rut.

Bring a large pot of water to a boil for the pasta. When it boils, season it liberally with salt, add the pasta, and cook to al dente; drain well.

While the water is heating, prepare the sauce. Heat 3 tablespoons of the EVOO in a large, deep skillet over medium heat. Add the chopped onions and garlic, cook for a couple of minutes to soften, then stir in the sardines. Chop and reserve a few tablespoons of the lacy green fennel fronds, then trim off the remainder of the fronds and quarter the fennel bulb. Cut the core away from each quarter, then very thinly slice the fennel and add it to the pan. Sauté the fennel with the sardines, onions, and garlic for 6 to 7 minutes, then stir in the raisins and wine. Add the chicken stock and tomatoes and season the sauce with salt and pepper to taste. Simmer for 4 to 5 minutes more.

While the sauce simmers, toast the pine nuts in a small dry skillet over low heat for 6 to 7 minutes or until golden. Transfer to a bowl and set aside.

In a salad bowl, whisk the mustard with the vinegar until combined. Stream in the remaining 3 tablespoons of EVOO, then add the spinach and red onions to the salad bowl. Toss to coat with the dressing.

Stir the butter into the sauce and turn off the heat. Add the drained pasta and toss to combine. Serve in shallow bowls with the toasted pine nuts and the fennel fronds on top. Serve the salad alongside.

SERVES 4

WILD MUSHROOM BEEF MEAT LOAF WITH HORSERADISH GRAVY AND ROASTED BROCCOLI

Who says meat loaf has to be mundane? Strap in for this spicy, saucy version.

Preheat the oven to 425°F.

Place about 1 cup of the stock in a sauce pot over high heat and bring up to a bubble. Place the dried mushrooms in a small heat-proof bowl, pour the boiling stock over the mushrooms, and cover with plastic wrap. Let the mushrooms steep for about 5 minutes or until soft. While the mushrooms are rehydrating, tear the slice of bread into small pieces and place them in a medium mixing bowl. Pour about 2 cups of stock over the bread, just to barely cover it, and let it soak for 5 to 10 minutes.

In another medium mixing bowl, combine the ground sirloin, thyme, sage, three quarters of the chopped onion, the garlic, and egg and season liberally with salt and pepper. With your hands, remove the soaked bread from the stock and gently squeeze out the excess liquid. Add the bread to the beef, and discard the soaking liquid. With a slotted spoon, remove the softened mushrooms from the stock to a cutting board, chop coarsely, and add to the beef, reserving the mushroom soaking liquid for the gravy. Mix the meat loaf ingredients together thoroughly. If you want to check the seasoning, make a thin quarter-size patty and cook it up in a skillet; taste and adjust the seasoning as needed. Transfer the meat mixture to a rimmed baking sheet and form a long, thin, oval-shaped loaf. Drizzle the loaf liberally with EVOO and roast for 45 minutes, or until the loaf is cooked through. Remove from the oven and let the meat loaf rest for about 5 minutes before slicing.

While the meat loaf is in the oven, work on the broccoli. Trim the very ends off of the broccoli stems with a peeler or a paring knife and remove the thick fibrous outer layer of the broccoli stems. Cut the broccoli lengthwise into large spears that look like long, skinny trees and arrange them on a baking sheet. Drizzle everything with EVOO and season with salt and pepper. Place the broccoli in the oven with the meat loaf for the last 25 to 30 minutes of cooking time, roasting until the broccoli is tender.

For the gravy, place a medium sauce pot over medium heat with the 3 tablespoons of EVOO. Add the reserved onion and the tomato paste and season with salt and pepper. Cook, stirring frequently, for 3 to 4 minutes or until the onions start to get soft. Sprinkle the flour over the onions, stir to

4 cups **beef stock**

2 ounces **dried mixed wild mushrooms**

1 large loaf of **crusty bread**, 1 slice (about 3 inches thick) for cooking and the remainder of the loaf for serving at the table

2 pounds lean **ground beef sirloin**

5 sprigs of fresh **thyme**, leaves removed and chopped

8 fresh **sage leaves**, chopped

1 large **onion**, finely chopped

3 **garlic cloves**, finely chopped or grated

1 **egg**, beaten

Salt and **pepper**

3 tablespoons **EVOO** (extra-virgin olive oil), plus some for drizzling

1 large head of **broccoli** or 2 small heads

1 tablespoon **tomato paste** (eyeball it)

2 tablespoons **all-purpose flour**

1 heaping tablespoon prepared **horseradish** (eyeball it)

1 tablespoon **Dijon mustard** (eyeball it)

1 handful of fresh flat-leaf **parsley** leaves, coarsely chopped

combine, and cook for 1 minute; if it seems too dry, add a little more EVOO. Whisk in the remaining 1 cup of stock, then carefully pour in the reserved mushroom steeping liquid, adding it slowly so that any grit from the mushrooms stays in the bottom of the bowl. Add the horseradish and mustard, bring up to a bubble, and cook over medium-low to medium heat until thickened, 5 to 7 minutes. Taste and adjust the seasonings, then stir in the parsley.

Serve the meat loaf topped with some of the horseradish gravy, with the roasted broccoli alongside. Pass the bread at the table.

SERVES 6

SLICED SKIRT STEAKS WITH DECONSTRUCTED GUACAMOLE

Marinated sliced steak is always a winner. Here it is topped with halved avocados that grill up to make a smoky, rich complement to the beef.

Bring the chicken stock and 1 tablespoon of the EVOO to a boil in a saucepan. Stir in the rice, bring to a boil, then cover, reduce the heat, and cook for about 12 minutes over low to medium-low heat. Stir in the scallions and black beans, replace the lid, and cook for 6 minutes more.

Heat an outdoor grill to medium-high. In a shallow dish, combine the hot sauce, Worcestershire, mustard, 3 tablespoons of the EVOO, and the grill seasoning. Coat the steak and marinate for 10 minutes.

Stick a toothpick through the side of each onion slice to keep the rings together. Brush the onions and jalapeños with a little EVOO and season with salt and pepper. Place the meat, onions, and jalapeño on the grill. Cook the meat for 5 to 6 minutes on each side for medium-cooked steak. After you turn the meat, onions, and jalapeño, halve and pit the avocados. Place the avocados on the grill for 3 to 4 minutes to char and mark. Remove the meat, onions, jalapeños, and avocados to a platter. Let the meat rest for a few minutes, tented with foil, to settle the juices.

To serve, thinly slice the steak on an angle. Divide the steak slices among 4 plates. Serve with an avocado half, a thick slice of onion, a jalapeño half, a sprinkle of cilantro, and a few halved tomatoes. Squeeze the juice of 1 lime over the vegetables and meat. Serve the black beans and rice alongside.

SERVES 4

2 cups **chicken stock**

4 to 5 tablespoons **EVOO** (extra-virgin olive oil)

1 cup **white rice**

4 **scallions**, chopped

1 (15-ounce) can **black beans**, drained

1 tablespoon **hot sauce**

2 tablespoons **Worcestershire sauce**

2 rounded tablespoons **grainy mustard**

1½ tablespoons **grill seasoning**, such as McCormick's Montreal Steak Seasoning, 1½ palmfuls

1¾ to 2 pounds **skirt steak**

4 (1-inch-thick) slices of **red onion**

2 **jalapeño peppers**, halved and seeded

Salt and **pepper**

2 ripe **Hass avocados**

A handful of chopped fresh **cilantro**

½ pint **multicolor cherry tomatoes**, halved

4 **limes**

STRIP STEAKS WITH GREEN OLIVE CHIMICHURRI AND CRIOLLA SALSA, ROASTED POTATO WEDGES, AND HEARTS OF PALM SALAD

I finally made it to a city I have always wanted to visit and eat my way through: Buenos Aires, Argentina. Bife de Chorizo, a thick-cut strip steak served with these great toppings, was my favorite take-away recipe.

Preheat the oven to 450°F. Halve each potato lengthwise, then cut each half into 3 fat wedges, 12 wedges total. Arrange the wedges on a rimmed baking sheet and coat them with a couple tablespoons of the EVOO. Finely chop the rosemary and thyme and reserve 1 teaspoon of each. Sprinkle the rest of the chopped herbs over the potatoes, then season them liberally with the grill seasoning. Roast the potatoes for 25 minutes.

Set out the steaks and let them come to room temperature. Season the meat with grill seasoning. Preheat an outdoor grill or heat a grill pan or cast-iron skillet over high heat.

Place the olives and yellow onion in a food processor and pulse until finely chopped and almost paste-like. Transfer to a small bowl. Grate 2 cloves of garlic into the olives and stir in the reserved rosemary, about 1 tablespoon of finely chopped red bell pepper, and about ⅓ cup of the EVOO. Set the olive chimichurri aside.

Chop the remaining piece of red bell pepper and place in a bowl. Add the chopped green bell pepper; the chopped red onion; hot pickled peppers; the remaining 2 cloves of garlic, grated or finely chopped; the chopped tomato; reserved chopped thyme; the juice of ½ lime; the red wine vinegar; and about ⅓ cup of the EVOO. Season the salsa with salt and pepper and set aside.

Grill the steaks for 3 to 4 minutes on each side, then set on the upper shelf of the grill for another 5 minutes for medium rare, 7 to 8 minutes for medium-well. If you are cooking on the stovetop, caramelize the meat in the hot pan for 3 to 4 minutes on each side, then transfer the pan to the oven for 8 to 12 minutes for medium-rare to medium-well doneness. Let the meat rest for 5 minutes.

While the meat cooks, place the sliced tomatoes in a bowl. Halve the avocado, remove the pit, then scoop the avocado from the skin. Quarter the avocado lengthwise and slice it thin, then add it to the tomatoes. Add

2 large Idaho **potatoes**, 1 pound each

About 1 cup **EVOO** (extra-virgin olive oil)

2 to 3 sprigs of fresh **rosemary**

5 to 6 sprigs of fresh **thyme**

Grill seasoning, such as McCormick's Montreal Steak Seasoning

4 (2-inch-thick) **strip steaks**

1 cup good-quality large pitted **green olives**

½ small **yellow onion**, peeled and coarsely chopped

4 **garlic cloves**, peeled

½ **red bell pepper**

1 small **green bell pepper**, seeded and chopped

1 small or medium **red onion**, ½ chopped, ½ thinly sliced

2 to 3 tablespoons sliced **hot pickled yellow peppers**, drained and chopped

3 small vine-ripe **tomatoes**, 1 seeded and finely chopped, 2 quartered and thinly sliced

2 **limes**

2 tablespoons **red wine vinegar**

Salt and **pepper**

1 firm but ripe **Hass avocado**

1 (14-ounce) can **hearts of palm**, drained

1 large bunch of **arugula**, coarsely chopped

the thinly sliced red onions to the bowl. Thinly slice the drained hearts of palm on an angle and add them to the salad as well. Scatter in the arugula and dress the salad with the juice of 1½ limes, a few tablespoons of EVOO, and salt and pepper.

Serve the steaks with 3 potato wedges and the salad alongside and pass the chimichurri and salsa at the table to dollop liberally on the steaks.

SERVES 4

SLICED GRILLED LIME-CILANTRO CHICKEN SAMMIES WITH PICO-GUAC

2 handfuls of fresh **cilantro**, finely chopped

4 **scallions**, finely chopped

2 tablespoons chopped fresh **thyme**, 5 to 6 sprigs

2 **limes**

2 teaspoons **hot sauce**

1 tablespoon **grill seasoning**, such as McCormick's Montreal Steak Seasoning

2 tablespoons **EVOO**

4 boneless skinless **chicken breast halves**, 6 ounces each

2 small to medium ripe **Hass avocados**

1 large **garlic clove**, grated or finely chopped

1 **lemon**

½ small to medium **red onion**, finely chopped

2 **jalapeño peppers**, seeded and finely chopped

2 small **plum tomatoes**, seeded and chopped

Salt

8 leaves of **green leaf** or **Bibb lettuce**

4 split **crusty rolls**

Fancy flavored **tortilla chips**

Who's not happy to find a new way to enjoy warm-weather faves: burgers and chicken-breast sammies? This tangy chicken sammie is topped with a spicy-cool combo of pico de gallo salsa and guacamole.

Heat an outdoor grill or stovetop grill pan to medium-high heat.

In a shallow dish, combine half the cilantro with the scallions, thyme, the zest and juice of 1 lime, the hot sauce, grill seasoning, and EVOO. Coat the chicken and let it marinate for 10 minutes, then grill the chicken for 12 minutes, 6 minutes on each side. Rest the chicken on a cutting board for a few minutes, then slice the breasts on an angle.

Split the avocados by halving them all the way around the pit. Scoop out the pit, then scoop the flesh into a bowl with a large spoon. Mash the avocados with the garlic and the juice of 1 lime and the lemon. Add the red onions, jalapeños, tomatoes, the reserved cilantro, and salt to taste, and mix well.

Place a couple of lettuce leaves on each bun bottom, top with sliced chicken breast, and spoon on a mound of pico-guac. Serve extra pico-guac with some chips for dipping.

SERVES 4

PAPRIKA CHICKEN SCHNITZEL WITH FRIED EGGS (À LA HOLSTEIN)

One year for the holidays my mom, brother, husband, and I visited Vienna, where menu items that say "Holstein" come topped with fried eggs. We all had our fill of schnitzel. Back home, I combined elements from a few versions with a twist or two of my own, for the best of both worlds (old and new!). This dish can be made with veal or chicken.

Preheat the oven to 200°F. Place a baking sheet in the oven to keep the cooked cutlets crisp.

Pressing the breast against the cutting board with the flat of your hand, cut horizontally into each chicken piece to butterfly it. Open the meat up like a book and place it between 2 sheets of plastic wrap. Gently pound out each piece into very thin, large cutlets. Pile the cutlets on a plate and season with salt and pepper.

Arrange a station for breading, putting the flour in one shallow bowl, 2 beaten eggs in a second, and the bread crumbs with the paprika, parsley, and lemon zest in a third.

Heat just enough EVOO to coat the bottom of a large nonstick skillet over medium to medium-high heat.

Dredge 2 of the cutlets in flour, then egg, and then bread crumbs. Cook for 2 to 3 minutes on each side and transfer to the oven to keep warm. Repeat with the remaining cutlets, adding a bit more oil to the pan if necessary. Wipe the pan clean, add 1 tablespoon of the EVOO, and heat over medium-high heat. Add the bell peppers and onions, season with salt and pepper, and cook until the peppers are wilted, 4 to 5 minutes.

While the peppers and onions are cooking up, heat 1 tablespoon of EVOO in a medium skillet over medium heat. Add the remaining 4 eggs and fry to desired doneness; season with salt and pepper.

Arrange some lettuce on each dinner plate, top with a cutlet, and squeeze the juice of ¼ lemon over each. Top each cutlet with some fried peppers and onions, a fried egg, 2 anchovy fillets, and 1 tablespoon of capers.

SERVES 4

4 small **boneles skinless chicken breast halves**, about 4 ounces each

Salt and **pepper**

All-purpose flour

6 large **eggs**

2 cups **bread crumbs**

2 tablespoons **sweet paprika**

A handful of fresh flat-leaf **parsley**

Zest and juice of 1 **lemon**

5 to 6 tablespoons **EVOO** (extra-virgin olive oil)

1 large **red bell pepper**, thinly sliced

1 **onion**, thinly sliced

1 **romaine lettuce heart**, shredded

8 **anchovy fillets**

4 tablespoons drained **capers**

APRICOT AND CIPOLLINI BRAISED CHICKEN OVER COUSCOUS WITH ESCAROLE SALAD

20 **cipollini onions**

4 tablespoons plus ⅓ cup **EVOO** (extra-virgin olive oil), plus more for drizzling

4 bone-in and skin-on **chicken breast halves**

Salt and **pepper**

7 to 8 sprigs of fresh **thyme**, leaves stripped and chopped

4 large **garlic cloves**, chopped

½ teaspoon **crushed red pepper flakes**

1 cup **white grape juice**

4½ cups **chicken stock**

20 **dried apricots**

Zest and juice of 1 **lemon**

Zest and juice of 1 **orange**

2 handfuls of fresh flat-leaf **parsley leaves**, coarsely chopped

1½ cups plain **couscous**

1 tablespoon **Dijon mustard**

1 large or 2 small heads of **escarole**, leaves separated, thoroughly washed, and torn into bite-size pieces

Apricot and chicken is a combo that I return to again and again. Here, little onions really sweeten the deal.

Bring a medium pot of water to a boil. Add the onions and blanch for 1 minute, then drain. Use a paper towel to wipe off the skins. Trim the root ends and leave the onions whole.

Heat a Dutch oven over medium-high heat. Add about 2 tablespoons of the EVOO. Season the chicken liberally with salt and pepper. Working in batches if necessary, brown the chicken in the hot oil, skin side first, until golden, about 5 minutes per side. Remove and reserve. Add another 2 tablespoons of the EVOO to the pan, along with the onions, thyme, garlic, and red pepper flakes. Season the mixture with salt and pepper, spread the onions in an even layer, and cook, stirring and flipping them over every now and then, until browned on all sides, about 10 minutes. Add the white grape juice, scraping up all the brown bits on the bottom of the pan with a wooden spoon. Add 3 cups of the chicken stock and the apricots and bring up to a bubble.

When the sauce is simmering, return the chicken to the pan, nestling it down into the liquid. Cover the pot, turn the heat down to medium, and simmer for about 15 minutes, flipping the chicken over in the sauce about halfway through. When the chicken is no longer pink inside, remove it to a plate and tent with foil to keep warm. Turn the heat under the pot to high and simmer the sauce until it thickens up slightly, 4 to 5 minutes.

Combine the lemon and orange zests and chopped parsley in a bowl.

When the chicken is about 10 minutes away from being done, bring the remaining 1½ cups of chicken stock to a boil in a sauce pot with a lid. Add a little salt and pepper and a small drizzle of EVOO, then stir in the couscous. Cover, turn off the heat, and let the couscous sit for 5 minutes.

For the salad, combine the lemon and orange juices in the bottom of a salad bowl. Add the mustard and whisk in about ⅓ cup of EVOO. Just before you are ready to serve, toss the escarole in the dressing.

Fluff the couscous with a fork, divide it among 4 serving plates, and top with a piece of braised chicken. Spoon some of the onions, apricots, and sauce over the chicken and sprinkle with some of the zest and parsley mixture. Serve the escarole salad alongside.

SERVES 4

TANGO JOES

This sloppy supper is my latest Ode to Joe and it packs a spicy kick: lots of chimichurri. In Argentina, this sauce is used in many recipes and also is a more common condiment than ketchup, used on anything and everything. There are endless versions of the sauce. Here, I used herbs that I thought complemented the meat best, but you can switch up the combo in any way you like.

Preheat the oven to 250°F.

Heat a large sauté pan over high heat and add the 1 tablespoon of EVOO. Add the meat and brown for 7 to 8 minutes. As it cooks, season it with salt and pepper and the paprika, and break it up with a spoon.

While the meat is browning, make the chimichurri. Place the rosemary, oregano, thyme and parsley leaves, garlic, onion, and vinegar into a food processor. Season with salt and pepper and pulse the machine to finely chop. With the machine running, stream in the ⅓ cup of EVOO.

Combine the Worcestershire, brown sugar, and tomato sauce in a small bowl. Pour the sauce over the meat in the skillet and stir. Bring to a bubble. Stir in half the chimichurri and simmer for 5 minutes.

Wrap the rolls in foil and heat in the oven for 3 or 4 minutes. Split the rolls open and slather the tops with the remaining chimichurri sauce. Pile the meat onto the bun bottoms and serve.

Pour a nice glass of Malbec to complement the Joes and you'll be tangoing in no time!

SERVES 4 REALLY HUNGRY ARGENTINES OR AMERICANS

⅓ cup plus 1 tablespoon **EVOO** (extra-virgin olive oil)

2 pounds **lean ground sirloin**
Salt and **pepper**

2 teaspoons **sweet smoked paprika**

2 sprigs of fresh **rosemary**, leaves removed

4 sprigs of fresh **oregano**, leaves removed

8 sprigs of fresh **thyme**, leaves removed

1 cup fresh flat-leaf **parsley leaves**, a couple handfuls

2 **garlic cloves**

½ small **onion**, coarsely chopped

3 tablespoons **red wine vinegar**, 3 splashes (eyeball it)

2 tablespoons **Worcestershire sauce** (eyeball it)

2 tablespoons **dark brown sugar**, packed

1 (8-ounce) can **tomato sauce**

4 **Portuguese rolls** (slightly sweet large, rectangular sandwich rolls)

CHOP ON!
LAMB CHOPS WITH GREENS AND CRISPY ORECCHIETTE PASTA WITH WALNUT-ROSEMARY PESTO

Salt

½ pound **orecchiette pasta**

1½ cups **walnuts**

7 to 8 stems of **rosemary**, ¼ to ⅓ cup leaves, loosely packed

2 **garlic cloves**, cracked from their skins, 1 clove cut in half

Black pepper

⅓ cup plus 5 tablespoons **EVOO** (extra-virgin olive oil)

4 shoulder **lamb chops**, 8 to 10 ounces each

Freshly grated **nutmeg**

1 **red onion**, thinly sliced

1 large head of **kale**, dinosaur kale, or chard, chopped

2 to 3 tablespoons **aged balsamic vinegar**

My friend Vince came up with the idea of crisping up the little ear-shaped pasta that is such a fave of mine. The nutty pasta tastes amazing with walnuts and rosemary.

Bring a pot of water to a boil for the pasta. Salt the water, add the pasta, and cook to al dente. Heads up: reserve ½ cup of the starchy pasta cooking water before draining the pasta.

Toast the walnuts in a dry skillet over medium heat until golden and fragrant, a few minutes, then cool. Place the nuts in a food processor with the rosemary, the whole garlic clove, salt, and pepper and turn on the processor. Stream ⅓ cup of the EVOO into the food processor and process until the pesto is fairly smooth.

Rub the chops with the cut clove of garlic, then season with salt and pepper. Heat 1 tablespoon of the EVOO in a large skillet over medium-high heat. Add the chops and cook for 4 minutes on each side for medium rare.

While the lamb cooks, drain the pasta and return the pot to the heat. Stir the reserved pasta cooking water into the pesto to thin it a bit. Heat 3 tablespoons EVOO in the pasta pot over medium heat. Return the pasta to the pot and cook for 4 to 5 minutes, to crisp and toast the pasta. Season the pasta with salt and pepper and a little nutmeg.

Remove the lamb from the skillet and tent with foil to let the juices settle. In a clean skillet, heat the remaining 1 tablespoon of EVOO over medium-high to high heat. Add the onions and kale and sear them. Season the greens with salt and pepper and wilt down, 3 to 4 minutes. Add the vinegar to the pan and turn the greens to coat.

Serve a chop alongside a pile of the greens. Top the greens with the toasted pasta and drizzle some pesto over everything.

SERVES 4

SALMON BURGERS WITH DILL MUSTARD

Salmon is probably right behind chicken in the list of food we can never have enough recipes for, and salmon is so meaty it makes for a perfect burger.

Preheat the broiler.

Place the fish in a food processor and pulse on and off until it forms small coarse pieces. Transfer it to a bowl and add the capers, lemon zest, parsley, and seafood seasoning. Add salt and pepper if your seafood seasoning is missing either. Mix the ingredients and form 4 salmon patties.

Heat the EVOO in a nonstick skillet over medium-high heat until the oil ripples. Add the burgers and cook for 4 minutes on each side, until cooked through.

While the burgers cook, in a bowl mix together the cucumber, tomatoes, and red onion. In a small bowl stir the Dijon together with the dill. Toast the rolls under the broiler until golden.

Squeeze the juice of the lemon half evenly over the cooked burgers and transfer to the bun bottoms. Top with the cucumber relish, lettuce, and bun tops slathered with dill mustard.

SERVES 4

1½ pounds skinless **salmon fillet**, cut into large chunks

2 tablespoons **capers**, drained and chopped

1 teaspoon grated **lemon zest**, plus ½ **lemon**

A handful of fresh flat-leaf **parsley**, finely chopped

2 teaspoons **Old Bay** or other seafood seasoning such as McCormick's Seafood Seasoning

Salt and **pepper**, if needed

1 tablespoon **EVOO** (extra-virgin olive oil)

¼ **seedless cucumber**, chopped

2 **plum tomatoes**, seeded and chopped

½ small **red onion**, chopped

½ cup **Dijon mustard**

3 tablespoons fresh **dill**, finely chopped

4 **Kaiser rolls**, split

Red leaf lettuce

FEEL-GOOD SUPPER
- GINGER-GARLIC FISH IN PARCHMENT
- LEMON CHIVE NOODLES

Next time you feel your jeans getting tight, check out this dish before you contemplate skipping meals altogether. To keep your metabolism up you need to eat dinner; just go lean. Parchment cooking is lean *and* delicious.

Ginger-Garlic Fish in Parchment

Preheat the oven to 375°F.

Rip off 4 pieces of parchment about 12 inches long to form packets. In a small bowl combine the honey, vinegar, and tamari.

Place a piece of parchment in a shallow baking dish for stability, then stack one quarter of the scallions and shiitakes in the center of the paper. Layer with slices of ginger and garlic and top with a fish fillet. Pour one quarter of the tamari mixture over the fish fillet. Season with pepper, then bring the parchment together over the fish and fold the top down twice to seal. Roll in the sides to form a sealed pouch. Repeat with the remaining ingredients. Arrange the parchment pouches on a baking sheet and roast for 12 to 14 minutes. Serve with lemon chive noodles as a starter or a side.

SERVES 4

3 tablespoons **honey**

2 tablespoons **rice wine vinegar**

3 tablespoons **tamari**

1 bunch of **scallions**, roots trimmed, cut into 3-inch pieces on an angle

¾ pound **shiitake mushrooms**, stemmed and sliced

3 to 4 inches of fresh **gingerroot**, peeled and thinly sliced

4 large **garlic cloves**, peeled and thinly sliced

4 **sea bass fillets**, 6 to 7 ounces each

Black pepper

Lemon Chive Noodles

Bring a large pot of water to a boil for the pasta. When it boils, salt it generously, then add the pasta and cook to just shy of al dente.

While the pasta water comes to a boil, combine the stock, tamari, oil, and lemon slices and cook over medium-high heat until slightly reduced, 7 to 8 minutes. Toss the cooked pasta with the sauce for 1 to 2 minutes to absorb the flavor, then add the lemon zest and chives and toss to combine. Serve the noodles as a first course or a side. If you prefer them a bit spicy, pass pepper or hot sauce at the table.

SERVES 4

Salt

1 pound **egg fettuccine** or pappardelle noodles

2 cups **chicken stock**

½ cup **tamari** (aged soy sauce)

1 tablespoon **vegetable oil**

1 **lemon**, zested and sliced

1 bunch of fresh **chives**, chopped into 1-inch lengths

Black pepper or **hot sauce** (optional)

FISH TACOS WITH QUICK SLAW, AVOCADO SAUCE, AND GREEN RICE

3 tablespoons **vegetable oil**, such as canola, plus more for drizzling

2 **jalapeño peppers**, seeds removed, finely chopped

1½ cups uncooked **rice**

3 cups **vegetable stock**

Zest and juice of 3 **limes**

¼ cup **honey**

2 tablespoons **hot sauce**

½ small head of **red cabbage**, shredded

1 small **red onion**, very thinly sliced

Salt and **pepper**

12 ounces **baby spinach**

½ cup fresh **cilantro leaves**

2 ripe **Hass avocados**, halved, pitted, and scooped out of the skin

½ cup **sour cream**

1 **garlic clove**, grated

4 firm **white fish fillets**, such as mahimahi, 8 ounces each

1 tablespoon **grill seasoning**, such as McCormick's Montreal Steak Seasoning

1 teaspoon **ground cumin**

1 teaspoon **ground coriander**

12 (6- to 8-inch) **flour tortillas**

It's a toss-up which fish tacos are better—these or the ones I've dedicated to my friend Charlie (see page 101). These are a little easier to make, so if you're feeling lazy, go for this recipe.

Preheat the broiler, grill, or a large nonstick skillet—whichever you prefer.

Heat 1 tablespoon of the oil in a medium pot over medium-high heat. Toss the jalapeños into the pan and cook until tender, 3 to 4 minutes. Add the rice and cook for about a minute (you're toasting it here, so you'll know it's ready when it starts to smell nutty). Add 2½ cups of the stock and bring it up to a bubble. Turn the heat down to medium-low, cover, and simmer the rice until tender, about 20 minutes.

Prepare the slaw by mixing together in the bottom of a salad bowl the juice of 2 limes, honey, hot sauce, and the remaining 2 tablespoons of oil. Add the cabbage and red onion to the bowl and toss to combine. Season with salt and pepper.

Grab your food processor bowl and make the "green" part of the rice by pureeing together the baby spinach, cilantro, and remaining ½ cup of vegetable stock. Put this mixture into a dish and save it until the rice is finished. Give your food processor bowl a quick rinse and make the avocado sauce by pureeing together the avocados, sour cream, garlic, and juice of the remaining lime. Season the sauce with salt and pepper and set aside.

Season the fish fillets on both sides with the lime zest, grill seasoning, cumin, and coriander. Lightly drizzle some oil over the fillets and broil, grill, or pan-fry the fish. If you're broiling, the fish should take about 6 minutes to cook (3 minutes per side); if you're grilling or cooking them on the stove-top, the fillets should take about 8 minutes to cook (4 minutes per side).

Warm the tortillas according to package directions.

Stir the reserved green sauce into the cooked rice and transfer to a serving bowl.

Serve each fillet of fish with 3 soft tortillas so each diner can shred the fish and fill each taco with a little fish, a few forkfuls of cabbage, and some avocado sauce on top. Serve the green rice alongside.

SERVES 4

MEALS FOR ONE

When I've lived alone I've often cooked for four because I loved the leftovers and I like to share my food with friends or neighbors. Still, many nights for budget's or time's sake, I would make single-serving meals—usually scrambled eggs with mix-ins or warm cereal (boo-hoo!). To make sure you don't find yourself in the same fix, here's a great collection of empowering and delicious meals for one. The smells from your kitchen are going to be so good, the neighbors will all be hinting for an invite. Table for one? Put some great music on and treat yourself, nightly, to the food you deserve.

ROASTED CAPRESE SPAGHETTI

I wrote this recipe for Duff, The Ace of Cakes on Food Network, who wanted an entreé that would be challenging to mimic as a cake—but it was easy for the Ace. This is as easy to make for many as it is for one, so multiply up as needed.

Salt

¼ pound **spaghetti** or thick spaghetti

½ pint **red grape tomatoes**

2 tablespoons **EVOO** (extra-virgin olive oil), plus some for drizzling

Black pepper

½ cup fresh **basil**, 10 to 12 leaves

¼ cup fresh **tarragon leaves**, 5 to 6 sprigs

2 tablespoons **pine nuts**, toasted (see Note, page 102)

1 teaspoon grated **lemon zest**

1 small **garlic clove**, grated or minced

¼ cup freshly grated **Parmigiano-Reggiano**

¼ pound fresh **mozzarella** cheese, diced into ½ inch pieces

Preheat the oven to 400°F.

Bring a large pot of water to a boil. Generously salt the water, add the spaghetti, and cook to al dente. Heads up: before draining the pasta, reserve about ⅓ cup of the starchy cooking water.

Place the grape tomatoes on a rimmed baking sheet and drizzle with a tablespoon of EVOO. Season with salt and pepper and roast until tender and bursting, 15 to 20 minutes.

Combine the basil, tarragon, pine nuts, lemon zest, garlic, and salt and pepper in a food processor or mini chopper. Pulse a few times, add the Parmigiano-Reggiano, then turn the processor on and drizzle in the remaining 2 tablespoons of EVOO.

Scoop the pesto into a pasta bowl, stir in the reserved pasta cooking water, then add the drained pasta, roasted tomatoes, and mozzarella. Toss to combine and adjust the salt and pepper.

SPINACH FETTUCCINE PRIMAVERA

Heads up: when making the veggie ribbons, discard the center of the squash if the flesh is too seedy.

Salt

¼ pound **spinach fettuccine**

1 small **carrot**, peeled

1 small **zucchini**, ¼ pound

1 tablespoon **EVOO** (extra-virgin olive oil)

1 tablespoon **butter**

1 **shallot**, thinly sliced

1 **garlic clove**, finely chopped

½ cup frozen **green peas**

½ cup **dry white wine** or vegetable or chicken stock

Black pepper

¼ cup freshly grated **Parmigiano-Reggiano**

2 tablespoons chopped fresh flat-leaf **parsley**

Bring a large pot of water to a boil for the pasta. Salt the water, add the pasta, and cook to al dente, 7 to 8 minutes. Using a vegetable peeler, make ribbons of the carrot and zucchini by holding the vegetables flat on a counter and running the peeler the length of the vegetable. Drop the carrot and zucchini ribbons into the boiling water with the pasta for the last 2 minutes of cooking time.

Heat a medium skillet over medium heat with the EVOO and butter. Add the shallots and garlic and sauté for 3 to 4 minutes, until softened. Add the peas and stir to heat through, about 2 minutes, then stir in the wine or stock. Add the drained pasta and vegetables and toss with the sauce. Season with salt and pepper, add the cheese and parsley, and toss again.

WILD MUSHROOM SPAGHETTI

Salt

¼ pound **whole wheat** or **whole grain spaghetti**

⅓ pound **mixed mushrooms** such as shiitake, cremini, or any that catch your eye at the market

¼ cup **EVOO** (extra-virgin olive oil)

1 **leek**

2 **garlic cloves**, finely chopped

Black pepper

1 tablespoon finely chopped fresh **thyme leaves**

½ cup **dry white wine**

2 to 3 tablespoons **heavy cream**

Grated **Pecorino Romano cheese**, for topping

Whole wheat and whole grain pastas pair well with earthy, woody flavors like those of mushrooms. This meal cooks down an enormous amount of 'shroom goodness into one delicious serving, sending you off to a food coma, full and happy.

Bring a pot of water to a boil for the pasta. Salt the water, add the pasta, and cook to al dente.

Wipe the mushrooms clean with a damp towel. Remove and discard the woody stems. Thinly slice the mushrooms.

Heat the EVOO in a large deep skillet over medium-high heat. Add the mushrooms and cook until tender and deeply golden, 7 to 8 minutes.

While the mushrooms cook, halve the leek lengthwise. Cut off a couple of inches of the tough tops and trim off the root end. Thinly slice the leek, then wash in a large bowl of cold water, swishing the leeks vigorously and separating all the layers to free the grit. Let the leeks stand in the water for 1 minute, then scoop them out and dry on a clean kitchen towel. Pour out the gritty water and wipe down your cutting board.

Add the leeks to the mushrooms along with the garlic and season with salt and pepper and the thyme. Cook for 3 to 4 minutes more, then add the wine. Cook for 30 seconds to reduce the wine a bit, then stir in the cream and heat through. Add the drained pasta to the mushroom mixture, toss to coat with the sauce, and adjust the seasonings. Top with grated cheese at the table.

PUTTANESCA FRESCA

Salt

¼ pound **penne rigate**

2 tablespoons **EVOO** (extra-virgin olive oil)

2 to 3 flat **anchovy fillets**

2 **garlic cloves**, finely chopped

¼ teaspoon crushed **red pepper flakes**

¼ cup chopped **kalamata olives**

1 tablespoon drained **capers**

½ pint **grape tomatoes**

Coarse black pepper

2 tablespoons chopped fresh flat-leaf **parsley**

This sauce is named for the ladies of the night, and like them it's spicy, fast, and easy (pardon the pun). This version is especially fresh-tasting because it uses sweet baby tomatoes rather than canned.

Bring a pot of water to a boil for the pasta. Salt the water generously, add the pasta, and cook to al dente.

Heat the EVOO over medium heat in a medium skillet. Add the anchovies, garlic, and red pepper flakes and cook until the anchovies melt into oil, 2 to 3 minutes. Add the olives, capers, tomatoes, and black pepper, turn the heat up to medium-high and cook for 4 to 5 minutes more, until the tomatoes burst. Toss the pasta with the fresh sauce and the parsley, and serve.

PASTA, PEAS, AND RICOTTA FAKE-BAKE

Baked ziti is something we associate with dinners at the VFW hall or an all-you-can-eat buffet—not exactly meal-for-one territory—but pastas *al forno* (from the oven) are just so comforting you shouldn't have to wait for a crowd to make them. These next two recipes are a great fake-out, cooked stovetop and just finished under the broiler, giving the illusion of a long-baked pasta. The recipes make a BIG portion; midnight snackers will love this one. You can substitute ¼ pound blanched asparagus or broccoli cut in small pieces for the peas.

Bring a pot of water to a boil for the pasta. Salt the water, add the pasta, and cook to al dente. Reserve ⅓ cup of the pasta cooking liquid before you drain the pasta.

Preheat the broiler.

Heat the EVOO and butter in a small or medium skillet. Add the scallions and garlic and sauté for 3 to 4 minutes, then add the peas and cook for 2 minutes to heat through. Season with salt, pepper, the lemon zest, and the thyme. Add the drained pasta and reserved cooking water to the skillet along with the ricotta and toss to combine; adjust the seasonings. Top the pasta with the grated cheese and place the skillet under the broiler to brown for 3 minutes.

Salt

¼ pound **penne** or rigatoni pasta or whole wheat pasta

1 tablespoon **EVOO** (extra-virgin olive oil)

1 tablespoon **butter**

2 **scallions**, finely chopped

1 **garlic clove**, finely chopped

½ cup **frozen peas**, a couple of handfuls

Black pepper

1 teaspoon grated **lemon zest**

1 tablespoon fresh **thyme leaves**, 3 to 4 sprigs, finely chopped

½ cup **ricotta cheese**

¼ cup freshly grated **Parmigiano-Reggiano**

SAUSAGE AND RIGATONI FAKE-BAKE

Bring a pot of water to a boil for the pasta. Salt the water, add the rigatoni, and cook to al dente. Preheat the broiler.

Heat the EVOO in a small or medium ovenproof skillet. Remove the sausage from its casing and add to the skillet, breaking it up with a spoon as it browns, 5 minutes. Add the garlic, cook for a minute or two more, then stir in the tomato sauce and cook just to heat through. Fold the basil into the sauce and stir in the cream. Simmer the sauce over low heat for 5 minutes. Add the drained pasta to the skillet and toss to coat with the sauce. Sprinkle the pasta with the cheese and place under the broiler until browned, 3 to 4 minutes.

Salt

¼ pound **rigatoni** or whole grain rigatoni

1 tablespoon **EVOO** (extra-virgin olive oil)

1 link of **sweet Italian sausage**

1 link of **hot Italian sausage**

1 large **garlic clove**, finely chopped or grated

1 (8-ounce) can **tomato sauce**

A handful of fresh **basil leaves**, torn

2 tablespoons **heavy cream**

¼ cup freshly grated **Parmigiano-Reggiano**

HAM STEAK WITH CHILI GRAVY AND CHEESY POLENTA

This meal has southern roots but polenta is even faster to make than grits and is sweeter, too. The polenta balances the spicy gravy.

1 tablespoon **vegetable, peanut, or canola oil**

½ pound **ham steak**

¼ small **onion**, finely chopped

1 **garlic clove**, finely chopped

¼ **bell pepper**, finely chopped

Salt and **pepper**

2 tablespoons **tomato paste**

1 tablespoon **chili powder**

½ cup **beef stock**

½ cup **milk**

⅓ cup **quick-cooking polenta**

1 tablespoon **butter**

½ teaspoon **hot sauce**, a few dashes

½ cup shredded **extra-sharp cheddar cheese**

Heat ½ tablespoon of the oil in a skillet over medium-high heat. Cook the ham steak for 3 minutes on each side to brown and heat through, then remove to a plate and cover to keep warm. Add the remaining ½ tablespoon of oil to the pan and add the onion, garlic, and bell pepper. Season with salt and pepper and cook for 4 to 5 minutes, until soft. Once the vegetables are tender, stir in the tomato paste and chili powder and cook for a minute, then stir in the stock and simmer for a couple minutes more.

While the gravy is working, bring the milk and ½ cup water to a boil in a small pot. Add the polenta and whisk for 2 to 3 minutes, until thickened. Melt the butter into the polenta and stir in the hot sauce and cheese; remove from the heat.

Top the ham steak with the chili gravy and serve the polenta alongside.

ORANGE-SESAME PORK CHOP WITH TERIYAKI WHOLE WHEAT NOODLES

Salt

¼ pound **whole wheat or whole grain spaghetti**

2 tablespoons **vegetable or light oil**

1 (1½-inches-thick) boneless **pork loin chop**

Black pepper

1 rounded tablespoon **orange marmalade**

5 tablespoons **teriyaki sauce**

1 teaspoon **sesame oil**

½ cup frozen shelled **edamame**

2 **scallions**, thinly sliced on an angle

1 tablespoon toasted **sesame seeds** (optional)

Bring a pot of water to a boil for the pasta. When it boils, salt the water, add the pasta, and cook to al dente.

While the pasta cooks, heat 1 tablespoon of the oil in a small skillet over medium-high heat. Season the chop with salt and pepper and cook for 6 minutes on the first side, 4 to 5 minutes on the second.

Remove the chop to a plate and tent loosely with foil to keep warm. Add the orange marmalade, a couple tablespoons of the teriyaki sauce, and a splash of water to the pan, bring the sauce to a bubble, and cook for 1 minute to combine. Stir in the sesame oil and remove from the heat.

While the chop cooks, heat a second skillet with the remaining tablespoon of vegetable oil over medium-high heat. Add the edamame and scallions and stir-fry for a couple of minutes. Stir in the remaining 3 tablespoons of teriyaki sauce. Add the drained pasta and toss to combine. Sprinkle the noodles with the sesame seeds, if using.

Slice the pork or leave the chop whole and top with the orange-sesame glaze. Serve the teriyaki noodles alongside.

SURF'S UP! SURF 'N' TURF FOR ONE
TENDERLOIN WITH RED WINE GRAVY AND CRACKED GARLIC JUMBO SHRIMP

1 (1½-inch-thick) **tenderloin steak**

EVOO (extra-virgin olive oil) for drizzling, plus 2 tablespoons

Salt and **pepper**

2 tablespoons **butter**

1 **shallot**, finely chopped

½ tablespoon **all-purpose flour**

½ teaspoon **Worcestershire sauce**, a few dashes

¼ cup **dry red wine**

¼ cup **beef stock**

2 large **garlic cloves**, cracked and peeled

2 jumbo or colossal **shrimp**, peeled and deveined

A couple of sprigs of fresh **thyme**, leaves finely chopped

½ teaspoon **hot sauce**

Juice of ½ **lemon**

A generous handful of fresh **spinach leaves**

Freshly grated **nutmeg**

1 slice **white bread**, toasted

Why wait for date night? I am rarely self-conscious, but asking for a table for one in some restaurants can be daunting. So stay in! Celebrate *you*. Crack open a split of champagne or a half-bottle of red. You are worth it. (Besides, if someone else happens along, it's easily made for two.)

Heat a small stainless-steel or cast-iron skillet over high heat. Preheat the oven to 400°F.

Drizzle the meat with a little EVOO and season it liberally with salt and pepper. Sear the meat in the skillet for 2 minutes on each side, then transfer to a baking sheet and roast in the oven for 5 minutes for medium rare. Cool the skillet for 1 minute, then return to the stovetop over medium heat. Add a drizzle more oil and 1 tablespoon of the butter and, when it melts, add the shallots and cook for 1 to 2 minutes. Add the flour to the shallots and cook for 30 seconds, then stir in the Worcestershire sauce and red wine. Stir for 30 seconds more, then whisk in the stock and season the sauce with salt and pepper.

While the meat cooks, heat the 2 tablespoons of EVOO and the remaining tablespoon of butter in a small skillet over medium-high heat. Add the cracked garlic and toss around the skillet for 1 minute. Season the shrimp with salt and pepper, add the shrimp to the skillet, sprinkle in the thyme and hot sauce, and cook for 3 minutes, until the shrimp are opaque. Douse the shrimp with the juice of the ½ lemon and remove to plate. Add the spinach to the same pan, season with salt, pepper, and nutmeg, and cook for 1 minute to wilt.

Cut the toasted white bread corner to corner, then set the meat on the toast points and pour the gravy over the top. Serve the spinach and shrimp alongside the meat.

GREEN EGGS 'N' HAM FOR 1

This is an homage to my favorte Dr. Seuss book and one of my favorite meals for one. Many friends and chefs I know make their own versions of this dish, adding pesto or chopped spinach.

2 tablespoons **EVOO** (extra-virgin olive oil)

½ pound **ham steak**

½ cup **chicken stock**

½ cup **baby spinach leaves**, a big handful from the bulk bin

¼ cup fresh **basil**, 5 to 6 leaves

1 tablespoon **pine nuts**, toasted (see Note, page 102)

Salt and **pepper**

1 small **garlic clove**, grated or minced

A handful of freshly grated **Parmigiano-Reggiano**

2 large **eggs**

A splash of **milk**

A couple of dashes **hot sauce**

Butter, for toast

Sliced bread, for toast

Heat ½ tablespoon of the EVOO in a skillet over medium-high heat. Add the ham steak and cook for 3 minutes on each side to brown and heat through. Add ¼ cup of the stock to the pan to loosen the browned bits and drippings, and transfer the ham to a plate. Tent with foil to keep hot.

While the ham cooks, in a blender, mini chopper, or food processor combine the remaining ¼ cup stock with the spinach, basil, pine nuts, salt and pepper, garlic, cheese, and about 1 tablespoon of the EVOO. Process to make a smooth pesto.

Once the ham is cooked, wipe out the pan and heat the remaining ½ tablespoon of EVOO over medium heat. Beat the eggs with the milk, salt and pepper, and hot sauce. Scramble the eggs to your preferred degree of doneness, remove from the heat, and stir in the pesto. Pile the green eggs on the ham and serve with buttered toast.

PORK CHOP WITH CIDER GRAVY, SAUTÉED APPLES, AND ONIONS

This meal will make you an official Walton—a member of a large farm family.

1 (1-inch-thick) **bone-in pork chop**

Salt and **pepper**

1 tablespoon **EVOO** (extra-virgin olive oil)

1 small **onion**, yellow or red, thinly sliced

1 Gala or Golden Delicious **apple**, thinly sliced

2 to 3 sprigs of fresh **thyme**, leaves finely chopped

½ **lemon**

1 tablespoon **butter**

1 tablespoon **all-purpose flour**

½ cup cloudy **apple cider**

½ cup **chicken stock**

1 **corn muffin**, split, buttered, and toasted

Season the chop with salt and pepper. Heat ½ tablespoon of the EVOO in a medium skillet over medium-high heat. Cook the chop until golden, 3 to 4 minutes per side, tenting loosely with foil once you turn the chop. Remove the cooked chop to a plate and cover to keep warm. Add the remaining EVOO and the onions and apples. Season with salt, pepper, and the thyme and cook until just tender, 5 to 6 minutes, stirring occasionally. Douse with juice of the ½ lemon and remove to the plate with the chop.

Add 1 tablespoon of the butter to the skillet and when it melts, whisk in the flour. Cook for 1 minute, stirring, then whisk in the cider and stock. Season the gravy with salt and pepper. Cook over medium-low heat for 3 to 4 minutes to thicken.

Serve the chop covered with apples and onions, the gravy poured down over the top, and the muffin alongside.

CHILI MAC FOR ONE

Salt

¼ pound **macaroni** or elbow pasta

1 tablespoon **EVOO** (extra-virgin olive oil)

⅓ pound **ground sirloin**

Black pepper

1 **jalapeño pepper**, seeded and thinly sliced

½ medium **onion**, chopped

1 **garlic clove**, finely chopped

1 tablespoon **chili powder**

½ teaspoon **ground cumin**

½ teaspoon **ground coriander**

2 tablespoons **tomato paste**

1 cup **beef stock**

½ cup shredded **cheddar cheese**

In a perfect world we could always buy fresh ground beef in just the quantity we need. But sometimes I have to take what's in the packaged case. Packaged ground meat generally comes in 1-pound packages and family packages of 3 to 5 pounds. These recipes roll over from one night to the next in order to use up all of a 1-pound package without resorting to leftovers: goulash to shepherd's pie, burgers to chili mac.

Bring a pot of water to a boil for the pasta. When it boils, salt the water, add the pasta, and cook to al dente.

While the pasta cooks, heat the EVOO in a skillet over medium-high heat. Add the meat and brown for 3 to 4 minutes, breaking it up as it cooks, and season with salt and pepper. Add the jalapeño, onions, and garlic and cook for 2 to 3 minutes more, then season with the chili powder, cumin, and coriander. Stir in the tomato paste, cook for 2 minutes, then stir in the stock and reduce the heat to low. Simmer the chili for 5 minutes. Stir in the pasta and cheese and serve.

1 large or 2 medium **Idaho potatoes**, peeled and diced

Salt

1 tablespoon plus 1 pat **butter**

2 tablespoons **sour cream**

¼ cup **milk**

3 tablespoons chopped **chives**

1 **egg yolk**

Dash of **hot sauce**

Black pepper

1 tablespoon **EVOO** (extra-virgin olive oil)

⅔ pound **ground sirloin**

1 **bay leaf**

1 small **garlic clove**, grated

½ medium **onion**, chopped

¼ cup shredded **carrots**, a handful, chopped into small bits

1 **celery stalk**, chopped

1 tablespoon **all-purpose flour**

½ cup **beef stock**

2 tablespoons **steak sauce**

A small handful of frozen **peas**

Paprika, for garnish

SINGLE GUY (OR GAL) SHEPHERD'S PIE

In a sauce pot, cover the potatoes with water and bring to a boil. Salt the water and cook the potatoes until tender, 12 to 15 minutes. Drain the potatoes and mash with 1 teaspoon of the butter, the sour cream, milk, chives, egg yolk, hot sauce, and salt and pepper.

While the potatoes cook, heat the EVOO in a medium skillet over medium-high heat. Add the meat and brown, breaking it into crumbles, for 3 to 4 minutes. Add the bay leaf, garlic if using, and onion, carrot, and celery, season with salt and pepper, and cook until the vegetables are tender, 4 to 5 minutes. Push the meat and vegetables off to the side of the pan and add the remaining 1 tablespoon of the butter to the middle of the pan. When it melts, stir in the flour, cook for 30 seconds, then whisk in the stock and steak sauce. Combine the gravy with the meat and vegetables, stir in the peas, and heat through for a minute or two. Taste to adjust the seasoning. Discard the bay leaf.

Preheat the broiler.

Transfer the meat mixture to a small casserole, large ramekin, or serving dish and top with the potatoes. Brown the potatoes for 3 to 4 minutes under the broiler and garnish with paprika.

ITALIAN BBQ CHICKEN
WITH POLENTA

1 bone-in **chicken thigh and leg** or **chicken breast**

Salt and **pepper**

1 teaspoon **poultry seasoning**

2 tablespoons **EVOO** (extra-virgin olive oil)

1 slice of **pancetta** or bacon, chopped (optional)

½ medium **red onion**, chopped

1 **garlic clove**, finely chopped

2 tablespoons **balsamic vinegar**

1 tablespoon **brown sugar**

1 teaspoon **Worcestershire sauce**

½ cup **tomato sauce**

1 cup **chicken stock**

½ cup **milk**

⅓ cup **quick-cooking polenta**

1 tablespoon **butter**

¼ cup freshly grated **Parmigiano-Reggiano cheese**

A few leaves of fresh **basil**, torn

Serve this with a green salad or steamed vegetables.

Preheat the oven to 400°F. Place a baking sheet in the oven to heat.

Season the chicken liberally with salt and pepper and poultry seasoning. Heat 1 tablespoon of the EVOO in a skillet and brown the chicken for a few minutes on each side to put some of its flavor and drippings into the pan, then transfer to the heated baking sheet and place in the oven. Roast the chicken for 15 minutes or until the juices run clear.

Meanwhile, add the remaining tablespoon of EVOO to the skillet and add the pancetta if using. Cook until crisp, 3 to 4 minutes, then add the onions and garlic and cook for 5 minutes. Add the vinegar, brown sugar, Worcestershire, tomato sauce, and ½ cup of the chicken stock, reduce the heat to low, and let the sauce simmer for 5 minutes more.

Bring the remaining ½ cup stock and the milk to a boil in a sauce pot. Whisk in the polenta and season with salt and pepper and cook, whisking, for 2 to 3 minutes, until it thickens. Stir in the butter and cheese and remove from the heat.

Serve the chicken oven polenta, topped with the barbecue sauce and basil.

CHICKEN AND DIJON-TARRAGON GRAVY OVER EGG NOODLES WITH ASPARAGUS TIPS

Bring a pot of water to a boil for the egg noodles.

While the water comes to a boil, heat the EVOO with the cracked garlic in a skillet over medium-high heat. Season the chicken with salt and pepper and cook in the garlic oil for 6 minutes on each side. Transfer the chicken to a plate and discard the garlic. Cover the chicken loosely with foil to keep warm. Add 1 tablespoon of the butter to the skillet the chicken was cooked in and reduce the heat a little. Whisk the flour with the melted butter for 1 minute, then whisk in the stock and simmer for 3 to 5 minutes, or until reduced and thickened. Season with salt and pepper.

Salt the boiling water and cook the egg noodles until al dente, 5 to 6 minutes. During the last minute or two of cooking, drop in the asparagus tips. Drain the noodles and asparagus and toss with the remaining ½ tablespoon butter.

Slice the chicken on an angle. Place the noodles and asparagus in a shallow bowl and top with the chicken.

Add the mustard and tarragon to the gravy, then stir in the cream and heat through. Pour the gravy over the noodles and chicken.

1 tablespoon **EVOO** (extra-virgin olive oil)

1 **garlic clove**, cracked away from the skin

1 boneless skinless **chicken breast half**

Salt and **pepper**

1½ tablespoons **butter**

1 tablespoon **all-purpose flour**

1 cup **chicken stock**

¼ pound **extra-wide egg noodles**

Half of a 10-ounce box **frozen tender asparagus tips**

1 rounded tablespoon **grainy Dijon mustard**

2 to 3 sprigs of fresh **tarragon**, leaves stripped from the stems and chopped

2 tablespoons **heavy cream** or half-and-half

CHICKEN AND BISCUIT

When the meat counter is closed or the line is too long, you are stuck buying packages of three pieces of chicken breast. Rather than making a big batch of something you'll reheat for the next three nights, use these next few recipes to rollover the extra breasts into new recipes. A family favorite of mine is the Italian BBQ Chicken (page 209), but these recipes are classic comforts, not to be ignored or replaced in your repertoire.

Heat the EVOO in a medium skillet over medium-high heat. Add the chicken, season with salt and pepper and sauté until lightly browned on each side, about 3 minutes. Add the thyme, mushrooms, and onions to the chicken and cook until the vegetables are tender, 5 minutes more. Add the peas and carrots to the pan, stir, and scoot the mixture to the sides of the pan. Add the butter to the space you've cleared and when it melts, whisk in the flour and cook, stirring, for 1 minute. Whisk in the stock and mix the sauce with the chicken and vegetables. Simmer everything together for a couple of minutes to thicken. Stir in the Dijon or hot sauce, if using, then transfer to a shallow bowl and top with the warm split biscuit, or split the biscuit and ladle the chicken mixture on top.

1 tablespoon **EVOO** (extra-virgin olive oil)

1 boneless skinless **chicken breast half**, diced into small bites

Salt and **pepper**

A few sprigs of fresh **thyme**, leaves stripped and finely chopped

3 to 4 **button mushrooms**, trimmed and thinly sliced

½ small **onion**, chopped

1 cup **frozen peas and carrots**

2 tablespoons **butter**

1 rounded tablespoon **all-purpose flour**

1 cup **chicken stock**

1 teaspoon **Dijon mustard** or 1 or 2 dashes of **hot sauce** (optional)

1 store-bought **biscuit**, warmed and split

M.Y.O.T.O.
DEVILISH SESAME CHICKEN WITH GREEN BEANS AND SCALLION RICE

If you walk on the spicy side, this one's for you! As always, the reason to make your own takeout is to take control of the fat and the quality of the ingredients. Plus, if you order Chinese food, you end up eating three or four portions rather than one.

In a small skillet heat ½ tablespoon of the oil over medium-high heat. Add the rice and toast for a minute or two, then add ½ cup of the chicken stock. Stir and reduce the heat to low, cover the pan with a small plate or aluminum foil, and cook until the rice is tender, about 17 minutes. Add the scallions to the rice in the last minute of cooking time.

Bring 1 inch of water to a boil in a second small pan and salt it. Add the beans and cook for 2 minutes, then drain them and run them under cold water to set the green color. Set aside.

When the rice has cooked for about 8 minutes, heat the remaining ½ tablespoon of oil in a skillet over high heat until it ripples. Add the chicken and cook until it is lightly golden, 3 to 4 minutes. Add the bell pepper and cook for 2 to 3 minutes more.

In a small bowl, mix together the hot sauce, mustard, tamari, honey, and the remaining ¼ cup of chicken stock.

Add the green beans to the chicken and peppers and toss for 1 minute. Pour the sauce over the chicken and vegetables and toss for a minute or two to heat through. Remove from the heat and drizzle sesame oil over the chicken.

Fluff the rice with a fork and transfer to a shallow bowl. Top with the chicken and garnish with the sesame seeds.

1 tablespoon **canola** or **vegetable oil**

¼ cup **white rice**

¾ cup **chicken stock**

2 **scallions**, finely chopped

Salt

A handful of **green beans**, trimmed

1 boneless skinless **chicken breast half**, thinly sliced

½ **red bell pepper**, seeded and thinly sliced

1 teaspoon **hot sauce**

1 rounded teaspoon **Dijon mustard**

1 tablespoon **tamari** (aged soy sauce)

1 tablespoon **honey**

1 teaspoon **sesame oil**

2 teaspoons toasted **sesame seeds**

Salt

¼ pound whole wheat **penne**

1 tablespoon **EVOO** (extra-virgin olive oil)

1 boneless skinless **chicken breast half**, thinly sliced

1 **portabella mushroom cap**, thinly sliced

½ **red bell pepper**, seeded and thinly sliced

¾ small **onion**, thinly sliced

1 **garlic clove**, chopped

A pinch of **crushed red pepper flakes**

Black pepper

¼ cup **dry red wine**

¼ cup **chicken stock**

1 (15-ounce) can **diced or crushed tomatoes**

1 tablespoon chopped fresh flat-leaf **parsley**

Pecorino Romano cheese, for grating

CHICKEN CACCIATORE WITH PENNE

In my family, hunter's chicken is served on the bone and flavored primarily with wild mushrooms and wine. Other Italian-American versions of cacciatore include peppers and onions and some have no mushrooms at all. Here, I make a fast version with the works— feel free to adjust as you see fit.

Bring a pot of water to a boil for the pasta. When it boils, salt the water, add the pasta, and cook to al dente.

While the water comes to a boil, heat the EVOO in a large skillet over medium-high heat. Add the chicken and lightly brown on both sides, 2 to 3 minutes, then add vegetables and cook until tender, 5 to 6 minutes. Season the vegetables with red pepper flakes, salt, and black pepper. Stir in the wine, then add the stock, stir, add the tomatoes, and stir in the parsley.

Drain the pasta, toss with the sauce, and add cheese to taste.

1 boneless skinless **chicken breast half**

½ teaspoon **ground cumin**

½ teaspoon **ground coriander**

½ teaspoon **chili powder**

Salt and **pepper**

Grated zest and juice of 1 **lime**

1 teaspoon **hot sauce**

1 tablespoon **canola or other vegetable oil**

1 small ripe **avocado**

1 **serrano chile**, seeded and finely chopped

1 small **garlic clove**, grated or minced

¼ small **onion**, finely chopped

1 small **plum tomato**, seeded and chopped

1 **crusty Kaiser roll**, split and lightly toasted

2 **lettuce leaves**, any variety

1 single-serving bag of **tortilla chips**

TEX-MEX CHICKEN SAMMIE

Tex-Mex and Mexican dishes are often translated into heavy, fat-laden food. This is a fun, fast, and healthful choice for supper, leaving you room (and calories) for an icy Corona or margarita.

Season the chicken breast with the cumin, coriander, chili powder, salt and pepper, 1 teaspoon of the lime zest, the hot sauce, and the oil. Heat a skillet or grill pan and cook the chicken over medium-high heat for 6 minutes on each side.

While the chicken cooks, mash the avocado with the lime juice, chopped serrano pepper, garlic, onion, and tomato, then season with salt.

Slice the cooked chicken on an angle. Pile the chicken slices on the bun bottom and top with lettuce, a generous scoop of the guacamole, and the bun top. Serve the remainder of the guac alongside with the chips.

SEARED SALMON WITH POTATO-CHORIZO RAGÙ

2 tablespoons **EVOO** (extra-virgin olive oil)

¼ pound **Spanish chorizo**, casings removed, chopped

1 large **Yukon Gold potato**, cut into quarters, then thinly sliced

½ small **onion**, chopped

¼ cup **dry white wine** (eyeball it)

¾ cup **chicken stock** (eyeball it)

1 (6-ounce) **salmon fillet**

Salt and **pepper**

A handful of fresh flat-leaf **parsley leaves**, coarsely chopped

Salmon is the perfect fish to cook for one, and so versatile as these four recipes show. The chorizo supper has a Spanish twist, creamy corn gives a wink to New England cookery, and the mango-lemon slaw brings out the tropical edge. These recipes are equally delish made with mahi mahi, orange roughy, halibut, snapper, or even sea bass, so go and hook whatever looks freshest at the market for any of these simple fishy suppers.

Preheat a small skillet over medium-high heat with 1 tablespoon of the EVOO. Once the oil is hot, add the chorizo and cook, stirring every now and then, for 2 to 3 minutes. Add the potatoes and onions and continue to cook for 8 to 10 minutes, or until the potatoes are tender. Add the wine and stock and simmer until lightly thickened, a couple of minutes.

Once you have the potatoes in the skillet with the chorizo, heat a second small nonstick skillet over medium-high heat with the remaining tablespoon of EVOO. While the skillet is heating, season the salmon with some salt and pepper. When the oil ripples, add the fish, skin side down, and cook for 3 to 4 minutes on each side.

Once the liquids in the skillet with the potatoes have thickened up, remove the skillet from the heat and stir in the parsley. Transfer the potato mixture to a plate and top with the seared salmon fillet.

SEARED SALMON FILLET WITH CUCUMBER DILL SALSA

1 tablespoon **EVOO** (extra-virgin olive oil)

1 (6-ounce) **salmon fillet**

Salt and **pepper**

1 slice of **rye bread**

1 **kirby cucumber**, quartered lengthwise and chopped

3 tablespoons fresh **dill**, chopped

2 tablespoons **sour cream**

¼ small **red onion**, finely chopped

¼ cup chopped fresh flat-leaf **parsley**

1 teaspoon grated **lemon zest** plus the **juice of ½ lemon**

What's cooler than a cucumber? This is: a really easy, really good-for-you, fast-to-prepare salmon supper.

Heat the EVOO in a small nonstick skillet over medium-high heat. While the skillet is heating, season the salmon with some salt and pepper. When the oil ripples, add the seasoned salmon skin side down, and cook for 3 to 4 minutes on each side.

While the salmon is cooking, toast up the rye bread and prepare the cucumber dill salsa. In a bowl stir together the chopped cucumber, dill, sour cream, red onion, parsley, lemon zest and juice, and a little salt and pepper.

Remove the salmon from the skillet to a plate and top with the cucumber dill salsa. Place the toast alongside.

CHILI-RUBBED SALMON STEAK WITH CREAMY SWEET CORN

For the creamy sweet corn, place a medium skillet over medium-high heat with 1 tablespoon of the EVOO. Once the oil is hot, add the onions and garlic and cook until the onions start to get tender, 3 to 4 minutes. Add the corn and jalapeño, season with salt and pepper, and cook for another 2 to 3 minutes. Add the chicken stock and half-and-half and simmer until the sauce has thickened and the corn is tender and cooked through, 5 to 6 minutes.

Once you have the onions working for the creamy corn, start the salmon. Drizzle the salmon steak with ½ tablespoon of the EVOO, season with a little salt and pepper, and sprinkle with the chili powder. Rub the salmon to make sure the chili powder coats it entirely. Preheat a small skillet over medium-high heat with the remaining ½ tablespoon of EVOO. Once you see a ripple in the oil, add the salmon steak and cook for 3 to 4 minutes on each side or until cooked through. Turn the heat off under the salmon and squeeze the ½ lime over the fish.

Place the creamy sweet corn on a plate, top with the salmon steak, and sprinkle with the chopped scallions.

- 2 tablespoons **EVOO** (extra-virgin olive oil)
- ½ small **onion**, finely chopped
- 1 **garlic clove**, grated or finely chopped
- 1 **ear of corn**, shucked and kernels cut off with a sharp knife
- 1 small **jalapeño pepper**, seeded and finely chopped
- **Salt** and **pepper**
- ½ cup **chicken stock**
- 2 tablespoons **half and half** or heavy cream
- 1 (6-ounce) **salmon steak**
- 1 teaspoon **chili powder**, ⅓ palmful
- ½ **lime**
- 1 **scallion**, chopped

BBQ SALMON WITH MANGO-LEMON SLAW

In a bowl combine the lemon juice with the mustard and whisk in 2 tablespoons of the EVOO. Add the red onion, cabbage, and mango. Season with some salt and pepper and toss to combine. Set the slaw to the side while you get the salmon together.

In a bowl, combine the barbecue sauce with the tamari and orange juice.

Preheat a small nonstick skillet over medium-high heat with 1 tablespoon of the EVOO. Season the salmon with some salt and pepper. Once you see the oil start to ripple in the skillet, add the seasoned salmon and cook for 3 minutes on one side. Flip the salmon over, cook for 2 minutes more, then pour the barbecue sauce over the salmon and cook for another 2 minutes.

Plate the barbecue salmon alongside the mango-lemon slaw.

- Juice of ½ **lemon**
- 1 rounded teaspoon **Dijon mustard**
- 3 tablespoons **EVOO** (extra-virgin olive oil)
- ¼ small **red onion**, thinly sliced
- 1 cup store-bought **shredded cabbage** for slaw salad
- 1 small **ripe mango**, peeled, flesh chopped into small pieces
- **Salt** and **pepper**
- 2 tablespoons of your favorite store-bought **barbecue sauce**
- 2 tablespoons **tamari**
- 2 tablespoons fresh **orange juice**
- 1 (6-ounce) **salmon fillet**

CRISPY THAI-STYLE SEARED SNAPPER IN COCONUT-LIME BROTH

3 tablespoons **vegetable oil**

½ small **onion**, thinly sliced

1 small **garlic clove**, grated or finely chopped

1 small **jalapeño**, seeded and thinly sliced

½ inch of fresh **gingerroot**, peeled and grated or minced

Salt and **pepper**

¼ cup **sweetened shredded coconut**, toasted (see Note)

1½ cups **chicken stock**

1 (6- to 8-ounce) **snapper fillet**

½ cup **cornstarch** (eyeball it)

1 handful of **sugar snap peas**, thinly sliced lengthwise

Grated zest and juice of 1 **lime**

A small handful of **cilantro leaves**, coarsely chopped

NOTE Toast coconut in a dry skillet over medium heat, stirring often, for 2 to 3 minutes.

EXOTIC! If you want to really sweeten up a ho-hum night, try this Thai-licious treat.

Heat 1 tablespoon of the oil in a medium skillet over medium heat. Add the sliced onion, garlic, jalapeño, and ginger. Season with some salt and pepper and cook for 3 minutes, stirring frequently. Add the toasted coconut and the chicken stock and bring up to a bubble, then turn the heat down to medium and simmer for 5 minutes.

Once you have the chicken stock in the skillet, start on the snapper. With a sharp paring knife, score the skin side of the fish with a crosshatch pattern. Place the cornstarch on a plate. Preheat a second small skillet over medium-high heat with the remaining 2 tablespoons of oil. Season the fish with some salt and pepper and then dredge it in the cornstarch, coating it evenly and shaking off the excess. Once the skillet is hot, add the fish, skin side down, pressing the fillet down onto the hot skillet to make sure that the entire skin side of the fish is making contact. Cook the fish for 3 to 4 minutes on each side or until golden and crispy.

Once you have flipped the snapper in the skillet, add the sugar snap peas to the simmering coconut broth. Add the lime zest and juice and the cilantro and remove from the heat. Transfer the brothy coconut sauce to a large shallow bowl and top with the crispy snapper.

MAHIMAHI MUCHO-GUSTO FISH BURRITO

1 (6-ounce) **mahimahi fillet**

2 tablespoons **vegetable oil**

2 **limes**

1 tablespoon **chili powder**

1 teaspoon **ground cumin**

Salt

1 cup shredded **cabbage**

1 small ripe **avocado**

1 **garlic clove**, peeled and grated

1 small **jalapeño** or serrano pepper

¼ red **onion**, finely chopped

1 large (12-inch) **flour tortilla**

Rub the fish with ½ tablespoon of the oil and season with 1 teaspoon of grated lime zest, the chili powder, cumin, and salt. Heat about ½ tablespoon of the oil in a small skillet over medium-high heat and cook the fish for 7 to 8 minutes, turning once. Break the fillet into flakes with a fork.

Place the avocado in a bowl and douse with the remaining juice of 1 lime. Grate the garlic into the avocado, mash the avocado with the jalapeño and onion, and season with salt. Dress the cabbage with the juice of 1 lime, the remaining tablespoon of vegetable oil, and a little salt.

Heat a large skillet over high heat. Add the tortilla and blister for 30 seconds on each side. Pile the cabbage onto the tortilla and top with the fish and the chunky guacamole. Wrap the burrito by tucking in the ends and rolling.

THYME AND GARLIC BUTTER BRAISED SKATE WITH ROASTED ASPARAGUS

Fish braised in butter is a delicate, rich preparation but it is also decidedly easy. If you want to feel like a multi-star chef for a night, give this one a try.

½ pound thin **asparagus spears**, trimmed of woody ends

1 tablespoon **EVOO** (extra-virgin olive oil)

Salt and **pepper**

1 (6- to 8-ounce) **skate fillet**

4 tablespoons (½ stick) **butter**

1 large **garlic clove**, cracked away from its skin

3 sprigs of fresh **thyme**

A chunk of **crusty bread**

Preheat the oven to 425°F.

Spread the trimmed asparagus spears on a rimmed baking sheet or in a small dish, drizzle with the EVOO, and season with salt and pepper. Roast the asparagus for 10 to 12 minutes, or until tender and starting to brown.

Once the asparagus is in the oven, season the skate with some salt and pepper. Place a small skillet over medium heat and add the butter, garlic, and thyme. When the butter has just melted and started to bubble, add the skate. Use a spoon to baste the fish with the butter every minute or so as it cooks, tilting the pan to scoop the butter up into the spoon. Keep basting the fish with the hot butter until the fish is cooked through, 7 to 8 minutes; the hot butter will cook the top of the fish so there will be no need to flip the fish in the skillet.

Transfer the fish to a plate and discard the remaining butter, garlic, and thyme sprigs; they've done their job. Serve with the roasted asparagus and a chunk of crusty bread.

DAL WITH RAITA AND FLATBREADS

Inexpensive, flavorful, and souful, this dish will convert anyone to the vegetarian way, at least for the night.

1 tablespoon **EVOO** (extra-virgin olive oil)

½ teaspoon **ground cumin**

½ **onion**, chopped

2 small **garlic cloves**, one crushed, one grated or finely minced

1 inch of fresh **gingerroot**, peeled and grated or finely chopped

Salt and **pepper**

½ cup red, brown, or yellow **lentils**

2 cups **vegetable stock**

1 **kirby cucumber**, finely chopped

½ small handful of fresh **mint leaves**, coarsely chopped

½ cup plain **Greek yogurt**

Whole wheat flatbreads such as pita bread

Heat the EVOO in a medium pot over medium heat. Add the cumin and the onions, the crushed garlic clove, the ginger, and some salt and pepper. Cook, stirring frequently, for 2 to 3 minutes. Add the lentils, stir to coat with the seasonings, then add the vegetable stock and bring up to a bubble. Partially cover the pot and simmer for 20 minutes, or until the lentils are tender.

While the lentils are cooking, prepare the raita. In a bowl combine the cucumber with the grated or minced garlic, the mint, yogurt, and some salt and pepper. Stir to mix thoroughly.

Warm the flatbreads in a toaster or in the oven.

Serve the dal topped with raita and eat with the warm flatbreads.

SUPERSIZED BEANS AND GREENS STOUP

2 tablespoons **EVOO** (extra-virgin olive oil)

2 ⅛-inch thick slices of **pancetta**, chopped

2 **garlic cloves**, finely chopped

1 small head of **escarole**, leaves separated and coarsely chopped

Freshly grated **nutmeg**

1 (15-ounce) can **butter beans**, rinsed and drained

Salt and **pepper**

2 cups **chicken stock**

1 teaspoon grated **lemon zest**

Crusty bread or roll

Freshly grated **Parmigiano-Reggiano**, for topping

I love to use gigante beans (also called butter beans) to give a fun twist to the old standby minestra, an Italian escarole and cannellini bean soup. If you cannot find butter beans in your market, by all means go traditional and use cannellini.

Heat the EVOO in a high-sided skillet over medium-high heat. Add the pancetta and cook until it starts to crisp, 3 to 4 minutes. Add the garlic and stir for 1 minute. Wilt in the escarole a handful at a time, and when it is all added, season with the nutmeg. Fold the beans into the escarole and season with salt and pepper. Stir in the chicken stock and bring to a boil. Stir in the lemon zest and remove from the heat. Serve in a large shallow bowl with the bread for mopping and the cheese for topping.

SAUSAGE WITH GARLIC LENTILS

¼ pound **lentils**

1 fresh or dried **bay leaf**

1 small **onion**, peeled and halved

2 **garlic cloves**, grated or minced

¼ cup **EVOO** (extra-virgin olive oil)

2 fresh **sausages**, pork, chicken, or lamb, hot or sweet

1 cup baby **arugula**

1 teaspoon **aged balsamic vinegar**

Salt and **pepper**

2 tablespoons finely chopped fresh flat-leaf **parsley**

This is pure comfort food. The garlic lentils are a fabulous first course for entertaining and with braised sausage of any kind they make a flavorful, hearty meal.

Place the lentils in a sauce pot with water to cover by 2 inches. Add the bay leaf and onion halves and bring to a boil. Boil the lentils for 20 to 22 minutes, until just tender but with a little bite left to them. Discard the bay leaf.

Once the lentils are cooking, combine the garlic and about 3 tablespoons of the EVOO in a shallow pasta bowl and let stand.

Place the sausages in a small pan and add ¼ inch water and 1 teaspoon EVOO, a little drizzle. Bring the water to a boil over high heat, then reduce the heat to medium-high. Let the water simmer away for 8 minutes or so, then cook for 3 to 4 minutes more to crisp the casings.

Dress the greens in the balsamic (just eyeball the amount), the remaining 2 teaspoons of EVOO, and salt and pepper.

Drain the lentils and add to the garlic oil along with the parsley. Toss to combine and serve with the sausages on top and the arugula alongside or on top for mixing in.

A LITTLE MORE THAN 30 MINUTES . . . BUT WORTH IT

Because my daytime show is an hour long I have gotten to expand my horizons a bit from my original 30-minute formula so for a couple of years now I've also been creating 60-minute meals. These recipes are no harder to make than 30-minute meals, they just take their time cooking.

I usually cook these recipes when I can take a day off or work from home—times when I can mellow out. In addition to my latest 60-minute meals I've included a few favorite dishes that take even longer but are worth the investment—even for me, the most impatient cook in the kitchen. The Braised Short Ribs with Roasted Beets and Polenta is probably the most complex recipe in this book, but I daydream about the results. I garnish the dish with bitter-sweet ruby pomegranate seeds; they are optional, but do try to find them even if you have to look at two stores. The jewellike tah-da they add is really something.

ELSA'S BEEF AND BURGUNDY

I've devoted a whole chapter of this book to recipes from my mom as well as my mother-in-law—their recipes, exactly the way they make them. This one is *my* best attempt (my fifth, actually) to get Mom's beef 'n' burgundy right—and I think I've finally done it.

3 tablespoons **EVOO** (extra-virgin olive oil), plus additional as needed

4 slices of **bacon**, chopped

2½ pounds **sirloin or sirloin tips**, cut into large, bite-size pieces

Salt and **pepper**

⅓ bottle (about 1 cup) **red burgundy wine**

2 cups **beef stock** (eyeball it)

1 package **frozen pearl onions**

2 teaspoons **sugar** (about ⅓ palmful)

5 tablespoons **butter**

½ pound **mushrooms**, quartered

1 pound **wide egg noodles**

A handful of fresh **chives**, minced

2 tablespoons **all-purpose flour**

1 teaspoon grated **orange zest**

Preheat the oven to 375°F.

Heat 2 tablespoons of the EVOO in a Dutch oven or oven-safe, heavy-bottomed pot over medium-high heat. Add the bacon and cook until crisp, 4 to 5 minutes. Remove the bacon to a paper-towel-lined plate.

While the bacon browns, season the chopped sirloin with salt and pepper. Working in 2 batches, brown the meat in the hot bacon fat, stirring occasionally, until deep golden brown, about 10 minutes. Transfer the browned meat to a plate as each batch is browned, adding more EVOO as needed.

Add the wine to the pot and deglaze the pan, scraping up any brown bits from the bottom of the pan with a wooden spoon. Bring the wine to a bubble and cook for a couple of minutes to reduce it, then add the beef stock. Return the meat and bacon to the pot, cover the pot, and transfer it to the oven. Bake for 90 minutes.

When the meat has cooked for 60 minutes, place the onions, sugar, and a splash of water in a small sauté pan. Cook over medium-high heat until the water has evaporated and the onions are tender and heated through, 4 to 5 minutes. Reserve and keep warm.

While the onions are cooking, heat a medium skillet with 1 tablespoon of the butter and the remaining tablespoon of EVOO, over medium-high heat. Add the mushrooms and cook until tender and golden brown, about 10 minutes, then season with salt and pepper. Reserve and keep warm.

Bring a large pot of water to a boil for the noodles. Add some salt and the noodles and cook to al dente. Drain the noodles and return them to the pot. Add 2 tablespoons of the butter and the minced chives; toss to combine.

After 90 minutes, remove the beef from the oven and place the pot over medium-high heat. Add the onions and mushrooms to the pot and bring the stew up to a bubble. Place the pan the mushrooms were cooked in over medium-high heat and melt the remaining 2 tablespoons of butter. Sprinkle the flour over the butter and cook the mixture for about 1 minute. Ladle about 1 cup of the liquid from the Dutch oven into the skillet with the roux and whisk to combine. Cook for a minute or two to thicken, then stir the sauce back into the stew. Simmer the stew until thickened, 5 to 6 minutes. Stir in the orange zest. Serve the stew over the buttered noodles.

SERVES 6

BIG BOY SUGO

Sugo is a thick meat sauce similar in consistency to Bolognese but made from pork rather than beef. The pork is hand-cut so the sauce is pretty labor-intensive and I only have the patience to make it a couple of times a year, but as far as I am concerned, it is the tastiest meat sauce you can belly up to. I serve it with either pasta or polenta; both options please me, so the decision comes down to the preferences of those I'm cooking for.

Place the mushrooms and stock in a medium pot. Bring to a bubble over high heat, then reduce the heat to low and let the mushrooms steep in the stock for 5 to 10 minutes.

Place a heavy-bottomed pot over medium-high heat and add the EVOO. Add the pancetta and cook until golden and crispy, 3 to 4 minutes, then remove it to a small plate, keeping as much of the fat in the pan as possible. Add the diced pork to the pan, season it with salt and pepper and the allspice, and cook until the pork is golden brown and a crust forms in the bottom of the pot.

Return the pancetta to the pan and add the onions, carrot, celery, garlic, portabellas, bay leaf, and sage. Cook this mixture until the veggies are very tender, about 10 minutes. Add the wine and stir with a wooden spoon to scrape up the crust from the bottom of the pan. Stir in the tomato paste and cook for 2 minutes. Lift the reconstituted mushrooms out of the stock with a slotted spoon and chop them. Add the mushrooms to the pot, then stir in the 3½ cups of mushroom-fortified stock a few ladles at a time. Reduce the heat under the sugo to low and simmer for 30 minutes.

Stir in the tomatoes, break them up with a wooden spoon, and simmer for 30 minutes more, or until the meat is very tender and the sauce is very thick. Discard the bay leaf and adjust the seasonings. The sugo should be thick but not stiff. If it is too thick, add more of the mushroom stock, leaving the last few spoonfuls of stock in the pot as the mushrooms may have released some grit while they were soaking.

To serve with pasta After the stew has been cooking for about 30 minutes, place a large pot of water over high heat and bring it to a boil. Salt the water, add the pasta, and cook to al dente. Drain the pasta and toss with half the sugo and the grated Parmigiano. Combine the ricotta with the parsley and honey. Serve the sugo and pasta in shallow bowls topped with extra sauce and a generous couple of spoonfuls of ricotta to stir in.

1 ounce **dried porcini mushrooms**

4 cups **chicken stock**

2 tablespoons **EVOO** (extra-virgin olive oil)

¼ pound sliced **pancetta**, chopped into fine dice

1½ pounds **pork shoulder**, some of the fat and all connective tissue removed, chopped into ¼-inch dice

Salt and **pepper**

½ teaspoon ground **allspice** (eyeball it in your palm)

1 large **onion**, finely chopped

1 **carrot**, peeled and finely chopped or grated

2 to 3 **celery stalks** from the heart, finely chopped

3 to 4 **garlic cloves**, finely chopped or grated

2 **portabella mushrooms**, chopped

1 fresh **bay leaf**

2 tablespoons finely chopped fresh **sage**, 7 to 8 leaves

1 cup **dry red wine** (eyeball it)

3 tablespoons **tomato paste** (eyeball it)

1 (28-ounce) can **San Marzano tomatoes** or other plum tomatoes

To serve the sugo with pasta

Salt

1 pound **rigatoni**, regular or whole wheat

½ cup grated **Parmigiano-Reggiano**, plus some to pass at the table

Ricotta cheese, to pass at the table

A handful of fresh flat-leaf **parsley**, finely chopped

A healthy drizzle of **honey**

To serve the sugo with polenta

1½ cups **chicken stock**

1½ cups **milk**

1 cup **quick-cooking polenta**

2 tablespoons **butter**

½ cup grated **Parmigiano-Reggiano**, plus some to pass at the table

A healthy drizzle of **honey**

To serve with polenta When the sauce is ready to serve, bring the chicken stock and milk to a boil over medium-high heat in a sauce pot. Whisk in the polenta and cook for 2 to 3 minutes until the polenta thickens. Stir in the butter, Parmigiano, honey, and salt and pepper to taste. Serve the polenta in shallow bowls topped with a generous ladle of sugo. Pass extra cheese at the table.

SERVES 4 BIG BOYS OR 6 NORMAL PEOPLE

SICILIAN MEATBALLS

6 slices of **white bread**, torn in pieces

1 cup **milk**

2 tablespoons **EVOO** (extra-virgin olive oil)

1 (28-ounce) can **San Marzano tomatoes** or other plum tomatoes

1 (15-ounce) can **San Marzano tomatoes** or other plum tomatoes

Salt and **pepper**

2½ pounds **ground sirloin**

6 **garlic cloves**, minced or grated

A generous handful of finely chopped fresh flat-leaf **parsley**

1 teaspoon dried **oregano**

1 teaspoon **crushed red pepper flakes**

½ teaspoon ground **allspice**

1 cup grated **Parmigiano-Reggiano**, 4 handfuls

⅓ cup **pine nuts**, a rounded handful, toasted (see Note, page 102) and chopped

¼ cup **currants**, a handful

1 **egg**, lightly beaten

1 loaf of **ciabatta bread** or other crusty bread

1 cup fresh **ricotta cheese**

¼ cup fresh **basil leaves**, 6 to 7 leaves, shredded or torn

These HUGE big-flavored beef meatballs are a spicy favorite of two guys I truly love, my husband, John, and our friend Danny DeVito, who really knows how to take a bite outta life.

Preheat the oven to 425°F.

Place the torn-up bread in a small bowl and pour the milk over it; set aside to soak.

Place a roasting pan on the counter. Add a healthy drizzle of EVOO to the pan, about 1 tablespoon. Add the canned tomatoes to the pan and crush with a potato masher or a wooden spoon. Season the tomatoes liberally with salt and pepper.

In a large bowl, using your hands, combine the ground sirloin, the remaining tablespoon of EVOO, the garlic, parsley, oregano, red pepper flakes, allspice, Parmigiano, pine nuts, currants, egg, and salt and pepper. Squeeze out the excess milk from the soaking bread—it should be loose and in small pieces—then add it to the meat mixture. Discard the milk.

Form the meatball mixture into 12 baseball-size balls, each about 3 inches in diameter, and place them in the roasting pan, nestling them into the tomatoes. Roast until the meatballs are brown and cooked through, about 30 minutes.

Place the ciabatta, unwrapped, in the oven to heat when the meatballs are just about done. Tear the warm, crusty bread into large pieces.

Remove the meatballs from the oven and arrange the torn pieces of crusty bread in and around the meatballs and sauce. Stir the ricotta cheese together with the basil, season with salt and pepper, and pass at the table. Complement each serving of 2 large meatballs with 2 to 3 tablespoons of cool ricotta spooned alongside.

SERVES 6

BRAISED SHORT RIBS WITH ROASTED BEETS AND CREAMY POLENTA

6 tablespoons **EVOO** (extra-virgin olive oil)

12 3-inch pieces of **beef short ribs**
Salt and **pepper**

½ cup plus 3 tablespoons **all-purpose flour**

1 (24-ounce) bottle **pomegranate juice**

1 tablespoon sweet **smoked paprika**, a palmful

1½ teaspoons **ground allspice**, ½ palmful

1 fresh **bay leaf**

6 cups **beef stock**

6 **red beets**, stems and root ends trimmed, tender greens cleaned and reserved (discard any tough or bruised greens)

1 large **red onion**, halved then cut into thick slices

5 to 6 **celery stalks** from the heart, cut into 3-inch pieces on an angle

2 large **carrots**, peeled and sliced into 2-inch slices on an angle

5 tablespoons **butter**

3 tablespoons sliced fresh **sage leaves**

2 cups **milk**

2 cups **chicken stock**

1⅓ cups **quick-cooking polenta**
Freshly grated **nutmeg**

½ cup grated **Parmigiano-Reggiano**, a couple handfuls
Juice of ½ **lemon**

½ cup **pomegranate seeds** for garnish (optional)

Aside from Thanksgiving, this meal is the first slow-cooked dish I've served to company in years! When I made it for some true foodies, a few great chefs among them, dinner was silent—a good sign, as they were all too busy eating to chat! My friend Fleur brought dessert, but for me the sweetest treat was the compliments to the chef. (I guess I'm not so bad at this cooking stuff after all.) This meal is time and labor intensive, but it is very much worth the effort, and if I can do it, you can, too.

Preheat the oven to 375°F.

Place a large, heavy-bottomed pan, such as a Dutch oven, over medium-high heat with 2 tablespoons of the EVOO. Generously season all sides of the short ribs with salt and pepper and dust with ½ cup of the flour. When the pan is scorching hot, add half the short ribs to the pan and sear them until deep golden brown all over, 8 to 10 minutes total, turning the ribs as each side becomes nice and brown. Remove the short ribs, wipe the pot clean, and heat another 2 tablespoons of EVOO. Brown the remaining short ribs.

Once all of the short ribs have been seared, add half of the pomegranate juice, the paprika, allspice, and bay leaf to the pan. Scrape up all the golden brown bits from the bottom of the pan with a wooden spoon and bring the juice up to a bubble. Boil until it reduces by about half, 4 to 5 minutes.

Return the seared ribs to the pot and add 4 cups of the beef stock. Cover the pot and transfer to the oven. Braise until the ribs are very tender, about 2 hours, leaving the pot undisturbed.

When the ribs have been braising for an hour, drizzle the beets with the remaining tablespoon of EVOO and season with salt and pepper. Wrap them in foil and place them into the oven along with the meat and roast until tender, about 45 minutes. Remove from the oven and let cool until you can handle them, about 10 minutes. Rub the beets gently with paper towels to remove their skins, cut them into quarters, and reserve.

About 30 minutes before the ribs are done, add the onions, celery, and carrots to the braising pot and replace the cover.

In a medium skillet, melt 3 tablespoons of the butter over medium-high heat. Stir in the 3 tablespoons of flour, cook for about 1 minute, then whisk in the remaining ½ bottle of pomegranate juice. Bring the sauce to a bubble

(continued)

and cook until it is reduced by half, 1 to 2 minutes. Stir in the remaining 2 cups of beef stock and season with salt and pepper.

When the ribs are finished braising, remove the pot from the oven and transfer the meat and veggies to a serving platter. Discard the bay leaf. Stir the gravy into the braising liquid and cook over medium-high heat until thickened, a couple minutes more.

About 10 minutes before you are ready to serve, place a medium pot over medium-high heat and melt the remaining 2 tablespoons of butter. Add the sage and cook until it is aromatic and lightly golden, 2 to 3 minutes. Add the milk and chicken stock to the pot and bring to a boil. When the liquids boil, whisk in the polenta and cook, continuing to whisk, until thickened, 2 to 3 minutes. Season the polenta with nutmeg, the grated Parm, and salt and pepper.

Coarsely chop the beet greens and dress with the lemon juice, the remaining tablespoon of EVOO, and salt and pepper.

To serve, ladle some polenta into a shallow bowl. Place two rib portions and some of the braised veggies and beets on top of the polenta and ladle some of the gravy over everything. Garnish each serving with some of the dressed beet greens and with pomegranate seeds, if you have them.

SERVES 6

TEX-MEX STUFFED POBLANO PEPPERS WITH MANCHEGO CHEESE SAUCE AND BLACK BEANS WITH ROASTED GARLIC

I am a fan of many of the Food Network chefs and this one's for you, Bobby Flay. I think of it as a tribute—kind of like a food version of a song cover. Come over for that supper we've owed each other for a long time and I'll make it for you and Stephanie.

1 large head of **garlic**

3 tablespoons **EVOO** (extra-virgin olive oil)

3 cups **chicken stock**

4 tablespoons (½ stick) **butter**

1 cup **white rice**

6 large **poblano peppers** (pick through to get the biggest available)

2 pounds **ground chicken**

2 tablespoons chopped fresh **thyme leaves**, 5 to 6 sprigs

1 tablespoon plus 1 teaspoon **ground cumin**

4 to 5 **scallions**, white and green parts finely chopped

Preheat the oven to 400°F.

Slice the top third off the entire head of garlic, exposing the cloves. Dress the garlic with a tablespoon of the EVOO and wrap in foil. Set aside.

In a sauce pot with a tight-fitting lid, bring 1½ cups of the stock, 1 tablespoon of the butter, and the rice to a boil. Reduce the heat to a simmer, cover the pot, and cook for 15 minutes; you want to slightly undercook the rice.

Salt and pepper

1 (15-ounce) can diced **fire-roasted tomatoes**

A generous handful of fresh **cilantro** or flat-leaf parsley, chopped

Juice of 1 **lime**

3 tablespoons **all-purpose flour**

2 cups **milk** (eyeball it)

2 cups grated **manchego cheese** or extra-sharp white cheddar

1 small **red onion**, chopped

2 (15-ounce) cans **black beans**, drained

Hot sauce

½ cup **green olives with pimientos**, chopped

To prepare the peppers for stuffing, lay them down on their sides and take a thin slice off the length of each pepper. Scoop out the seeds. Your peppers should look like empty boats. Chop the slices you have removed.

Heat 1 tablespoon of the EVOO in a large skillet over medium-high heat. Add the chicken and cook for 5 to 6 minutes to brown, breaking it up with a wooden spoon. Stir in the chopped poblanos, the thyme, 1 tablespoon of the cumin, the scallions, and salt and pepper. Cook the chicken for 5 to 6 minutes more, transfer to a mixing bowl, and stir in the semi-cooked rice, tomatoes, cilantro or parsley, and lime juice. Combine the ingredients thoroughly.

Using a spoon or your hands, mound the stuffing into the pepper boats. Once they're filled, arrange the peppers in a 9 x 13-inch casserole dish, alternating the stem ends so that they all fit snugly in the pan. Add a splash of water or chicken stock to the pan and cover with aluminum foil. Place the peppers and the foil-wrapped garlic in the oven and roast for 45 minutes. Remove the garlic from the oven, uncover the peppers, and cook for an additional 5 to 10 minutes, until nicely browned and cooked through. When the garlic is cool enough to handle, squeeze the roasted pulp into a small bowl and set aside.

About 10 or 15 minutes before the peppers come out of the oven, make the cheese sauce: Melt the remaining 3 tablespoons of butter in a medium sauce pot over medium-high heat. Add the flour and cook for 1 minute. Whisk in 1 cup of the chicken stock and the milk, bring up to a bubble, and cook until thickened. Season with some salt and pepper, turn the heat down to low, and stir in the cheese with a figure-eight motion until melted.

For the beans, place another medium sauce pot over medium heat with the remaining tablespoon of EVOO. Add the red onions, salt and pepper, and the remaining teaspoon of cumin and cook, stirring every now and then, for 6 to 7 minutes. Add 1 can of the beans and all of the roasted garlic pulp, mashing the onions, beans, and garlic together. Fold in the remaining can of black beans and the remaining ½ cup of chicken stock, add hot sauce to taste, then simmer for 5 minutes to thicken.

Cover each dinner plate with some cheese sauce. Spoon some beans in a line across the plate. Place a pepper on the plate perpendicular to the beans and garnish the plate with chopped olives.

SERVES 6

DINNER-SIZE TEXAS CHILI CHEESE FRIES

4 BIG **Idaho potatoes**, cut lengthwise into 8 wedges each

2 tablespoons **grill seasoning**, such as McCormick's Montreal Steak Seasoning

2 tablespoons plus ¼ cup **EVOO** (extra-virgin olive oil), plus more for drizzling the fries

2 to 2½ pounds **ground sirloin** or turkey

1 large **onion**, chopped

3 to 4 **garlic cloves**, finely chopped or grated

1 **jalapeño pepper**, seeded and chopped

2 tablespoons **chili powder**

2 teaspoons **ground cumin**

Salt and **pepper**

3 tablespoons **tomato paste**

Hot sauce

2 tablespoons **Worcestershire sauce**

1 bottle **dark beer**, such as Negra Modelo, or 1½ cups **beef** or **chicken stock**

3 tablespoons **butter**

3 tablespoons **all-purpose flour**

3 tablespoons **yellow mustard**

1 cup **milk**

1 cup **chicken stock**

1½ to 2 cups shredded **sharp cheddar cheese**

2 tablespoons **red wine vinegar**

1 head of **romaine lettuce**, chopped

1 **seedless cucumber**, chopped

One night my husband asked me, "Could you make cheese fries into a simple supper . . . that won't kill me?" Here's my answer.

Preheat the oven to 450°F.

Place the potatoes on a rimmed baking sheet. Sprinkle them with the grill seasoning and give them a good drizzle of EVOO; toss to coat. Roast the potatoes until crispy golden brown, about 40 minutes, turning them once halfway through the cooking time.

While the potatoes are roasting, place a large, heavy-bottomed pot over medium-high heat with the 2 tablespoons of EVOO. Add the ground meat to the pan and cook until brown, 6 to 7 minutes, using a potato masher or the back of a wooden spoon to break it up into small pieces as it cooks.

Push the meat to one side of the pan and add the onions, garlic, jalapeño, chili powder, and cumin to the pot. Cook until the veggies soften, 5 to 6 minutes, and season with salt and pepper.

Add the tomato paste to the pot and cook for about 1 minute, until it smells sweet and has caramelized slightly. Add hot sauce to taste, the Worcestershire, and the beer or stock. Bring everything up to a bubble, then reduce the heat and simmer the chili until thickened, about 10 minutes.

While the chili is simmering, melt the butter in a medium pot over medium-high heat. Sprinkle the flour over the melted butter and cook it for about a minute, stirring. Stir the mustard into the roux, then whisk in the milk and chicken stock. Continue whisking the sauce until it has thickened up, then remove the pot from the heat and stir in the cheese in a figure-eight motion until it melts. Season the cheese sauce with salt and pepper and set aside.

In a large salad bowl, whisk together the remaining ¼ cup of EVOO along with the red wine vinegar and salt and pepper. Add the lettuce and cucumber to the bowl and toss to combine. To serve, divide the fries among 4 plates and top each serving with some chili and some cheese sauce. Serve the salad alongside.

SERVES 4

GREEK BEEF TENDERLOIN IN TOGAS WITH MEDITERRANEAN ORZO AND GREEK SALAD

6 **beef tenderloin medallions**, 4 to 6 ounces each and 1 to 1½ inches thick, at room temperature

5 tablespoons **EVOO** (extra-virgin olive oil), plus some for drizzling

Salt and **pepper**

1 small or medium **onion**, finely chopped

2 **garlic cloves**, finely chopped or grated

1 pound **spinach**, tough stems removed, chopped

Freshly grated **nutmeg**

¾ cup **feta cheese** crumbles

¼ cup **milk**

1 teaspoon dried **oregano**

1 package store-bought **phyllo dough** (at least 24 sheets), defrosted

4 tablespoons (½ stick) **butter**, melted

½ pound **orzo pasta**

4 **scallions**, thinly sliced

½ cup chopped fresh flat-leaf **parsley**, a couple of handfuls

Zest and juice of 1 **lemon**

¼ cup **pine nuts**, toasted (see Note, page 102)

1 **English cucumber**, cut into quarters lengthwise then into bite-size pieces

3 **plum tomatoes**, cored and cut into bite-size pieces

1 **green bell pepper**, seeded and chopped into bite-size pieces

1 **red onion**, chopped

½ cup pitted **kalamata olives**, coarsely chopped

5 to 6 **peperoncini peppers**, drained and coarsely chopped

2 tablespoons **red wine vinegar**

This menu is a fancy fake for entertaining—it looks very sophisticated, yet it is very simple to put together.

Preheat the oven to 425°F and bring a pot of water to a boil over high heat.

Place a large skillet over high heat. Drizzle the meat sparingly with EVOO and season it with salt and pepper. When the pan is very hot add the tenderloins and sear until golden brown, 1 to 2 minutes on the top and the bottom plus another minute for the sides. Reserve the seared meat on a plate and return the skillet to the stovetop.

Reduce the heat under the pan a bit and drizzle in a tablespoon of EVOO. Add the onions and garlic and cook until the onions are tender, 5 to 6 minutes. Add the spinach and toss with a pair of tongs until it wilts down, about 3 minutes. Season with nutmeg, salt, and pepper.

In a food processor combine the feta cheese, milk, and oregano and give it a zap to make a smooth puree. Set aside while you assemble the toga packets.

Lay down a sheet of phyllo dough on the counter and dot it with melted butter. Top that sheet with a second sheet of phyllo rotated about 25 degrees; you don't want the corners to line up. Add 2 more sheets of phyllo, dotting each with butter and placing each one at a bit of an angle.

Place a beef medallion atop the phyllo stack and top with a generous spoonful of the cheese mixture, then some of the spinach. Brush the very edges with melted butter, then gather them up and twist the dough around the meat. Transfer to a baking sheet. Repeat, making 6 phyllo-wrapped bundles in all. Bake the bundles until the dough is golden brown, 12 to 15 minutes.

While the toga-wrapped medallions are baking, salt the boiling water and add the orzo; cook it to al dente.

Return the skillet you cooked the greens in to the stovetop over medium-high heat with 1 tablespoon of EVOO. Toss the scallions into the pan and cook them until tender, 2 minutes. Drain the pasta and toss it in with the scallions. Stir in the parsley, lemon zest and juice, and pine nuts.

In a mixing bowl combine the cucumbers, tomatoes, bell peppers, red onions, olives, and peperoncini. Toss with the red wine vinegar and the remaining 3 tablespoons of EVOO and season with salt and pepper.

Serve the toga beef with a side of orzo and a scoop of cool, bright salad.

SERVES 6

"NEW" BRUNSWICK STEW

Brunswick stew is a southern country fave that can be made of squirrel meat or chicken. This is my "new" version of the classic recipe, a more northern take on the original—hold the squirrel.

Preheat the oven to 450°F.

Place a heavy-bottomed sauce pot or a Dutch oven over medium-high heat with a drizzle of EVOO. Add the bacon to the pan and cook until crispy and golden brown, 3 to 4 minutes.

While the bacon is cooking, season the chicken with salt and pepper. Combine the flour and poultry seasoning and sprinkle it over the meat, tossing it lightly to coat.

Remove the crisp bacon from the pan and reserve it on a paper-towel-lined plate. In two batches, cook the seasoned chicken in the same pan, adding 1 tablespoon EVOO to the pot, about 1 turn of the pan, with each batch. Cook until golden brown, 5 to 6 minutes. Remove the browned chicken from the pot and reserve it on a paper-towel-lined plate.

Add the remaining tablespoon of EVOO to the pot and toss in the onions, celery, bell pepper, garlic, and bay leaf. Season the veggies with salt and pepper and cook until tender, 8 to 10 minutes.

While the veggies are cooking, combine the biscuit mix, milk, 2 tablespoons of the chives, the smoked paprika, and reserved crisped bacon in a medium mixing bowl. Drop 8 biscuits onto a nonstick or lightly greased baking sheet and bake until light golden brown, about 10 minutes. When the biscuits are done, remove them from the oven and allow them to cool on the baking sheet.

Once the veggies are softened, add the hot sauce, chicken stock, stewed tomatoes, and Worcestershire to the pot and bring up to a bubble. Add the reserved chicken, the butter beans, and corn to the pot, and simmer until the chicken is cooked through and the stew is slightly thickened, 5 to 8 minutes. Discard the bay leaf.

Serve the stew topped with the remaining chives and with the sliced scallions, if using, and pass the biscuits.

SERVES 4

3 tablespoons **EVOO** (extra-virgin olive oil), plus some for drizzling

3 slices of **center-cut bacon**, chopped

3 pounds boneless skinless **chicken breasts and thighs**, cut into 2-inch pieces

Salt and **pepper**

1 cup **all-purpose flour**

1 tablespoon **poultry seasoning**

1 large **onion**, chopped into big pieces

3 to 4 **celery stalks** from the heart, chopped into big pieces

1 large **green bell pepper**, seeded and chopped into big pieces

3 to 4 **garlic cloves**, finely chopped or grated

1 **bay leaf**

2¼ cups **biscuit mix**

⅔ cup **milk**

3 tablespoons chopped fresh **chives** or scallions, divided

1 teaspoon smoked **paprika** (add more or less depending on your taste)

1 teaspoon **hot sauce** (add more or less depending on your taste)

2 cups **chicken stock**

1 (15-ounce) can **stewed tomatoes**

1 tablespoon **Worcestershire sauce**

1 (15-ounce) can **butter beans**, drained

1 (10-ounce) box frozen **corn**

2 to 3 **scallions**, sliced thin on the bias (optional)

APPLE-FENNEL STUFFED PORK TENDERLOIN

2 **pork tenderloins** (1 package), 2 to 2½ pounds total

Salt and **pepper**

3 tablespoons **EVOO** (extra-virgin olive oil), plus extra for drizzling

1 small **fennel bulb**, cored and chopped, plus a handful of the fronds, chopped

1 small **onion**, chopped

3 **garlic cloves**, finely chopped or grated

1 firm **apple** such as Gala or Honey Crisp, peeled, cored, and sliced

4 to 5 sprigs of **thyme**, leaves removed and chopped

½ cup **apple juice** or cider

1 cup fresh **bread crumbs**

½ pound **extra-wide egg noodles**

10 ounces **baby spinach**

2 tablespoons **butter**

½ cup chopped fresh flat-leaf **parsley**, about 2 handfuls

NOTE The tenderloins also grill up wonderfully. Preheat your grill to medium heat and secure the rolled tenderloins closed with a few toothpicks. Rub them down with some EVOO, salt, and pepper and grill them, turning frequently so they cook evenly, for 20 minutes with the lid down. Remove the tenderloins from the grill, tent them with foil, and allow them to rest for about 10 minutes before slicing.

Pork tenderloin is like a chicken breast—a lean, high-protein blank canvas. This stuffing paints a portrait of sweet, fragrant flavors, year-round. Serve this with the roasted vegetable of your choice.

Preheat the oven to 400°F.

Trim the tenderloins of any remaining silver skin, then butterfly them by cutting into and across but not all the way through each one. Open the tenderloins up like a book and cover with a piece of plastic wrap, then pound out to ¼-inch thickness. Season with salt and pepper.

Place a skillet over medium-high heat with 2 tablespoons of the EVOO. Add the fennel, onion, ⅔ of the garlic, and the apple, season with salt and pepper and the thyme, and sauté until soft, 7 to 8 minutes. Add the apple juice to the pan and then the bread crumbs and mix thoroughly to form a stuffing for the tenderloins.

Bring a large pot of water to a boil over high heat for the egg noodles.

Divide the stuffing between the two tenderloins, spreading it in an even layer up to within 1 inch of each long edge. Roll the tenderloins up like a jelly roll and place them seam side down on a baking sheet. Lightly drizzle some EVOO over the tenderloins and season with salt and pepper. Roast the meat for 30 minutes, or until the rolls have browned. When the meat comes out of the oven, cover it with a piece of aluminum foil and let it rest for 10 minutes to allow the juices to settle.

While the meat is resting, salt the boiling water, add the noodles, and cook them to al dente. While the pasta cooks, heat the remaining tablespoon of EVOO in a skillet over medium heat. Add the remaining garlic, stir for a minute or two, then add the spinach a handful at a time, adding more as each batch wilts into the pot and turning to cook evenly. Keep warm. Drain the noodles and return them to the pot they were cooked in. Toss the butter and parsley into the pot and toss to melt the butter and coat the noodles.

To serve, slice the tenderloins, divide among 4 plates, and serve the noodles and spinach alongside.

SERVES 4

WINTER WHITE LASAGNA

As with burgers and mac 'n' cheese, lasagnas—whether quick-cooking twists or more traditional takes—remain a category of recipe for which I cannot write enough versions to satisfy the demand from viewers and readers alike. This one is a bit unusual and very delicious.

Preheat the oven to 375°F.

Heat the EVOO in a large skillet over medium-high heat. Add the sausage and cook, breaking it up with a spoon, until the meat is crumbled and golden brown, about 10 minutes. Add the mushrooms to the pan and cook until golden brown, 5 to 6 minutes. Season the mixture with salt and pepper and reserve.

While the meat is browning up, place a large sauce pot over medium heat and melt the butter. Sprinkle the flour over the butter and cook it for about 1 minute, stirring. Whisk in the milk and chicken stock and bring the sauce up to a bubble. Season the sauce with nutmeg and salt and pepper, then simmer until it thickens, 3 to 4 minutes.

Assemble the lasagna by ladling a small amount (about ½ cup, just eyeball it) of the sauce into the bottom of a 13 x 9-inch baking dish. Lay 3 of the lasagna noodles over the sauce and top them with about one third of the sausage-mushroom mixture. Top with about 1 cup of the sauce and 1 cup of the shredded cheese (about 2 generous handfuls). Make 2 more layers, laying down 3 lasagna noodles, about one third of the meat-mushroom mixture, 1 cup of the sauce, and about 1 cup of the shredded cheese for each layer. Top the lasagna off with the last 3 noodles, the remaining sauce, and the remaining shredded cheese.

Cover the pan with aluminum foil and bake the lasagna for 30 minutes. Remove the foil and bake for another 15 minutes, or until the cheese is melted and the sauce is bubbly.

SERVES 6 TO 8

2 tablespoons **EVOO** (extra-virgin olive oil)

2½ pounds fresh **sweet or hot Italian chicken sausage,** removed from the casings

1 pound **button mushrooms,** sliced

Salt and **pepper**

4 tablespoons (½ stick) **butter**

4 tablespoons **all-purpose flour**

2 cups **milk**

2 cups **chicken stock**

A generous dash of freshly grated **nutmeg**

1 box no-boil **lasagna noodles**

4 cups shredded **Italian Four Cheese blend** or shredded provolone

BOURBON ORANGE SKILLET BBQ CHICKEN WITH CORN BREAD TOPPER

This is a go-to recipe in my family and I've added a corn bread topper to turn it into a groovy deep-dish skillet supper. When I taught this dish on air I got a HUGE response, so if you missed it that day, check this out!

Preheat the oven to 375°F.

Heat 1 tablespoon of the EVOO in a medium sauce pot over medium-high heat. Add the onions and garlic to the pan and cook until tender, 4 to 5 minutes. Season the onions with salt and pepper and stir in the tomato paste and smoked paprika. Cook the mixture for 1 to 2 minutes, then add the Worcestershire, hot sauce, brown sugar, orange zest, orange juice, and chicken stock to the pan. Bring everything up to a bubble, then reduce the heat to medium and simmer the sauce until thickened, about 5 minutes.

While the sauce is simmering, place a large cast-iron skillet over medium-high heat with the remaining 2 tablespoons of EVOO. Season the chicken with salt and pepper and cook it until golden brown on all sides, 5 to 6 minutes. When the chicken is golden brown, pour the thickened barbecue sauce into the cast-iron skillet and add the bourbon, but don't stir it in. Remove the pan from the heat and very carefully flame the alcohol using a match or a barbecue lighter. Return the pan to the heat and allow the alcohol to cook out of the bourbon; it'll be ready when the flames die away. Remove the skillet from the heat and reserve on a heat-safe surface while you prepare the corn bread.

In a medium mixing bowl prepare the corn bread batter according to the package directions. Fold the scallions and ½ cup of the cheese into the corn bread batter and spoon it evenly over the top of the barbecue chicken. Sprinkle the rest of the shredded cheese over the corn bread and transfer the skillet to the oven. Bake until the corn bread is golden brown and baked through, about 15 minutes. Serve immediately.

SERVES 6

3 tablespoons **EVOO** (extra-virgin olive oil)

1 large red **onion**, finely chopped

3 to 4 **garlic cloves**, finely chopped or grated

Salt and **pepper**

3 tablespoons **tomato paste**

1½ tablespoons **smoked paprika**, ½ palmful

2 tablespoons **Worcestershire sauce** (eyeball it)

3 tablespoons **hot sauce**

¼ cup **brown sugar**

1 tablespoon grated **orange zest**

Juice of 2 large **oranges**

3 cups **chicken stock**

3 pounds boneless skinless **chicken breasts and thighs**, cut into large chunks

¼ cup **bourbon**

2 boxes **corn bread mix**, such as Jiffy

Milk, as needed for the corn bread, per package directions

Eggs, as needed for the corn bread, per package directions

4 **scallions**, thinly sliced

1 cup shredded **cheddar cheese**

ROASTED CITRUS CHICKEN WITH LEMON-THYME GRAVY, SMASHED POTATOES, AND GREEN BEANS

4 **chicken leg quarters** plus 4 **chicken breast halves** on the bone

8 **garlic cloves**, crushed, skins removed

8 fresh **bay leaves**

2½ **lemons**, 2 thinly sliced

1 cup **green** or **green, red, and black Cerignola olives** or large green Sicilian olives

1 large red **onion**, quartered and thinly sliced

4 tablespoons **EVOO** (extra-virgin olive oil)

Salt and **pepper**

4 large **Idaho potatoes**, peeled and cut into 1-inch cubes

2 cups **chicken stock**, plus a splash for the potatoes

½ cup part-skim or **whole-milk ricotta cheese**

A generous handful of grated **Parmigiano-Reggiano**

¼ cup finely chopped fresh flat-leaf **parsley**

2 pounds **green beans**, trimmed

2 tablespoons **butter**

2 tablespoons **all-purpose flour**

About 2 tablespoons finely chopped fresh **thyme**

Like families pretty much everywhere, mine adores a good roasted chicken. Generally we roast ours with lots of garlic and rosemary and some small potatoes, then splash the bird with a little hot pepper juice when it comes out of the oven. We serve it with parsley and some chopped hot peppers on top. From time to time, though, I like to stray from the old reliable and come up with new twists on this family mainstay.

Preheat the oven to 450°F.

Arrange the chicken pieces in a roasting pan with the garlic, bay leaves, lemon slices, olives, and onions. Drizzle about 2 tablespoons of the EVOO over the mixture and season with salt and pepper. Roast the chicken, turning the pieces occasionally, until the juices run clear and the skin is deeply golden brown, 45 to 50 minutes.

While the chicken is roasting, place the potatoes in a pot of cold water. Bring the water to a bubble over medium-high heat and cook the potatoes until tender, about 15 minutes. Drain the potatoes and return them to their cooking pot to dry off and cool down slightly. Add a splash of chicken stock, the ricotta, Parmigiano, and parsley to the potatoes and smash them to your preferred consistency. Season with salt and pepper. Place the lid on the pot to keep them warm and reserve.

When the chicken has roasted for about 25 minutes, arrange the green beans on a rimmed baking sheet. Drizzle them with the remaining 2 tablespoons of EVOO, season with salt and pepper, and place in the oven with the chicken. Roast the beans for about 20 minutes, until brown at the edges and very tender.

When the chicken is almost done, place a medium pot over medium heat and add the butter. When it melts, sprinkle the flour into the pot and whisk for 1 minute. Whisk the 2 cups of chicken stock into the roux along with the thyme. Season the gravy with salt and pepper and squeeze in the juice of the remaining ½ lemon.

Serve the chicken directly from the baking dish—it's so pretty to look at! Be careful of roasted olive pits (Cerignolas do not come pitted!) and discard the bay leaves. Pass the gravy to top the chicken and potatoes and serve the green beans alongside.

SERVES 4

CHICKEN CUTLETS AND SPAGHETTI WITH PEPPERS AND ONIONS

This meal was created with my sister in mind. She loves chicken cutlets, so I made up a deluxe version: the cutlets are rubbed with garlic paste and herbs, then coated in flour, egg, and cheesy parsley-lemon bread crumbs. To go along with it, I serve up a huge portion of pepper and onion spaghetti just the way our mama has always made it for us. It was always Ria's favorite spaghetti. The sauce is more like a vegetable course because it is so laden with thinly sliced sweet peppers and onions. The spaghetti is tossed with butter and cheese, then combined with the sauce—wow! This one's as special as my sister Maria.

Preheat the oven to 250°F.

Place a large pot of water over high heat and bring it to a boil. When the water boils, salt it liberally, add the pasta, and cook to al dente.

Mash together 4 of the garlic cloves with a generous pinch of salt to make a paste, either by squishing and smoothing them under the flat side of your chef's knife, or by mashing them in a small bowl with the back of a spoon. Mix the rosemary, thyme, and some black pepper into the paste.

Butterfly each piece of chicken breast by cutting horizontally into the side of the breast, almost but not all the way through. Open the breast meat up like a book. Place each piece of breast between layers of plastic wrap or wax paper and pound it out nice and thin, between ⅛ and ¼ inch thick, giving it a couple of whacks with a small pan, mallet, or rolling pin. Rub each pounded cutlet with one quarter of the herb and garlic paste.

Set up a breading station in 3 shallow dishes: flour in one, eggs beaten with a splash of milk in another, and the bread crumbs combined with the lemon zest, parsley, and half the cheese in the third.

Heat about ¼ cup of the EVOO in a large skillet. Coat the cutlets first in the flour, then in the egg and bread crumbs. Cook the cutlets 2 at a time until golden on both sides, about 6 minutes total. Keep the finished cutlets warm in the oven while you cook the remaining batch.

While the cutlets are cooking, heat the remaining 2 tablespoons of EVOO in a deep skillet over medium-high heat. Add the peppers and onions and the remaining 2 cloves of garlic. Season with salt and pepper and cook for about 8 minutes to soften. Stir in the stock and add the tomatoes. Mash the tomatoes with a potato masher or the edge of a wooden spoon and stir to combine. Simmer for a few minutes. Stir in the basil just to wilt it.

Salt

1 pound **spaghetti** or whole wheat spaghetti

6 **garlic cloves**, finely chopped or grated

2 sprigs of fresh **rosemary**, leaves removed and finely chopped

5 to 6 sprigs of fresh **thyme**, leaves removed

Black pepper

4 boneless skinless **chicken breast halves**, 6 to 8 ounces each

1 cup **all-purpose flour**

2 **eggs**

Splash of **milk**

1 cup **bread crumbs**

Zest of 1 **lemon**

¼ cup fresh flat-leaf **parsley**, finely chopped

About ¾ cup grated **Parmigiano-Reggiano**

6 tablespoons **EVOO** (extra-virgin olive oil)

1 **red bell pepper**, seeded and thinly sliced

1 **green bell pepper**, seeded and thinly sliced

1 **cubanelle pepper** (light green mild Italian frying pepper), seeded and thinly sliced

1 large **onion**, thinly sliced

1 cup **chicken stock**

1 (28-ounce) can **San Marzano** or other **plum tomatoes**

½ cup fresh **basil**, 10 to 12 leaves, torn or coarsely chopped

2 tablespoons **butter**, cut into small pieces

Drain the pasta and return it to the pot it was cooked in and toss it with the butter and the remaining cheese. Add half of the prepared peppers and onions and toss again.

To serve, divide the pasta among 4 plates and accompany with 1 chicken cutlet per person. Divide the remaining sauce among the plates.

SERVES 4 TO THE POINT OF BLISSFUL DISCOMFORT

BUFFALO CHICKEN POTPIE

4 tablespoons **EVOO** (extra-virgin olive oil)

2 pounds boneless skinless **chicken breast** or **chicken tenders**, chopped into bite-size pieces

Salt and **pepper**

1 large **onion**, chopped

2 **carrots**, peeled and chopped

3 to 4 **celery stalks** from the heart, chopped

1 fresh **bay leaf**

3 to 4 **garlic cloves**, grated or finely chopped

4 tablespoons (½ stick) **butter**

4 tablespoons **all-purpose flour**

2 cups **chicken stock**

¼ to ⅓ cup **hot sauce** for medium to spicy heat level

2 boxes **corn bread mix**, such as Jiffy brand

Eggs, as needed for the corn bread, see package directions

Milk, as needed for the corn bread, see package directions

1½ cups crumbled **blue cheese**

Buffalo Chicken Chili was the number-one-most-downloaded recipe from season one of my daytime talk show. It obviously struck a chord, so I play with the flavor combination as many ways as possible. Here's another spin-off. This one I cooked up for spicy Teri Hatcher—and she baked dessert, of course!

Preheat the oven to 375°F.

Heat 2 tablespoons of the EVOO in a large skillet over medium-high heat. Add the chopped chicken, season with salt and pepper, and sauté until golden brown all over, 3 to 4 minutes. Remove the chicken chunks from the skillet and reserve on a plate.

Add the remaining 2 tablespoons of EVOO to the same pan along with the onions, carrots, celery, bay leaf, and garlic. Season with salt and pepper and cook, stirring occasionally, until the vegetables are tender, 7 to 8 minutes.

While the veggies are cooking, melt the butter in a medium saucepan over medium heat. Whisk in the flour and cook for about 1 minute, then whisk in the chicken stock and hot sauce and bring it to a boil. Simmer the gravy until thickened, about 3 minutes.

Return the reserved chicken chunks to the skillet with the cooked vegetables and add the gravy, stirring to combine. Discard the bay leaf. Transfer everything to a 9 x 11-inch casserole dish and set aside while you prepare the topping.

In a medium mixing bowl, prepare the corn bread according to package directions, using the eggs and milk. Stir the blue cheese crumbles into the corn bread batter and drop the batter by spoonfuls onto the top of the casserole, covering it completely.

Bake the potpie until the corn bread is baked through, 18 to 20 minutes.

SERVES 6

CIDER HOUSE CHICKEN

My mom is something else. One winter night I came in from the cold and sat down to this creation. The sauce looks like a creamy version of traditional poultry gravy but—surprise—it is tangy, rich, slightly sweet, and deeply comforting.

Preheat a large, heavy-bottomed pot over high heat with 2 tablespoons of the EVOO. While the EVOO is heating up, season the chicken with salt and pepper. Once the oil starts to ripple, add the chicken breasts, skin side down, and brown them on both sides, 4 to 5 minutes. Remove to a plate and reserve. Add the remaining 2 tablespoons of EVOO to the pot and repeat with the dark meat.

To the chicken drippings add 1 tablespoon of the butter and the carrots and onions. As the veggies cook, tie the bay leaves, thyme, and parsley sprigs together into a neat little bundle with some kitchen twine and toss it in the pot. Season with salt and pepper and cook the vegetables until tender, 7 to 8 minutes.

Add the ½ cup of Calvados to the vegetables. Remove the pan from the heat and, using a lighter or a long match, carefully ignite the brandy to burn off the alcohol.

Let the flame burn out, then return the pot to the stove and add the cider and vinegar or hard cider. Cook over medium-high heat until the liquid has reduced by half. Fish out the herb bundle and reserve, then puree the vegetables and liquid in a food processor or a blender. Return the vegetable puree to the pot along with the herb bundle and browned chicken, season with hot sauce and nutmeg, and adjust the seasonings. Simmer over low heat for 10 minutes, stir in the cream, and cook the sauce for a few minutes more to thicken.

While the chicken is cooking, melt the remaining 2 tablespoons of butter in a skillet over medium-high heat. Add the apples and sauté until lightly browned; don't overcook them, they should remain crispy. Add the remaining 2 tablespoons of Calvados, remove the pan from the heat, and ignite the brandy. Let the alcohol cook out, and reserve the apples for garnish.

Serve the chicken and sauce in shallow bowls with slices of baguette. Top the chicken with a few slices of sautéed apple and a garnish of chopped parsley.

SERVES 4

¼ cup **EVOO** (extra-virgin olive oil)

2 organic **baby chickens**, 2 to 3 pounds each, cut into pieces

Salt and **pepper**

3 tablespoons **butter**

2 medium **carrots**, peeled and chopped

2 medium **onions**, chopped

2 fresh or dried **bay leaves**

5 to 6 sprigs of fresh **thyme**

6 sprigs of fresh flat-leaf **parsley**, plus a handful of chopped leaves

½ cup plus 2 tablespoons **Calvados** or other apple brandy

1 cup unfiltered **apple cider** (see Note)

1 tablespoon **white wine vinegar**

A few dashes of **hot sauce**

Freshly grated **nutmeg**

½ cup **heavy cream**

3 Honey Crisp **apples**, sliced through the equator (core and all) into 1-inch disks

1 **multigrain baguette**

NOTE If you prefer, you can substitute 1 cup hard cider for the cider and vinegar.

TURKEY, BACON, AND SCALLION STUFFED TATERS

4 BIG **Idaho potatoes**

1 tablespoon **EVOO** (extra-virgin olive oil), plus some for drizzling

Salt and **pepper**

6 strips of **turkey bacon**

¼ pound deli-sliced **smoked turkey breast**, chopped

1 cup **sour cream**

½ cup **chicken stock**

4 **scallions**, thinly sliced

1½ cups shredded **sharp cheddar cheese**

I saw a personal trainer in a TV commercial one night promoting the health benefits of baked potatoes. Hey, sign me up! Serve the spuds with a side salad for a well-rounded supper. If this is your kind of meal, check out the Ranch-Style Stuffed Taters (page 163) and Broccoli and Cheddar Stuffed Taters (page 162) in the Vegetarian Meals chapter of this book.

Preheat the oven to 425°F.

Scrub the potatoes and prick them each several times with a fork. Place them on a rimmed baking sheet, drizzle with EVOO, and season with salt and pepper, rolling them around on the sheet to coat them with the oil. Bake the potatoes until tender, 45 to 60 minutes, depending on the size of the potatoes. Let the potatoes cool for 5 or 10 minutes, until cool enough to handle, leaving the oven on.

While the potatoes are cooling, heat a medium skillet over medium-high heat with 1 tablespoon of EVOO. Add the turkey bacon and cook until crispy golden brown and cooked through, about 3 minutes per side. Transfer the cooked bacon to a paper-towel-lined plate to drain off any excess grease and cool. Add the chopped turkey to the same skillet and toss over medium heat for 1 to 2 minutes to heat through, then remove from the heat and reserve. Chop up the cooled bacon.

Once the potatoes are cool enough to handle, cut each one in half lengthwise and scoop out the insides into a mixing bowl, leaving a thin layer of flesh intact. Try not to pierce the skin of the potato. Add the sour cream, stock, and scallions and about ½ cup of the cheddar to the bowl and mash the potatoes; season with salt and pepper. Fold the turkey and bacon into the mashed potatoes and mound the filling into the potato skins. Top with a little extra cheese, a couple of tablespoons per skin. Return them to the oven for 5 minutes to melt the cheese. Serve them up with your favorite salad alongside.

SERVES 4

CHICKEN FRA DIAVOLO WITH FENNEL, ONIONS, AND POTATOES AND WARM ROASTED TOMATO AND GARLIC SAUCE

I do not dine out often, because I prefer to make dinner with my family and eat in. So when I find a new place that feels as comfortable as home to me, and that serves food my family enjoys as much as home cooking, it matters. Dell'anima, a small Italian restaurant in New York, is one of those places; and, ironically, we've tried to re-create a few of their dishes ourselves—so we can stay home. Oh well. They have a great devilish chicken under a brick with anise and hot pepper that's red as can be. Here's our sinful attempt at working with our spice rack. We serve ours with a heavenly white roasted vegetable medley and a sweet, warm roasted garlic and tomato salsa on top.

Preheat the oven to 400°F.

Bring a medium pot of water to a boil over high heat to blanch the cipollini onions.

While the water is coming to a boil, combine the smoked paprika, grill seasoning, chili powder, ground fennel, and poultry seasoning in a small bowl. Drizzle the chicken halves with some EVOO, a couple of tablespoons total, then coat the chicken halves with the spice mixture: they will be deep red in color.

Drop the onions in the boiling water for 1 minute. (Blanching the onions for 1 minute will allow you to wipe away their skins with a kitchen towel rather than peeling them—easy!) Drain and peel the onions, then trim the tops and root ends with a sharp paring knife. Place the onions in a roasting pan.

Quarter each fennel bulb lengthwise and cut out the cores. Halve each piece again and add to the roasting pan. Add the potatoes to the fennel and onions, toss the vegetables with a couple more tablespoons of EVOO, and season with salt and pepper. Arrange the chickens atop the vegetables in the center of the pan; the red chickens will be surrounded by the white vegetables.

Cut off the top third of the head of garlic to expose the cloves. Drizzle the cut surfaces with a little oil and wrap the head in foil.

Roast the garlic and the chicken and vegetables for 45 to 55 minutes, or until the juices from the thigh meat run clear.

When the chicken has roasted for about 25 minutes, place the tomatoes on a rimmed baking sheet and coat with a tablespoon of EVOO. Season with salt and pepper, then roast in the oven for 20 to 25 minutes, until they burst.

3 tablespoons **sweet smoked paprika**

3 tablespoons **grill seasoning**, such as McCormick's Montreal Steak Seasoning

3 tablespoons **chili powder** (the redder the chili powder you choose, the redder the Diavolo will be)

1½ tablespoons ground **fennel seed**

1 tablespoon **poultry seasoning**

2 small **spring chickens**, 3 to 3½ pounds, split, backbone removed (ask your butcher to do this for you)

5 to 6 tablespoons **EVOO** (extra-virgin olive oil) for liberal drizzling

16 **cipollini onions** or 4 medium **onions**, root end intact and quartered lengthwise

2 **fennel bulbs**, trimmed of fronds

1½ to 2 pounds small **Yukon Gold potatoes**, halved

Salt and **pepper**

1 head of **garlic**

2 pints **grape tomatoes**

A handful of fresh **basil leaves**, coarsely chopped

A handful of fresh flat-leaf **parsley**, coarsely chopped

Squeeze the roasted garlic cloves from their papery skins into a bowl and mash with a fork. Stir in the roasted tomatoes, basil, and parsley. Adjust the salt and pepper.

Serve each chicken half with some of the fennel, onions, and potatoes alongside and top with a liberal mound of the roasted tomato and garlic salsa.

SERVES 4

FROM MY FAMILY TO YOURS

The recipes in this chapter were contributed by my mom, Elsa Scuderi, and Vicki Cusimano, my mother-in-law (with an assist from John's aunt, Annette Dickman). These are the dishes we ask for time and again and we never get tired of them. Maybe it's the family associations that make them especially delicious—each one has its own story—but I think you'll agree that they are all simple, satisfying, and super tasty. So here you go, from my family to yours!

A note from my mom: Rachael and her siblings grew up eating the foods I grew up eating, very humble yet irresistible foods. The table, both inside and outside, was the center of our family's interaction. Sometimes we sat around the dinner table for hours, for thanks and to review our day (our daily adventures were often a source of good belly laughs!). Our meals were complete with a salad, potatoes, rice or pasta, a meat or fish, fruit and cheese, and Mom's special pastry, all made fresh. I now realize we ate daily what many consider a festive meal. It is amazing what they had time to do besides their work. Many of the dishes are served up on our dining tables today. Enjoy.

ELSA'S BAKED ZITI

No leftovers with this pasta! It's easy, easy, and delish! We ate ziti or rigatoni with cheeses and light tomato sauce, made creamy with ricotta. We went to bed happy after this dinner. —Rach

Preheat the oven to 375°F.

Bring a big pot of water to a boil for the pasta. Salt the water, add the pasta, and cook to al dente.

Drain the ricotta cheese in a strainer or a colander lined with paper towels. Place the drained ricotta in a 9 x 13-inch casserole dish and season with some grill seasoning and a few handfuls of Parm cheese.

While the pasta cooks, heat the EVOO in a small pan over medium heat. Add the garlic and a pinch or two of red pepper flakes and sauté for a minute or two, then stir in the tomatoes and basil. Reduce the heat to low.

Drain the pasta and toss with the cheese mixture. Add the tomato sauce, top the pasta with more Parm, and bake until the cheese browns, about 15 minutes.

SERVES 4 TO 6

Salt

1 pound **ziti rigate** (with ridges) or rigatoni

2 cups **ricotta cheese**

Grill seasoning, such as McCormick's Montreal Steak Seasoning

A couple of handfuls of grated **Parmigiano-Reggiano**

1 tablespoon **EVOO** (extra-virgin olive oil)

1 to 2 **garlic cloves**, chopped

Crushed red pepper flakes

1 cup **crushed tomatoes** or tomato sauce

A few fresh **basil** leaves, torn or chopped

BASIL CREAM SAUCE WITH PASTA

This is a Friday meal I made because Rachael's sister Maria, my older daughter, does not like basil pesto but she does like basil, and she is fond of white sauces. This is a combo she *devours*. —Elsa

Bring a big pot of water to a boil for the pasta. Salt the water, add the spaghetti, and cook to al dente.

Melt the butter in a large skillet over medium heat. Make a roux, whisking together the melted butter and flour for 1 minute, then add the wine and cook down for 1 minute. Add the stock and season with salt and pepper. Cook for another couple of minutes to thicken. Stir the chicken and prosciutto into the white sauce. Add the peas and lemon zest, combine, then add pesto to taste. Heat through.

To serve, toss the sauce with the drained spaghetti. Garnish with the chopped herbs.

SERVES 4

Salt

1 pound thin **spaghetti**

2 tablespoons **butter**

2 tablespoons **all-purpose flour**

½ to ¾ cup **dry white wine** (eyeball it)

¾ cup **chicken stock**

Black pepper

½ pound cooked **chicken breast**, julienned

¼ pound sliced **prosciutto**, julienned

1 cup **frozen tiny green peas**

2 teaspoons **lemon zest**

¼ cup **basil pesto**

A handful of fresh **mint leaves**, chopped

A handful of fresh flat-leaf **parsley**, chopped

A handful of fresh **basil**, chopped

CHICKEN CHASSEUR

This is a version of another classic that we gobbled! Chicken cooked with tomatoes, herbs, shallots, and mushrooms makes a great brothy sauce to serve along with fine spaghetti and crusty bread. This is a kids' yum-o meal! —Rach

1 cup **all-purpose flour**
Salt and **pepper**
1 teaspoon **ground thyme**
3 pounds bone-in, skin-on **chicken pieces**
¼ cup **EVOO** (extra-virgin olive oil)
4 tablespoons (½ stick) melted **butter**
¼ cup chopped **shallots**
¼ pound **mushrooms**, sliced
½ cup **dry white wine**
3 to 4 stems of fresh **tarragon**, chopped
1 (15-ounce) can **diced tomatoes**, drained
A handful of fresh flat-leaf **parsley**, chopped

Preheat the oven to 325°F.

Season the flour with salt and pepper and the thyme. Dredge the chicken in the seasoned flour. Heat the EVOO and butter in a large Dutch ovenover medium to medium-high heat. Add the chicken and brown on all sides. You may need to do this in 2 batches; if so, use half of the oil and butter for each batch. Remove the chicken and reduce the heat a bit. Add the shallots and mushrooms to the pot and cook for 3 to 4 minutes, until softened. Stir in the wine and cook for 1 minute to reduce, then stir in the tarragon, reserving a little for garnish, and the tomatoes. Return the chicken to the pot. Cover and bake in the oven until the chicken is done, 45 minutes to an hour. Garnish with the parsley and reserved tarragon. Serve with salad and a side of pasta tossed in the pan sauce.

SERVES 6

BEEF WITH BEER AND MUSTARD MASHED POTATOES

If you prefer, serve the stew with crusty bread spread with mustard butter made by stirring together 3 tablespoons of butter and a rounded tablespoon of grainy mustard. —Elsa

3 tablespoons **EVOO** (extra-virgin olive oil)
1½ to 2 pounds **sirloin**, cut in cubes
1 **garlic clove**, crushed
1 **onion**, chopped
1 large **carrot**, peeled and chopped
2 rounded tablespoons **all-purpose flour**
Salt and **pepper**
2 tablespoons **tomato paste**
1½ cups **beer**
½ cup **beef stock**
1 sprig of fresh **rosemary**, finely chopped

Mustard mashed potatoes

2 pounds peeled **potatoes**
2 tablespoons **butter**
⅓ cup **half-and-half** or whole milk
2 tablespoons **grainy mustard**

Preheat the oven to 375°F.

Heat the EVOO in a large, heavy pot over medium-high heat. When it is hot, add the sirloin cubes and brown on all sides, about 5 minutes. Add the garlic, onions, and carrots to the pot and cook to soften, about 5 minutes. Sprinkle the meat and veggies with the flour and with salt and pepper, stir for 1 minute, then add the tomato paste. Stir in 1 cup water, the beer, beef stock, and rosemary and bring to a boil. Cover the pot and transfer to the oven to bake for 90 minutes. Serve the beef over the mustard mashed potatoes.

When the beef has cooked for 1 hour, place the potatoes in a pot with water to cover. Bring to a boil, salt the water, then reduce the heat and simmer until the potatoes are fork tender, 15 to 17 minutes. Drain the potatoes and return to the hot pot. Add the butter, half-and-half, and mustard, and mash to your preferred consistency.

SERVES 4

CLASSIC HADDOCK
OR COD DUGLIERE

8 tablespoons (1 stick) **butter**

1 small **onion**, finely chopped

2 pounds thick **haddock** or cod fillets

Salt and **pepper**

1 **lemon**

3 chopped **tomatoes** or 1 (15-ounce) can diced tomatoes, drained

⅓ cup **fish stock** or clam juice

⅔ cup dry **white wine**

1 fresh **bay leaf**

1 to 2 sprigs of fresh **tarragon**, finely chopped

Cayenne pepper

A handful of fresh flat-leaf **parsley**, finely chopped

The aromas wafting to the lakeshore from her open kitchen window told us when she was baking fish. The casserole of fish cooked with onions, tomatoes, and wine was brought to the table with crusty bread to soak up the juices. Wearing her food-spattered apron, Tia Patrina would gather my siblings and me into a circle and teach us a folk song and dance from the old country. We would dance barefoot in the sand and eat at the long picnic table outside. There were always extra plates on the dining table for visitors on Sunday, and those plates were used! —Elsa

Preheat the oven to 400°F.

Place 4 tablespoons of the butter in a metal baking pan just large enough to hold the fish, and place it in the oven to melt.

When the butter has melted, stir in the onions. Sprinkle the fish with salt, pepper, and the juice of ½ lemon. Arrange the fish over the onions, spooning some of the melted butter over the top. Add the chopped tomatoes to the dish, then pour the fish stock and wine over the fish. Add the bay leaf and tarragon. Cover the dish with foil and bake for 20 minutes, or until cooked through.

When the fish is cooked, transfer it to a platter and cover with foil. Place the pan on the stovetop and cook for 2 to 3 minutes over medium-high heat to reduce the sauce. Season with salt, pepper, the juice of ½ lemon, and cayenne pepper to taste. Add the remaining 4 tablespoons of butter in small pieces and swirl the pan to melt the butter into the sauce. Discard the bay leaf. Pour the sauce over the fish and garnish with the parsley.

SERVES 4

ELSA'S FAVORITE FISH

2 tablespoons **EVOO** (extra-virgin olive oil)

4 **scallions**, thinly sliced

½ cup fresh flat-leaf **parsley**, a couple of handfuls, finely chopped

1 teaspoon **fennel seeds**

½ to ¾ cup **dry white wine** (eyeball it)

1 (15-ounce) can diced **tomatoes**

½ cup **clam juice** or seafood stock

Salt and **pepper**

2 pounds center-cut **cod** or haddock fillets

1 pound **fettuccine** or linguine

3 tablespoons **butter**, softened

3 tablespoons **all-purpose flour**

2 tablespoons **balsamic vinegar**

¼ cup **heavy cream**

1 cup fresh **basil**, 20 leaves, shredded or torn

As part of a Roman Catholic family, I grew up eating fish on Fridays. This fish dish is made with many of the "always-on-hand" ingredients in the kitchen. It was no problem to get my kids to enjoy a fish dish when it was seasoned with favorite flavors, wine, and tomatoes. —Elsa

Preheat the oven to 350°F and bring a large pot of water to a boil over high heat for the pasta.

Heat the EVOO in a large ovenproof skillet over medium-high heat. Add the scallions, parsley, and fennel seeds and cook until the scallions are tender, about 1 minute. Add the wine and let it reduce for 1 minute. Add the tomatoes and clam juice, stir, and season with salt and pepper. Bring the mixture to a bubble. Season the fish with salt and pepper and nestle it into the sauce. Place a lid on the pan or cover it tightly with foil, and transfer the pan to the oven. Bake until the fish has just about cooked through, 15 to 18 minutes.

Salt the pasta water and drop in the pasta. Cook to al dente.

Carefully tranfer the fish to a warm platter and tent with foil. Return the skillet to the stovetop and cook the sauce over medium-high heat for 2 to 3 minutes. In a small bowl stir the softened butter together with the flour. Whisk the butter-flour mixture into the sauce, cook for 1 minute, then stir in the balsamic vinegar and cream. Bring to a bubble and remove from the heat. Stir in the basil.

Toss the drained pasta with half of the sauce. Divide among 4 plates and top with a fish fillet and the remaining sauce.

SERVES 4

CRUNCHY GREEN BEAN SIDE DISH

1 pound **green beans**, trimmed

Salt

3 tablespoons **butter**

¼ cup sliced **almonds**, toasted (see Note, page 102)

My parents took time to cook our veggies with great flavor. Green beans were always welcome at our meals, cooked with onions, bacon, nuts, or herbs. Here's one of our favorite versions. —Elsa

In a medium pot cook the green beans in salted water until al dente. In a small skillet melt the butter over medium heat. Sauté the sliced almonds in the melted butter. Toss with the green beans and serve.

SERVES 4 TO 6

SHRIMP WITH GARLIC

The Friday-night number-one meal. Pans full of shrimp in a bubbly garlic wine sauce. Yum-o! We would serve it with sautéed escarole and crusty bread. Three heavy oval-shaped copper pans of this meal were spaced equally down the table; otherwise our brothers would have devoured it all! —Rach

Heat the EVOO in a large skillet over medium heat. Add the garlic and red pepper flakes and cook for 2 minutes. Raise the heat to high and add the shrimp, sherry, and paprika. Cook, stirring, until the shrimp are pink, about 3 minutes. Season with salt, pepper, parsley, and lemon juice to taste. Serve.

SERVES 4

¼ cup **EVOO** (extra-virgin olive oil)

4 large **garlic cloves**, minced

1 teaspoon **crushed red pepper flakes**

1 pound large **shrimp**, peeled and deveined

2 tablespoons **dry sherry**

½ teaspoon **paprika**

Salt and **pepper**

A generous handful of fresh flat-leaf **parsley**, finely chopped

1 **lemon**

BROILED EGGPLANT SIDE DISH

Our roots are in Sicily, and I am told that because many of our ancestors were poor, eggplant stood in for meat and fish. Today, we cook eggplant many different ways, often because we prefer it to meat—"thanks" to our Sicilian relatives. —Elsa

Preheat the broiler.

In a small bowl combine the onion and half the garlic with the ½ cup EVOO. Season with salt and pepper. Place the eggplant slices in a single layer on a baking sheet. Brush the eggplant with the onion-garlic oil and broil 5 inches from the heat for 4 to 5 minutes, then turn and brush the other side. Broil for a few more minutes, until brown and tender.

While the eggplant cooks, heat the 1 tablespoon EVOO in a medium skillet over medium heat, add the remaining garlic and the red pepper flakes, and cook for 2 minutes or so. Stir in the tomatoes and heat through, then fold in the basil and reduce the heat to warm.

Serve the broiled eggplant with the spicy tomato sauce.

Optional: Top the eggplant with cooked, chopped bacon and asiago or Parmigiano-Reggiano cheese, or melt your favorite cheese into the tomato sauce.

SERVES 4 TO 6

1 small **onion**, grated

3 to 4 **garlic cloves**, grated or minced

½ cup plus 1 tablespoon **EVOO** (extra-virgin olive oil)

Salt and **pepper**

1 large, firm **eggplant**, peeled and cut into ½-inch-thick slices

1 teaspoon crushed **red pepper flakes**

2 cups **crushed or diced tomatoes**

A few leaves of fresh **basil**, torn or chopped

SPECIAL-EVENT MEAL

- ROASTED STRIP LOIN OF BEEF
- YORKSHIRE PUDDING AND BORDELAISE SAUCE
- TOMATO AND MUSHROOM SIDE STUFFING
- CAESAR SALAD WITH BACON

Buy a whole bone-in sirloin strip roast and have the butcher trim the excess fat and remove any veined meat at the end; keep this meat to trim out for beef stew. Have the roast boned and tied. Allow the meat to sit out for 1 to 2 hours before cooking. Sometimes we add ¼ pound of mushrooms that have been sautéed in butter to the bordelaise sauce. —Elsa

Roasted Strip Loin of Beef

Preheat the oven to 450°F. Rub the sirloin roast with EVOO and salt and pepper. Make slits close to the bone and place the crushed garlic in the slits along the bone. Place the roast on a rack on a roasting pan, uncovered.

Roast for 25 minutes, then lower the oven temperature to 325°F and cook to the desired doneness. Do not baste. Allow 16 to 18 minutes per pound for rare (140°F), and 20 to 22 minutes per pound for medium (160°F). When the roast is cooked, remove it from the oven, tent with foil, and allow it to rest for 20 minutes. When ready to serve, run a sharp, thin knife between meat and bone, lift out the roast, and slice for service. The meat's temperature will increase by 5 degrees as it rests after cooking.

SERVES 8

Sirloin strip roast, boned and tied

EVOO (extra-virgin olive oil)

Salt and **pepper**

15 **garlic cloves**, peeled and crushed

Yorkshire Pudding

Preheat the oven to 450°F.

Beat the eggs with the milk. Add the salt to the flour in a medium bowl. and stir the flour mixture into the egg mixture. Melt the butter and spread it around a medium baking dish. If using meat drippings, remove most of the fat from the meat-roasting pan first, and add about ¼ cup of drippings to the baking dish. Pour in the pudding mix. Bake for 10 minutes. Lower the oven temperature to 350°F and let the pudding cook for 15 to 20 minutes, until it is puffed and golden brown. The pudding can bake while the meat rests.

SERVES 8

2 **eggs**

1 cup **milk**

½ teaspoon **salt**

1 cup **all-purpose flour**

4 tablespoons (½ stick) **butter** or drippings from a beef roast

2 tablespoons **butter**

2 tablespoons minced **shallots**

¾ cup **dry red wine**

2 tablespoons **lemon juice**

2 tablespoons minced fresh flat-leaf **parsley**

Salt and **pepper**

Cayenne pepper

Bordelaise Sauce

In a medium sauté pan, melt the butter and sauté the shallots. Add the wine and simmer to reduce by half, about 5 minutes. Add the lemon juice, parsley, salt and pepper, and cayenne to taste. You can add ¼ pound sliced mushrooms cooked in butter if you'd like.

MAKES 1 CUP

3 tablespoons **EVOO** (extra-virgin olive oil)

½ **red onion**, chopped

¼ **green bell pepper**, diced small

1 **celery stalk**, finely chopped

4 **garlic cloves**, finely chopped

½ teaspoon **crushed red pepper flakes**

¾ pound **button or cremini mushrooms**, chopped

1 **bay leaf**

Salt and **pepper**

1 (14-ounce) can diced **tomatoes**, drained and juice reserved

2 tablespoons chopped fresh flat-leaf **parsley**

A handful of fresh **basil** leaves, shredded

¾ cup **bread crumbs**

½ cup grated **Parmigiano-Reggiano**

Tomato and Mushroom Side Stuffing

Preheat the oven to 400°F.

Heat the EVOO in a skillet over medium to medium-high heat. Add the onions, bell peppers, celery, garlic, and red pepper flakes and cook for 5 minutes to soften. Add the mushrooms, bay leaf, and salt and pepper and cook until the mushrooms are just about tender, 6 to 7 minutes. Stir in the tomatoes and heat through. Add the parsley, basil, bread crumbs, and cheese and moisten with the reserved tomato juice, stirring to combine.

Place in a buttered shallow casserole and bake until crusty and hot throughout. Discard the bay leaf. Serve warm or at room temperature.

SERVES 8

8 slices of **bacon**

2 teaspoons **anchovy paste**

2 **garlic cloves**, minced or grated

Juice of 1 **lemon**

1½ tablespoons **Worcestershire sauce**

½ cup **EVOO** (extra-virgin olive oil)

½ cup grated **Parmigiano-Reggiano**

2 large hearts of **romaine lettuce**

Black pepper

1 cup **croutons**

4 hard-boiled **eggs**, chopped

Caesar Salad with Bacon

Cook up the bacon in a large skillet until crisp; drain on paper towels and when cool, chop into small bits and reserve.

Mix the anchovy paste, garlic, lemon juice or vinegar, and Worcestershire sauce in a salad bowl. In a small saucepan, heat the EVOO nearly to a boil, then stream the hot oil into the bowl, whisking to combine. Stir in half the cheese. Tear the lettuce into bite-size pieces and add to the bowl; toss to combine. Season with pepper. Toss with the bacon and croutons, and serve garnished with chopped eggs and the remaining grated cheese.

SERVES 8

COOKED DARK GREENS—OFTEN SERVED AT THE SCUDERI TABLE

As a young woman, I spent as much of my time outside as I could. I loved to jump and could do quite a high jump, always reaching for the sky. My dad said over and over again that it was because I ate my dark greens—escarole, endive, and dandelions. I loved them all! —Elsa

2 pounds **greens**, such as chard, escarole, or dandelions, well cleaned and stems discarded

Salt

¼ cup **EVOO** (extra-virgin olive oil)

6 to 8 **garlic cloves**, finely chopped

A generous handful of fresh flat-leaf **parsley**, chopped

½ teaspoon **crushed red pepper flakes**

Black pepper

Freshly grated **nutmeg**

Zest of 1 **lemon**

¼ cup slivered **almonds** or pine nuts, toasted (see Note, page 102)

Bring a medium pot of water to a boil.

Strip the leaves from thick stems such as chard; if you're using dandelion greens, remove the stems and chop them along with the greens. Salt the boiling water, then add the stems (if using), and then the leaves. Blanch for 2 to 3 minutes, transfer to a colander, rinse with cold water, and drain well.

Heat the EVOO in a large pan over medium heat. Add the garlic, parsley, and red pepper flakes and cook for a minute or two. Add the drained greens, toss to heat through, and season with salt, black pepper, nutmeg, and the lemon zest. Top with the toasted almonds and serve.

SERVES 8

CLASSIC ANNA

Our favorite potato dish! When Daddy served this, all of us kids ate it as the main event, ignoring anything else on our plates. —Elsa

2½ pounds **potatoes**

8 tablespoons (1 stick) **butter**, melted

¼ cup grated **onion**

Salt and **pepper**

Preheat the oven to 400°F.

Peel and very thinly slice the potatoes.

Generously brush a high-sided 8-inch baking pan or ovenproof skillet with butter. Arrange overlapping slices of potato around the side of the pan. Cover the bottom of the pan with potato slices, overlapping them; brush with butter, sprinkle with grated onion, and season with salt and pepper. Repeat until the pan is filled. Cover the pan with foil or with the lid if using a skillet. Bake the potatoes for 30 minutes, or until the potatoes are golden brown.

SERVES 4

CREAMY BAKED POTATO CASSEROLE

Butter, to grease the pan

5 large **russet potatoes**, scrubbed or peeled and thinly sliced

Salt and **pepper**

Freshly grated **nutmeg**

3 **garlic cloves**, minced

½ cup diced **onion**

3 generous handfuls of grated **Parmigiano-Reggiano** (½ to ¾ cup)

2 cups **heavy cream**

At the end of the summer my family was involved in the preserving of fruits, vegetables, and chicken. Potatoes also were put away for the winter months, stored in bins in our stone basement. This classic potato casserole needed no accompaniment to constitute a meal—even though it was the starch we often served with our fish dinners. We heaped our plates over and over again until all the potatoes were gone. —Elsa

Preheat the oven to 350°F.

Grease a shallow casserole with butter. Arrange a layer of potatoes in the casserole and season with salt and pepper and a little nutmeg. Sprinkle one third of the minced garlic, one third of the onions, and a handful of the Parmigiano over the potatoes. Repeat to make 2 more layers.

In a bowl, stir together the cream and ½ cup water. Pour the mixture over the potatoes and cover the dish with foil. Bake for 90 minutes, then remove the foil and bake until the top is brown and the potatoes are tender when pierced with the tip of a paring knife. Let the casserole stand for a few minutes before serving.

SERVES 8

EVOO MASHED POTATOES

2 pounds **potatoes**, peeled and cut in chunks

Salt

1 cup hot **milk**

¼ cup **EVOO** (extra-virgin olive oil)

Black pepper

Freshly grated **nutmeg**

2 tablespoons chopped fresh **chives**

2 tablespoons chopped fresh flat-leaf **parsley**

Place the potatoes in a pot with water to cover. Bring to a boil, salt the water, and cook until the potatoes are tender, 10 to 12 minutes. Drain the potatoes and return them to the pan. Mash the potatoes over low heat, adding the hot milk, EVOO, salt, pepper, nutmeg, chives, and parsley.

SERVES 4

GRANDMA ROSE'S COLD EGGPLANT CASSEROLE

When we were growing up, we loved this as a sandwich on Wonder Bread. If we took it to school we had to eat it quickly, because all of our friends wanted to trade their sandwiches for ours. Our mother had quite the reputation as an excellent cook. —Vicki and Annette

1 large **eggplant**, peeled and thinly sliced

EVOO (extra-virgin olive oil)

Salt

1½ cups **marinara sauce**

2 tablespoons **Romano** cheese, grated

2 hard-boiled **eggs** sliced in ¼-inch rounds (an egg slicer works great!)

Place the eggplant slices in a strainer or colander and place a weight, such as a plate with some heavy cans, on top. Press the eggplant until most of the moisture is released, about 15 minutes. Heat some EVOO in a large sauté pan. Salt the eggplant slices lightly and add to the skillet, cooking in batches if necessary. Cook until the eggplant is tender and brown, adding more oil as needed. Remove from the skillet.

Place slices of eggplant in a single layer in a 8 x 8-inch baking dish, then alternate thin layers of marinara sauce, eggplant, grated cheese, and sliced hard-boiled egg. Refrigerate until cold, about 2 hours, or overnight.

Serve cold on crusty Italian bread with a tossed green salad.

SERVES 4 TO 6

EMMANUEL'S ARTICHOKES

My grandpa Emmanuel was a fantastic cook because the food he made was filled with his love of food itself; the land it comes from; and the people he was feeding: his family. My mom is lucky (and I am lucky to be her child) because she was my grandpa's first born, and the older kids got to spend the most time in the kitchen with Emmanuel. My mom has taught everyone in our family to make this recipe and we will be making it for generations to come. At every holiday or gathering we serve each person half of a large artichoke as an appetizer, but they are huge, so unless you are a relative of mine, make one for every four guests. —Rach

3 large **male** (tall and pointy) **artichokes**

2 **lemons**

½ cup **EVOO** (extra-virgin olive oil), plus some for drizzling

1 (2-ounce) thin flat **anchovy fillets**, drained

8 **garlic cloves**, finely chopped

½ teaspoon **crushed red pepper flakes**

2 cups **bread crumbs**

1 bunch of fresh flat-leaf **parsley**, chopped

1½ to 2 teaspoons **coarse black pepper**

1 cup grated **Parmigiano-Reggiano**

Preheat the oven to 400°F.

Trim the artichokes by cutting off the stems and tops with a knife. Snip the tips of the side leaves with scissors. Rub all the cut surfaces with cut lemon halves. Squeeze the lemons into a large pot, add the juiced lemon halves, and fill the pot halfway with water. Bring to a boil. Add the artichokes to the boiling water and place a small kitchen towel on top; this will keep them submerged. Boil the artichokes until tender, 12 to 15 minutes, then remove them with tongs and place them upside down on a towel to cool. When they are cool enough to handle, use a teaspoon to scoop out the spiny choke.

While the artichokes cook, heat the ½ cup of EVOO in a skillet over medium-low heat. Add the anchovies, garlic, and red pepper flakes and cook for 3 to 4 minutes, until the anchovies melt away. Add the bread crumbs and toast until deeply golden. Season with parsley and lots of black pepper. Remove from the heat, add the cheese, and toss to combine.

Add ¼ inch water to a shallow baking dish and arrange the artichokes in the pan. Spoon the filling into each leaf and the center of the artichokes. Drizzle more EVOO over the stuffed artichokes, cover the pan with foil, and bake for 15 minutes to set the stuffing. Remove the foil and bake for another 10 minutes uncovered to crisp up the tops.

Serve out of the hot baking dish with a bowl alongside to catch the leaves.

SERVES 6 AS AN APPETIZER

POTTED BEEF SIRLOIN

EVOO (extra-virgin olive oil), for browning the meat

2 pounds (1½-inch-thick) **beef sirloin**, cut into 4- to 6-ounce chunks

1 large **garlic clove**, crushed plus 6 chopped **garlic cloves**

Grill seasoning, such as McCormick's Montreal Steak Seasoning

2 pounds peeled **potatoes**, thinly sliced

2 medium **onions**, thinly sliced

1 (28-ounce) can diced **tomatoes**, drained

A couple of handfuls of grated **Parmigiano-Reggiano**

A couple of handfuls of fresh flat-leaf **parsley**, finely chopped

On cold winter nights we gathered in the dining room near the wood-burning stoves, and we would spend our time listening to stories and eating braised casseroles. This is one such meal. We loved this garlicky, spicy meat and potato casserole—a holiday version of potatoes Anna. ——Vicki and Annette

Preheat the oven to 400°F.

Heat the EVOO in a heavy-bottomed roasting pan. Brown the beef in batches, making sure to brown all sides. Return all the meat to the pan, add the crushed garlic, and sprinkle with grill seasoning. Make layers over the meat in this order: potatoes, onions, diced tomatoes with the chopped garlic, Parmigiano-Reggiano, and parsley. Continue layering to use all ingredients, then cover the pan with foil and roast to 150 to 160°F, 40 to 50 minutes. Uncover for the last 10 minutes.

SERVES 4 TO 6

VERY EASY BEEF BRISKET

John has always been a big beef eater, but his brother Andy, who loves beef now, never liked the texture as a youngster. This recipe was hearty enough for John, tender and tasty enough for Andy, and super easy for a busy mom (Dad always seems content). —Vicki and Annette

1 (2½-pound) **beef brisket**

1 (1-pound) bag **baby carrots**

6 **russet potatoes**, peeled and quartered

1 (26-ounce) jar of **marinara sauce**

1 packet of **onion soup mix**

Preheat the oven to 350°F.

Line a roasting pan with enough aluminum foil to wrap the entire brisket. Place the meat in the middle of the pan. Surround the meat with the carrots and potatoes.

In a bowl, mix the marinara sauce and onion soup mix. Pour the mixture over the meat and vegetables. Carefully fold the foil over the meat, veggies, and sauce, and fold to seal. Cook for 2 to 2½ hours, until the meat is fork tender.

SERVES 4 TO 6

ROASTED LOIN OF PORK WITH APPLES

This is the first dinner I made for Rachael when John brought her home to Poughkeepsie. Even after all those years of cooking for friends and family, I was more than a little rattled. Among other things, I forgot to marinate the meat and to season the asparagus. It was one of the blandest meals I ever made! —Vicki and Annette

1 (2- to 2½-pound) **loin of pork**

1 (10-ounce) bottle **light teriyaki sauce**

Sweet-and-sour sauce with apricots

8 to 10 small **red potatoes**, partially peeled and cut in quarters

1 (1-pound) bag **baby carrots**

3 **apples**, each quartered and cored

With a skewer or the tip of a sharp knife, pierce the pork in a few places to allow the marinade to be absorbed into the meat. Place the meat in a resealable plastic bag with the teriyaki sauce and marinate in the refrigerator for about 2 hours, turning once or twice.

Preheat the oven to 350°F. Remove the meat from the marinade and place it in a roasting pan. Cover it with the sweet-and-sour sauce. Transfer to the oven and roast for about 2 hours total, basting occasionally.

When the meat has cooked for 45 minutes, scatter the potatoes and baby carrots around the meat and return to the oven. After another 30 minutes, add the apples to the pan. Continue to roast for 45 minutes, or until the meat reaches 160°F on an instant-read thermometer and the veggies are tender.

SERVES 6 TO 8

POTTED CHICKEN WITH RICE

2 medium or 1 large **onion**, chopped

Salt and **pepper**

3 cups **chicken stock**

¾ cup **Sauternes wine**

1¼ cups **white rice**

4 tablespoons (½ stick) **butter**

1 **bay leaf**

1 **carrot**, peeled and chopped

1 **garlic clove**, smashed

1 (2½- to 3-pound) **chicken**

1 cup frozen green **peas**

A handful of fresh flat-leaf **parsley**, chopped

Another easy but good one from John's mom! —Rach

Fill a large Dutch oven to the rim with hot water for several minutes to heat it. Combine the onions, salt and pepper, chicken stock, wine, rice, butter, bay leaf, carrots, and garlic in a bowl.

Empty the water from the pot and place the chicken in the warm pot. Season the chicken with salt and pepper inside and out, then add the rice mixture to the pot, placing it around the chicken. Cover the pot, place it on a baking sheet in a cold oven, and turn the oven to 350°F. Cook for 2 hours, or until very tender. Just before serving, discard the bay leaf, stir in the peas and parsley, and cook just to heat through.

SERVES 4

SPAGHETTI AND CLAMS

3 dozen small **clams**

EVOO (extra-virgin olive oil)

Minced **garlic**

1 small **onion**, peeled and diced

Chopped fresh flat-leaf **parsley**

Salt

1 pound **spaghetti**

This was always a Friday-night dish at our house. While other families kept it simple on Fridays, our mother was straining clam juice through cheesecloth. We felt so deprived, because our friend's mother worked and they actually ate TV dinners on certain Fridays. How lucky we thought she was because she got to eat her dinner out of an aluminum plate with separate compartments for each food. It just seemed so modern! —Vicki and Annette

Clean and rinse the clams. Place the clams in 2 inches of water in a pot, cover, and cook over medium heat until the clams open. Remove the clams and set aside. (Discard any that do not open.) Pour the clam juice through cheesecloth and set the juice aside.

Place a separate pot over low heat and add enough EVOO to coat the bottom. Add the garlic and onion and lightly brown. Add the clam juice and parsley. Cook for 30 minutes. Add the clams and simmer for 15 minutes.

Bring a large pot of water to a boil for the spaghetti. When the water boils, add salt and the pasta. Cook to al dente and drain.

Serve the clam sauce over the hot spaghetti.

SERVES 4 TO 6

GRANDPA VIC'S XMAS EVE SEAFOOD SALAD

In our youth, Christmas Eve was a major family event, spent at our grandmother's house. Fish and seafood were the mainstay of the traditional dishes served that evening. It was quite a scene, with our mother, grandmother, and all of our aunts cooking for hours on end. Lots of female bonding was taking place, which is the best part of cooking with family for family.

Our parents always brought the seafood salad, which our father prepared ahead of time. Everyone loved it. It was his signature dish and he served it with great pride. Long after our mother passed away, he continued to bring it to family functions. The year before he died, we had Christmas Eve at our sister's house. We all noticed that his seafood salad was not up to par. Tactfully, we asked what recipe he had used and he told us that his fish store had made the salad for him. For the first and only time it was store bought. It was quite a revelation. —Vicki and Annette

4 (1¼-pound) **lobsters**

5 pounds large **shrimp**, peeled and deveined

3 pounds **bay scallops**

2 pounds **calamari**

6 **celery stalks**, diced

8 **garlic cloves**, thinly sliced

½ cup chopped fresh flat-leaf **parsley**

Juice of 8 to 10 **lemons**

2 cups **EVOO** (extra-virgin olive oil) plus more as needed

Fill a large pot halfway with water and bring to a boil. Add the lobsters and cook until the shells are bright red, 10 to 12 minutes. Use tongs to remove the lobsters from the pot and let them cool.

While the lobsters cool, add half the shrimp to the same pot the lobsters were cooked in and cook for 2 minutes or until they are just pink; use a slotted spoon to transfer the cooked shrimp to a bowl to cool. Repeat with the remaining shrimp. When all the shrimp are cool, cut them in half and place them in a large mixing bowl.

In the same pot, cook the scallops for 5 minutes, or until tender. Scoop from the water with a slotted spoon and let cool. Repeat with the calamari, cooking for 5 minutes or until tender. Scoop from the water with a slotted spoon and let cool. Discard all but 2 cups of the cooking water.

When the lobsters are cool enough to handle, crack the shells and remove the meat. Cut it into bite-size pieces and add it to the bowl with the shrimp. Add the cooled scallops and calamari.

Stir together the chopped celery, garlic, and parsley and add them to the bowl, stirring to distribute them throughout the seafood. Add the juice of 8 lemons, the EVOO, and the cooled seafood-cooking liquid and stir again. Refrigerate the salad, stirring every 6 to 8 hours. Just before serving add more lemon juice and EVOO to taste.

SERVES 20 TO 25

GRANDMA ROSE'S SUNDAY SAUCE

When we were growing up, a pot of this sauce would always be on the stove when we got home from church. Sunday dinner was served at about two o'clock, so preparations started at about eight in the morning. Every time we walked by the stove one of us would take a sample of a meatball from the pot or dip a piece of bread into the sauce, sprinkle it with cheese, and munch away. John's grandma Rose (our mother) always made plenty, knowing that a good portion of it would disappear before it ever made it to the dinner table. —Vicki and Annette

½ cup **EVOO** (extra-virgin olive oil)

2 **onions**, 1 coarsely chopped, 1 finely chopped

3 **garlic cloves**, minced

4 (28-ounce) cans **crushed tomatoes**

1 pound **Italian sausage links**

1 pound **ground beef**

1 **egg**

½ cup **bread crumbs**

½ cup grated **Romano cheese**

8 teaspoons dried **oregano**

4 teaspoons **salt**

4 teaspoons **black pepper**

1 pound thinly sliced **round steak**

3 tablespoons chopped fresh flat-leaf **parsley**

1 hard-boiled **egg**

3 fresh **basil leaves**

Heat the EVOO in a large, wide pot. Add the coarsely chopped onion and 2 of the minced garlic cloves and cook over medium-high heat until lightly browned, 5 to 6 minutes. Stir in the tomatoes with their juices, and bring to a simmer.

Prick the sausages 6 or 8 times with a fork and place them in a frying pan with ½ inch of water. Bring to a simmer over medium heat and cook until the water evaporates, turning the sausages frequently. When the water has cooked off, cook the sausages a minute or two longer to brown, then add them, whole, to the sauce.

To make the meatballs, mix the ground beef, half the finely chopped onion, the raw egg, bread crumbs, cheese, 2 teaspoons of the oregano, 1 teaspoon salt, and 1 teaspoon pepper. Mix the ingredients well and shape into 2-inch meatballs. Add them to the simmering sauce.

Using a mallet, pound the round steak until it is uniformly thin. Sprinkle with 1 teaspoon salt, 1 teaspoon pepper, 2 teaspoons of the oregano, 1 tablespoon of parsley, and the remaining minced garlic, and finely chopped onion. Crumble the hard-boiled egg over the meat. Roll the meat into a log and tie with string or secure with wooden toothpicks. Add the rolled steak to the sauce.

Sprinkle the remaining 2 teaspoons of salt, 2 teaspoons of pepper, 4 teaspoons of oregano, and 2 tablespoons of parsley, and the basil over the sauce. Cook on low to medium heat for 4 to 6 hours, stirring every 30 minutes. Serve with your favorite pasta.

You can add any leftover meat from the refrigerator such as pork chops, chicken, or veal cutlets to the pot, and you can also add pork or beef ribs. For this particular dish, the more meat the merrier!

SERVES 10 TO 12

GRANDMA ROSE'S
RED FISH SAUCE

¼ cup **EVOO** (extra-virgin olive oil)

4 **garlic cloves**, chopped

1 large **onion**, coarsely diced

2 (28-ounce) cans **crushed tomatoes**

1 (28-ounce) can **whole tomatoes**

2 1½-pound **lobsters**

1 pound large **shrimp**, peeled and deveined

1 dozen littleneck **clams**, scrubbed and rinsed

1 dozen **mussels**, scrubbed and rinsed

1 pound **calamari** bodies, cut into rings

1 pound **scallops**, rinsed

2 tablespoons dried **oregano**

¼ cup chopped fresh flat-leaf **parsley**

3 **bay leaves**

1 teaspoon **salt**

1 teaspoon **black pepper**

Whenever people say someone was a "saint," our mother always comes to mind. She was a wonderfully easygoing person and a very docile and domesticated wife (after all, it was the fifties). We all loved this dish and it was served not only for the family, but also for company. In retrospect, her patience must have been stretched to the limit during the preparation of this and a few other dishes that our father felt needed his attention, and he would always oversee any recipes that involved cleaning seafood. On those occasions the kitchen became a battleground, with her against her four offspring looking for a sample (clams, either cooked or raw, were our favorite) and our father "helping" her clean the calamari—whether she was ready or not—and giving instructions to a woman who basically didn't need any! —Vicki and Annette

Heat the EVOO in a large, wide pot over low heat. Add the garlic and onion and cook for 5 to 7 minutes, until lightly browned; do not burn the garlic. Add the crushed tomatoes, raise the heat to medium, and simmer for 15 minutes. While the sauce cooks, break the whole tomatoes into pieces with a wooden spoon.

Split the lobsters and clean out the body cavity. Cut the lobster halves in pieces and crack the claws. Add the lobster, shrimp, clams, mussels, calamari, and scallops to the sauce. Add the oregano, parsley, bay leaves, and salt and pepper. Bring to a gentle simmer and cook on low to medium heat for 45 minutes. Serve over the pasta of your choice.

SERVES 4 TO 6

STARTERS AND SNACKS

There's enough stress in life that we cannot escape; why invite it into your kitchen—or your next party? The whole key to cooking when it comes to entertaining is keeping it simple. Just like the holiday meals and my family's recipes that are included in this book, all of the tasty treats in this chapter are low maintenance and foolproof and are just as appropriate for a cocktail party or first course of a big dinner as they are for an afternoon of watching old movies or the big game.

STUFFED EGGS

I love deviled eggs; they are my signature appetizer. Instead of cutting them in half lengthwise I cut just enough off the top to remove the yolk and serve the stuffed eggs whole. Still, even the above-average devilish egg becomes a bit of a bore after a while so I like to play around with the flavors in the stuffing. These are some of my favorite variations. To fill the eggs, spoon the egg yolk mixture into a plastic food storage bag and squeeze it into one corner. Snip a small hole in the corner of the bag and pipe the filling into the egg whites. For perfect hard-boiled eggs every time, put the eggs in a saucepan, reserving the egg carton. Cover the eggs with cold water and bring to boil over high heat. Turn off the heat, cover the pot, and let the eggs stand for 10 minutes. Drain off the hot water and refill the pot with cold water to cool the eggs completely. Drain the water out of the pot, place the lid on the pot again, and shake the pot to crack the eggs. Peel the eggs under gently running cold water.

Deviled Ham and Eggs

Cut the fat rounded ends off the eggs, scoop the yolks into a bowl, and stand the hard-boiled egg whites upright in the egg carton. If you prefer to serve the eggs on a platter, trim a small piece of egg off the pointed ends so they will stand upright.

Place the ham in a food processor and grind or very finely chop it. Add the ham to the yolks along with the mayo, mustard, hot sauce, and relish. Grate 3 to 4 tablespoons of onion directly over the bowl so that all of the onion juice falls into the eggs. Add the parsley, dill, and salt and pepper. Mash everything together to make a smooth filling, adding a little extra mayo if necessary.

Overstuff the eggs; you will have plenty of filling.

MAKES 1 DOZEN

12 large hard-boiled **eggs**, peeled

¼ pound **deli-sliced ham**, coarsely chopped

3 to 4 tablespoons **mayonnaise**, just enough to bind

2 rounded tablespoons **yellow mustard**

2 teaspoons **hot sauce**

2 tablespoons **pickle relish**

½ small **onion**

2 tablespoons finely chopped fresh flat-leaf **parsley**

2 tablespoons finely chopped fresh **dill**

Salt and **pepper**

Deviled Eggs with Green Olives

Cut the fat rounded ends off the eggs, scoop the yolks into a bowl, and stand the hard-boiled egg whites upright in the egg carton. If you prefer to serve the eggs on a platter, trim a small piece of egg off the pointed ends so they will stand upright.

Break the egg yolks up a little bit using a fork. Add the olives, mayo, mustard, and hot sauce. Grate 3 to 4 tablespoons of the onion into the bowl so that you catch all of the onion juice. Add some salt and pepper to the yolks, then mash until smooth and check the seasonings.

Fill the eggs, overstuffing them a little. Garnish with a dash of paprika.

MAKES 1 DOZEN

12 large hard-boiled **eggs**, peeled

½ cup well-drained **green olives with pimientos**, finely chopped

3 to 4 tablespoons **mayonnaise**, just enough to bind

2 tablespoons **yellow** or Dijon **mustard**

1 teaspoon **hot sauce**

½ small **onion**

Salt and **pepper**

Sweet paprika, for garnish

Carbonara Stuffed Eggs

½ tablespoon **EVOO** (extra-virgin olive oil)

¼ pound sliced **pancetta**, chopped

12 large hard-boiled **eggs**, peeled

1 small **garlic clove**

3 to 4 tablespoons **Parmigiano-Reggiano**

3 to 4 tablespoons **mayonnaise**, just enough to bind

1 teaspoon **coarse black pepper**

Hot sauce

2 tablespoons fresh flat-leaf **parsley**, finely chopped

Heat the EVOO in a small skillet over medium heat. Add the pancetta and cook until crisp, 3 to 4 minutes. Drain the pancetta on a paper-towel-lined plate.

Cut the fat rounded ends off the eggs, scoop the yolks into a bowl, and stand the hard-boiled egg whites upright in the egg carton. If you prefer to serve the eggs on a platter, trim a small piece of egg off the pointed ends so they will stand upright.

Break the egg yolks up a little bit using a fork. Grate the garlic into the bowl, then add the crispy pancetta, the cheese, mayo, pepper, and a few dashes of hot sauce. Mash until smooth and check the seasonings.

Fill the egg whites, overstuffing them a little. Garnish with parsley.

MAKES 1 DOZEN

Bacon and Deviled Eggs

12 large hard-boiled **eggs**, peeled

8 slices of good quality **smoky bacon**

3 to 4 tablespoons **mayonnaise**

1 teaspoon **sweet smoked paprika**

2 tablespoons **yellow mustard**

½ small **onion**

1 teaspoon **hot sauce**

Salt and **pepper**

4 **grape** or **cherry tomatoes**

1 **romaine lettuce leaf**, finely chopped

Preheat the oven to 375°F.

Cut the fat rounded ends off the eggs, scoop the yolks into a bowl, and stand the hard-boiled egg whites upright in the egg carton. If you prefer to serve the eggs on a platter, trim a small piece of egg off the pointed ends so they will stand upright.

Bake the bacon on a slotted pan for 15 minutes, or until crisp. Drain and cool the bacon on paper towels, then chop it fine.

Break the egg yolks up a little bit using a fork. Add three quarters of the chopped bacon, the mayo, paprika, and mustard. Grate 3 to 4 tablespoons of onion and juice directly into the bowl, and add the hot sauce and salt and pepper. Mash and taste the filling for seasoning, adding salt to taste if necessary.

Fill the egg whites, overstuffing them a little. Garnish the eggs to look like BLTs. Trim the ends off the tomatoes, then cut each tomato into 3 slices. Top each egg with the remaining bacon bits, some chopped lettuce, and a slice of tomato.

MAKES 1 DOZEN

Uptown Stuffed Eggs with Caviar

12 large hard-boiled **eggs**, peeled

3 to 4 tablespoons **mayonnaise**, just enough to bind

1 tablespoon **Dijon mustard**

Juice of ½ **lemon**

A few dashes of **Worcestershire sauce**

½ small **onion**

Salt and **pepper**

¼ cup **crème frâiche**

1 ounce **sevruga caviar** or other caviar of choice

1 tablespoon finely chopped fresh **chives**, optional

Cut the fat rounded ends off the eggs, scoop the yolks into a bowl, and stand the hard-boiled egg whites upright in the egg carton. If you prefer to serve the eggs on a platter, trim a small piece of egg off the pointed ends so they will stand upright.

Break the egg yolks up a little bit using a fork. Add the mayo, mustard, lemon juice, and Worcestershire. Grate in about 3 tablespoons of onion and juice, working directly over the bowl. Season the filling with salt and pepper, mix to combine, and check for seasoning.

Fill the egg whites, overstuffing them a little. Garnish the eggs with small dollops of crème fraîche and caviar and sprinkle with chives.

MAKES 1 DOZEN

Caesar Stuffed Eggs

12 large hard-boiled **eggs**, peeled

1 small **garlic clove**

2 teaspoons **anchovy paste**

A handful of grated **Parmigiano-Reggiano**, 3 to 4 tablespoons

3 to 4 tablespoons **mayonnaise**, just enough to bind

1 teaspoon **Worcestershire sauce**

Juice of ½ **lemon**

1 teaspoon **coarse black pepper**

2 **romaine lettuce leaves** from the heart, finely chopped

This is the one I am famous for, and it's by far my most requested stuffed egg. It tastes exactly (or, eggs-actly) like a Caesar salad.

Cut the fat rounded ends off the eggs, scoop the yolks into a bowl, and stand the hard-boiled egg whites upright in the egg carton. If you prefer to serve the eggs on a platter, trim a small piece of egg off the pointed ends so they will stand upright.

Break the egg yolks up a little bit using a fork. Grate the garlic directly over the bowl, then add the anchovy paste, Parmigiano, mayo, Worcestershire, lemon juice, pepper, and half the finely chopped lettuce. Mash until smooth and check the seasonings.

Fill the egg whites, overstuffing them a little. Garnish with the remaining finely chopped greens.

MAKES 1 DOZEN

Lemon-Caper Stuffed Eggs

Cut the fat rounded ends off the eggs, scoop the yolks into a bowl, and stand the hard-boiled egg whites upright in the egg carton. If you prefer to serve the eggs on a platter, trim a small piece of egg off the pointed ends so they will stand upright.

Break the egg yolks up a little bit using a fork. Grate the garlic into the egg yolks, then grate about 2 tablespoons of onion juice into the bowl. Add the capers, 1 teaspoon of lemon zest, the juice of the lemon, a few dashes of hot sauce, the mayo, pepper, and half of the parsley. Mash until smooth and check the seasonings.

Fill the egg whites, overstuffing them a little. Garnish with the remaining parsley.

MAKES 1 DOZEN

12 large hard-boiled **eggs**, peeled

1 small **garlic clove**

¼ small **onion**

2 tablespoons **capers**, drained and chopped (or soaked in milk and drained if using salt-packed capers)

Zest and juice of 1 **lemon**

Hot sauce

3 to 4 tablespoons **mayonnaise**, just enough to bind

1 teaspoon coarse **black pepper**

3 tablespoons fresh flat-leaf **parsley**, finely chopped

Asian Stuffed Eggs

Cut the fat rounded ends off the eggs, scoop the yolks into a bowl, and stand the hard-boiled egg whites upright in the egg carton. If you prefer to serve the eggs on a platter, trim a small piece of egg off the pointed ends so they will stand upright.

Break the egg yolks up a little bit using a fork. Add the ginger, scallions, garlic, tamari, hot sauce, mayo, and pepper. Mash until smooth and check the seasonings.

Fill the egg whites, overstuffing them a little. Garnish the eggs with whole cilantro leaves or finely chop the cilantro and sprinkle it over the eggs.

MAKES 1 DOZEN

12 large hard-boiled **eggs**, peeled

1 inch of fresh **gingerroot**, peeled and finely grated

2 to 3 thin **scallions**, finely chopped

1 **garlic clove**, grated

2 tablespoons **tamari** (aged soy sauce)

1 teaspoon **hot sauce**

3 to 4 tablespoons **mayonnaise**, just enough to bind

Black pepper

Fresh **cilantro**, chopped or whole leaves, for garnish

Curry Stuffed Eggs

12 large hard-boiled **eggs**, peeled

1 inch of fresh **gingerroot**, peeled and finely grated

2 to 3 thin **scallions**, finely chopped

1 **garlic clove**, grated

1 rounded tablespoon **curry powder** or mild curry paste, such as Patak's

3 to 4 tablespoons **mayonnaise**, just enough to bind

Salt and **pepper**

2 tablespoons finely chopped **red bell pepper**

1 tablespoon finely chopped fresh **cilantro**

Cut the fat rounded ends off the eggs, scoop the yolks into a bowl, and stand the hard-boiled egg whites upright in the egg carton. If you prefer to serve the eggs on a platter, trim a small piece of egg off the pointed ends so they will stand upright.

Break the egg yolks up a little bit using a fork. Add the ginger, scallions, garlic, curry powder, mayo, and salt and pepper. Mash until smooth and check the seasonings.

Fill the egg whites, overstuffing them a little. Garnish the eggs with the red bell pepper and cilantro.

MAKES 1 DOZEN

Crabby Eggs

12 large hard-boiled **eggs**, peeled

3 to 4 tablespoons **mayonnaise**, just enough to bind

1 tablespoon **Dijon mustard**

Juice of ½ **lemon**

1 teaspoon **Worcestershire sauce**

1 teaspoon **hot sauce**

½ small **onion**

¼ cup **celery leaves**, a handful, finely chopped

1 tablespoon fresh **thyme leaves**, finely chopped

6 ounces **lump crabmeat**, picked over for shells

2 teaspoons to 1 tablespoon **Old Bay seasoning**

Black pepper

2 tablespoons finely chopped **red bell pepper**

2 tablespoons finely chopped fresh **chives**

Cut the fat rounded ends off the eggs, scoop the yolks into a bowl, and stand the hard-boiled egg whites upright in the egg carton. If you prefer to serve the eggs on a platter, trim a small piece of egg off the pointed ends so they will stand upright.

Break the egg yolks up a little bit using a fork. Add the mayo, mustard, lemon juice, Worcestershire, and hot sauce. Grate in about 3 tablespoons of onion and juice, working directly over the bowl. Add the celery leaves and thyme to the bowl, then break up the crab as you add it. Season the crab with a couple teaspoons of Old Bay and some pepper, then mix to combine the filling and check for seasoning.

Fill the egg whites, overstuffing them a little. Garnish the crabby eggs with the red bell pepper and chives.

MAKES 1 DOZEN

SWEET BAKED BRIE

Preheat the oven to 350°F.

Spread the puff pastry sheet onto a counter and roll it to ⅛ inch thick. Trim a few inches of the dough off the ends to square it off (save the scraps). Cut the Brie through the equator into two disks, and place one half on the puff pastry, cut side up. Spread the jam on the cheese, and sprinkle with the almonds. Replace the top half of the Brie. Wrap the dough up and over the Brie, and brush with egg wash to secure. Place the Brie package on a nonstick baking sheet, seam side down. Cut designs of your choice from the dough scraps and decorate the top of the dough, then brush with the egg wash. Bake for 18 to 20 minutes, or until golden brown.

Serve with the crackers.

SERVES 8

1 sheet of frozen **puff pastry**, 11 x 17 inches, defrosted

1-pound wheel of **Brie cheese**, about 5 inches in diameter

2 tablespoons **raspberry jam**

¼ cup sliced **almonds**, toasted (see Note, page 102)

1 **egg**, beaten with a splash of water

1 box **water crackers**

VARIATION: SAVORY BAKED BRIE

Instead of jam and nuts, fill the Brie with finely chopped giardiniera (hot pickled vegetables) or chopped olives, capers, and sun-dried tomatoes.

EGGPLANT CAVIAR

The seeds of the eggplant make this rich and healthful spread resemble caviar eggs.

Preheat the oven to its highest setting, at least 500°F.

Cut 2 or 3 slits into the eggplant and place it directly on the oven rack in the middle of the oven. Roast the eggplant until it is tender, about 25 minutes. The roasted eggplant should look like a flat tire when you (carefully!) remove it from the oven. Set it aside to cool for 10 minutes or so.

When the eggplant is cool enough to handle, use a sharp knife to peel the skin away from the eggplant flesh. Place the cooked eggplant flesh and the lemon juice in a food processor and add the garlic, salt and pepper, herbs, and EVOO. Pulse to puree the eggplant into a smooth dip. Transfer to a serving bowl and surround the bowl with pita chips.

SERVES 8

1 medium, firm **eggplant**

Juice of ½ **lemon**

1 **garlic clove**, cracked away from its skin

Salt and **pepper**

A few sprigs of fresh flat-leaf **parsley**

A couple of fresh **basil leaves**, torn

2 to 3 tablespoons **EVOO** (extra-virgin olive oil), a healthy drizzle

Pita chips, for dipping

RANCHORAMA
RANCH DIP AND VARIATIONS

For your dippin' pleasure I challenged myself to see how many different ways I could jazz up this perennial crowd-pleaser, a tangy blend of buttermilk and fresh herbs. The beauty of buttermilk is that it is made with skim or low-fat milk, yet it tastes thick and creamy. It's fermented—a little like yogurt. One cup has two-thirds the calories of whole milk and less than one-third of the fat (and less than an eighth of the calories of heavy cream). To make this into ranch salad dressing, just change the ratio of buttermilk and sour cream, using 1 cup of buttermilk and just ¼ cup sour cream.

¾ cup **buttermilk**

¾ cup **sour cream**

1 tablespoon fresh **lemon juice**

1 **garlic clove**, grated or finely chopped

A few dashes of **hot sauce**

A handful of fresh flat-leaf **parsley**, chopped

A handful of fresh **dill**, chopped

A handful of fresh **chives**, chopped

Salt and **pepper**

In a medium bowl, stir together the buttermilk, sour cream, lemon juice, garlic, hot sauce, parsley, dill, and chives. Season the dip with salt and pepper, adding more hot sauce to taste if needed.

MAKES 1½ CUPS

RANCH DIP MIX-INS

RANCHAMOLE: Stir together a mashed ripe avocado and 1 recipe of ranch dip. Serve with whole grain tortilla chips.

TEX-MEX RANCHER: Stir ½ cup salsa—chipotle, verde, any kind you like—into 1 recipe of ranch dip. Serve with whole grain tortilla chips.

TANGY RANCHER: Stir ½ cup prepared barbecue sauce into 1 recipe of ranch dip and serve with breaded chicken tenders and veggies.

ITALIAN RANCHER: Stir ½ cup prepared pesto into 1 recipe of ranch dip and serve with pita chips.

SPINACH-ARTICHOKE RANCH: Stir ½ cup finely chopped artichoke hearts and 1 package frozen chopped spinach, defrosted and squeezed dry in a clean kitchen towel, into 1 recipe of ranch dip; top with shredded asiago cheese. Serve with pita chips or bread sticks.

WEEKEND SALMON DIP: Finely chop ¼ pound smoked salmon and stir into 1 recipe of ranch dip. Top with 2 to 3 tablespoons of capers and 1 finely chopped shallot. Serve with toasted party-size rye or pumpernickel slices and cucumber sticks or slices.

FOUR-LAYER MEDITERRANEAN DIP

1 family-size (17-ounce) container of **hummus**

1 cup **pickled vegetable salad**, such as giardiniera, drained and chopped

1 cup pitted **kalamata olives**, chopped

1 (12-ounce) jar **roasted red peppers**, drained and chopped

Pita chips, cucumber slices, and **celery**, for dipping

Scoop the hummus into a small or medium bowl and spread the giardiniera over it. Top with the olives, spreading them in an even layer, then with the roasted red peppers. Place the bowl on a serving platter and surround with pita chips, cucumber, and celery for dipping.

SERVES 8 TO 10

ROASTED VEGGIE DIP

1 **fennel bulb**, cored and chopped

1 small **onion**, chopped

3 **garlic cloves**, smashed

½ small **eggplant**, peeled and chopped

1 small **zucchini**, trimmed, cut in half lengthwise, then cut into thick half-moons

3 tablespoons **EVOO** (extra-virgin olive oil)

3 tablespoons **aged balsamic vinegar**

Salt and **pepper**

20 fresh **basil leaves**, coarsely chopped

¼ cup fresh flat-leaf **parsley leaves**, chopped

Next time you make a turkey sandwich, slap some of this veggie dip on the bread rather than mayo for a lighter and more flavorful lunch. Or serve it with baked pita chips, celery sticks, and carrot sticks for a healthy snack.

Preheat the oven 400°F.

Place the veggies on a rimmed baking sheet, drizzle with the EVOO and balsamic vinegar, and season liberally with salt and pepper. Toss to coat thoroughly, then roast the veggies for 30 to 40 minutes until brown and tender, turning them once or twice as they roast. Cool and transfer to a food processor with the basil and parsley. Pulse the vegetables to make a smooth puree. Transfer to a bowl and season with salt and pepper to taste.

MAKES 2 CUPS

BLT GUACAMOLE DIP

½ pound **bacon**

3 ripe **Hass avocados**

2 **garlic cloves**

2 **jalapeño peppers**, seeded and
finely chopped

¼ **red onion**, finely chopped

2 **lemons**

Salt

1 small **heart of romaine lettuce**,
chopped

1 cup **chopped tomatoes**
(3 to 4 seeded Roma or plum
tomatoes)

Fancy whole grain or blue
corn **tortilla chips**

Preheat the oven to 350°F.

Place the bacon on a slotted pan and bake for about 15 minutes, or until
crisp. Drain on a paper-towel-lined plate and when it is cool, coarsely chop.

Halve and pit the avocados and scoop the flesh into a bowl. Grate the
garlic directly into the bowl, add the jalapeños and red onion, and squeeze
the juice of the 2 lemons over the avocados. Mash to the desired consistency and season with salt. Top the guac with the bacon, lettuce, and
tomatoes and serve with the tortilla chips.

SERVES 8

MEDITERRANEAN FETA DIP

1½ cups **feta cheese** crumbles,
plain or with Mediterranean
herbs

½ cup **whole milk**

½ cup toasted **walnut pieces**,
toasted (see Note, page 102)

1 teaspoon dried **oregano**,
⅓ palmful

1 teaspoon coarse **black pepper**

Juice of ½ **lemon**

1 teaspoon **hot sauce**

1 **roasted red pepper**, chopped,
for garnish

½ cup pitted **kalamata olives**,
chopped, for garnish

Seedless cucumber slices, for
dipping

Crispy flatbreads such as
lavash or pita chips, for dipping

In a food processor, combine the feta, milk, walnuts, oregano, pepper,
lemon juice, and hot sauce. Puree until smooth and creamy. Scrape the feta
dip into a serving bowl and garnish with the red peppers and olives. Serve
with cucumbers and crispy flatbreads for dipping.

SERVES 8

ITALIAN NACHOS

2 tablespoons **EVOO** (extra-virgin olive oil)

1 pound **ground sirloin**

1 small **onion**, finely chopped

1 small **carrot**, peeled and grated or finely chopped

4 **garlic cloves**, minced

1 **bay leaf**

½ cup **dry red wine**

Salt and **pepper**

1 teaspoon **Worcestershire sauce**

½ cup **beef** or **chicken stock**

1 (15-ounce) can **crushed tomatoes**

1 (8-ounce) can **tomato sauce**

2 tablespoons chopped fresh **basil**

2 tablespoons chopped fresh **flat-leaf parsley**

1 large bag **yellow corn chips**

2 cups **smoked scamorza cheese**, grated

½ cup **yellow hot pepper rings**

1 cup **kalamata olives**, pitted and chopped

Preheat the oven to 350°F.

Heat the EVOO in a large saucepan over medium-high heat. Add the meat and brown it to the point where it is becoming a little on the crispy side, 10 to 12 minutes, breaking it up with a wooden spoon as you go. This will give the sauce a deep flavor. Move the browned meat over to one side of the pan and add the onions, carrots, garlic, and bay leaf to the empty side of the pan. Cook until the veggies are softened, about 5 minutes.

Deglaze the pan with the wine, scraping up all the browned bits of meat and veggies from the bottom of the pan. Raise the heat to high and add the salt, pepper, Worcestershire sauce, stock, crushed tomatoes, and tomato sauce. Cook until the sauce starts to thicken, 6 to 7 minutes. Remove from the heat and stir in the basil and parsley.

Spread half the corn chips on a rimmed baking sheet and top with half of the sauce (do your best to cover the chips). Top with half the cheese, then repeat with a second layer of chips, sauce, and cheese. Place in the oven to melt the cheese for just a couple of minutes. Top with the hot pepper rings and kalamata olives and serve hot.

SERVES 8

CURRY CHICKPEAS

1 (15-ounce) can **chickpeas**, drained

1 teaspoon **curry powder**

2 pinches of **cayenne pepper**

Pinch of **cinnamon**

Salt and **pepper**

Serve these spicy, crunchy bites as a healthy snack or in place of toasted nuts as a party nibble.

Place the chickpeas in a medium, dry skillet. Season with the curry powder, cayenne, cinnamon, and salt and pepper and toast over medium-high heat for 8 to 10 minutes, until deep golden brown in color and crispy.

MAKES 1½ CUPS

PIGSKIN PANINIS

These are a hit for football season! Porchetta sandwiches, made with thinly sliced roast pork, are a favorite of my husband's. Add provolone for a cheesy combo panini.

Preheat the oven to 400°F.

Cut 6 slits in the pork loin and nestle the garlic cloves into the slits. In a small bowl, combine the rosemary, thyme, EVOO, and grill seasoning. Rub the herb mixture into the pork loin, making sure to coat all sides. Place in a roasting pan or on a rimmed baking sheet and roast until the internal temperature reads 155°F on an instant-read thermometer, about 1 hour. Remove the pork to a cutting board and tent with foil. Let it rest for 15 minutes. Slice the pork loin thin.

While the pork is roasting, drain the giardiniera and place it in a food processor. Pulse the vegetables to finely chop into relish.

Spread the rolls with the giardiniera relish. Add some of the pork slices and set the roll top in place. Press in a panini maker until toasty and golden brown (see Tip).

SERVES 8

1 boneless **pork loin roast**, 3½ to 4 pounds

6 **garlic cloves**, cracked away from their skins

4 sprigs of fresh **rosemary**, leaves removed and finely chopped

10 to 12 sprigs of fresh **thyme**, leaves removed and chopped

2 tablespoons **EVOO** (extra-virgin olive oil)

2 tablespoons **grill seasoning**, such as McCormick's Montreal Steak Seasoning

1½ to 2 cups **giardiniera** (hot pickled vegetables), drained

8 **Kaiser rolls**, split

TIP If you do not have a panini press, cook the sandwiches in a large skillet and weight the sandwiches down with a smaller heavy skillet with a heavy can or two in it. Turn the sammie after 3 to 4 minutes.

GRAPE BITES WITH PROSCIUTTO CREAM

In a bowl, stir together the mascarpone and prosciutto and season with some black pepper. Spoon or pipe a small amount of the prosciutto cream mixture onto the cut side of a grape and sandwich the cream with the other half of the grape. Continue until you have used up all the cream.

SERVES 6

1 cup **mascarpone cheese**

¼ pound sliced **prosciutto**, chopped

Black pepper

1 bunch of large **green or red seedless grapes**, halved lengthwise

SMOKY STUFFED DATES

Cut the dates in half and stuff each half with a smoked almond. Garnish with the chives.

16 **pitted dates**

32 **smoked almonds**

2 tablespoons finely chopped **fresh chives**

4 (8-ounce) logs of **goat cheese**

FLAVORED GOAT CHEESE BALLS

For rolling

¼ cup **poppy seeds**

¼ cup finely chopped fresh **herbs** of any variety

¼ cup **chili powder**

¼ cup toasted **sesame seeds** spiked with granulated garlic

Slice each log into 8 pieces. Wet your hands with warm water, and roll each piece of cheese into a ball, rewetting your hands as needed. Coat each piece in one of the flavorings, making 8 of each. Arrange on a platter and serve.

MAKES 32 BALLS

BABY PEARS AND FIGS WITH GORGONZOLA

Ripe **pears**

Ripe **fresh figs**

1 **lemon**

Aged balsamic vinegar

Gorgonzola dolce

Walnut halves

Finely chopped **chives** or sage leaves

This is a method more than a recipe—make as many or as few as you like.

Preheat the oven to 400°F.. Halve small ripe pears or fresh large figs. Sprinkle the cut sides with lemon juice to prevent them from browning and arrange in a baking dish, cut sides up. Drizzle the fruit with aged balsamic vinegar and top with spoonfuls of Gorgonzola dolce (a young, mild, and creamy version of Gorgonzola cheese). Top the cheese with walnut halves and bake for 5 minutes. Garnish with finely chopped chives or slivered sage leaves.

CHEESE AND NUT BALLS

8 ounces **cream cheese**, softened

4 tablespoons (½ stick) **butter**, softened

10 ounces shredded **extra-sharp cheddar cheese**

⅓ cup **mango chutney**, chopped

1 cup **macadamia nuts**, chopped

2 handfuls of fresh flat-leaf **parsley**, chopped

You'll need to put this spread out on a table that can be surrounded. Friends and relatives tend to lounge near this quick and easy cheese and nut appetizer. If you don't have time to chill the mixture so it can be rolled into balls, serve it as a dip, garnished with nuts and additional chutney.

Beat the cream cheese and butter together in a mixing bowl with a wooden spoon or a handheld mixer. Add the cheddar, chutney, half the nuts, and half the parsley and combine thoroughly. Chill the mixture overnight, or until very firm. The next day, scoop the mixture out by tablespoons and form into balls. Roll the balls in the reserved nuts and parsley. Small balls can be served over mild greens and fruit or salad.

SERVES 8

LEAN, MEAN, SPICY BEEF SATAY STICKS

Pop the beef in the freezer for 15 to 20 minutes to make slicing easier.

Preheat a grill pan or a griddle over medium-high heat.

Place the beef strips in a medium-large casserole dish. Stir together 1 cup of the teriyaki sauce, the crushed garlic, and the chili oil and pour over the beef strips, stirring to coat. Set aside while you make the dipping sauce.

In a small sauce pot, combine the remaining ¼ cup teriyaki sauce, the apple juice, and the chunk of ginger and bring the mixture to a boil. Once it reaches a boil, turn off the heat and let it sit for 2 to 3 minutes to infuse with the ginger flavor. Discard the ginger. Place the peanut butter in a medium mixing bowl and whisk in the zest of one lime and the hot teriyaki–apple juice mixture until smooth. Transfer to a pretty serving dish.

Thread the beef strips onto wooden skewers and grill for 2 minutes on each side for medium. Douse with fresh lime juice. Garnish the meat with the scallions and toasted sesame seeds.

SERVES 8

1 pound **top round steak** cut against the grain into thin 1½-inch-wide strips (about 20 slices)

1¼ cups **teriyaki sauce**

4 **garlic cloves**, crushed

3 teaspoons **hot chili oil**

½ cup **apple juice**

1 inch piece of fresh **gingerroot**, peeled

1 cup **peanut butter**, chunky or smooth

2 **limes**

4 **scallions**, thinly sliced

3 tablespoons toasted **sesame seeds**

BUFFALO CHICKEN MEATBALLS

Preheat the oven to 400°F.

Place the chicken in a mixing bowl and add the egg and bread crumbs. Grate 3 to 4 tablespoons of onion directly into the bowl, then grate in the garlic. Add the parsley and season with salt and pepper. Use your hands to mix the ingredients thoroughly but don't overmix. Press the meat down in the bowl and score it in 4 equal portions using the side of your hand. Form each portion into 4 meatballs for 16 meatballs total. Arrange the meatballs on a nonstick rimmed baking sheet and coat with the EVOO. Bake the meatballs until cooked through and golden brown, 12 to 15 minutes.

While the meatballs are baking, melt the butter in a large skillet over medium heat. Add the hot sauce and whisk to combine. Toss the baked meatballs in the hot sauce and roll them around in the sauce to coat.

Transfer the meatballs to a serving platter and spike each one with a toothpick or serving fork. In a small bowl combine all but ½ tablespoon of the scallions with the sour cream, buttermilk, and blue cheese crumbles. Garnish the blue cheese dressing with the reserved scallions and serve alongside the meatballs with the celery and carrot sticks.

SERVES 6 TO 8

1 pound **ground chicken**

1 **egg yolk**

A generous handful of **bread crumbs**

½ small **onion**

2 **garlic cloves**, peeled

A handful of fresh flat-leaf **parsley**, finely chopped

Salt and **pepper**

1 tablespoon **EVOO** (extra-virgin olive oil)

2 tablespoons **butter**

½ cup **hot sauce**, such as Frank's RedHot

2 **scallions**, finely chopped

½ cup **sour cream**

½ cup **buttermilk** or cream

½ cup **blue cheese** crumbles

A couple handfuls of **celery sticks**

A couple handfuls of **carrot sticks**

CRAB-STUFFED MUSHROOMS WITH BÉCHAMEL SAUCE

Preheat the oven to 400°F.

Place the mushroom caps on a lightly oiled rimmed baking sheet and roast gill side down until tender, about 10 minutes.

While the mushrooms are roasting, melt the butter in a medium skillet over medium-high heat. Add the onions, shallots, garlic, celery, bell pepper, and parsley and cook until softened, about 5 minutes. Deglaze the pan with the wine, scraping up the brown bits from the bottom of the pan with a wooden spoon, and cook for another minute. Add the toast crumbs, thyme, and salt and pepper. Mix to combine thoroughly. Gently fold in the crabmeat. Divide the stuffing among the mushroom caps and return them to the baking sheet. Bake until the mushrooms are tender and the stuffing is browned, about 25 minutes. Remove the mushrooms and turn the oven to broil.

While the mushrooms bake, prepare the béchamel: In a skillet, melt the butter over medium heat. Whisk in the flour and cook for 1 minute, then add the wine, stock, and milk. Whisk and cook for 3 to 4 minutes, until thickened. Season the sauce with salt, pepper, and nutmeg.

Top the mushrooms with a bit of béchamel sauce and sprinkle with grated Parm. Slide under the broiler for a minute to brown the sauce. Serve hot.

MAKES 2 TO 2½ DOZEN MUSHROOMS

2 pounds large **button mushrooms**, stems removed

4 tablespoons (½ stick) **butter**

1 medium **onion**, finely chopped

1 **shallot**, finely chopped

1 large **garlic clove**, finely chopped

1 **celery stalk** from the heart, finely chopped

¼ **red bell pepper**, finely chopped

¼ cup fresh flat-leaf **parsley** leaves, chopped

¼ cup **dry white wine**

2 slices **white sandwich bread**, toasted and buttered then finely chopped

¼ teaspoon ground **thyme**

Salt and **pepper**

1½ cups **fresh or canned lump crabmeat**, picked over for shells and cartilage

For the béchamel

3 tablespoons **butter**

3 tablespoons **all-purpose flour**

A splash of **white wine**

¼ cup **fish stock** or clam juice

1 cup **milk**

Salt and **pepper**

Freshly grated **nutmeg**

¼ cup grated **Parmigiano-Reggiano**

WONTON CUPS

24 **wonton wraps** (a 12-ounce package), such as Nasoya brand

2 tablespoons **vegetable oil**, plus some for brushing

½ pound medium **shrimp**, peeled, deveined, and chopped

¼ head of **napa cabbage**, shredded

3 inches of fresh **gingerroot**, peeled and grated

1 large **garlic clove**, finely chopped

5 **scallions**, green and white parts, thinly sliced

¼ cup fresh **cilantro leaves**, chopped

2 hard-boiled **eggs**, chopped (in the salad bar section of your supermarket)

Juice of 1 **lime**

¼ cup **tamari** (aged soy sauce)

3 tablespoons toasted **sesame seeds**

These taste like egg rolls; if you like these, check out the Thai-flavored version that follows.

Preheat the oven to 375°F.

Brush each wonton wrapper with a little vegetable oil, then nestle each one into one of the cups of a 24-cup nonstick mini muffin tin. Bake the wonton cups until golden brown and crisp, about 6 minutes.

While the cups are baking, put together the filling: Place a large nonstick skillet over medium-high heat with the 2 tablespoons of vegetable oil. Add the chopped shrimp and cook for 1 minute, then add the cabbage, ginger, garlic, and scallions. Cook for another minute, stirring constantly. Stir in the cilantro and eggs and cook for another minute. Add the lime juice, tamari, and sesame seeds to the mixture and stir to combine. Heat through, about a minute, and remove the mixture from the heat.

Transfer the wonton cups to a serving platter. Fill each cup with 1 to 2 tablespoons of the shrimp and cabbage mixture, and serve.

MAKES 24 PIECES

THAI-STYLE SHRIMP WONTON CUPS

24 **wonton wraps** (a 12-ounce package), such as Nasoya brand

2 tablespoons **vegetable oil**, plus some for brushing

¼ head of **napa cabbage**, shredded

3 inches of fresh **gingerroot**, peeled and grated

2 large **garlic cloves**, finely chopped

½ pound medium **shrimp**, peeled, deveined, and chopped

Zest and juice of 1 **lemon**

¼ cup **rice wine vinegar**

¼ cup fresh **basil**, 6 to 7 leaves, chopped

¼ cup fresh **mint leaves**, chopped

2 **scallions**, green and white parts, thinly sliced

¼ cup **almonds**, toasted (see Note, page 102), chopped

Preheat the oven to 375°F.

Brush each wonton wrapper with a little vegetable oil, then nestle each one down into one of the cups of a 24-cup nonstick mini muffin tin. Bake the wonton cups until golden brown and crisp, about 6 minutes.

While the wontons are baking put together the filling: Heat the 2 tablespoons of oil in a large nonstick skillet over medium-high heat. Add the cabbage, ginger, and garlic and cook for 3 to 4 minutes, or until slightly wilted. Add the shrimp and cook for another 3 to 4 minutes or until cooked through. Add the lemon zest and juice and the vinegar, and cook for another minute. Add the basil, mint, and scallions to the mixture and give a quick stir to combine.

Transfer the browned wonton cups to a serving platter. Fill each cup with 1 to 2 tablespoons of the shrimp and cabbage mixture, sprinkle with the toasted almonds, and serve.

MAKES 24 PIECES

CROSTINI ALLA NORMA

Pasta alla Norma is a fave of mine: eggplant, basil, tomato, and ricotta salata over pasta. Here's a snackable version.

Preheat an outdoor grill or grill pan to medium-high heat and preheat the broiler.

Square off the eggplant by cutting a long strip off each side so it sits flat. Cut the eggplant lengthwise into ½-inch-thick slices. Season the sliced eggplant with salt and pepper, and brush with ¼ cup of the EVOO. Place on the hot grill and cook for 3 to 4 minutes per side or until completely cooked. Transfer the grilled eggplant to a platter to cool, then cut the slices into ½-inch dice.

While the eggplant is cooling, paste the garlic by mashing it with some salt with the side of your chef's knife. Scrape the paste into a mixing bowl and stir in a generous drizzle of EVOO. Toss the tomatoes and basil with the garlic oil, then add the chopped eggplant.

To slice the bread, hold your serrated knife at a 45-degree angle and slice ½ inch thick—you'll get larger rounds. Arrange the bread slices on a baking sheet (you should have 14 to 16 pieces) and toast on both sides under the broiler, a minute or two per side. Drizzle the toasts with EVOO and season with salt and pepper. Top with the eggplant and tomato mixture and with a bit of ricotta salata and serve.

MAKES 14 TO 16 CROSTINI

1 medium **eggplant** (choose one that is long and narrow)

Salt and **pepper**

⅓ to ½ cup **EVOO** (extra-virgin olive oil)

1 **garlic clove**, grated

4 **plum tomatoes**, seeded and chopped

10 to 12 fresh **basil** leaves, chopped

1 **baguette**

½ pound **ricotta salata cheese**, crumbled

BAKED JALAPEÑO POPPERS

Preheat the oven to 425°F.

Working lengthwise, slice off the top quarter of each jalapeño. Using a small spoon or paring knife, scrape the seeds and ribs out of each jalapeño, making little jalapeño canoes. Finely chop the tops and place in a mixing bowl. Add the cream cheese, manchego, green olives, parsley, and salt and pepper to the mixing bowl with the chopped jalapeños. Use a small spoon to fill the peppers or transfer the mixture to a plastic bag, squeeze the mixture to one of the bottom corners of the bag, then trim the corner off and squeeze the mixture into the hull of your jalapeño canoes. Arrange the filled canoes on a baking sheet and roast for 15 minutes. Serve hot.

MAKES 12 POPPERS

12 large **jalapeños**

4 ounces **cream cheese**, softened

4 ounces **manchego cheese**, grated

2 to 3 tablespoons **green olives with pimientos**, finely chopped

2 tablespoons chopped fresh **parsley** or cilantro

Salt and **pepper**

"BA-DA-BING" ITALIAN CHICKEN CIGARS

2 tablespoons **EVOO** (extra-virgin olive oil)

1 small **onion**, finely chopped

2 **garlic cloves**, grated or finely chopped

1 pound **ground chicken**

¼ cup **sun-dried tomatoes**, softened in hot water, drained and finely chopped

½ cup fresh **basil** (about 10 leaves), chopped

1 teaspoon dried **oregano**

1 tablespoon **fennel seeds**

1 teaspoon **crushed red pepper flakes**

¼ cup grated **Parmigiano-Reggiano**

Salt and **pepper**

4 sheets frozen **phyllo dough**, defrosted

4 tablespoons (½ stick) **butter**, melted

Preheat the oven to 425°F.

Heat a medium skillet over medium-high heat with the EVOO. Once it is hot, add the onions and garlic and cook until soft, 6 to 7 minutes. Remove the pan from the heat, scrape the onions and garlic into a medium-size mixing bowl, and let cool. Once the mixture is cool, add the chicken to the bowl along with the sun-dried tomatoes, basil, oregano, fennel, red pepper flakes, cheese, and salt and pepper. Combine well.

Place a piece of phyllo on a nonstick baking sheet and brush with the melted butter. Top with a second sheet of phyllo and brush with butter again. Divide the chicken mixture in half and form one portion into a 1-inch-thick log the length of the long side of the phyllo dough. Place the filling log along one long edge of the dough and wrap it tightly in the phyllo. Cut the chicken-filled phyllo into 3 "cigars" and brush with more butter. Repeat with the remaining 2 sheets of phyllo and the rest of the chicken mixture to make a total of 6 chicken and phyllo cigars. Bake for 12 to 15 minutes, until the pastry is golden brown and the filling is cooked through.

MAKES 6 CIGARS

THE ULTIMATE CHICKEN LIVERS

8 tablespoons (1 stick) **butter**

2 softball-size **onions**, thinly sliced

1 fresh **bay leaf**

Salt and finely ground **black pepper**

1 pound **chicken livers**, cleaned and patted dry

½ teaspoon ground **thyme**

1 loaf of party-size **rye**, **pumpernickel**, or **whole grain bread**, lightly toasted

1 large **shallot**, very thinly sliced or finely chopped

¼ cup of **specialty mustard**, such as cassis mustard or cranberry mustard

1 small jar of **cornichons**

This is my mom's recipe and I've made it for years without making a single adjustment—it's that good, just the way she makes it. Serve the livers warm or chill and serve at room temperature.

Heat the butter in a large skillet over medium heat. When it has melted, add the onions and bay leaf and season with a little salt and pepper. Cook the onions for 20 to 25 minutes, until caramelized and sweet. Scoot the onions off to one side of the pan and raise the heat to medium-high. Add the livers and season with the thyme. Cook until firm and cooked through; cut one of the chicken livers open to be sure it's no longer pink inside. Remove and discard the bay leaf, then transfer the contents of the skillet to a food processor. Process the livers and onions into a spread as coarse or as smooth as you like; taste to check the seasonings. Serve the liver mixture smeared on a slice of bread and topped with finely chopped shallots, a dab of mustard, and halved cornichons.

SERVES 6 TO 8

CAESAR-FILLED FRICOS

1¾ cups shredded **Parmigiano-Reggiano**

1 tablespoon **all-purpose flour**

2 teaspoons **anchovy paste**

Juice of 1 **lemon**

A few dashes of **Worcestershire sauce**

1 small **garlic clove**, grated or very finely chopped

1 teaspoon **pepper**

⅓ cup **EVOO** (extra-virgin olive oil)

2 small **hearts of romaine** or 1 large heart, chopped

When melted on a baking sheet, grated Parm takes on a crisp, cracker-like consistency, and it can be molded into different shapes when warm. I like to press the fricos into an egg carton to make little cups; they make my favorite Caesar salad into a great finger food!

Preheat the oven to 400°F.

In a small bowl, combine 1½ cups of the Parmigiano and the flour.

To make the fricos, use about 2 tablespoons of the cheese mixture to make a circle about 3 inches across on a nonstick baking sheet. Repeat with the remaining cheese to make 24 fricos; you'll need to use 2 or more baking sheets. Bake the fricos until they start to smell nutty and the cheese is melted and golden brown, about 10 minutes.

Working quickly, lift the cheese rounds off the baking sheet with a small spatula and transfer them to the cups of an egg carton; use your fingers to press them into the cups and shape them into small bowls. Let cool.

Combine the anchovy paste, lemon juice, Worcestershire, garlic, and pepper in a bowl, then whisk in the EVOO. Stir in the remaining ¼ cup of grated cheese. Toss the lettuce with the dressing and overfill the cups.

MAKES 24 CUPS; SERVES 8 TO 12

BRAZILIAN VATAPA

⅓ cup smooth **peanut butter**

¼ loaf of stale **French bread**, cut into chunks

1 (13.5-ounce) can **coconut milk**

1-inch piece of fresh **gingerroot**, peeled and grated

2 **garlic cloves**, grated

1 teaspoon **hot sauce**

¼ cup chopped fresh **cilantro**

Zest and juice of 2 **limes**

2 **scallions**, thinly sliced

½ cup **chicken stock**

1 tablespoon **EVOO** (extra-virgin olive oil)

Salt and **pepper**

2 pounds jumbo **shrimp**, peeled, deveined, and tails removed

This recipe was developed for Helio Castroneves, the Indy 500 and *Dancing with the Stars* champion. It is an exotic starter for any lovers of Brazilian food and music—and it will make your mouth dance.

In a blender or food processor, combine the peanut butter, bread, coconut milk, ginger, garlic, hot sauce, cilantro, lime zest and juice, scallions, chicken stock, EVOO, and salt and pepper. Puree the mixture until smooth and transfer to a medium skillet.

Place the skillet of sauce over medium-high heat and bring up to a simmer. Drop the shrimp into the sauce and simmer until cooked through, 2 to 3 minutes. Serve the warm shrimp and sauce in a dish with tooth picks or forks.

SERVES 8

CHICKEN PARM BITES

1 cup **all-purpose flour**

2 **eggs**, lightly beaten

¾ cup **bread crumbs**

¾ cup grated **Parmigiano-Reggiano**

1 teaspoon **granulated garlic** or garlic powder

2 teaspoons grated **lemon zest**

¼ cup fresh flat-leaf **parsley**, a handful, finely chopped

2 pounds **chicken tenders**, each cut in thirds

Salt and **pepper**

3 tablespoons **EVOO** (extra-virgin olive oil)

1 (15-ounce) can **crushed tomatoes**

¼ cup homemade **basil pesto** or store-bought

These mini cutlets on a toothpick are popular party fare. In the interest of full disclosure, at an office cook-off, one of my television producers, Andrew Goldman, presented a delicious parm bite of his own (see page 296) that rivaled my version. Read through both before you decide which one's for you. Frankly, I'm torn.

Arrange 3 shallow bowls on the counter and fill one with the flour, one with the eggs, and one with a mixture of the bread crumbs, cheese, garlic, lemon zest, and parsley.

Season the chicken pieces with salt and pepper, and coat each first in the flour, then in the egg, and finally in the bread-crumb mixture. Set the coated chicken pieces on a baking sheet.

Place a large pan over medium-high heat with the EVOO. Cook the chicken bites in 2 batches, turning once, until golden brown and cooked through, 5 to 6 minutes.

While the chicken bites are cooking, place a small pot over medium heat with the crushed tomatoes and bring up to a bubble. Remove the pot from the heat and stir in the pesto.

Serve the chicken bites with the tomato-pesto sauce alongside.

SERVES 8

GOLDMAN'S CHICKEN PARM BITES

These are like little chicken parm–stuffed calzones. I take my hat off to you, Goldman!

Preheat the oven to 375°F.

Preheat a large skillet over medium-high heat with the EVOO. Add the ground chicken to the skillet and cook until golden, 6 to 7 minutes, breaking it up with a spoon as it cooks.

Once the chicken has browned, add the onions and garlic, and cook until softened, 4 to 5 minutes. Add the tomatoes, half of the parsley, half of the oregano, half of the basil, and salt and pepper. Cook for 4 to 5 minutes to combine the flavors. Remove from the heat and mix in the mozzarella and half of the Parmigiano. Set aside to cool.

Once the filling has cooled, place the pizza dough on a clean, flat work surface that has been dusted with flour. Roll out the dough into a large rectangle, about 12 x 10 inches. Cut the rectangle in half lengthwise, then cut each strip in half again, leaving you with 4 long strips. Cut all the strips in half widthwise, then cut each piece in half again, leaving you a total of 16 squares.

In a small mixing bowl, whisk up the egg with the milk to make a wash and set aside. Place a heaping tablespoon of filling in the middle of each dough square, leaving a small border around the filling. Using a pastry brush or the back of a spoon, brush the border with the egg wash. Fold all the sides inward, one at a time, as if you were closing a box. Once the filling is enclosed, lightly pinch the seam closed. Transfer to a nonstick baking sheet, seam side down, and repeat this process with the remaining dough squares and filling.

In a medium-size mixing bowl, combine the remaining Parmigiano, oregano, basil, and parsley and mix thoroughly. Brush the tops of each chicken parm bite with the remaining egg wash and sprinkle some of the cheese-herb mixture over each. Bake the bites until uniformly golden brown, 12 to 15 minutes.

MAKES 16 BITES; SERVES 8

2 tablespoons **EVOO** (extra-virgin olive oil)

¾ pound **ground chicken**

1 small **onion**, chopped

2 **garlic cloves**, finely chopped or grated

1 (15-ounce) can **diced tomatoes**

¼ cup fresh flat-leaf **parsley**, a handful, chopped

2 teaspoons chopped fresh **oregano**

½ cup fresh **basil leaves**, chopped and divided

Salt and **pepper**

½ cup shredded **mozzarella**

½ cup grated **Parmigiano-Reggiano**

1 **pizza dough**, from a pizzeria or the grocery store

All-purpose flour, for dusting

1 **egg**

A splash of **milk**

INDIVIDUAL CHICKEN POTPIE POCKETS

2 tablespoons **butter**, plus more to grease the baking sheet

2 tablespoons **all-purpose flour**, plus more for dusting

½ cup **chicken stock**

¼ cup **milk** or half-and-half

Salt and **pepper**

1 teaspoon **Dijon mustard**

1 cup finely chopped cooked **chicken meat** from a rotisserie chicken, leftovers, or deli sliced

2 **scallions**, finely chopped

¼ cup frozen tiny **green peas**

1 small **carrot**, grated and finely chopped

2 tablespoons fresh **dill**, finely chopped

2 sheets prepared **puff pastry**, defrosted

1 **egg**, lightly beaten with a splash of water

Occasionally on my daytime show I will cook for a Mystery Taster—a guest whose identity remains a secret through the first half of the show. While I play "twenty questions" with the MT, I prepare a snack or an appetizer, and I have to go for crowd-pleasers, since I have no idea about the likes or dislikes of my guest. If the guests at your next party are a bit of a mystery to *you*, try this. (P.S. The guest I made these for turned out to be Diane Sawyer, and she really liked them.) Add a green salad if you are serving these as an entrée.

Preheat the oven to 400°F.

Heat the 2 tablespoons of butter in a small skillet over medium heat. When it melts, whisk in the flour and cook for 1 minute, then whisk in the stock and milk. Season with salt and pepper, cook for a couple of minutes until thickened, then stir in the mustard. Remove from the heat.

Combine the chicken, scallions, peas, carrots, and dill in a mixing bowl. Pour the sauce over the mixture and stir to combine.

Grease a baking sheet lightly with butter. Dust your work surface lightly with flour and roll out one sheet of dough to the thickness of a nickel, and cut into quarters. Cut each quarter into 2 triangles. Transfer the triangles to the baking sheet and make 8 more triangles with the second sheet of dough. Divide the filling among the triangles on the baking sheet, leaving a little room at the edges to seal the pockets. Brush the edges with egg wash and place a second triangle on top; press the edges to seal or crimp with the tines of a fork. Brush the tops of the pockets with more egg wash and cut a small x in the top of each one to vent. Bake for 20 minutes, or until deeply golden and crisp. Serve hot.

MAKES 8 APPETIZERS OR SERVES 4 AS AN ENTRÉE, 2 POCKETS PER PERSON

OVEN-BAKED SAMOSAS

I consider this the finest vegetarian starter in the book, and it is a perennial best seller in our green room when we make it for visitors appearing on my show. Once, for a friend observing Passover I made the shells out of matzo by breaking them into triangles and forming a pyramid around the filling and the samosas still passed muster. Thanks to Kara, a fine young chef in our show kitchen, for developing this recipe; I love these!

Preheat the oven to 400°F.

Cook the potatoes in a large saucepan of boiling, salted water until tender, 5 to 7 minutes. Drain and reserve in the same pot you cooked them in.

Heat the EVOO in a large skillet over medium-high heat. Add the onions and cook until soft, 5 minutes, then add the jalapeño, ginger, garlic, coriander, curry powder, cumin, allspice, cinnamon, and salt and pepper, and cook for about 3 minutes more. Stir in the drained potatoes, tomato, and peas, and cook for another minute. Stir in enough of the stock to moisten the mixture, then remove it from the heat and let cool.

On a lightly floured surface, unroll the pie dough. Cut each dough round into 8 equal wedges, like a pizza. Spoon 1 tablespoon of the potato filling onto the middle of each wedge. Brush the edges of the dough with the egg wash and fold up, bringing the three points together over the filling, then pinching at the seams to form a small pyramid. Transfer to a baking sheet and brush the samosas with the egg wash. Bake for 15 to 20 minutes, until golden brown.

While the samosas bake, make the dipping sauce: Combine the mint, cilantro, jalapeño, sugar, salt, lime juice, 1 tablespoon water, and the EVOO in the bowl of a food processor. Grate the garlic and ginger directly into the bowl, then puree until smooth. Transfer to a small serving bowl.

Serve the samosas hot out of the oven with the mint-cilantro dipping sauce.

MAKES 16 SAMOSAS; SERVES 8

2 **Idaho potatoes**, peeled and diced

Salt

1 tablespoon **EVOO** (extra-virgin olive oil)

1 small **onion**, finely chopped

½ **jalapeño pepper**, seeds and stem removed, finely chopped

½ inch of fresh **gingerroot**, peeled and grated

1 **garlic clove**, grated or finely chopped

1 teaspoon **ground coriander seeds** or ground coriander

2 teaspoons **curry powder**

1 teaspoon **ground cumin**

¼ teaspoon **ground allspice**

⅛ teaspoon **cinnamon**

Black pepper

1 **plum tomato**, seeded and finely chopped

¼ cup frozen **peas**, a handful

¼ to ½ cup **vegetable stock**

All-purpose flour, for rolling the dough

1 package (two 9-inch rounds) refrigerated **ready-made pie dough**

1 **egg**, beaten with a splash of water

Mint-Cilantro Dipping Sauce

1 bunch of fresh **mint**, leaves stripped from the stems

1 bunch of fresh **cilantro**, leaves stripped from the stems

1 **jalapeño pepper**, seeds and stem removed

1 teaspoon **sugar**

Salt

Juice of 2 **limes**

1 tablespoon **EVOO** (extra-virgin olive oil)

1 **garlic clove**

1 inch of fresh **gingerroot**

ARANCINI WITH TOMATO DIPPING SAUCE

4 cups **chicken** or **vegetable stock**

¼ cup **EVOO** (extra-virgin olive oil)

1 small **onion**, finely chopped

2 **garlic cloves**, grated or finely chopped

1½ cups **arborio rice**

1 cup **white wine**

Salt and pepper

2 tablespoons **butter**

1½ cups grated **Parmigiano-Reggiano**

1 cup fresh **mozzarella**, cut into ¼-inch cubes

2 cups **all-purpose flour**

2 **eggs**, lightly beaten

1½ cups **bread crumbs**

2 teaspoons **orange zest**

¼ teaspoon freshly grated **nutmeg** (eyeball it)

Olive oil, for frying

Tomato Dipping Sauce

¼ cup **EVOO** (extra-virgin olive oil)

1 small **onion**, finely chopped

2 **garlic cloves**, grated or finely chopped

2 tablespoons fresh **thyme** leaves, chopped

½ small **carrot**, grated and finely chopped

1 (28-ounce) can peeled **whole tomatoes**

Salt

Basil leaves, for garnish

The literal transaltion of these golden-brown rice balls is "little oranges"; a bit of orange zest in the bread crumbs makes this version extra special and also gives a wink and a nudge to the fruit they resemble.

Heat the stock in a small sauce pot over low heat. Once it is bubbling, turn off the heat and keep the stock warm on the stovetop.

Heat the EVOO in a large, deep saucepan over medium-high heat. Add the onions and garlic, and cook for 5 minutes. Add the rice and stir for a few minutes to toast the grains, then stir in the wine and cook until it is absorbed, a couple of minutes. Season the rice with salt and pepper. Add the warm stock to the rice a ladle or two at a time, waiting until each addition is absorbed before adding more, and stirring frequently. The risotto will cook in about 18 minutes total. Stir in the butter and half of the Parmigiano. Spread the risotto on a baking sheet to cool it quickly.

When the rice is cool enough to handle, grab a small amount and roll it into a 2-inch ball. Make a small indentation in the rice ball's center and insert a cube of mozzarella, then cover the hole up with more rice. Repeat until you've used up all of the risotto; you should have 24 cheese-filled balls.

Set up a breading station with 3 shallow bowls: one with the flour, one with the beaten eggs, and a third with the bread crumbs seasoned with the orange zest, nutmeg, and the remaining Parmigiano. Roll each risotto ball in the flour, then in the egg, then in the bread-crumb mixture. Reserve the coated balls on a rimmed baking sheet and place them in the refrigerator until you're ready to fry them.

For the dipping sauce: In a saucepan, heat the EVOO over medium heat. Add the onions and garlic and cook until soft and light golden brown, 8 to 10 minutes. Add the thyme and carrot and cook for 5 minutes more, or until the carrot is quite soft. Add the tomatoes and their juices crushing the tomatoes with your hands, and bring to a boil; reduce the heat and simmer for 20 minutes. Season the sauce with salt, then transfer to a blender and puree. Keep warm while you fry up the arancini.

In a large, heavy pan heat 1 inch of olive oil (not EVOO, which is too heavy for frying) over medium to medium-high heat. You'll know it's ready when bubbles run rapidly around a wooden spoon handle when you dip it in the oil. Fry the risotto balls, 5 at a time, until golden brown, 3 to 4 minutes. Remove with a slotted spoon and drain on a paper-towel-lined plate. Serve hot garnished with the basil, and with the tomato sauce alongside for dipping.

MAKES 24 BALLS

HOLIDAY MENUS

I cannot write or say it enough—when it comes to holidays or entertaining of any kind, keep it simple. Do not try out new recipes or complicated dishes under already nerve racking circumstances unless you are the kind of person who thrives on that kind of thing. For most of us, the best advice is cook what you know or what you can envision yourself preparing easily, and when possible break up one big party into a few little parties. I like throwing "smallidays," small holiday gatherings of 6 to 8 friends or family at a time. It is easier to control costs, manage time, and you'll be more apt to actually sit down and enjoy your guests rather than serving them nonstop. When I do cook for a large crowd, I find it easier to cook dishes in multiple batches and combine them once prepared than to overcrowd my pots and pans and multiply ingredient amounts to jumbo batches. Remember, the more people you have coming the easier the menu should be and tell everyone YES, they can bring something, when they ask. (Assign them whatever you're afraid of making—for me, it's the baked goods!) Happy holidays! Take it easy!

SPEEDY AND SPECIAL

- SEAFOOD PASTA WITH SHERRY TOMATO CREAM SAUCE
- HEARTS OF ROMAINE, PALM, AND ARTICHOKE WITH CITRUS DIJON DRESSING
- LOVE BIRDS (CHICKEN IN PASTRY)

This menu of chicken in pastry and soft, sexy pasta is perfect for any anniversary or romantic get-together for eight. It can be made in truly short order. Round out the party with store-bought cheeses, pâtés, and olives. For sweets, serve store-bought mini cupcakes and long-stem berries. Chilled prosecco is the appropriate beverage for a gala spread like this.

Seafood Pasta with Sherry Tomato Cream Sauce

Bring a pot of water to a boil for the pasta. When the water boils, salt it liberally, add the pasta, and cook to al dente.

Heat a large, deep skillet over medium heat with the EVOO. Add the shiitakes, shallots, garlic, and red pepper flakes and sauté for 5 minutes. Raise the heat a bit, then add the seafood and season with the lemon zest and salt and pepper. Heat through (if already cooked) or cook until just about firm and opaque, a couple of minutes; do not overcook. Deglaze the pan with the sherry, stir in the stock and tomatoes, and bring to a bubble. Stir in the cream and reduce the heat to a simmer.

Drain the pasta and toss with the sauce and herbs. Adjust the seasonings and serve.

SERVES 8 TO 10 AS A FIRST COURSE OR PART OF A PARTY BUFFET; SERVES 6 AS AN ENTRÉE

Salt

1½ pounds **bow-tie pasta** or penne rigate (with ridges)

3 tablespoons **EVOO** (extra-virgin olive oil)

½ pound **shiitake mushrooms**, stemmed and sliced

2 large **shallots**, chopped

3 to 4 **garlic cloves**, finely chopped or grated

A pinch or two of **crushed red pepper flakes**

1 pound **seafood** such as cooked lobster meat, quartered sea scallops, or peeled deveined shrimp—your choice

1 teaspoon grated **lemon zest**

Black pepper

½ cup **dry sherry**

½ cup **seafood** or chicken stock

1 (15-ounce) can **crushed tomatoes**

½ cup **heavy cream**

A handful of chopped fresh **chives** or flat-leaf parsley or both

Hearts of Romaine, Palm, and Artichoke with Citrus Dijon Dressing

2 hearts of **romaine lettuce**, chopped

1 (15-ounce) can **hearts of palm**, drained and sliced on an angle in 1-inch pieces

1 (15-ounce) can quartered **artichoke hearts** in water, drained well

A handful of fresh flat-leaf **parsley leaves**

¼ cup **orange marmalade**

Juice of 1 **lemon**

1 small **shallot**, peeled

2 teaspoons **Dijon mustard**

Salt and **pepper**

⅓ cup **EVOO** (extra-virgin olive oil)

¼ cup sliced **almonds**, toasted (see Note, page 102)

Arrange the romaine, hearts of palm, and artichokes on a large platter and sprinkle with the parsley. Combine the marmalade with the lemon juice in a bowl. Grate the shallot directly into the bowl, then add the mustard and season with salt and pepper. Whisk in the EVOO in a steady stream. Pour the dressing evenly over the salad just before serving and garnish with the almonds.

SERVES 8

Love Birds (Chicken in Pastry)

4 boneless skinless **chicken breast halves**, 6 to 8 ounces each

Salt and **pepper**

2 to 3 sprigs of fresh **rosemary**, finely chopped

1 tablespoon **EVOO** (extra-virgin olive oil)

1 11 x 17-inch sheet of frozen **puff pastry**

8 ¼-inch-thick slices **Italian fontina cheese**, 2 to 3 inches square

½ cup **fig preserves**

1 **egg**, beaten with a splash of water

Preheat the oven to 400°F.

Halve each piece of chicken crosswise, giving you 8 equal portions. Season the chicken with salt, pepper, and the rosemary. Heat the EVOO in a non-stick skillet over medium-high heat. Lightly brown the chicken on both sides, 5 minutes total (it will cook further in the oven). Remove from the heat.

Line a baking sheet with parchment paper. Cut the pastry into 8 equal pieces and place a piece of cheese in the center of each. Top with a spoonful of fig preserves and a piece of chicken. Fold the dough up and over the meat and cheese and pinch the edges to seal. Brush the seams with egg wash, flip the pastry packets over, and brush the tops with the remaining egg wash. Bake for 12 to 15 minutes, or until golden all over and heated through.

NOTE For entrée portions, simply leave the chicken breasts whole and cut the pastry into quarters to make 4 packets. Trim off excess dough and use it to decorate the pastry with small cutouts, such as heart shapes.

SERVES 8 AS A FIRST COURSE OR 4 AS AN ENTRÉE

MOTHER'S DAY PASTA SAMPLER

Salt

2 pounds **bow-tie pasta**

Pasta with Peas

1 tablespoon **butter**

1 small **onion**, chopped

½ cup **chicken** or **vegetable stock**

2 teaspoons **lemon zest**

1 (10-ounce) box frozen **peas**

Salt and **pepper**

1 cup fresh **ricotta cheese**

10 fresh **basil leaves**, torn or shredded

A handful of fresh **mint leaves**, finely chopped

Pasta with Carrots

1 tablespoon **butter**

2 tablespoons **honey**

1 cup **chicken** or **vegetable stock**

1 (10-ounce) box frozen cooked **carrots** or **baby carrots**

½ teaspoon **curry powder**

A few dashes of **hot sauce**

3 tablespoons chopped fresh **chives**

Salt and **pepper**

Grated **Parmigiano-Reggiano**

Pasta with Peppers

5 or 6 jarred **roasted yellow** or **red peppers**

2 tablespoons **EVOO** (extra-virgin olive oil)

3 to 4 **garlic cloves**, grated or finely chopped

½ teaspoon **crushed red pepper flakes**

Salt and **pepper**

1 tablespoon **aged balsamic vinegar**

A handful of chopped fresh flat-leaf **parsley**

Grated **Parmigiano-Reggiano**

We love you, Mom!

My mom loves both pasta and Tuscany and this trio of pasta dishes is a tribute to a place called Acqua al Due in Florence (they have a sister restaurant in San Diego as well). The chef, Stefano, uses vegetable purees to dress some of his pasta starters. I'm sure his mama is well fed and that his dishes are tastier than mine, but I think this is a pretty fair substitute—no need for a plane ticket.

Bring a large pot of water to a boil, salt it, and cook the pasta to al dente. Heads up: each of the 3 sauces will require a ladle of the starchy pasta cooking water taken just before the pasta is drained.

While the pasta cooks, set up 3 small skillets or pots and a food processor nearby. Set up 3 serving dishes near the stove.

In the first skillet, melt the butter over medium heat. Add the onions and sweat them for 5 to 6 minutes, until quite soft. Add the stock and zest and bring to a boil, then add the peas, season with salt and pepper, and heat through for 2 minutes. Transfer the peas and onions to a food processor and puree, adding some of the cooking liquid as needed to make a smooth sauce. Transfer to a bowl, mix with the ricotta, basil, and mint, and adjust the salt and pepper. Rinse the processor bowl and dry; return it to its base. When the pasta is ready, add a ladle of water and one third of the pasta to the bowl. Toss the pasta with the pea sauce.

In the second skillet while the peas are cooking, heat the butter, honey, and stock and bring to a boil. Add the carrots, curry, hot sauce, chives, and salt and pepper and simmer to heat through, 10 minutes.

While the carrots are cooking, process the roasted peppers into a paste in the food processor. Heat the EVOO in the third pan over medium-low heat and sauté the garlic and red pepper flakes; stir in the ground roasted peppers and season with salt and pepper. Rinse the processor bowl and return to its base to puree the carrots when they are tender. When the roasted peppers are hot, stir in the balsamic vinegar and parsley and let simmer over low heat. Stir in the starchy cooking liquid, scrape the sauce into a serving dish, and toss with one third of the pasta and the cheese until well coated.

Process the carrots into a smooth paste and transfer to a serving dish. Thin the carrot sauce with the starchy liquid and toss with the remaining pasta and the cheese.

SERVES 6 TO 8

SAINT PATRICK'S DAY MENU

- REUBEN HASH
- RADLER OR IRISH TEA

To go along with the hash (and better than green beer!), try one of the drinks that follows.

Reuben Hash

Place the potatoes into a large pot and fill it with cold water. Bring to a bubble over high heat, then turn the heat down to medium and cook the potatoes until tender but not falling apart, about 10 minutes. Drain the potatoes and return them to the pot they were cooked in to dry out for a few minutes.

Place a large cast-iron pan over medium-high heat with 2 tablespoons of the butter and the EVOO. Add the potatoes to the pan and cook them until they start to get golden brown, about 5 minutes.

Add the onions and corned beef to the pan along with the potatoes. Cook until the onions are tender and the beef starts to brown, 4 to 5 minutes. Stir the sauerkraut, mustard, and Guinness into the pan and cook until heated through, about 2 minutes. Season the hash with salt and pepper. Sprinkle the cheese evenly over the hash and cover the pan with aluminum foil to melt the cheese, 3 minutes or so.

While the cheese is melting, place a medium skillet over medium-low heat with the remaining tablespoon of butter. When the butter melts, add the eggs and cook however you or your guests like them. When the eggs are finished, remove the foil from the pan and spoon the eggs onto the hash. Cut the buttered toasts in half and line them up around the pan. Serve directly from the skillet.

SERVES 4

1 pound baby white **potatoes** such as Yukon Gold, quartered

3 tablespoons **butter**, plus additional for the toast

1 tablespoon **EVOO** (extra-virgin olive oil)

1 medium **onion**, chopped

1 pound **corned beef** left over from dinner or thinly sliced from the deli counter, cut or torn into bite-size pieces

1 package (about 1 pound) **sauerkraut**, drained, rinsed, and squeezed dry

¼ cup **spicy brown mustard** (eyeball it)

1 cup **Guinness beer** (eyeball it)

Salt and **pepper**

2 cups (an 8- to 10-ounce block) grated **Blarney cheese** or Swiss cheese

4 **eggs**

4 slices of **rye bread**, toasted and buttered

Radler (aka Shandy)

Divide the beer between 2 large drinking glasses. Top each one off with the lemonade, garnish with a lemon slice, and serve.

SERVES 2

1 bottle of **lager beer**, such as Corona

1½ cups **lemonade**, chilled

2 **lemon** slices

Irish Tea

Divide the beer between 2 large drinking glasses. Top each one off with the sweet tea, garnish with a lemon slice, and serve.

SERVES 2

1 bottle of **Guinness stout**

1½ cups purchased **sweet tea** or sweetened iced tea, chilled

2 **lemon** slices

TEA PARTY

- FRUIT AND NUT SCONES WITH HONEY BUTTER
- HAM, CHEESE, AND CHIVE SCONES
- SOUR CREAM AND DILL SCONES WITH SMOKED SALMON

I made these scones the day Julie Andrews returned to our show to discuss her memoir, *Home*. Julie Andrews gives me chicken skin—maybe you call them goose bumps. She is so wonderful, caring, honest, and genuinely funny that spending any amount of time with her makes me feel a better person for it. Her book is as rich and wonderful as she. These scones were a tasty treat for all and, complemented with a selection of fine teas, this would be a lovely menu for a book club meeting, a weekend brunch, or an afternoon tea.

Fruit and Nut Scones

2 cups **baking mix**, such as Bisquick, plus a little extra for dusting

¼ cup **sugar**

½ cup **currants**, a couple of handfuls

Zest of 1 **lemon**

¼ teaspoon freshly grated **nutmeg**

½ cup chopped **walnuts**

1 **egg**

½ cup **heavy cream**

4 tablespoons (½ stick) **butter**, softened

¼ cup **honey**

Preheat the oven to 425°F.

In a large mixing bowl combine the baking mix, sugar, currants, lemon zest, nutmeg, and half the nuts. (The nuts in the scones will remain buttery. The remaining nuts will top the scones and they will toast and get crunchy and deepen in flavor.)

In a small bowl combine the egg and cream. Grab a small dish or coffee cup and set aside about a teaspoon of the liquid, then add the remainder to the bowl of dry ingredients. Give it a gentle stir with a fork or a rubber spatula until a soft dough forms.

Sprinkle a little bit of baking mix onto your work surface and turn the dough out onto it. Give it a quick knead (about 10 turns should do the trick). Transfer the dough to a baking sheet and use your hands to shape it into a round that is 1 inch thick and 8 inches across. Brush the dough with the reserved egg mixture and sprinkle with the remaining chopped walnuts. Use a long knife to cut the round into 8 wedges. Separate the wedges and bake until the edges of the scones are golden brown, 12 to 15 minutes.

While the scones are baking, combine the softened butter and honey in a small mixing bowl.

Serve the scones with the honey butter.

MAKES 8 SCONES

Ham, Cheese, and Chive Scones

Preheat the oven to 425°F.

In a large mixing bowl combine the baking mix, sugar, chopped ham, about ½ cup of the shredded cheese, and the chives. In a small bowl, combine the egg and milk. Grab a small dish or coffee cup and set aside about a teaspoon of the liquid, then add the remainder to the bowl of dry ingredients. Give it a gentle stir with a fork or rubber spatula until a soft dough forms.

Sprinkle a little bit of baking mix onto your work surface and turn the dough out onto it. Give it a quick knead (about 10 turns should do the trick). Transfer the dough to a baking sheet and use your hands to shape it into a round that is 1 inch thick and about 8 inches across. Brush the dough with the egg liquid that you reserved, then sprinkle with the remaining cheese. Use a long knife to cut the round into 8 wedges; separate the wedges and bake for 12 to 15 minutes, until golden brown.

While the scones are baking, combine the softened butter and mustard in a small bowl.

Serve the scones with the mustard butter.

MAKES 8 SCONES

2 cups **baking mix**, such as Bisquick, plus a little extra for dusting

¼ cup **sugar**

10 slices of **deli ham**, chopped

½ cup plus 2 tablespoons shredded **cheddar cheese**

¼ cup chopped fresh **chives**

1 **egg**

½ cup **milk**, half-and-half, or cream (whichever you put into your morning coffee)

4 tablespoons (½ stick) **butter**, softened

¼ cup **Dijon mustard**

Sour Cream and Dill Scones with Smoked Salmon

Preheat the oven to 425°F.

In a large mixing bowl combine the baking mix, sugar, and dill. In a small bowl, stir together the egg, sour cream, and milk. Grab a small dish or coffee cup and set aside about a teaspoon of the liquid, then add the remaining egg mixture to the bowl of dry ingredients. Give it a gentle stir with a fork or a rubber spatula until a soft dough forms.

Sprinkle a little bit of baking mix onto your work surface and turn the dough out onto it. Give it a quick knead (about 10 turns should do the trick). Transfer the dough to a baking sheet and use your hands to shape it into a large round, about 8 inches wide and 1 inch thick. Brush the top with the reserved egg mixture and use a long knife or pizza wheel to cut the round into 8 wedges. Separate the scones and pop the pan into the oven to bake until the edges of the scones are golden brown, 12 to 15 minutes.

Serve the scones with extra sour cream, salmon, and sliced cucumber.

MAKES 8 SCONES

2 cups **baking mix**, such as Bisquick, plus a little extra for dusting

¼ cup **sugar**

3 tablespoons chopped fresh **dill**

1 **egg**

⅓ cup **sour cream**, plus some to pass at the table

2 tablespoons **milk**, half-and-half, or cream (whichever you put into your morning coffee)

1 pound very thinly sliced **smoked salmon**

¼ **English cucumber**, thinly sliced

PASSOVER FEAST

- SWEET HERBAL POT ROAST
- POTATO CAKES FLORENTINE
- GREENS AND MUSTARD DRESSING
- STORE-BOUGHT DESSERTS OR SELECTION OF FRESH AND DRIED FRUITS

Oy, is this a meal! Loosen those belts, kids!

Sweet Herbal Pot Roast

Preheat the oven to 300°F.

Heat the oil in a large Dutch oven with a tight-fitting lid over medium-high heat. Season the roast liberally with salt and pepper. Once you see a ripple in the oil, add the roast to the pan and brown on all sides, 8 to 10 minutes. Remove the roast to a plate and add the onions, carrots, celery, garlic, bay leaves, rosemary, thyme, and tomato paste to the Dutch oven. Cook, stirring frequently, for about 5 minutes, or until the onions are just on the verge of becoming tender. Add the wine and stir to scrape up any brown bits from the bottom of the pot. Add the prunes, then return the browned roast to the pot, nestling it down into the veggies. Add enough chicken stock to come halfway up the side of the roast and bring up to a bubble over medium-high heat. Cover the pot with the lid and transfer to the middle of the oven. Cook the roast, turning it every 30 to 40 minutes, for about 3½ hours or until a roasting fork inserted into the meat is easily pulled out. (Try doing this about an hour into the roasting so that when it is ready you really understand the difference.)

Remove the roast to a cutting board and cover with foil to keep warm. Discard the bay leaves. Place the Dutch oven over medium-high heat and simmer the juices until they are just slightly thickened. Stir in the lemon juice along with the parsley to freshen the flavor.

Remove the strings from the roast, slice the meat, and arrange on a platter. Cover with some of the sauce and pass the remainder in a gravy boat.

SERVES 6 TO 8

3 tablespoons **vegetable** or **olive oil**

1 (3- to 3½-pound) boneless **chuck eye roast**, tied

Salt and **black pepper**

2 large **onions**, sliced

1 large **carrot**, peeled and grated

3 **celery stalks** from the heart, chopped

5 large **garlic cloves**, chopped

2 fresh or dried **bay leaves**

4 sprigs of **rosemary**, leaves removed and chopped

7 to 8 sprigs of fresh **thyme**, leaves removed and chopped

3 tablespoons **tomato paste** (eyeball it)

1 cup **dry white wine** (eyeball it)

5 pitted **prunes**, chopped

3 to 4 cups **chicken stock** (eyeball it)

Juice of ½ **lemon**

2 large handfuls of fresh flat-leaf **parsley leaves**, coarsely chopped, about ½ cup

Potato Cakes Florentine

2 (10-ounce) boxes frozen **chopped spinach**

2½ pounds **Yukon Gold potatoes**, scrubbed clean, grated

1 medium **onion**, grated

2 **garlic cloves**, grated or finely chopped

3 **eggs**, lightly beaten

4 to 5 tablespoons **matzo meal**

Salt and **pepper**

Freshly grated **nutmeg**

Vegetable or **light olive oil**, for frying

Preheat the oven to 200°F.

Heat each package of spinach in the microwave for 5 minutes on high to defrost. Squeeze the defrosted spinach in a clean kitchen towel to remove as much liquid as possible. Transfer the squeezed-out spinach to a bowl and break it up thoroughly so it will mix well with the rest of the ingredients. Add the potato, onion, garlic, eggs, and matzo meal and season liberally with salt and pepper and a little nutmeg. Mix until combined.

Place a large skillet over medium-high heat and add enough oil to coat the bottom of the pan. Once you see a light ripple in the oil, working in batches, add the potato mixture in mounds of 2 heaping tablespoons each, flattening each mound a bit with the back of a spoon. Cook the cakes until golden brown on both sides and cooked through, 2 to 3 minutes per side. Transfer to a rack set over a baking sheet and keep warm in the oven while you cook the remaining batches. Continue until all the potato mixture is used; you should have 16 cakes in all.

SERVES 8

Greens and Mustard Vinaigrette

2 tablespoons **grainy mustard** (eyeball it)

2 tablespoons **white wine vinegar** (eyeball it)

⅓ cup **EVOO** (extra-virgin olive oil)

Salt and **pepper**

1 small head of **escarole**, leaves separated and chopped

1 heart of **romaine lettuce**, cored and chopped

In a salad bowl, whisk together the mustard and vinegar. Pour in the EVOO in a slow steady stream, whisking constantly, and season with some salt and pepper. Just before serving, add the greens and toss to coat with the dressing.

SERVES 6 TO 8

EASY SPRING MENU FOR FOUR

- SKILLET ROSEMARY-LEMON LAMB CHOPS WITH ROASTED TOMATO CHUTNEY
- SPRING PEA AND ASPARAGUS RISOTTO WITH CRISPY PROSCIUTTO CHIPS AND BABY ARUGULA
- STORE-BOUGHT DESSERT, SUCH AS SORBETS AND FRESH BERRIES WITH MINT OR A FRUIT TART AND CRÈME FRAÎCHE

This is a new take on a leg of lamb dinner for smaller gatherings. Whether it's a mini-Easter celebration or Mother's Day, this is a festive, elegant menu for four guests. It's not much work for such a big-meal feeling: it can be made in about an hour or less. You can marinate the lamb the day before, but definitely give it at least 45 minutes in the marinade. Make and serve the risotto, roast the tomatoes, and then, just before you're ready to serve, cook the chops.

Skillet Rosemary-Lemon Lamb Chops with Roasted Tomato Chutney

Preheat the oven to 400°F.

In a resealable plastic bag, combine about 3 tablespoons of the EVOO, the rosemary, half of the garlic, the lemon zest, and lots of coarse black pepper. Add the chops, turn to coat, and refrigerate.

Arrange the tomatoes on a rimmed baking sheet, drizzle with 1 tablespoon of the EVOO, and season with salt and pepper. Roast for 20 to 25 minutes, until the tomatoes have burst and are taking on a little brown color.

Heat the remaining 2 tablespoons of EVOO in a medium skillet over medium-high heat. Add the shallots, the remaining garlic, the honey, thyme, and a little salt and pepper. Cook, stirring frequently, until the shallots are tender and brown, about 10 minutes. Add the sherry vinegar, stir, then stir in the chicken stock. Bring to a bubble and simmer for 5 to 6 minutes more. Stir in the roasted tomatoes and the parsley.

Preheat a large ovenproof skillet over medium-high heat. Sprinkle the marinated lamb chops with some salt and place in the hot skillet; you may need to work in batches, depending on how big your skillet is. Brown the chops on each side for about 2 minutes. Once all of the chops have been browned, return them all to the skillet, squeeze the juice of the lemon over them, and transfer to the oven to roast for about 5 minutes for medium-rare. Serve 2 chops per person in a pool of the tomato chutney.

SERVES 4

6 tablespoons **EVOO** (extra-virgin olive oil)

4 sprigs of fresh **rosemary**, leaves removed from the stem and finely chopped

4 large **garlic cloves**, finely chopped

Zest and juice of 1 **lemon**

Salt and **pepper**

8 **lamb rib chops**, frenched (ask your butcher to do this for you)

2 pints **grape tomatoes**

6 large **shallots**, sliced

2 tablespoons **honey** (eyeball it)

4 sprigs of fresh **thyme**, leaves removed and chopped

3 tablespoons good-quality **sherry vinegar** (eyeball it)

1 cup **chicken stock** (eyeball it)

2 handfuls of fresh flat-leaf **parsley leaves**, coarsely chopped, about ½ cup

Spring Pea and Asparagus Risotto with Crispy Prosciutto Chips and Baby Arugula

6 cups **chicken stock**

1 bunch of **thin asparagus**, trimmed of woody ends, stalks cut into 2-inch pieces

3 tablespoons **EVOO** (extra-virgin olive oil), plus some for drizzling on the salad

8 slices of **prosciutto**

2 **shallots**, finely chopped

2 **garlic cloves**, finely chopped

4 to 5 sprigs of fresh **thyme**, leaves removed and chopped

1½ cups **arborio rice**

½ cup **dry white wine** (eyeball it)

1 cup frozen **peas**, 3 or 4 generous handfuls

2 tablespoons **butter**

1 cup freshly grated **Parmigiano-Reggiano**, 3 to 4 generous handfuls

4 cups **baby arugula**

2 teaspoons **aged balsamic vinegar** (eyeball it)

Salt and **pepper**

Pour the stock into a sauce pot and bring up to a bubble over high heat. Place the asparagus pieces in a sieve or small colander with a handle and dunk the asparagus into the boiling stock, submerging it completely. Cook for 1 minute, then remove. (If you don't have a sieve or small colander that will fit, simply drop the asparagus into the boiling stock for a minute and fish the pieces out with tongs or a slotted spoon.) Turn the heat down to low and keep the stock warm for use in the risotto. Chop the asparagus into bite-size pieces.

Heat 2 tablespoons of the EVOO in a large skillet with high sides over medium-high heat. Working with a couple of slices of prosciutto at a time, lay the slices in the hot skillet, browning and crisping them up on both sides. As they get crisp, remove the slices to a paper-towel-lined plate and reserve. Repeat until you have crisped up all the prosciutto.

To the same skillet add the remaining tablespoon of EVOO, then add the shallots, garlic, and thyme and sauté for 2 minutes. Add the rice and sauté for 2 or 3 minutes more. Add the wine and cook until it has been fully absorbed. Add a couple of ladles of the hot stock, just enough to cover the rice, and continue to cook and stir, adding more hot stock once the rice has soaked up the last batch you added. Continue until you have used up all but the last ladle of stock. Add the peas, asparagus, and butter along with the last of the stock, stirring to combine, and cook for another minute or so. Remove from the heat and stir in the grated Parmigiano. The total cooking time for the risotto is 18 minutes.

Once the risotto is done, dress the arugula with the balsamic and a drizzle of EVOO, and season with some salt and pepper.

Divide the risotto among 4 shallow serving bowls. Break each crispy prosciutto slice into a couple of pieces and distribute them among the risotto bowls, piling some of the dressed arugula on top. Serve immediately.

4 SERVINGS

OSCAR NIGHT MENU

- WILD MUSHROOM BEEF SLIDERS
- ASIAN TUNA SLIDERS
- PROSCIUTTO AND ARUGULA PIZZA
- CARAMELIZED ONION PIZZA
- FLAVORED POPCORNS
- GOLDEN ICE CREAM CAKES

Wild Mushroom Beef Sliders

1 1-ounce package dried **wild mushrooms**

2¼ pounds **ground sirloin**

¼ cup chopped fresh flat-leaf **parsley**

2 tablespoons **Worcestershire sauce** (eyeball it)

Salt and **pepper**

3 tablespoons **EVOO** (extra-virgin olive oil)

6 **shallots**, thinly sliced

¼ cup **dry sherry** (eyeball it)

1 tablespoon **butter**, cut into small bits

16 **small buns**, about 3 inches in diameter, split

½ **romaine lettuce heart**, chopped or shredded

Preheat the broiler or oven to 400°F.

Place the dried mushroms in a spice mill or a coffee grinder and grind to a powder. Transfer to a medium mixing bowl and add the ground beef, parsley, Worcestershire sauce, and salt and pepper. Combine the mixture well with your hands, then pat it down in the bowl and score the meat into 4 sections with the side of your hand. Form 4 small patties from each section, for 16 patties total, making them a bit thinner in the center for even cooking.

Heat 1 tablespoon of the EVOO in a medium skillet. Add the shallots to the hot oil, season with salt and pepper, and cook until softened and caramelized, 8 to 10 minutes. Stir the sherry into the skillet and turn off the heat. Add the butter to the pan and toss until it melts.

Heat the remaining 2 tablespoons of EVOO in a large skillet over medium-high heat. When the oil is hot, place the sliders in the pan (as many as will fit comfortably, don't crowd the party!). For medium doneness, cook the patties for 2 minutes on each side.

Meanwhile arrange the buns on a baking sheet and lightly toast them under the broiler.

Pile a little lettuce on each bun, add a patty, and top with a hearty scoop of the carmelized shallots and a bun top. Serve each person 4 sliders and enjoy the show!

MAKES 16 PATTIES

Asian Tuna Sliders

Place the cubed tuna in the bowl of a food processor and pulse it to coarsely grind the fish.

Transfer the tuna to a medium mixing bowl and add the garlic, tamari, chives, and some salt and pepper. Pat the meat down in the bowl and use the side of your hand to roughly score the mixture into 4 equal portions. Form 4 small patties from each portion, each 2½ to 3 inches in diameter and ½ inch thick, 16 in all.

Place a large skillet over medium-high heat with the EVOO. When the oil is hot, place the sliders in the pan (as many as will fit comfortably—don't crowd the party!). Cook until golden brown on the outside, 1 minute on each side for pink centers, 2 minutes on each side for cooked-through fish.

While the burgers are cooking, heat the broiler. Split the buns, arrange them on a baking sheet, and toast them lightly under the broiler.

Assemble the sliders by placing a patty on each bun bottom and topping with pickled ginger, cucumber, and duck sauce or plum sauce. Set the bun tops in place.

MAKES 16 SLIDERS

2¼ pounds fresh **tuna steaks**, cut into bite-size cubes

3 **garlic cloves**, finely chopped or grated

2 tablespoons **tamari** (aged soy sauce; eyeball it)

2 tablespoons finely chopped fresh **chives**

Salt and **pepper**

2 tablespoons **EVOO** (extra-virgin olive oil)

16 small **rolls**, about 3 inches in diameter

½ cup **pickled ginger**, found on the international food aisle

½ **seedless cucumber**, thinly sliced

1 cup **duck sauce** or plum sauce, found on the international food aisle

Prosciutto and Arugula Pizza

Preheat the oven to 400°F.

Pop open the tubes of pizza dough and unroll them onto baking sheets. Sprinkle the garlic evenly over the dough. Cover the pizzas with the shredded cheese and top each pizza with 8 slices of prosciutto, overlapping at the edges. Bake until crisp, 15 minutes.

Toss the arugula with the lemon juice, EVOO, and salt and pepper.

When the pizzas come out of the oven, top them with the greens, cut each pie into 16 pieces, and serve.

MAKES 32 PORTIONS

2 tubes of refrigerated **pizza dough**

6 **garlic cloves**, finely chopped or grated

4 cups shredded **fontina cheese**

16 slices of **prosciutto**

2 bunches of **arugula**, stem ends removed

Juice of 1 **lemon**

2 tablespoons **EVOO** (extra-virgin olive oil)

Salt and **pepper**

Caramelized Onion Pizza

2 tablespoons **butter**

2 tablespoons **EVOO** (extra-virgin olive oil)

2 large softball-size **onions**, quartered lengthwise then thinly sliced

Salt and **pepper**

2 tubes of **refrigerated pizza dough**

2 cups shredded **provolone cheese**

1 cup **blue cheese** or Gorgonzola crumbles

½ cup grated **Parmigiano-Reggiano**

2 tablespoons thinly sliced fresh **sage leaves**

A handful of fresh flat-leaf **parsley**, finely chopped

Preheat the oven to 425°F.

Preheat a large skillet over medium heat with the butter and EVOO. When the butter melts into the oil, add the onions, season with salt and pepper, and cook, stirring frequently, for 25 minutes or until caramelized.

Unroll the pizza dough onto baking sheets. Top each pizza with equal amounts of the cheeses and the caramelized onions. Sprinkle the sage over the pizzas and bake until brown and crisp, 15 to 18 minutes. Cut each pizza into 16 squares and garnish with the parsley.

MAKES 32 PORTIONS

Black Pepper and Parm Cheesy Popcorn

½ cup **popcorn kernels**

¼ cup **vegetable oil**

2 tablespoons hot melted **butter**

2 teaspoons **coarse black pepper**

¾ cup grated **Parmigiano-Reggiano**

Combine the popcorn and oil in a large kettle or pot with a tight-fitting lid and place over medium-high heat. When the corn begins to pop, shake the pot constantly. When the popping slows, remove the pan from the heat. Pour the hot butter over the popcorn, sprinkle with the pepper and cheese, and toss well.

MAKES 2 QUARTS POPPED CORN

Curried Salt Popcorn

½ cup **popcorn kernels**

¼ cup **vegetable oil**

2 tablespoons hot melted **butter**

2 teaspoons **ground turmeric**

1 tablespoon **mild or hot curry powder**

2 teaspoons **salt**

Combine the popcorn and oil in a large kettle or pot with a tight-fitting lid and place over medium-high heat. When the corn begins to pop, shake the pot constantly. When the popping slows, remove the pot from the heat and pour the butter over the top. Combine the spices and toss with the popped corn.

MAKES 2 QUARTS POPPED CORN

Golden Ice Cream Cakes

Line a 12-cup muffin tin with plastic wrap.

Slice 2 of the pound cakes into twelve ½-inch slices. Using a small round cookie cutter or a rinsed-out 5-ounce can (such as a tomato paste can), cut 12 circles from the cake slices. With the remaining 12 slices, use a 15-ounce can to make slightly larger circles of cake for the tops. You should end up with 12 small circles and 12 large circles.

Slice both of the remaining 2 pound cakes lengthwise into 6 slices about ¼ inch thick, then cut those slices into strips about an inch wide.

Set the small circles of cake into the muffin tins. Bend the long strips of cake to line the sides of each tin. Fill each cake cup with a scoop of ice cream and place the larger circles of cake on top to form a lid. Wrap the whole tin in plastic wrap and place in the freezer for at least an hour to firm up.

To serve, gently lift each individual ice cream cake out of the tin, using the plastic wrap to help release it. Invert each cake onto a dessert plate. Squirt some whipped cream on top. Heat up the caramel or butterscotch sauce and drizzle it over the cakes.

MAKES 12 ICE CREAM CAKES

4 store-bought **pound cakes**

2 pints **French vanilla ice cream**, slightly softened

2 cans real **whipped cream**

2 jars **caramel or butterscotch sauce**, whichever you prefer

ULTIMATE BBQ BURGER
- THE ULTIMATE BBQ BURGER WITH CHIPOTLE RANCH SAUCE
- NOT POTATO SALAD
- RED, WHITE, AND BLUE SLAW

The spice blend in this burger gives the meat the sweet-smoky flavor of barbecue, while the chipotle ranch sauce heats things up and then cools them off. This one will be a summertime hit at your next backyard barbecue. Serve with a super simple and tangy red, white, and blue slaw, and a gnocchi salad—a potato salad without—the fuss of peeling the spuds. Try it on the Fourth for some real fireworks!

The Ultimate BBQ Burger with Chipotle Ranch Sauce

1 tablespoon **sugar**

1 tablespoon **grill seasoning**, such as McCormick's Montreal Steak Seasoning

1 tablespoon **chili powder**

2 teaspoons **sweet smoked paprika**

1 teaspoon **ground cumin**

½ teaspoon **ground allspice**

2 pounds lean **ground sirloin**

1 tablespoon **EVOO** (extra-virgin olive oil)

8 slices of **cheddar cheese**

⅓ cup **buttermilk**

⅓ cup **sour cream**

1 **chipotle in adobo**, seeded and finely chopped, plus 1 tablespoon adobo sauce

2 tablespoons chopped fresh **dill**

2 tablespoons chopped fresh flat-leaf **parsley**

2 tablespoons chopped fresh **chives**

Salt and **pepper**

4 **Kaiser rolls**, lightly toasted

Leaf lettuce, for topping

1 **beefsteak tomato**, sliced

½ **red onion**, sliced into rings

1 large **deli pickle**, thinly sliced lengthwise

In a mixing bowl combine the sugar, grill seasoning, chili powder, smoked paprika, cumin, and ground allspice. Add the ground meat to the bowl and mix with your hands. Press the meat down in the bowl and score it into 4 portions using the side of your hand. Form 4 burgers, making them thinner in the middle than at the edges for even cooking and to produce flat burgers once they bulge up during cooking.

Heat the EVOO in a large skillet over medium-high heat. Add the burgers and cook for 3 to 4 minutes on one side. Flip the burgers and top each with 2 slices of cheese. Tent the pan with foil to help melt the cheese, and cook for 3 minutes more. You can also cook the burgers on a preheated grill over a medium-high flame; once you top them with cheese, close the lid to melt the cheese.

While the burgers are cooking, combine the buttermilk, sour cream, chipotle, adobo sauce, dill, parsley, and chives in a small mixing bowl. Season the sauce with salt and pepper.

When the burgers are ready, load them onto some toasted Kaiser rolls with lettuce, tomato, red onion, pickles, and a big dollop of the chipotle ranch sauce.

SERVES 4

Not Potato Salad

Salt

2 pounds **gnocchi**

3 tablespoons **Dijon mustard**

2 tablespoons **white wine vinegar**

⅓ cup **EVOO** (extra-virgin olive oil), plus a drizzle for serving

Black pepper

4 **celery stalks** from the heart, finely chopped

½ **red onion**, finely chopped

2 **roasted red peppers**, chopped

1 (14-ounce) jar **marinated mushrooms**, drained

½ cup fresh flat-leaf **parsley**, a couple of handfuls, chopped

Bring a large pot of water to a boil over high heat for the gnocchi. Once the water is boiling, salt it, add the gnocchi, and cook them for 3 minutes or until they float to the surface.

With your gnocchi cooking, grab a large mixing bowl and whisk together the Dijon and white wine vinegar. Stream the EVOO into the bowl while whisking and then season the dressing with salt and pepper. Add the veggies and parsley to the mixing bowl. Drain the gnocchi well and toss directly into the dressing while they are still hot, so they will soak up the dressing. You can serve the salad now or let it chill out in the refrigerator for a couple of hours to develop the flavors more. Freshen it up with an extra drizzle of EVOO when you are ready to serve.

SERVES 6 TO 8

Red, White, and Blue Slaw

3 tablespoons **white wine vinegar**

1 tablespoon **sugar**

⅓ cup **EVOO** (extra-virgin olive oil)

Salt and **pepper**

1 cup crumbled **blue cheese**

2 cups shredded **red cabbage**

4 cups **shredded white cabbage**, available in the produce section

1 bunch of **scallions**, thinly sliced

In a large mixing bowl, whisk together the vinegar, sugar, and EVOO with some salt and pepper. Stir the crumbled blue cheese into the dressing, and then add the cabbages and scallions to the bowl and give everything a hearty toss.

You can serve the salad now or let it chill out in the refrigerator for a couple of hours to develop the flavors more.

SERVES 6 TO 8

OCKTOBERFEST

- BOCKWURST IN CREAMY MUSTARD SAUCE WITH SMASHED POTATOES AND BROCCOLINI
- BRATWURST REUBENS
- GERMAN CHEESE AND BEER FONDUE

This menu is a wurst celebration. Bockwurst is made from a combination of veal and pork, with the emphasis on veal, and bratwurst combines veal, pork, and beef. I get all of my sausages and smoked meats from Oscar's Smokehouse in Warrensburg, New York. They ship anywhere, so try some!

Bockwurst in Creamy Mustard Sauce with Smashed Potatoes and Broccolini

Place the potatoes in a medium saucepan with water to cover. Bring to a boil and cook the potatoes for 10 minutes, or until fork tender. Drain the potatoes, then return them to the hot saucepan to dry out.

Pierce the casings of the bockwurst and arrange the sausages in a medium skillet. Add 1 inch of water and the EVOO and bring to a simmer over medium heat. Keep simmering until the water completely evaporates, about 10 minutes. Continue to cook to let the skins crisp up.

While the wurst are cooking, add the butter to a medium sauce pot over medium heat. When the butter melts add the shallots and sauté until soft and translucent, a couple of minutes. Add the flour and cook for 1 minute, then add the stock and bring to a boil. Cook the sauce until it thickens, about 2 minutes, then add the cream, nutmeg to taste, and the mustard. Cook for 2 minutes more and season with salt and pepper. Turn the heat off, and cover to keep the sauce warm while you prepare the broccolini.

Trim and discard the bottom ½ inch from the broccolini stems, then cut the broccolini into 1-inch pieces. Place the broccolini in a small skillet with ½ inch of boiling water, cover, and steam over medium-high heat for 3 minutes, just until tender. Drain and, just before serving, squeeze the juice of ½ lemon over the top.

Add half of the creamy mustard sauce to the cooked potatoes and mash. Season the potatoes with salt and pepper and stir in the chopped chives.

Spoon a generous portion of the creamy mustard smash onto each plate and place a bockwurst on top. Top with a large spoonful of the reserved creamy mustard sauce and serve the steamed broccolini alongside.

SERVES 4

4 large **Idaho potatoes**, peeled and quartered

4 **bockwurst** links

1 tablespoon **EVOO** (extra-virgin olive oil)

2 tablespoons **butter**

2 **shallots**, finely chopped

2 tablespoons **all-purpose flour**

2 cups **chicken stock**

1 cup **heavy cream**, half-and-half, or milk

Freshly grated **nutmeg**

3 tablespoons **grainy mustard**

Salt and **pepper**

1 bunch of **broccolini**

½ **lemon**

¼ cup chopped fresh **chives**

Bratwurst Reubens

4 smoked **bratwurst** links

1 tablespoon **EVOO** (extra-virgin olive oil)

1 package (about 1 pound) **sauerkraut**, drained

½ cup **sweet red pepper relish** or sweet pickle relish

Butter, softened

8 slices of **onion rye**, rye, or pumpernickel bread

¼ cup **grainy or German mustard**

8 slices of **Havarti cheese with dill**

Place the links in a skillet and add 1 inch of water and the EVOO. Bring to a simmer over medium heat, and keep simmering until the water completely evaporates, about 10 minutes. Continue to cook to let the skins crisp up. Cut the brats open but not all the way through and turn cut side down in the pan to crisp the insides.

Preheat a griddle pan or a large skillet over medium heat.

Combine the sauerkraut and relish in a bowl. Cover loosely with plastic wrap and microwave on high for 1 minute to warm through. Lightly butter 4 of the bread slices, then flip them over and spread with mustard. Top each with a slice of cheese, a brat, some kraut, and another slice of cheese. Set a second slice of bread on top and lightly butter it.

Cook the Reuben sammies until they are golden and the cheese melts, turning once. Halve the sammies and serve.

SERVES 4

German Cheese and Beer Fondue

1 head of **cauliflower**, separated into florets

1 tablespoon **vegetable oil**

6 **bacon** slices, chopped

1 cup shredded **cheddar cheese**

1 cup shredded **smoked Gruyère cheese**

1 cup shredded **Swiss cheese**

1 rounded tablespoon **all-purpose flour**

1½ cups **German lager**

2 tablespoons **hot mustard**

A few drops of **hot sauce**

A few drops of **Worcestershire sauce**

Cooked **wursts** (knock, brat, or brot), cubed or thickly sliced

1 small jar **mini gherkins**, drained

1 small jar **pickled onions**

1 small round **loaf of rye**, pumpernickel, or sourdough bread, cubed

Bring a medium pot of water to a boil. Add the cauliflower florets and blanch for 2 minutes; drain.

Heat a small skillet over medium heat with the vegetable oil. Once it is hot, add the bacon and cook, stirring every now and then, until crispy, 3 to 4 minutes. Remove from the skillet, drain on a paper-towel-lined plate, and reserve.

Combine all three cheeses in a bowl and toss together with the flour. Pour the beer into a small pot and bring up to a bubble over medium heat. Reduce the heat to a simmer and add the cheese in batches, stirring the pot in a figure-eight pattern with a wooden spoon. When all the cheese has been incorporated fully, stir in the mustard, hot sauce, and Worcestershire sauce. Transfer the cheese mixture to a warm fondue pot and sprinkle with the reserved bacon.

To serve, arrange the cauliflower, wursts, pickles, onions, and cubed bread around the fondue pot.

SERVES 6

Turkey Sweet Potato Shepherd's Pie

Preheat the oven to 425°F.

In a deep ovenproof skillet or a Dutch oven, heat the EVOO over high heat. Add the turkey and break it up with a wooden spoon; season with salt and pepper and the poultry seasoning.

Place the sweet potatoes in a pot with water to cover. Cover the pot, bring to a boil, then salt the water and cook the potatoes for 15 minutes, or until tender.

Grate the onion and carrots directly into the skillet with the turkey. Add the celery, stir, and cook for 5 minutes. While the vegetables are cooking, heat 2 tablespoons of the butter in a small pot over medium heat. Add the flour to the melted butter and whisk for 1 minute, then whisk in the stock and season with salt, pepper, and Worcestershire. Cook for a few minutes, until thickened then add to the turkey mixture. Stir in the peas into the turkey mixture and turn off the heat.

Drain the potatoes and return the hot pot to the heat. Add the remaining 2 tablespoons of butter and melt over medium heat. Add the banana and potatoes to the pot and season with salt, pepper, and hot sauce. Mash the potatoes and banana to combine, and adjust the seasoning.

Spoon the potatoes onto the meat, and cover the potatoes with the cheese. Bake uncovered for 5 minutes to melt the cheese.

SERVES 4

2 tablespoons **EVOO** (extra-virgin olive oil)

2 pounds **ground turkey** or chopped leftover turkey

Salt and **pepper**

2 teaspoons **poultry seasoning**

2½ pounds **sweet potatoes**, peeled and cubed

1 **onion**, peeled

2 **carrots**, peeled

4 **celery stalks** from the heart, chopped

4 tablespoons (½ stick) **butter**

2 tablespoons **all-purpose flour**

2 cups **turkey** or **chicken stock**

A few dashes of **Worcestershire sauce**

1 (10-ounce) box frozen **peas**

1 very ripe **banana**, sliced

A few dashes of **hot sauce**

2 cups shredded sharp yellow **cheddar cheese**

Cran-Applesauce Sundaes

For dessert, combine the applesauce and cranberry sauce and warm in the microwave or in a small pot over low heat. Season with the cinnamon and orange zest. For each sundae, place a little cran-applesauce in the bottom of a sundae dish, top with 2 scoops of ice cream, drizzle with more sauce, and top with whipped cream. Garnish with the chopped pecans.

SERVES 4

1½ cups all-natural **applesauce**

½ cup good-quality whole-berry **cranberry sauce**, such as Ocean Spray (sold in tubs on the canned food aisle)

2 pinches of **ground cinnamon**

2 teaspoons grated **orange zest**

2 pints **French vanilla ice cream**

Whipped cream

¼ cup chopped **pecans**, toasted (see Note, page 102)

HOLIDAY MENU IN 30

- BUTTERNUT SQUASH RISOTTO
- ROASTED BROCCOLINI AND BEANS
- HERB-APRICOT CHICKEN
- CHOCOLATE HAZELNUT TART

Between mid-November and the first week of the New Year we all gather and entertain family and friends in a seemingly endless stream—and sometimes these get-togethers can sneak up on us. This menu is fancy, fabulous, and a necessity for any holiday menu arsenal!

Butternut Squash Risotto

4 cups **chicken stock**

2 tablespoons **EVOO** (extra-virgin olive oil)

1 small **onion**, chopped

2 **garlic cloves**, grated or finely chopped

2 cups **arborio rice**

1 cup **dry white wine**

1 (10-ounce) box frozen **butternut squash puree**

Freshly grated **nutmeg**

Salt and **pepper**

2 tablespoons **butter**, cut into small pieces

10 fresh **sage leaves**, slivered

1 cup grated **Parmigiano-Reggiano**

Bring the stock and 1 cup water to a simmer in a sauce pot, then reduce the heat to low and keep warm.

Heat the EVOO in a medium skillet over medium-high heat. When the oil ripples, add the onions and garlic and cook for 2 to 3 minutes to soften. Add the rice and toast for 2 to 3 minutes more. Add the wine and let it cook off completely, stirring occasionally, 2 to 3 minutes. Start ladling in the stock, a couple of ladles at a time, allowing the stock to be absorbed by the rice before each addition and stirring frequently. The risotto will take about 18 minutes to cook, total, from the first addition of liquid.

While the risotto is cooking, defrost the squash in your microwave (place it in a dish to collect any liquids) for about 7 minutes on the defrost setting. Stir the defrosted squash into the risotto for the last 3 minutes of cooking time. Season the risotto with nutmeg and salt and pepper. In the last minute of cooking time, stir in the butter, sage, and cheese. Serve.

SERVES 6

Roasted Broccolini and Beans

2 bundles of **broccolini**, ends trimmed

1 pound **string beans**, ends trimmed

4 **garlic cloves**, crushed

3 tablespoons **EVOO** (extra-virgin olive oil)

Salt and **pepper**

Heat the oven to 425°F. Arrange the broccolini and beans on a rimmed baking sheet. Scatter the garlic around. Drizzle the EVOO over the vegetables and toss to coat; season with salt and pepper. Roast the vegetables for 15 to 18 minutes, until nutty and crispy at the edges. Check once halfway through the roasting and turn the veggies if they are getting too dark.

SERVES 6

Herb-Apricot Chicken

3 tablespoons **EVOO** (extra-virgin olive oil)

3 pounds boneless skinless **chicken breasts and thighs**, cut into large chunks

Salt and **pepper**

¼ cup **aged balsamic vinegar**

1½ cups **chicken stock**

20 to 24 **dried apricots**, chopped

5 to 6 sprigs of fresh **thyme**

2 to 3 tablespoons brown sugar

A generous handful of fresh flat-leaf **parsley**, chopped

3 tablespoons chopped fresh **chives**

2 teaspoons grated zest and the juice of 1 **lemon**

In a large skillet with high sides, heat the EVOO, 3 turns of the pan, over medium-high heat. Season the chicken liberally with salt and pepper. When the oil ripples, add the chicken and brown it on both sides, 7 to 8 minutes total. Add the balsamic vinegar and stir for 30 seconds, then add the stock, apricots, and thyme. Sprinkle in the sugar and stir to combine. Reduce the heat to medium-low, cover the pan, and simmer for 10 minutes. Take the lid off, stir the chicken and apricots, and add the parsley, chives, and lemon zest and juice. Turn off the heat, let stand for a couple of minutes, and serve.

SERVES 6

Chocolate Hazelnut Tart

2 cups **heavy cream**

2 shots of **hazelnut liqueur** such as Frangelico (try buying a nip— the size served on airplanes)

1 large store-bought **chocolate tart**

1 small bar of **bittersweet chocolate**, for shaving

Whip the cream with a whisk or electric beater until soft peaks form. Whisk in the liqueur. Slather the cream over the tart and use a vegetable peeler to shave chocolate curls on top as garnish. Serve.

SERVES 6

HOLIDAYS IN 60-ISH MINUTES

- OLIVE AND GARLIC SOFT CHEESE SPREAD
- ORANGE BALSAMIC CORNISH HENS
- SWEET AND SPICY BRUSSELS SPROUTS
- BRAISED CARROTS AND FENNEL
- PUMPKIN PIE WITH ALMOND–SPICE WHIPPED CREAM

A few years ago Food Network challenged me, their 30-minute girl, to come up with a 60-minute holiday meal for a seasonal special. The special was so well received and the recipes were so often requested, that we have filmed several similar specials since. I had to make the whole menu in 60 minutes, literally, but I recommend that you take a breath, open some wine, and give yourself 75 to 80 minutes—trust me! (P.S. These menus feed a small group of 6 to 8 people. If you are feeding more and doubling the recipes, add an extra half hour of chopping time to your schedule.)

Olive and Garlic Soft Cheese Spread

Preheat the oven 425°F.

Toast the bread slices on a baking sheet for 5 to 10 minutes to crisp lightly. While they toast, place the olives in the bowl of a food processor and grate the garlic directly into the bowl. Add the cream cheese and ricotta cheese. Pulse the cheese and olives into a fairly smooth spread. Transfer to a serving bowl and top with the hazelnuts. Surround the spread with the toasted bread, pita crisps, and celery.

SERVES 6

1 **whole grain baguette**, sliced
1 cup large **green olives with pimientos**
1 **garlic clove**, peeled
8 ounces **cream cheese**, softened
1 cup **ricotta cheese**
½ cup chopped **hazelnuts**, toasted (see Note, page 102)
   Parmesan pita crisps, store-bought
1 **celery heart**, cut into sticks

Orange Balsamic Cornish Hens

Preheat the oven to 425°F.

Line 2 rimmed baking sheets with foil to make cleanup easier. Set a baking rack in each pan. Using poultry shears or a sharp chef's knife, cut along both sides of each hen's backbone and discard. Open the birds up and turn skin side up, pressing lightly on the breastbones to flatten them a bit. Arrange 3 hens on each baking rack, skin side up, and season liberally with salt and pepper. Mix the orange juice concentrate, balsamic vinegar, and EVOO and pour evenly over the hens, and sprinkle with the rosemary. Roast the hens for 15 minutes at 425°F, then reduce the heat to 375°F and roast for 30 minutes more, or until the juices run clear. Let the hens rest for 5 minutes before serving.

SERVES 6

6 **Cornish hens**, rinsed and patted dry
   Coarse salt
   Coarse black pepper
1 cup defrosted **orange juice concentrate**
1 cup **aged balsamic vinegar**
3 to 4 tablespoons **EVOO** (extra-virgin olive oil)
7 to 8 stems fresh **rosemary**, chopped

Sweet and Spicy Brussels Sprouts

3 tablespoons **white wine vinegar**

3 tablespoons **honey**

1 cup **chicken stock**

1 fresh **bay leaf**

½ **red onion**, chopped

½ **red bell pepper**, seeded and chopped

1 teaspoon **mustard seeds**

¼ teaspoon **ground turmeric**

2 tubs of fresh **Brussels sprouts**

Celery salt

Black pepper

In a skillet, whisk together the vinegar, honey, and stock. Stir in the bay leaf, onion, bell pepper, mustard seeds, and turmeric and bring to a boil. Trim the Brussels sprouts and halve them. Add to the skillet and season with celery salt and pepper. Bring back to a boil, then cover the skillet, reduce the heat, and simmer for 15 minutes, until cooked through. Uncover the pan and cook for 5 minutes more, until golden. Discard the bay leaf before serving.

SERVES 6

Braised Carrots and Fennel

6 large **carrots**, peeled

2 large **fennel bulbs**

1 large **onion**, peeled

1 teaspoon **sugar**

Salt

2 tablespoons **EVOO** (extra-virgin olive oil)

3 tablespoons chopped fresh **chives**

3 tablespoons chopped fresh **dill**

Slice the carrots ½ inch thick on an angle. Quarter the fennel bulbs lengthwise, cut into the bulb to remove the core, and thinly slice the fennel. Chop ¼ cup of the fennel fronds and reserve them. Halve and slice the onion.

Fill a skillet with ¼ inch of water. Add the vegetables, then sprinkle them with the sugar and salt and drizzle with the EVOO. Cover and bring to a boil, then reduce the heat and simmer for 20 minutes, until tender Uncover and simmer for another 5 minutes to cook down the liquid; adjust the salt. Toss the vegetables with the reserved fennel fronds and the chives and dill.

SERVES 6

Pumpkin Pie with Almond-Spice Whipped Cream

1 store-bought **pumpkin pie**

1½ cups **heavy cream**

1 shot (about 1 ounce) **almond liqueur** such as Amaretto or 1 teaspoon almond extract

Freshly grated **nutmeg**

2 pinches of **ground cinnamon**

Preheat the oven to 350°F. Place the pie in the oven to crisp the crust.

In a medium bowl, whisk the cream until soft peaks form, a couple of minutes. Whisk in the almond liqueur and season with nutmeg and cinnamon. Slice the pie and serve with a generous dollop of whipped cream.

SERVES 6

- AUTUMN POTATO GRATIN
- SWEET GREEN BEANS
- HERB-ROASTED TURKEY BREAST WITH CIDER PAN GRAVY
- PUMPKIN SOUP WITH CHILI CRAN-APPLE RELISH
- APPLE AND ONION STUFFIN' MUFFINS
- STORE-BOUGHT PIES AND WHIPPED CREAM

Autumn Potato Gratin

Preheat the oven to 400°F.

Halve the potatoes and toss them into a large buttered baking dish. Season with salt and pepper.

Meanwhile, put the cream, butter, herbs, and garlic in a small saucepan and bring to a simmer over medium heat. Cook for about 5 minutes, to infuse the cream with flavor. Season with salt and pepper.

Pour the hot cream mixture through a strainer over the potatoes (discard the herbs and garlic). If there is not enough cream to cover the potatoes about three quarters of the way, pour in some additional cream to make up the difference. Sprinkle the Parmigiano evenly over the top. Bake for 30 to 35 minutes, until the potatoes are cooked through and the top begins to brown. Cover and keep warm until ready to serve.

SERVES 8

4 pounds mixed **baby potatoes**, such as Red Bliss, Peruvian purples, and fingerlings

4 tablespoons (½ stick) **butter**, plus more for buttering the baking dish

Salt and **pepper**

2 cups **heavy cream**, plus more as needed

2 sprigs of fresh **thyme**

2 sprigs of fresh **sage**

2 sprigs of fresh **rosemary**

2 **garlic cloves**, cracked

½ cup grated **Parmigiano-Reggiano**

Sweet Green Beans

Put the beans in a large microwave-safe bowl with a few tablespoons of water. Cover loosely with plastic wrap, and microwave on high for 5 minutes. Uncover and stir the beans, then cover again and microwave on high for 4 to 7 minutes more, until the desired doneness, from still-crisp to tender, but with a bite.

Heat a small skillet over medium-low heat. Add a drizzle of EVOO and the onions and cook until they begin to caramelize, about 10 minutes, stirring frequently. Add the cider, raise the heat to medium-high, and cook until the liquid is reduced and syrupy, about 5 minutes.

Season the beans with salt and pepper and add them to the pan with the onions and cider. Toss to coat and keep warm until ready to serve.

SERVES 8

2 (16-ounce) bags whole frozen **green beans**

EVOO (extra-virgin olive oil), for liberal drizzling

1 small **yellow-skinned onion**, finely chopped

¾ cup cloudy **apple cider**

Salt and **pepper**

Herb-Roasted Turkey Breast with Cider Pan Gravy

Although sage is the herb most used with turkey, I especially love the flavor and aroma of fresh bay (laurel) leaves with turkey. Fresh bay leaves are now widely available in supermarkets. Since the leaves are a bit woody, and no fun to eat, I baste my turkey with bay-infused butter and roast the breasts right on top of the leaves, which perfumes the meat.

3 tablespoons **EVOO** (extra-virgin olive oil), plus more for the roasting pan

1 small (golf ball–size) **onion**, peeled and coarsely chopped

Zest of 1 **lemon**

12 fresh **sage leaves**

Large handful of fresh flat-leaf **parsley**

Salt

8 fresh **bay leaves**

4 tablespoons (½ stick) **butter**

2 boneless **turkey breast halves**, skin on (2 to 2½ pounds each)

Black pepper

3 tablespoons **all-purpose flour**

¼ cup **apple brandy** such as Calvados, or regular brandy

2 cups cloudy **apple cider**

Preheat the oven to 450°F. Oil a roasting pan and set it aside.

Combine the onions and the zest of the lemon in a food processor. Chop the mixture very fine. Add the sage, parsley, EVOO, and 1 teaspoon salt and pulse until they form a coarse paste.

Put 2 of the bay leaves and the butter into a small pan and melt over medium-low heat until the butter is bubbling. Remove from the heat and set aside.

Put the turkey breasts on a work surface. Season the skin liberally with salt and pepper. Carefully work your fingers between the skin and the flesh from one end to create a pocket, being careful not to pull the skin off completely. Stuff half of the herb paste under the skin of each breast and spread it evenly. Scatter the remaining bay leaves in the roasting pan and place the breasts on top of the leaves. Using a pastry brush, baste the breasts with half of the bay butter.

Roast the turkey breasts for 20 minutes, then reduce the heat to 400°F, baste the turkey breasts with the remaining butter, and roast for an additional 20 to 25 minutes, until cooked through and an instant-read thermometer placed in the thickest part of the breast registers 170°F. Remove the turkey from the oven, transfer to a platter, cover, and let rest for 10 minutes while you make the gravy.

Put the roasting pan over a burner on medium heat. Sprinkle the flour over the pan juices and cook, stirring, for a few minutes. Add the apple brandy and scrape the pan with a wooden spoon to lift the bits that are stuck to the bottom. Cook for a minute to burn off the alcohol, then whisk in the apple cider. Bring to a simmer and stir until the gravy is thickened. Season the gravy with salt and pepper.

Slice the turkey breast on the diagonal, and serve with the warm gravy.

SERVES 8

Pumpkin Soup with Chili Cran-Apple Relish

1 tablespoon **EVOO** (extra-virgin olive oil)

2 tablespoons **butter**

1 fresh **bay leaf**

2 **celery stalks**, finely chopped

1 medium **onion**, finely chopped

Salt and **pepper**

3 tablespoons **all-purpose flour**

2 teaspoons **poultry seasoning**

2 teaspoons **hot sauce**, or to taste

6 cups **chicken stock**

1 (28-ounce) can **pumpkin puree**

2 cups **heavy cream**

½ teaspoon freshly grated **nutmeg**

Relish

1 **crisp apple**, finely chopped

¼ **red onion**, finely chopped

2 tablespoons fresh **lemon juice**

½ cup **dried sweetened cranberries**, chopped

1 teaspoon **chili powder**

2 teaspoons **honey**

½ teaspoon **ground cinnamon**

Heat a medium soup pot over medium to medium-high heat. Add the EVOO and butter, and when the butter melts, add the bay leaf, celery, and onions. Season the veggies with salt and pepper and cook for 6 or 7 minutes, until tender. Add the flour, poultry seasoning, and hot sauce, then cook for a minute. Whisk in the chicken stock and bring the liquid to a bubble. Whisk in the pumpkin in large spoonfuls to incorporate it into the broth. Simmer the soup for 10 minutes to thicken a bit, then add the cream and nutmeg. Reduce the heat to low and keep warm until ready to serve.

While the soup cooks, assemble the relish: Combine the apple, onion, lemon juice, cranberries, chili powder, honey, and cinnamon in a bowl and mix thoroughly.

Adjust the seasonings in the soup and relish. Discard the bay leaf. Ladle the soup into shallow bowls and top with a few spoonfuls of relish.

SERVES 8 AS A STARTER, 4 AS AN ENTRÉE

Apple and Onion Stuffin' Muffins

2 tablespoons **EVOO** (extra-virgin olive oil)

8 tablespoons (1 stick) **butter**, softened

1 fresh **bay leaf**

4 **celery stalks** from the heart with leafy tops, chopped

1 medium **onion**, chopped

3 or 4 **McIntosh apples**, quartered and chopped

Salt and **pepper**

2 tablespoons **poultry seasoning**

¼ cup chopped fresh flat-leaf **parsley leaves**

8 cups cubed **stuffing mix**

2 to 3 cups **chicken stock**

Preheat the oven to 375°F.

Heat a large skillet over medium-high heat. Add the EVOO and 4 tablespoons of the butter to the skillet. When the butter melts, add the bay leaf and the celery, onions, and apples as you chop them. Sprinkle the vegetables and apples with salt, pepper, and the poultry seasoning. Cook for 5 to 6 minutes to begin to soften the vegetables and apples, then add the parsley and stuffing cubes to the pan and combine. Moisten the stuffing with stock until all of the bread is soft but not wet.

Butter 12 muffin cups liberally with the remaining 4 tablespoons of butter. Use an ice cream scoop to mound the stuffing into the muffin tins. (Remove the bay leaf from the stuffing when you come upon it.) Bake the stuffin' muffins until set and crisp on top, 10 to 15 minutes. Remove them to a platter and serve hot or at room temperature.

MAKES 12 STUFFIN' MUFFINS

HOLIDAY MEAL IN 60-ISH #3

- SPICED NUTS
- STORE-BOUGHT MARINATED BOCCONCINI AND ASSORTED SALAMI
- TRICOLORE SALAD WITH FENNEL
- BEEF TENDERLOIN WITH ROASTED PEPPER AND BLACK OLIVE SAUCE
- ASPARAGUS WITH GREMOLATA
- EGGNOG PANETTONE BREAD PUDDING

Spiced Nuts

This recipe makes a double batch, giving you 3 cups to serve and 3 cups to gift away. Buy nuts from the bulk bins in your market; they are better priced than the packaged nuts on the baking aisle.

Combine the walnuts, hazelnuts, cashews, and pecans in a large skillet and place over moderate heat for 7 to 8 minutes, shaking the pan or stirring often, until golden and well toasted; your nose will know when they are done. Transfer the nuts to a plate and add the smoked almonds. Return the pan to the stovetop, add the butter to the pan and melt it over medium-low heat. Stir in the anise, cinnamon, pepper, and nutmeg. Let the butter infuse with the spices for a minute over low heat, then pour over the nuts. Stir to coat with the butter.

MAKES 6 CUPS

2 cups **walnut halves**

1 cup peeled **hazelnuts**

1 cup whole **unsalted cashews**

1 cup **pecan halves**

1 cup **smoked almonds**

3 tablespoons **butter**, cut into pieces

1 teaspoon **ground anise**

1 teaspoon **ground cinnamon**

1 teaspoon **coarse black pepper**

½ teaspoon freshly grated **nutmeg** (eyeball it)

Tricolore Salad with Fennel

Combine the lettuces in a large salad bowl. Place the fennel fronds in a small bowl. Zest the orange over the fronds and add the shallots. Add the vinegar to the shallots and let stand for 10 minutes. Cut the remaining peel and white pith off the orange and chop the orange into bite-size pieces. Add the sliced fennel and oranges to the salad. Whisk the EVOO into the shallot dressing and pour over the salad. Toss and season with salt and pepper.

SERVES 8

2 hearts of **romaine lettuce**, trimmed and chopped

2 heads of **radicchio**, cored and sliced

1 large **fennel bulb** and a few of the fronds (fronds chopped, fennel cored and thinly sliced)

1 **navel orange**

1 small **shallot**, finely chopped

3 tablespoons **red wine vinegar** (eyeball it)

⅓ cup **EVOO** (extra-virgin olive oil)

Salt and **pepper**

Beef Tenderloin with Roasted Pepper and Black Olive Sauce

2 (2- to 2½-pound) center-cut pieces of **beef tenderloin**

3 tablespoons **EVOO** (extra-virgin olive oil), plus more for coating the beef

Grill seasoning, such as McCormick's Montreal Steak Seasoning

5 roasted **red peppers** from a jar, well drained, patted dry, and coarsely chopped

2 **garlic cloves**, cracked away from their skins

A handful of fresh flat-leaf **parsley**

1 cup good-quality **pitted black olives** such as kalamata, drained well

Salt and **pepper**

Crusty bread, sliced

Ask the butcher to give you 2 pieces of tenderloin for use in a Chateaubriand recipe.

Preheat the oven as high as it goes, at least 500°F.

Liberally coat the meat with EVOO and grill seasoning. Place the meat on a roasting rack or in a roasting pan and place in the oven. If you are cooking in a pan with no rack, add a splash of water to the pan. Roast the meat for 10 minutes without opening the oven door, then reduce the oven temperature to 350°F and roast for 30 minutes more, for rare. Remove the meat from the oven and tent with foil. Let the meat rest for 10 minutes.

Place the roasted peppers in a food processor and add the garlic, parsley, olives, and salt and pepper. Turn the processor on and stream in the 3 tablespoons of EVOO.

Slice the meat thin against the grain and serve with the crusty bread and sauce.

SERVES 8

Asparagus with Gremolata

2½ pounds **thin asparagus**, tough ends trimmed

Salt

EVOO (extra-virgin olive oil), for drizzling

6 **garlic cloves**, peeled and crushed

Zest of 2 **lemons**

8 to 10 **anchovies**, 1 (2-ounce) tin, drained (use ½ cup pitted green olives if you do not care for anchovies)

½ cup fresh flat-leaf **parsley leaves**, a couple of generous handfuls

Bring a shallow pan of water to a simmer. Add the asparagus and some salt and simmer for 5 minutes, until cooked through but still with a little bite. Drain the asparagus, arrange on a platter, and drizzle with EVOO.

While the asparagus cooks, make a pile of garlic, lemon zest, anchovies, and parsley on your cutting board. Finely chop all of the ingredients together to form a paste; this is the gremolata.

Sprinkle the gremolata liberally over the hot asparagus and drizzle with EVOO. Serve hot or at room temperature.

SERVES 8

Eggnog Panettone Bread Pudding

Preheat the oven to 475°F.

Place a kettle of water on to boil. With a serrated knife, remove the side crusts from the panettone. Cut the bread into ¾- to 1-inch dice. You should have 5 cups. Place the cubed panettone in a large mixing bowl.

In another bowl, thoroughly whisk together the eggs, egg yolks, sugar, half-and-half, rum, vanilla, and a healthy grating of fresh nutmeg. Pour this over the bread cubes.

Spray a 12-cup muffin tin with vegetable cooking spray. Ladle the bread-eggnog mixture gently and evenly into the muffin cups. Some big cubes sticking up look nice. Place the filled muffin tin in a high-rimmed baking sheet or a large roasting pan. Transfer to the preheated oven and carefully pour the hot water from the kettle into the pan, creating a water bath for the muffin tin to sit in.

Bake for 15 to 20 minutes, until the tops are nicely browned and a toothpick inserted in the center comes out clean.

Bread pudding may be served warm or cold. Vanilla ice cream or whipped cream would be great accompaniments.

NOTE If you prefer you can cook the bread puddings on top of the stove. Place the muffin tin in a roasting pan set over a burner. Pour in up to 1 inch of boiling water. Cover the pan with foil and cook over medium-high heat for 15 to 20 minutes. The puddings will puff and a toothpick will come out clean from the center. The tops won't brown with this method; perhaps a sprinkle of cinnamon sugar at serving time would be nice.

SERVES 12

1 loaf of **panettone** (Italian holiday bread)

3 whole **eggs**

3 **egg yolks**

¾ cup **sugar**

2 cups **half-and-half**

¼ cup **dark rum**

1 teaspoon **vanilla extract**

⅛ to ¼ teaspoon freshly grated **nutmeg**

Vegetable cooking spray

Optional accompaniments

Vanilla ice cream

Whipped cream

HOLIDAY IN 60-ISH #4

- SPANISH NIBBLES
- CHEDDAR SOUP WITH TORTILLA CRUNCHIES
- PARSLEY-PAPRIKA POTATOES
- PRESSED HERBS AND SPICES TURKEY BREAST, PUMPKIN-ZUCCHINI MUFFIN STUFFIN' WITH CHIPOTLE GRAVY
- ORANGE-SCENTED GREEN BEANS
- PECAN PIE WITH CHOCOLATE-CINNAMON WHIPPED CREAM

SPANISH NIBBLES
Hot Olives with Citrus and Spice, Marcona Almonds, Paprika Toasted ChickPeas

4 cups mixed good-quality **olives**

3 to 4 strips of **orange zest**

3 to 4 strips of **lemon zest**

1 teaspoon crushed **red pepper flakes**

1 teaspoon **fennel seeds**, ⅓ palmful

2 to 3 tablespoons **EVOO** (extra-virgin olive oil)

2 cups **Marcona almonds** (available in bulk food section of your market), or toasted peeled whole almonds

2 (15-ounce) cans **chickpeas**, rinsed and drained

2 teaspoons **sweet smoked paprika**

Salt and **pepper**

Preheat the oven to 400°F or preheat an outdoor grill.

Make a large double layer of foil and set the olives in the center. Add the citrus zest, red pepper flakes, and fennel seeds, then top with the olive oil. Bring the sides together and fold, then fold up the ends to make a pouch. Shake the pouch to distribute the spices and oil. Set the pouch on a baking sheet and place in the oven, or place the pouch on the grill, to heat through, 8 to 10 minutes.

Place the almonds in a small decorative serving dish.

Place the chickpeas in a medium skillet over medium heat and cook for 15 minutes, or until crisp and dry. In the last 5 minutes, season the chickpeas with the paprika and salt and pepper. (If you season them up too soon, the paprika will blacken and become bitter.) Place the chickpeas in a small serving bowl. Place the pouch of olives on a platter and cut the pouch open to expose them. Arrange the dishes of nuts and chickpeas alongside the olives, as well as a ramekin or a small cup for the olive pits.

SERVES 8

Cheddar Soup with Tortilla Crunchies

Melt the butter in a medium soup pot over medium heat. Add the onions and cook for 5 minutes. Add the garlic and peppers and cook for 2 to 3 minutes more. Add the flour and cook for 1 minute. Whisk in the stock slowly and stir in the cream.

Bring the soup to a bubble and reduce the heat to a simmer. Stir in the cheese and season the soup with salt, pepper, the chili powder, and the cumin. Let the soup reduce for 10 to 15 minutes over low heat, then serve with the crushed chips and dollops of salsa.

SERVES 8

3 tablespoons **butter**

1 medium **onion**, finely chopped

2 to 3 **garlic cloves**, finely chopped

1 **jalapeño pepper**, seeded and chopped

½ **red bell pepper**, seeded and very thinly sliced

3 tablespoons **all-purpose flour**

6 cups **chicken stock**

2 cups **heavy cream**

6 cups grated good-quality **cheddar cheese**

Salt and **pepper**

1 tablespoon **chili powder**, a palmful

1½ teaspoons **ground cumin**, ½ palmful

4 cups lightly crushed **tortilla chips**, blue or yellow corn

2 cups store-bought chunky-style **salsa**, any variety

Parsley-Paprika Potatoes

Place the potatoes in a deep pot and cover with water. Cover the pot and bring to a boil over high heat. When the water boils, salt the water and cook the potatoes until tender, about 15 minutes. Drain the potatoes and return to the hot pot. Add the butter, stock, parsley, hot sauce, and paprika and smash the potatoes to the desired consistency. Season the potatoes with salt and pepper to taste.

SERVES 8

4 pounds baby **red-skinned** or **baby Yukon gold potatoes**, halved if large

Salt

4 tablespoons (½ stick) **butter**, cut into small pieces

1 cup **chicken stock**

½ cup fresh flat-leaf **parsley leaves**, a couple of handfuls, finely chopped

2 teaspoons **hot sauce**

1 tablespoon **sweet paprika**, a palmful

Black pepper

Pressed Herbs and Spices Turkey Breast, Pumpkin-Zucchini Muffin Stuffin' with Chipotle Gravy

3 tablespoons **grill seasoning**, such as McCormick's Montreal Steak Seasoning, 3 palmfuls

1 tablespoon **ground cumin**, a palmful

1 tablespoon sweet **smoked paprika**, a palmful

1 tablespoon **ground coriander**, a palmful

4 tablespoons fresh **thyme** leaves

½ cup fresh **cilantro leaves**, 2 handfuls, or ½ cup fresh **basil leaves**

1 cup loosely packed fresh flat-leaf **parsley leaves**, 4 handfuls

1 cup shelled **natural pistachios**

EVOO (extra-virgin olive oil), for generous drizzling

2 boneless **turkey breast halves**, about 3 pounds each

8 tablespoons (1 stick) **butter**

1 fresh or dried **bay leaf**

6 **celery stalks** from the heart, with leafy tops, chopped

2 to 3 **McIntosh apples**, quartered, cored, and chopped

2 medium **onions**, chopped, the other finely chopped

1 medium **zucchini**, chopped

Salt and **pepper**

6 store-bought **pumpkin muffins**, crumbled

½ cup **sunflower seeds**

2 tablespoons **poultry seasoning**

6 cups **chicken stock**

2 slightly rounded tablespoons **all-purpose flour**

1 canned **chipotle chile in adobo**, seeded and finely chopped, plus 2 rounded teaspoonfuls of the adobo sauce

Heads up: you need a couple of bricks covered in foil to press these breasts.

Preheat the oven to 450°F.

Preheat a 14-inch skillet or medium roasting pan over medium heat on your largest burner. Mix the grill seasoning, cumin, paprika, and coriander in a small bowl. Place the thyme, cilantro, parsley, and pistachios in a food processor and process into a paste.

Drizzle EVOO generously over the breasts to coat the skin. Loosen the skin of the breasts with a small sharp knife but don't detach it entirely. Use a rubber spatula to scrape the herb and nut paste out of the processor bowl and divide it between the two breasts, using your hands to move the paste around under the skin to distribute the mixture evenly and to coat the skin as well. Sprinkle the skin with the spice mixture.

Set the coated breasts into the hot skillet or roasting pan, skin side down. Wash your hands. Set a second, slightly smaller skillet or pan on top of the breasts and weight it down with a couple of foil-wrapped bricks. Crisp the skin for 8 to 10 minutes, then transfer the pan to the oven and roast for 35 to 40 minutes, or until an instant-read meat thermometer registers 165 to 170°F. Let the turkey rest, tented with foil.

While the turkey roasts, melt 5 tablespoons of the butter in a second large, deep skillet over medium to medium-high heat. Add the bay leaf, celery, apples, chopped onion, and zucchini. Season the vegetables liberally with salt and pepper. Cook for 10 minutes or until softened. Add the crumbled muffins and the sunflower seeds to the pan and combine with the vegetables. Season the stuffing with the poultry seasoning, then adjust the salt and pepper. Moisten the stuffing with 1½ to 2 cups of the stock. Pile the stuffing into a baking dish. Place in the oven along with the turkey just long enough to crisp up the top of the stuffing. Or, if the pan does not fit, switch on the broiler when the turkey comes out and crisp the top of the stuffing; it should take only a couple of minutes.

(continued)

In a sauce pot, melt the remaining 3 tablespoons of butter over medium heat. Add the finely chopped onion and sweat it in the melted butter for 5 to 6 minutes to make it nice and sweet. Sprinkle the flour into the skillet and cook, whisking, for 1 minute. Add the chipotle and adobo sauce, then whisk in the remaining 4 to 4½ cups of chicken stock. Cook the gravy for 8 to 10 minutes to thicken it, then season with salt.

Let the roasted turkey rest to distribute the juices, then slice thin and serve with mounds of stuffing and lots of gravy.

SERVES 8

TIP An ice cream scoop is an easy way to portion out stuffing on dinner plates.

Orange-Scented Green Beans

Fill a pan with 2 inches of water and bring to a boil. Add the orange zest and the beans and cook for 5 to 6 minutes. The beans should remain bright green with a snap to them. Drain the beans and return them to the pan; discard the zest. Toss with the butter, salt, and chives, then transfer to a serving dish.

SERVES 8

Zest of 1 **orange**, removed in strips with a vegetable peeler

2 pounds trimmed **green beans** (available in the produce department)

2 tablespoons **butter**

Salt

3 tablespoons snipped fresh **chives**

Pecan Pie with Chocolate-Cinnamon Whipped Cream

Melt the chocolate in a medium bowl in the microwave for about 45 seconds, checking it every 10 seconds and stirring often. Set aside until cool to the touch.

Combine the cream, liqueur, cinnamon, and chili powder in a mixing bowl. Whisk or beat until stiff peaks form. Stir one quarter of the whipped cream into the chocolate until totally combined, then fold in the rest of the whipped cream in small batches. Serve wedges of the pie topped with a dollop of the chocolate spiced cream.

SERVES 8

1 (3-ounce) bar of **semisweet chocolate**, chopped

2 cups **heavy cream**

1 shot of **Grand Marnier** or other orange liqueur (buy a tiny bottle, a nip, if you like)

¼ teaspoon **ground cinnamon** (eyeball it in your palm)

2 pinches of **chili powder** or ground cayenne pepper

1 store-bought **pecan pie**, warm or chilled, as you like

RECIPES FOR THE DAY AFTER TURKEY DAY

- TURKEY FRITTATA
- TURKEY PASTA
- TURKEY STOUP
- TURKEY HASH

Turkey Frittata

12 **eggs**

¼ cup **heavy cream**

2 tablespoons **EVOO** (extra-virgin olive oil)

6 **scallions**, chopped

1 **yellow bell pepper**, seeded and cut into medium dice

2 medium **tomatoes**, seeded and diced

3 cups **leftover turkey**, shredded

Salt and **pepper**

1½ cups shredded **cheddar cheese**

Set the oven rack in the lowest position and preheat the broiler to high.

Crack the eggs into a bowl and whisk in the cream until well combined.

Heat the EVOO in a medium nonstick skillet with an oven-safe handle over medium-high heat. Once the oil is hot, add the scallions and bell pepper and cook for 2 to 3 minutes. Add the tomatoes, turkey, and salt and pepper. Pour the egg and cream mixture into the veggies and turkey, add the cheese, and stir to combine. Using a rubber spatula, stir the eggs until the mixture is about one quarter set. The eggs should look lumpy and runny at the same time. Pop the skillet under the broiler and cook until firm, 4 to 5 minutes.

SERVES 4

Turkey Pasta

Salt

1 pound **penne pasta**

2 tablespoons **EVOO** (extra-virgin olive oil)

½ cup diced **pancetta**, from 3 or 4 ½-inch slices

1 medium **onion**, chopped

2 **garlic cloves**, finely chopped

1 fresh or dried **bay leaf**

1 cup **heavy cream**

2 cups shredded **cooked turkey**

Freshly grated **nutmeg**

Black pepper

1 cup grated **asiago cheese**

½ head of **radicchio**, shredded

Place a large pot of water over high heat and bring to a boil for the pasta. Once it is boiling, add some salt and the pasta and cook to al dente. Drain the pasta, reserving ¼ cup of the starchy cooking water.

While the water is coming to a boil, start the sauce. Place a large nonstick skillet over medium-high heat with the EVOO. Add the pancetta and cook for 3 to 4 minutes to render some of the fat. Add the onions, garlic, and bay leaf and cook until nice and soft, 5 to 6 minutes, then add the turkey and cook for 5 minutes more. Stir in the cream, nutmeg, and salt and pepper and cook until the cream has reduced by half, 4 to 5 minutes.

Add the pasta to the creamy turkey sauce, mix, and add the reserved pasta water. Plate the pasta in a large serving dish and top with the cheese and radicchio.

SERVES 4

Turkey Stoup

2 tablespoons **EVOO** (extra-virgin olive oil)

1 large **onion**, chopped

4 **celery stalk**s from the heart, chopped

2 medium **carrots**, peeled and chopped

3 **garlic cloves**, chopped

1 fresh or dried **bay leaf**

1 (15-ounce) can **tomato sauce**

4 cups **chicken** or **turkey stock**

5 cups shredded **cooked turkey**

Salt and **pepper**

1 package small fresh **cheese ravioli**, from the dairy aisle

½ cup fresh **basil leaves**, torn or chopped, a couple of handfuls

¼ cup grated **Parmigiano-Reggiano**

Heat the EVOO in a large soup pot over medium-high heat. Add the onions, celery, carrots, garlic, and bay leaf and cook until soft and fragrant, 4 to 5 minutes. Add the tomato sauce, stock, and turkey and simmer for 10 minutes; season with salt and pepper. Add the ravioli to the stoup and cook according to the package directions. Stir in the basil and serve each bowl of turkey stoup with a sprinkle of Parmigiano.

SERVES 4

Turkey Hash

2 tablespoons **EVOO** (extra-virgin olive oil)

4 ounces **Mexican (raw) chorizo**, casings removed

1 large **sweet white onion**, chopped

1 **red bell pepper**, seeded and chopped

4 baking **potatoes**, peeled and shredded

1 cup shredded cooked **turkey**

2 tablespoons **white wine vinegar** (eyeball it)

4 **eggs**

Preheat a medium skillet over medium-high heat with the EVOO. Add the chorizo and cook, stirring frequently, to render the fat, about 5 minutes. (If there is a lot of fat in the pan, pour most of it out.) Add the onions, peppers, and potatoes and cook until the potatoes get some color and are crispy around the edges, 8 to 10 minutes.

Add the turkey and heat through. While the potatoes are cooking, bring a high-sided skillet of water to a boil over medium-high heat. Once the water is at a bubble, pour the vinegar into the simmering water. Crack an egg into a small bowl and gently slide the egg into the simmering water. Repeat with the remaining 3 eggs. Poach the eggs for about 2 minutes for runny yolks, or about 4 for solid yolks. Do not allow the water to boil. Carefully remove the eggs with a slotted spoon to a towel-lined plate to drain.

Divide the hash among 4 serving plates. Place a poached egg on each serving and cut into it so the yolk runs over the hash like a sauce.

SERVES 4

- ROASTED PORTABELLA MUSHROOM SALAD WITH POTATO CROUTONS
- CAULIFLOWER-CHICKPEA STEW
- EGGPLANT-BEET ROSES WITH GARLIC AND HERB CHEESE
- STORE-BOUGHT DESSERTS

Here's a meatless menu that is hearty, flavorful, and colorful—nice and festive for any holiday! If you want to get ahead, you can roast the eggplant and sauté the beets in advance and just warm them up when you are ready to assemble the dish. Serve this beefy-tasting salad hot or at room temperature.

Roasted Portabella Mushroom Salad with **Potato Croutons**

Preheat the oven to 450°F.

Place a large rimmed baking sheet in the oven and let it get hot while you get the potatoes together. In a large bowl drizzle the potatoes with a liberal amount of EVOO, season with some salt and pepper and the thyme, and toss to coat. Open the oven and drop the potatoes onto the hot baking sheet, spreading them out in an even layer. Try to do this quickly so the baking sheet and the oven stay really hot. Roast for 40 minutes, or until the potatoes are really brown and crispy; toss the potatoes around on the baking sheet once about halfway through the cooking.

Once you have the potatoes in the oven, season up the mushrooms. In a shallow dish combine the garlic, balsamic, 3 tablespoons of EVOO, and some salt and pepper. Add the mushrooms and coat thoroughly in the mixture. Arrange them on a rimmed baking sheet, gill side up, and roast in the oven for about 12 minutes, or until the mushrooms are tender.

While the potatoes and the mushrooms are working in the oven, prepare the dressing. In a salad bowl combine the mustard, shallots, vinegar, and some salt and pepper. Pour in the ¼ cup of EVOO in a slow, steady stream while whisking.

Once the potatoes and mushrooms are done, remove from the oven, slice the mushrooms, and add to the dressing along with the potatoes and the escarole. Toss to combine and serve immediately.

SERVES 8

3 pounds large **Yukon Gold potatoes**, scrubbed clean, then cut into ½-inch dice

¼ cup plus 3 tablespoons **EVOO** (extra-virgin olive oil), plus some for drizzling

Salt and **pepper**

3 tablespoons chopped fresh **thyme leaves**

2 large **garlic cloves**, grated or finely chopped

¼ cup **aged balsamic vinegar** (eyeball it)

8 **portabella mushroom caps**

2 tablespoons **grainy mustard**

1 large **shallot**, finely chopped

2 tablespoons **white wine vinegar** (eyeball it)

2 small heads of **escarole**, thoroughly washed, dried, then torn into small pieces

Cauliflower-Chickpea Stew

3 tablespoons **EVOO** (extra-virgin olive oil), plus more as necessary

1 large head of **cauliflower**, cut into florets

Salt and **pepper**

1 large **onion**, sliced

4 large **garlic cloves**, chopped

3 **celery stalks** from the heart, leaves reserved, stalks chopped

1 **fennel bulb**, halved, cored, and thinly sliced

2 tablespoons fresh **thyme leaves**, chopped

1 teaspoon crushed **red pepper flakes**, ⅓ palmful

1 cup **dry white wine** (eyeball it)

4 cups **vegetable stock**

3 tablespoons **honey**

2 handfuls of fresh flat-leaf **parsley leaves**, chopped

Zest and **juice** of 1 **orange**

1 (16-ounce) jar of **roasted red peppers**, seeded and chopped

½ cup **green olives**, coarsely chopped

1 (28-ounce) can **chickpeas**, drained

Place a large Dutch oven over medium-high heat with 2 tablespoons of the EVOO. Once you see a ripple in the oil, add the cauliflower and brown, 7 to 8 minutes. Season with some salt and pepper, and add the remaining tablespoon EVOO to the pot along with the onions, garlic, chopped celery, fennel, thyme, red pepper flakes, and some salt and pepper. Cook, stirring frequently, for 8 to 10 minutes, or until the veggies start to take on a little color.

Once the veggies are lightly browned, add the wine and scrape up any brown bits that are on the bottom of the pot. Add the stock, honey, parsley, orange zest and juice, roasted red peppers, green olives, and chickpeas and continue to simmer for a couple of minutes to let the flavors come together and get everything to heat through. Taste, and adjust the seasoning with salt and pepper.

SERVES 8

Eggplant-Beet Roses with Garlic and Herb Cheese

1 large **eggplant**, stem end trimmed

2 tablespoons **EVOO** (extra-virgin olive oil), plus more for drizzling

Salt and **pepper**

2 pounds **red beets**, skin removed and discarded, flesh grated

1 large **garlic clove**, grated or finely chopped

½ cup **dry white wine** (eyeball it)

1 (6-ounce) container **garlic and herb cheese**, such as Boursin, at room temperature

Preheat the oven to 400°F.

Cut a strip off each side of the eggplant to square it off, then cut lengthwise into 8 ½-inch-thick slices.

Arrange the eggplant slices on a rimmed baking sheet, drizzle with a little EVOO, season with some salt and pepper, transfer to the oven, and roast for 15 minutes, flipping the slices over halfway through the cooking time.

Once the eggplant is in the oven, place a skillet over medium-high heat with the 2 tablespoons of EVOO. Once it is hot, add the grated beets and garlic and cook, stirring frequently, for about 10 minutes. Add the wine, salt and pepper, and cook for another few minutes or until the beets are tender.

To assemble, spread some of the garlic and herb cheese on each of the slices of eggplant. Top with some of the sautéed beet mixture, spreading it out from end to end. Roll the eggplant up and transfer to a platter to serve.

SERVES 8

CHRISTMAS DAY DINNER

- GARLIC-THYME ROASTED BEEF TENDERLOIN WITH HORSERADISH SAUCE
- TWO-TIMES THE WILD: WILD MUSHROOM WILD RICE
- LEMON-TARRAGON ROASTED STRING BEANS AND TOMATOES
- STORE-BOUGHT WARM GINGERBREAD CAKE WITH WHIPPED CREAM

Heads up: Combine the meat with the marinade on Christmas Eve, because it should soak up the flavors overnight. Leave a note for Santa and the reindeers to keep their hooves off! For the dessert, make a store-bought mix according to the package directions, and garnish with whipped cream and grated nutmeg when ready to serve.

Garlic-Thyme Roasted Beef Tenderloin with Horseradish Sauce

To marinate the beef, combine the thyme, garlic, pepper, and EVOO in a small bowl. Place the beef on a rimmed baking sheet, pour the marinade over it, and rub the meat all over to coat it completely. Wrap the beef tightly in plastic wrap and refrigerate overnight.

About an hour before you are ready to cook, remove the beef from the refrigerator to let it come to room temperature. Preheat the oven to 400°F.

Unwrap the beef, season it with some salt, and place on a rimmed baking sheet or in a roasting pan. Roast the beef for 10 minutes, then reduce the heat to 350°F and roast for 30 minutes more, or until an instant-read thermometer registers 125°F.

Transfer the roast to a cutting board, cover with a piece of foil, and let it rest for at least 10 minutes; the beef will continue to cook as it rests and will be medium-rare at the center, medium at the ends.

While the beef is in the oven, put together the horseradish sauce. In a bowl combine the sour cream, horseradish, applesauce, bread crumbs, and salt and pepper to taste. Garnish the sauce with the chives.

Slice up the beef to the desired thickness and arrange on a platter. Serve the horseradish sauce alongside.

8 SERVINGS, WITH SECONDS

12 sprigs of fresh **thyme**, leaves removed and chopped

5 large **garlic cloves**, grated or finely chopped

2 tablespoons **coarse black pepper**

3 tablespoons **EVOO** (extra-virgin olive oil)

1 (4- to 4½-pound) **beef tenderloin**, trimmed and tied (your butcher can do this for you)

Salt

2 cups **sour cream**

¼ cup prepared **horseradish**

¼ cup unsweetened **applesauce**

½ cup **bread crumbs**

2 tablespoons finely chopped fresh **chives**

Two-Times the Wild:
Wild Mushroom Wild Rice

5 cups **chicken stock**

2 cups **wild rice**

Salt and **pepper**

½ pound **button mushrooms**, wiped clean, stems trimmed, and halved

¾ pound **cremini mushrooms**, wiped clean, stems trimmed, and halved

½ pound **shiitake mushrooms**, wiped clean, stems removed, and halved

¼ to ⅓ cup **EVOO** (extra-virgin olive oil)

4 **scallions**, finely chopped

A handful of fresh flat-leaf **parsley leaves**, about ¼ cup, chopped

Preheat the oven 350°F.

In a medium sauce pot heat the chicken stock to a boil over high heat. While the stock is heating, place the wild rice on a rimmed baking sheet and give it a good once-over, picking out any small pebbles or debris. Put the rice in a sieve or small-holed colander and rinse under cold water for about 1 minute. Add the rice to the boiling stock along with some salt and pepper. Cover the pot with a lid, turn the heat down to low, and cook the rice for 45 minutes. You'll know the rice is done if the grains are just starting to crack open and are tender but not mushy.

Once you have the rice going, place the mushrooms on a rimmed baking sheet. Drizzle them liberally with EVOO and season with salt and pepper. Roast the mushrooms for 25 to 30 minutes, or until the mushrooms are tender and lightly browned.

Stir the roasted mushrooms, the scallions, and the parsley into the cooked wild rice and stir with a fork until the mushrooms are distributed. Taste and add more salt and pepper if necessary.

8 SERVINGS

Lemon-Tarragon Roasted
String Beans and Tomatoes

1½ pounds **string beans**, trimmed of the stem ends

1 pint **grape tomatoes**

2 tablespoons **EVOO** (extra-virgin olive oil)

Salt and **pepper**

Juice of 1 **lemon**

4 sprigs of fresh **tarragon**, leaves removed and chopped

Preheat the oven to 350°F.

Place the string beans and tomatoes on a rimmed baking sheet, drizzle with the EVOO, season with salt and pepper, and toss to coat. Roast for 25 to 30 minutes, until the beans are browned and nutty and very tender. Remove from the oven, squeeze the juice of the lemon over them, and sprinkle with the tarragon. Toss to combine, and serve.

8 SERVINGS

LEMON-CREAM CHICKEN WITH CHAMPAGNE RISOTTO AND ASPARAGUS WITH PANCETTA

There are a few overlapping steps going on here, but as fancy suppers go, this is still pretty simple. Read through the method a time or two to get the timing down before you start cooking, and you should have no problems. There is champagne in the risotto but it doesn't have to be of the very finest quality; buy a small split of good-quality but affordable dry sparkling wine for cooking and a big bottle of the good stuff to drink.

Heat 3 cups of the stock in a small pot over low heat; keep warm over very low heat or place on a pot holder and keep covered.

Heat 2 tablespoons of the EVOO in a skillet over medium-high heat. Add the onions and garlic and sauté to soften, 3 to 4 minutes. Add the rice and toss to coat; season with salt and pepper. Pour in the sparkling wine and stir, allowing it to cook off, 1 minute or so. Stir in a couple of ladles of the warm stock and cook until the liquids are absorbed, stirring occasionally. Continue adding the stock a few ladles at a time, until the rice is creamy and just tender. Total cooking time for the risotto will be about 18 minutes.

While the risotto cooks, heat the cream in a small pot with a 3-inch piece of lemon zest and a pinch of cayenne pepper. Cook gently over medium-low heat for 15 minutes, until the cream is reduced by about half and slightly thickened.

Season the chicken breasts with salt and pepper. Heat 2 more tablespoons of the EVOO in a nonstick skillet over medium-high heat. Add the chicken and cook for 6 minutes on each side. Remove the cooked chicken to a cutting board to rest. Add the remaining ½ cup of chicken stock to the skillet and stir to deglaze the pan, then stir the pan juices into the risotto. Remove the lemon zest from the cream.

In a medium skillet, heat the remaining tablespoon of EVOO over medium-high heat. Add the pancetta and cook for 3 to 4 minutes. Trim off the tough ends of the asparagus and cut the spears on an angle into 1-inch pieces. Add the asparagus and shallots to the skillet with the pancetta and cook for 3 minutes more. Turn off the heat.

To serve, stir the Parmigiano and thyme into the risotto and spoon generous portions into shallow bowls or deep dinner plates. Slice the chicken breasts on an angle and fan them over the risotto; spoon the reduced cream over the top. Cut the lemon in half and douse the asparagus with a little juice to cut the pancetta's richness. Toss the asparagus to coat, and spoon it around the edges of the risotto.

SERVES 2

3½ cups **chicken stock**

5 tablespoons **EVOO** (extra-virgin olive oil)

1 **onion**, chopped

2 **garlic cloves**, chopped

1 cup **arborio rice**

Salt and **pepper**

1 split of **sparkling wine** (see headnote)

¾ cup **heavy cream**

1 **lemon**

A pinch of **cayenne pepper** or crushed red pepper flakes

2 boneless skinless **chicken breast halves**

3 (⅛-inch-thick slices) **pancetta** or 2 slices thick-cut bacon, chopped

1 small bundle of **asparagus**, ⅔ to ¾ pound

1 large **shallot**, thinly sliced

½ cup grated **Parmigiano-Reggiano**

3 to 4 sprigs of fresh **thyme**, leaves stripped and chopped

Rosemary Roasted Leg of Lamb with Green Romesco Sauce

Preheat the oven to 450°F.

Season the lamb liberally on both sides with salt and pepper. Drizzle with some EVOO and rub to coat. Turn the meat fat side down on the work surface and rub the top side with the lemon zest. Arrange the rosemary down the center of the meat, then fold in the sides over the rosemary like a letter. Transfer the meat to a roasting pan and roast for 15 minutes, then reduce the heat to 350°F and roast for another hour. Because the thicknesses of the meat varies these directions will give you some meat cooked to medium and some cooked to medium-rare. If you prefer your lamb medium to well-done, add 20 minutes to the cooking time at 350°F. Remove the meat from the oven, tent with foil, and let it rest for at least 10 minutes before slicing.

While the lamb is roasting, prepare the green romesco. In a food processor, combine the mint, parsley, basil, pine nuts, garlic, lemon juice, matzo, and some salt and pepper. Pulse until well ground, then let the machine run while you add the ⅓ cup of EVOO in a slow, steady steam. The mixture should be thick but smooth. Transfer to a serving bowl.

Slice the lamb against the grain (but don't make yourself crazy slicing it; a leg of lamb is not easy to slice perfectly). Arrange the slices on a platter and serve the sauce alongside.

SERVES 8

1 (5-pound) boneless **leg of lamb**, butterflied

Salt and **pepper**

⅓ cup **EVOO** (extra-virgin olive oil), plus some for drizzling

Zest and juice of 2 **lemons**

5 sprigs of fresh **rosemary**

2 cups fresh **mint leaves**, about 8 handfuls

1 cup fresh flat-leaf **parsley leaves**, about 4 handfuls

1 cup fresh **basil leaves**, about 4 handfuls

½ cup **pine nuts**, about 2 handfuls, toasted (see Note, page 102)

1 **garlic clove**

1 **matzo**, broken into pieces, or 1 slice of bread, toasted and then torn into pieces

Spicy Roasted String Beans

Preheat the oven to 400°F.

Trim the stem ends of the green beans and wax beans and place them on a rimmed baking sheet. Coat with the EVOO, and season with salt, pepper, the red pepper flakes, and the garlic. Roast for 25 to 30 minutes, until very tender and lightly browned, stirring the beans once after 15 minutes. Serve immediately.

SERVES 8

1½ pounds green **string bean**

1 pound **wax beans**

3 tablespoons **EVOO** (extra-virgin olive oil)

Salt and **pepper**

1 teaspoon **crushed red pepper flakes**, ⅓ palmful

3 **garlic cloves**, crushed

Barley Salad

Place the stock and ½ cup water in a sauce pot with a lid. Add the garlic and a little pepper and bring up to a bubble over high heat. Add the barley, return to a boil, then cover the pot and reduce the heat to low. Cook until the barley is tender and has soaked up all the liquid, about 45 minutes.

While the barley is cooking, whisk together the mustard and vinegar in a salad bowl. Whisk in the EVOO in a slow, steady stream, and season with salt and pepper.

Once the barley is cooked, fish out the garlic cloves and discard. Transfer the barley to a colander and rinse under cold water for about 1 minute, swooshing it around with your hand; drain thoroughly. Add the barley to the bowl with the dressing and toss to coat. Add the celery, tomatoes, and onions, toss to combine, and adjust the seasonings.

SERVES 8

4 cups **chicken stock**

2 **garlic cloves**, cracked from their skins and lightly crushed

Black pepper

1½ cups **pearl barley**

1 tablespoon **Dijon mustard**

2 tablespoons **white wine vinegar** (eyeball it)

⅓ cup **EVOO** (extra-virgin olive oil)

Salt

5 **celery stalks** from the heart with leafy tops, finely chopped

2 **plum tomatoes**, seeded and finely chopped

½ small **red onion**, finely chopped

INDEX